Microsoft® Office xp

Illustrated Brief

Michael Halvorson
Marjorie Hunt

COURSE
TECHNOLOGY
™
THOMSON LEARNING

Australia • Canada • Mexico • Singapore • Spain • United Kingdom • United States

Microsoft Office^{xp} - Illustrated Brief

Mike Halvorson • Marjorie Hunt

Managing Editor:
Nicole Jones Pinard

Production Editor:
Kristen Guevara

QA Manuscript Reviewer:
Nick Atlas
Shawn Day
Vitaly Davidovitch

Senior Product Manager:
Rebecca Berardy

Developmental Editor:
Mary-Terese Cozzola

Text Designer:
Joseph Lee, Black Fish Design

Editorial Assistant:
Christina Kling Garrett

Composition House:
GEX Publishing Services

The Illustrated Series Vision

Teaching and writing about computer applications can be extremely rewarding and challenging. How do we engage students and keep their interest? How do we teach them skills that they can easily apply on the job? As we set out to write this book, our goals were to develop a textbook that:

▶ works for a beginning student

▶ provides varied, flexible and meaningful exercises and projects to reinforce the skills

▶ serves as a reference tool

▶ makes your job as an educator easier, by providing resources above and beyond the textbook to help you teach your course

Our popular, streamlined format is based on advice from instructional designers and customers. This flexible design presents each lesson on a two-page spread, with step-by-step instructions on the left, and screen illustrations on the right. This signature style, coupled with high-caliber content, provides a comprehensive yet manageable introduction to Microsoft Office XP—it is a teaching package for the instructor and a learning experience for the student.

—The Illustrated Series

ACKNOWLEDGMENTS

Publishing a detailed and up-to-the-minute computer book requires a huge team effort. The authors would like to acknowledge many of the people that made this book a fun and satisfying project to work on. Thank you to Nicole Pinard, Managing Editor at Course Technology, for encouraging us to participate as co-authors on this project. Nicole's professionalism, vision, and friendship have made this project a great experience. Thanks, too, to Rebecca Berardy, Senior Product Manager, who did an excellent job keeping the project on track and keeping us all enthused and motivated. In addition, the authors warmly thank M.T. Cozzola, Development Editor, whose creative ideas, insightful comments, and thoughtful edits improved the manuscript significantly. Thanks also to the book's careful reviewers: Rick Sheridan and Susan Jarvie, and to the book's eagle-eyed testers: Shawn Day, Vitaly Davidovitch, and Nick Atlas. The authors would also like to send a special thank you to Kathie Werner, who revised the PowerPoint and Integrating units in this book, and shared her Office XP experience with us generally. Finally, Marjorie would like to thank her husband, Cecil, and her two sons Trey and Stephen, for their constant love, support, and inspiration, and for giving the necessary space to finish the manuscript during late nights and early mornings. In addition, Marjorie thanks Michael Halvorson for the opportunity to work on this book and renew their friendship—working together again has been a real pleasure. Michael would also like to thank his family for their love and encouragement. He thanks Kim for her patience and support, and Henry and Felix for their hugs and many smiles at the end of the day. He especially encourages all of the students out there who are about to learn Microsoft Office XP—you can do it!

Preface

Welcome to *Microsoft Office^XP – Illustrated Brief*. Each lesson in the book contains elements pictured to the right in the sample two-page spread.

► How is the book organized?
This book is organized into sections, by application, illustrated by the brightly colored tabs on the sides of the pages: Office XP, Word, Excel, Access, PowerPoint, and Integration.

► What kinds of assignments are included in the book? At what level of difficulty?
The lessons use Outdoor Designs, a company that sells do-it-yourself kits for recreational products, as the case study. The assignments on the blue pages at the end of each unit increase in difficulty. Project files and case studies, provide a great variety of interesting and relevant business applications for skills. Assignments include:

• **Concepts Reviews** include multiple choice, matching, and screen identification questions.

• **Skills Reviews** provide additional hands-on, step-by-step reinforcement.

Each 2-page spread focuses on a single skill.

Concise text that introduces the basic principles in the lesson and integrates the brief case study (indicated by the paintbrush icon).

Excel 2002

Entering Numbers and Labels

You enter numbers and labels into a worksheet by typing data in cells. You must select a cell before you can enter data in it. ▰▰▰ You decide to practice entering numbers and labels into the worksheet by entering a product order from a sales representative. The completed product order will serve as an internal tracking sheet that the Outdoor Designs accounting department will use to process the order.

Steps

1. In cell **A1** type **Outdoor Designs Product Order**
   As you type, the text appears in cell A1 and in the Formula bar, as shown in Figure A-3. The text you typed is a **label**, data that serves as a description instead of a calculation. Labels can extend into neighboring cells that don't contain data, so the text "Outdoor Designs Product Order" extends into cells B1 and C1, but it is contained only in cell A1.

2. Press **[Enter]**
   Pressing [Enter] causes Excel to accept your entry and activate the next cell in the column.

3. Press **[↓]** to move to cell **A3**
   Cell A3 is selected and "A3" appears in the name box, identifying your current location. You can use the arrow keys to accept an entry and move to the next cell in the direction of the arrow key. However, when you are entering data in multiple columns, it is easier to press [Enter] after the last column because this moves you to the first column, as you will see in Step 4.

4. Type these four lines, remembering to press **[Enter]** after each line
   Sales rep: Kimberly Ullom
   Store: Mountain Air, North Bend, WA
   Order date: June 30, 2003
   Terms: Payment 30 days after receipt (Net 30)

   QuickTip
   Pressing [Tab] is the same as pressing [→] in the worksheet. You might find that using [Tab] is more convenient for entering multiple columns of data.

5. Press **[Enter]** until cell **A8** is the active cell, then type the following text in columns **A** through **D** of rows **8** and **9**, pressing **[Tab]** to move to the next cell in a row, and pressing **[Enter]** at the end of each row
   Kit num Kit name   Price   Quantity
   #401   Cascade Ski Sack   19.95   5
   Pressing [Enter] at the end of a row of data activates the first cell in the row below the data, rather than activating the next cell in the current column. When you typed "19.95" in cell C9, the text in cell B9 was cut off. When text is wider than a cell, it spills into the adjacent cell unless that cell has data in it. (But the data hasn't been deleted, it is just not visible now.) You'll widen the necessary cells later to display the data again.

6. Beginning with cell **A10**, continue typing the following data in the worksheet; remember to press **[Tab]** to move one cell to the right and **[Enter]** to move to the next row
   #501   Coastal Parafoil Kite   22.95   1
   #502   Puget Sound Delta Kite   24.95   2
   #801   Olympic Rain Tent   79.95   2
   #802   Tent Vestibule   19.95   1
   The text is entered in the worksheet, as shown in Figure A-4.

7. Click the **Save button** 🔲 on the Standard toolbar

► EXCEL A-4   **CREATING AND ENHANCING A WORKSHEET**

Hints as well as troubleshooting advice, right where you need it — next to the step itself.

Every lesson features large, full-color representations of what the screen should look like as students complete the numbered steps.

FIGURE A-3: Worksheet text in Formula bar and in neighboring cells

Name box displays name of selected cell

Cell A1

Formula bar displays contents of selected cells

FIGURE A-4: Worksheet after entering product order data

Data that extends beyond the width of a column is hidden because cells to the right contain data; you'll fix this later

Excel 2002

- **Independent Challenges** are case projects requiring critical thinking and application of the unit skills. The Independent Challenges increase in difficulty, with the first one in each unit being the easiest (most step-by-step with detailed instructions). Independent Challenges 2 and 3 become increasingly open-ended, requiring more independent problem solving.

- **E-Quest Independent Challenges** are case projects with a Web focus. E-Quests require the use of the World Wide Web to conduct research to complete the project.

- **Visual Workshops** show a completed file and require that the file be created without any step-by-step guidance, involving problem solving and an independent application of the unit skills.

CLUES TO USE

Using data entry keys

As you enter data in your worksheets, you can use some keyboard keys to work more effectively. Pressing [Caps Lock] configures your keyboard to enter text labels in all uppercase characters. Pressing [Num Lock] configures the keys on the numeric keypad to insert numbers and mathematical operators. If you enter lengthy data in Excel, [Num Lock] can speed the process significantly.

CREATING AND ENHANCING A WORKSHEET EXCEL A-5 ◀

Clues to Use boxes provide concise information that either expands on the major lesson skill or describes an independent task that in some way relates to the major lesson skill.

The pages are numbered according to unit. Excel indicates the section, A indicates the unit, 5 indicates the page.

Instructor Resources

The Instructor's Resource Kit (IRK) CD is Course Technology's way of putting the resources and information needed to teach and learn effectively into your hands. All the components are available on the IRK (pictured below), and many of the resources can be downloaded from www.course.com.

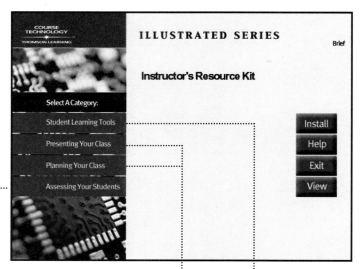

ASSESSING YOUR STUDENTS

Solution Files
Solution Files are comprehensive answers. Use these files to evaluate your students' work. Or, distribute them electronically or in hard copy so students can verify their own work.

ExamView
ExamView is a powerful testing software package that allows you to create and administer printed, computer (LAN-based), and Internet exams. ExamView includes hundreds of questions that correspond to the topics covered in this text, enabling students to generate detailed study guides that include page references for further review. The computer-based and Internet testing components allow students to take exams at their computers, and also save you time by grading each exam automatically.

PRESENTING YOUR CLASS

Figure Files
Figure Files contain all the figures from the book in .jpg format. Use the figure files to create transparency masters or in a PowerPoint presentation.

STUDENT LEARNING TOOLS

Project Files and Project Files List
To complete most of the units in this book, your students will need **Project Files**. Put them on a file server for students to copy. The Project Files are available on the Instructor's Resource Kit CD-ROM, the Review Pack, and can also be downloaded from www.course.com.

Instruct students to use the **Project Files List** at the end of the book. This list gives instructions on copying and organizing files.

PLANNING YOUR CLASS

Instructor's Manual
Available as an electronic file, the Instructor's Manual is quality-assurance tested and includes unit overviews, detailed lecture topics for each unit with teaching tips, comprehensive sample solutions to all lessons and end-of-unit material, and extra Independent Challenges. The Instructor's Manual is available on the Instructor's Resource Kit CD-ROM, or you can download it from www.course.com.

Sample Syllabus
Prepare and customize your course easily using this sample course outline (available on the Instructor's Resource Kit CD-ROM).

Brief Contents

Contents

Office XP

Word 2002

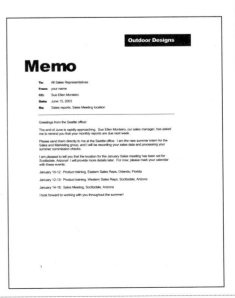

Contents

Enhancing a Document WORD B-1

Adding Special Elements to a Document WORD C-1

Excel 2002

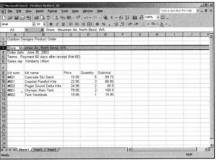

Contents

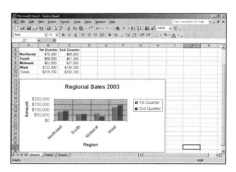

Access 2002

Creating a Database   ACCESS A-1

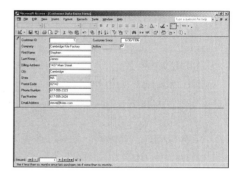

Working with Forms and Data   ACCESS B-1

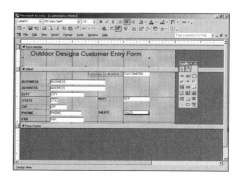

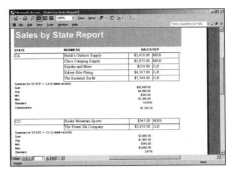

PowerPoint 2002

Contents

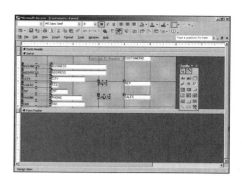

Integration

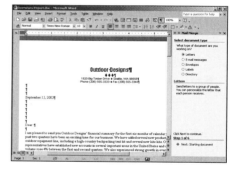

Read This Before You Begin

Tips for Students

Software Information and Required Installation

This book was written and tested using Microsoft Office XP Professional Edition, with a typical installation on Microsoft Windows 2000.

What are Project Files?

To complete many of the units in this book, you need to use Project Files. You use a Project File, which contains a partially completed document used in an exercise, so you don't have to type in all the information you need in the document. Your instructor will either provide you with a copy of the Project Files or ask you to make your own copy. Detailed instructions on how to organize your files, as well as a complete listing of all the files you'll need and will create, can be found in the back of the book (look for the yellow pages) in the Project Files List.

Why is my screen different from the book?

1. Your Desktop components and some dialog box options might be different if you are using an operating system other than Windows 2000.
2. Depending on your computer hardware capabilities and the Windows Display settings on your computer, you may notice the following differences:
   - Your screen may look larger or smaller because of your screen resolution (the height and width of your screen).
   - The colors of the title bar in your screen may be a solid blue, and the cells in Excel may appear different from the purple and gray because of your color settings.
3. Depending on your Office settings, your toolbars may display on a single row and your menus may display with a shortened list of frequently used commands. Office menus and toolbars can modify themselves to your working style by displaying only the most frequently used buttons and menu commands, as shown here.

Toolbars in one row

To view buttons not currently displayed, click a Toolbar Options button ⟫ at the end of either the Standard or Formatting toolbar. To view the full list of menu commands, click the double arrow at the bottom of the menu.

In order to have your toolbars display on two rows, showing all buttons, and to have the full menus display, you must turn off the personalized menus and toolbars feature. Click Tools on the menu bar, click Customize, select the show Standard and Formatting toolbars on two rows and Always show full menus check boxes on the Options tab, then click Close. This book assumes you are displaying toolbars on two rows and full menus.

Toolbars on two rows

An important note on closing files in Access

In the Access units, you will open and close files much like you do in the other sections of this book. When you work with Access, however, it is extremely important to close database files before copying or moving them, or before ejecting the Project Files floppy disk from the disk drive. Not doing so could result in corrupting the database so that it is no longer usable.

Why does this happen? Access is a multi-user application, which means that it allows multiple users to work with the same database file at the same time. In order to keep track of each file in use, Access creates temporary files. These temporary files automatically close when Access closes. However, if these files are open when you attempt to move or copy the database file using My Computer or Windows Explorer, they could cause serious damage to the database.

Make sure to close both the database file and the Access program window before moving, copying, or e-mailing database files. Also, make sure to eject the floppy disk containing your Project Files only after you have closed both the database file and the Access program window.

Access 2000 file format

As you begin the Access section, you might notice that the figures in these units and your own Access program window show "Access 2000 file format" in the title bar. This is because Access 2002 saves all files in Access 2000 format by default. This has the advantage of allowing users of previous versions of Access to view database files created using Access 2002. So, while it might appear at a glance that these units cover the previous version of Access, in fact they cover the latest version of Access (2002).

Unit
A

Getting
Started with Microsoft Office XP

Objectives

- ► **Understand Office XP Professional**
- ► **Start an Office program**
- ► **Use menus, toolbars, and the task pane**
- ► **Save, print, and close a file**
- ► **Use Help**
- ► **Create a new file with a wizard**
- ► **Exit an Office program**

Microsoft Office XP, often referred to as simply "Office," is a collection (or **suite**) of programs that you can use to produce a wide variety of documents, including letters, balance sheets, mailing lists, graphics presentations, Web pages, and comprehensive reports that combine all of these elements. Office comes in several **editions**, or product configurations. The Professional Edition includes Word, Excel, PowerPoint, Access, and Outlook. Among other editions are the Standard Edition, which does not include Access, and the Developer Edition, which includes FrontPage and the Microsoft Office Developer tools. The staff at Outdoor Designs, a company that sells do-it-yourself kits for recreational products, uses Office XP Professional to write memos and reports, manage inventory and sales data, track customers, and create business presentations. Sue Ellen Monteiro, the sales manager, has asked you to begin preparing a memo to the sales force using Office XP.

Office XP

Understanding Office XP Professional

Microsoft Office XP Professional Edition comes with a variety of programs and tools you can use to create documents, analyze data, and complete almost any business task. The programs you will learn about in this book include Word, Excel, Access, and PowerPoint. Sue Ellen suggests that you familiarize yourself with the programs and tools in Office XP Professional before starting work on your memo.

The following programs are contained in Office XP Professional:

▶ **Microsoft Word** is a word-processing program you can use to create text-based documents, such as letters, term papers, and reports. Figure A-1 shows an example of a letter. You also can use Word to add pictures, drawings, tables, and other graphical elements to your documents. At Outdoor Designs, you'll create memos, letters, flyers, and reports in Word to communicate with staff, customers, and distributors.

▶ **Microsoft Excel** is a spreadsheet program you can use to manipulate, analyze, and chart quantitative data, particularly financial information. Figure A-2 shows an example of a spreadsheet and chart. In your work at Outdoor Designs, you'll use Excel to create product order worksheets, shipping tickets, sales reports, and charts to help the Sales and Marketing Departments track sales and make informed business decisions.

▶ **Microsoft Access** is a database management program you use to store, organize, and display information, such as names and addresses, product inventories, and employee data. At Outdoor Designs, you'll use Access to create customer and product databases, data entry forms that others can use to input additional data, and reports the staff can use to spot important trends in the data.

▶ **Microsoft PowerPoint** is a presentation graphics program you can use to develop materials for presentations, including slide shows, computer-based presentations, speaker's notes, and handouts. An example of a presentation slide is shown in Figure A-3. The staff at Outdoor Designs is preparing for the fall season, so you'll use PowerPoint to create a sales presentation for the Sales Department and an informative presentation for the fall company meeting.

▶ **Microsoft Outlook** is an e-mail and information manager you use to send and receive e-mail, schedule appointments, maintain to do lists, and store contact information.

▶ **Microsoft Office Tools** are tools that facilitate working with the Office suite. The tools include **Microsoft Photo Editor**, which you can use to view and edit digital photographs and images, **Microsoft Binder**, which you can use to collect and store documents, images, and other useful information, and **Microsoft Office Application Recovery**, which allows you to restart an Office program that has stopped working unexpectedly. Additional Office tools include **Microsoft Access Snapshot Viewer**, which you can use to view and transmit Microsoft Access reports using less disk space, **Microsoft Office Language Settings**, which you can use to enable editing and related tools for working in other languages in Office documents, **Microsoft Office Shortcut Bar**, a toolbar that contains buttons for starting Office programs and performing other common Office tasks, **Server Extensions Administrator**, a tool for network administrators managing Office on a network, and **Microsoft Clip Organizer**, a tool that helps you organize picture, sound, and animated files.

FIGURE A-1: Document created in Microsoft Word

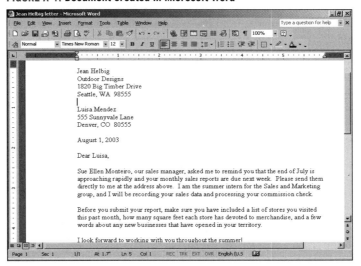

FIGURE A-2: Worksheet with a chart created in Microsoft Excel

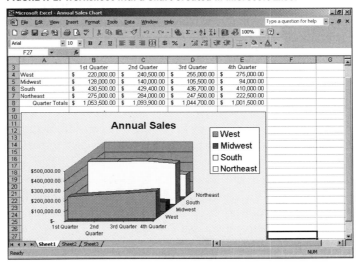

FIGURE A-3: Presentation created in Microsoft PowerPoint

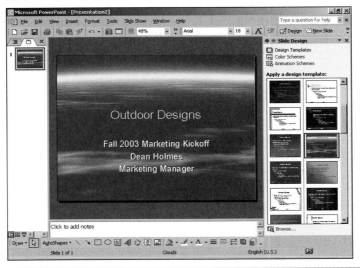

Unit A
Office XP

Starting an Office Program

As with many tasks you perform in Office, there are several ways you can start an Office program. One of the more basic methods is to use the Start menu on the taskbar. ✐ You decide to familiarize yourself with Office by starting Word and getting acquainted with the main screen elements, many of which are shared by all Office applications.

Steps

1. Click the Start button [Start] on the taskbar

The Start menu opens. Your screen should look similar to Figure A-4, however the items on your Start menu will probably be different.

QuickTip

If this is your first time using Word, you may see a dialog box that welcomes you to the Word program. If you do, click the Start button to start Word and then close the Office Assistant.

2. Point to Programs, then click Microsoft Word

Microsoft Word starts and displays a blank document on the screen, as shown in Figure A-5. The Word program window contains several elements common to all Office programs. The Word window displays the following elements, many of which are common to all Office applications:

- The **title bar** is the bar at the top of the Word window that contains the name of the document (with the temporary name "Document1" currently assigned to it) and the name of the application (currently Microsoft Word). The title bar also contains the **Minimize**, **Restore**, and **Close buttons** at its far right end.

- The **menu bar** is directly below the title bar, and includes the names of each Word menu, each of which contain commands you can click to perform tasks. Clicking a menu name opens its menu.

- At the far right of the menu bar is the **Ask a Question box**, which provides fast access to the Office XP Help system. If you need help on how to complete a task, you can type a question in this box and the Help System for that application will display a list of possible solutions to get you back on track.

- All Office applications have toolbars. A **toolbar** is a customizable set of buttons that provide rapid access to the most commonly used commands in a program. Buttons on a toolbar are often easier to remember than their menu counterparts because they display a picture illustrating their function. The **Standard toolbar**, located directly below the menu bar, contains buttons that perform the most common tasks in a program, such as opening, saving, and printing a document. The **Formatting toolbar**, just below the Standard toolbar, contains buttons that help you enhance the look of your document. The **Drawing toolbar**, at the bottom of the window, provides tools for drawing and working with graphical elements.

- The **task pane** is a window on the far right of an Office application window that provides access to the most commonly used commands in that application. The task pane changes depending on what task you are performing. At the moment, the **New Document task pane** is open, providing commands for creating a new document or opening an existing one.

- The **document window** is the area within the program window that contains your document. The **insertion point** is a flashing vertical line in the document window that indicates where text will be inserted when you type. The **status bar** is located at the bottom of the screen and displays information such as the current page and the location of the insertion point on the screen. It also displays important messages such as the status of the current print job.

FIGURE A-4: Start menu

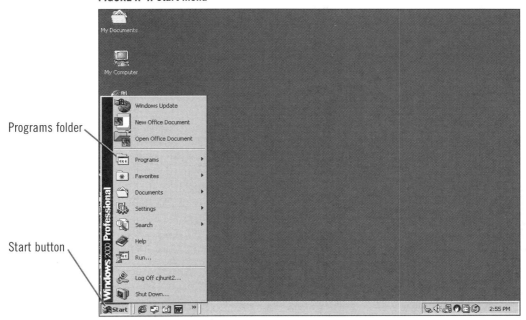

Programs folder

Start button

FIGURE A-5: Word window with New Document task pane open

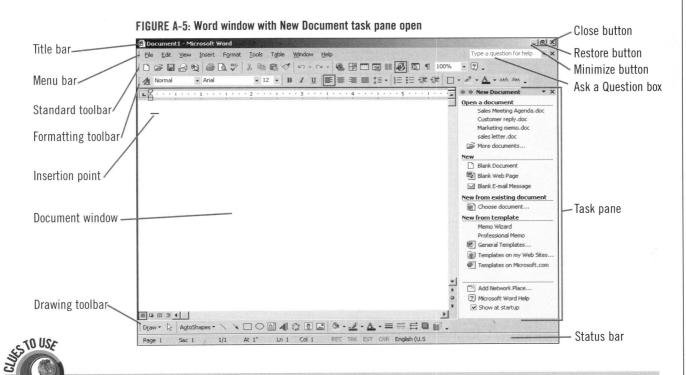

Title bar

Menu bar

Standard toolbar

Formatting toolbar

Insertion point

Document window

Drawing toolbar

Close button

Restore button

Minimize button

Ask a Question box

Task pane

Status bar

Starting an Office program with the New Office Document dialog box

If you prefer to work in a more **document-centric** environment, meaning that you like to focus on documents rather than the programs used to create them, you might prefer to start an Office program using the New Office Document dialog box. To use the New Office Document dialog box, click the Start button on the taskbar, then click New Office Document. The New Office Document dialog box opens, containing tabs for different types of documents. Depending on the type of document you click, Office starts the necessary program. If the Office Shortcut Bar is installed on your system, you can open the New Office Document dialog box by clicking the New Office Document button on the Office Shortcut Bar. To display the Office Shortcut Bar, click the Start button on the taskbar, point to Programs, click Microsoft Office Tools, then click Microsoft Office Shortcut Bar. If prompted, insert your Office XP CD to complete the installation.

Using Menus, Toolbars, and the Task Pane

All Office applications share similar tools that help you complete tasks. Menus, toolbar buttons, and the task pane are common to most Office programs and contain buttons or commands that you select to perform a task. If Office needs more information in order to carry out a particular command from a menu or toolbar, it displays a **dialog box** that presents available options for you to select to complete the task. Once you learn how to use these tools to select commands in Word, you will be able to use them in any Office application. You decide to use the task pane, menus, and toolbars to create a simple to do list for yourself.

Steps

1. Click **Blank Document** in the New section of the New Document task pane
   A new, blank document appears in the document window with the temporary name "Document2," and the task pane closes, giving you more space to work. The insertion point blinks at the top of the document.

2. With the insertion point at the top of the Word document window, press **[Enter]** four times
   The insertion point moves down four lines.

3. Click **Insert** on the Menu bar
   The Insert menu opens, as shown in Figure A-6, displaying a short list of commands relating to inserting various elements in a document. Office program menus are **personalized** to suit the way you work. When you first use an Office program, the menus display the most commonly used commands. Other commands are available on the **full menu**, which you can see by clicking the arrows at the bottom of a menu or double-clicking the menu name. When you use commands from the long menu, they are added to the short menu.

4. Click the **arrows** at the bottom of the Insert menu, then click **Date and Time** in the menu
   The Date and Time dialog box opens, showing options for inserting the date and time.

5. Click the **third format** in the Available formats list, as shown in Figure A-7, verify that the **Update automatically check box** contains a check mark, then click **OK**
   Today's date appears in the document. Because the Update automatically check box contains a check mark, the date will change to reflect today's date whenever you open this document.

6. Press **[Enter]** twice, type **To Do List**, then press **[Enter]** twice

7. Click the **Undo button** on the Standard toolbar
   The words you typed, "To Do List," are deleted, and the insertion point moves back up to the date. The Undo button reverses your last action. You can click the Redo button to restore your document to the state it was in before you clicked the Undo button.

8. Click the **Redo button** on the Standard toolbar, then type the following text, pressing **[Enter]** at the end of each line:

   Write memo to sales reps

   Schedule meeting with Lisa Allen in Human Resources

   Meet for lunch with other interns
   Compare your screen to Figure A-8.

Click arrows to open
the full menu

FIGURE A-7: Date and Time dialog box

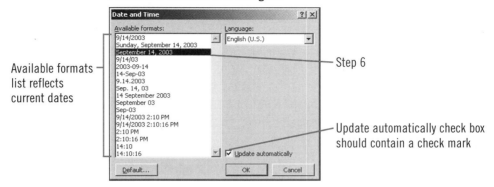

Available formats
list reflects
current dates

Step 6

Update automatically check box
should contain a check mark

FIGURE A-8: Completed To Do list

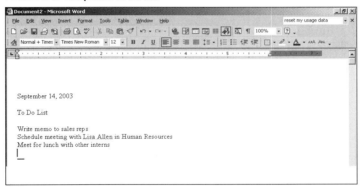

Customizing toolbars and menu commands

You can customize your toolbars and menus to suit your preferences by using the Customize dialog box. To open the Customize dialog box, click Tools on the menu bar, then click Customize. The Customize dialog box contains three tabs, as shown in Figure A-9. Use the Toolbar tab to choose which toolbars you want to display. Use the Commands tab to drag your favorite toolbar buttons from the dialog box to any location on a toolbar on your screen. You can also get full descriptions of each toolbar button's function on this tab. Use the Options tab to personalize certain aspects of how your toolbars and menus appear on-screen. For instance, you can specify that full menus should always be shown, or that the Standard and Formatting toolbars should be displayed on one row (instead of two, which is the default). You can also click the Reset my usage data button, which restores the configuration of the menus and toolbars to their default state.

Clicking this button is a good idea if you share your computer with others; it ensures that the most commonly used buttons will be available on-screen before you start working. Office will then personalize the menus and toolbars based on your actions.

FIGURE A-9: Customize dialog box

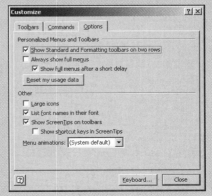

Saving, Printing, and Closing a File

When you enter data into a computer, it is stored in the computer's **random access memory (RAM)** until you turn off your computer, at which point the computer's RAM is erased. To store your work permanently, you must save it as a **file** (an electronic collection of data). When you save a document, you must assign it a unique **filename**, a name for the file so you can identify it later. You must also specify where you want to save the document (on a floppy disk or on the computer's hard disk, and in what folder, if any). Before you save a document, Office assigns it a temporary filename, such as "Document1" or "Book1," which reflects the type of document it is (the number is assigned in case you create more than one unsaved document during a work session). You decide to save your to do list.

1. **Click File on the menu bar, then click Save As**
   The Save As dialog box opens, showing the list of folders and files in the current folder. At the bottom of the dialog box is the File name box, where you enter the name you want for the file. By default, Word always suggests a filename based on the first text in the document, which is the date you inserted.

2. **Select all the text in the File name box if necessary, then type To Do List**
   The filename "To Do List" appears in the File name box, as shown in Figure A-10.

3. **If the Files of type list box does not display "Word Document," click the Files of type list arrow, scroll if necessary, then click Word Document**

4. **Click the Look in list arrow at the top of the dialog box, then navigate to the drive and folder where your Project Files are located**

5. **Click Save**
   The Save As dialog box closes, and your memo is saved to the drive and folder you specified. Notice that the title bar now displays the new filename.

6. **Click the Print button 🖨 on the Standard toolbar**
   Clicking this button prints the document using the program's default print settings—usually a single copy of the complete file.

7. **Click File on the menu bar, then click Close**
   The To Do List document closes. The temporary document "Document1" is still open in the document window.

Saving a File as a Web page

You can save almost any Office document as a Web page . To do this, click File on the menu bar, then click Save As Web Page. When the Save As dialog box opens specify a name and location for the file, then click OK. Saving a file as a Web page can be very helpful for distributing your file electronically or posting it on a Web site so that people can access it easily. If necessary, Office will open a dialog box showing what formatting elements will not be displayed in this file format. When you save a file as a Web page, it is saved in HTML format, the standard language for viewing documents over the Web. Once your page is saved as a Web page, it can be viewed in a Web browser, such as Internet Explorer or Netscape Navigator.

FIGURE A-10: Save As dialog box

Current drive or folder

File name box

Save as type box

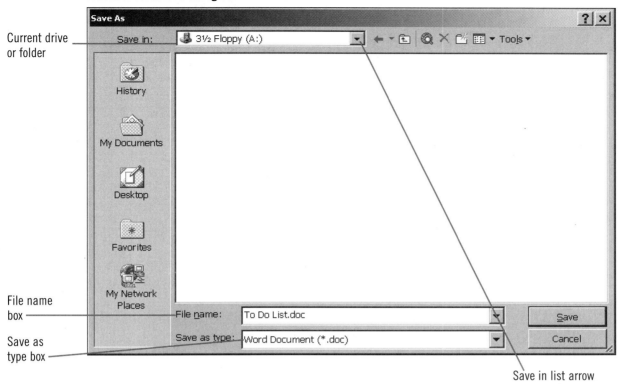

Save in list arrow

Naming files

A valid filename in an Office file can be up to 255 characters, but descriptive titles with fewer than 20 characters are easier to work with. You can use uppercase and lowercase letters in a filename, plus spaces and most symbols you can type on your keyboard. When you save your file, the proper program type is automatically associated with it so that even if you open it later using the Document menu on the Start menu, Windows Explorer, or some other means, the proper program starts and opens the file. When you name your files, try to use precise names that you'll remember later. Make sure you know in what drive and folder you are saving your files so that you can quickly find them when you need them.

Using Help

Office has an extensive Help system you can use to guide you through using almost any feature or completing any procedure. It has both step-by-step instructions and explanations of difficult concepts. The variety of Help tools available suits many different situations and work styles. You can access Help quickly by typing a question in the **Ask a Question box**, which searches the Help database for keywords related to your question; you can open the Help dialog box and scan the entire Help index or table of contents to look for answers; you can respond to Help given by the **Office Assistant**, which is an animated character that appears on screen and provides tips and alerts as you work. You can also get a quick explanation of almost any screen element by pointing to it with the What's This? pointer, available through the Help menu. Finally, you can obtain assistance and information on the World Wide Web. Familiarize yourself with the Help system now by learning about some formatting features in preparation for the documents you will be creating in Word.

1. Click in the **Ask a Question box**, type **how do I get help?**, then press **[Enter]**

   A list opens, showing several topics related to your entry. See Figure A-11.

2. Click **About getting help while you work**, then click the **Contents tab** in the Microsoft Word Help dialog box

   The Help dialog box displays a table of contents for Help topics on the left, and the topic you selected on the right, as shown in Figure A-12. You see two other tabs in this dialog box. The Answer Wizard tab lets you ask a question and preview the related topics it finds in the right pane, and the Index tab lets you search for topics based on key words.

3. Click the heading **Ask a Question box** in the right pane, read the text that appears, then click **Ask a Question box** again

   The text under the Ask a Question box heading collapses. You can click any link in the right pane to read more about the topic or term, then click it again to collapse the text.

4. Click the **Close button** in the Help dialog box

5. Click **Help** on the menu bar, then click **What's This?**

   The pointer changes to ⟨?. When this pointer is active and you click a screen element or command for which a ScreenTip is available, the ScreenTip opens in a shaded box. A **ScreenTip** is a concise explanation of the selected screen element. You can also click the What's This? pointer on text in your documents to view the text's current formatting.

6. Click the **status bar** at the bottom of the Word window, read the ScreenTip that appears, then click anywhere to close the ScreenTip

7. Click **Help** on the menu bar, then click **Show the Office Assistant**

   The Office Assistant appears on your screen. It may look like an animated paper clip character or it may be a different character.

8. Click the **Office Assistant**, type **saving a file** in the text box at the bottom of the Help bubble as shown in Figure A-13, then click **Search**

   The Assistant displays a list of Help topics.

9. Right-click the **Office Assistant**, then click **Hide** on the pop-up menu

   The Assistant swirls around the screen for a moment and then disappears.

QuickTip

Many dialog boxes also contain a Help button ? on the right side of the title bar that you can click to activate the What's This? pointer. Using this pointer to click the elements of the dialog box helps you learn about the options available and when to use them.

QuickTip

To close a ScreenTip, turn off the What's This? pointer, or close an Office Assistant bubble, press [Esc].

FIGURE A-11: Ask a Question list box

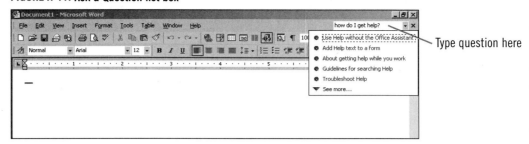

Type question here

FIGURE A-12: Microsoft Word Help dialog box

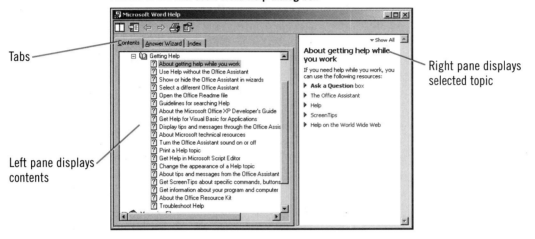

Tabs

Left pane displays contents

Right pane displays selected topic

FIGURE A-13: The Microsoft Office Assistant

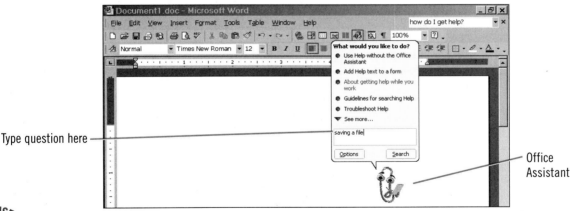

Type question here

Office Assistant

CLUES TO USE

Using the Office Assistant

Using the Office Assistant is a fun and easy way to find information. You can ask it questions or set it to provide tips and guidance while you work. To ask a question when the Assistant is open, click the Assistant, then type your question. Clicking outside the Assistant window closes the window, but the Assistant stays on your screen. To reopen the window, just click the Assistant and type another question. You can drag the Assistant to a new location if it's in the way (it also moves automatically when you enter data near it). To move the Assistant off your screen entirely, right-click the Assistant and then click Hide. You can also customize how the Assistant looks, to suit your personality (there's an Einstein image, a cat and dog, a smiley face, and other graphics). To change the way the Office Assistant works, display the Office Assistant if necessary, right-click it, then click Options and choose the appropriate settings in the Office Assistant dialog box.

Creating a New File with a Wizard

A **wizard** is a series of dialog boxes that guides you step by step through the process of creating a new document or completing a task. A **template** is a special file that contains predesigned formatting, text, and other tools for creating common business documents, such as letters, business presentations, and invoices. By creating a new document using a wizard or template, you can save formatting time and be assured that the finished document will look professional. When you start a new document using a wizard, you first supply specific information, usually using dialog boxes, so that Office can prepare the initial document for your review and modification. When you start a new document using a template, the document opens immediately on your screen, ready for you to customize and save it. ◄━━ Sue Ellen asks you to create a memo to the sales reps, informing them of the summer sales department outing. You decide to begin creating the memo with the Memo Wizard.

Steps

1. Click **File** on the menu bar, then click **New**
The New Document task pane opens.

2. Click **General Templates** in the New from template section of the task pane
The General Templates dialog box opens, displaying tabs for various types of documents, as shown in Figure A-14.

3. Click the **Memos tab,** then double-click the **Memo Wizard icon**
The first dialog box in the Memo Wizard opens, as shown in Figure A-15. The dialog boxes in a wizard are easy to navigate; after you finish reading or completing the current dialog box, click Next. To return to a previous dialog box to change information, click Back.

4. Click **Next**
The next dialog box opens, where you choose a style for the memo. Notice that the chart on the left side of the wizard dialog box tracks your progress through the document creation process, so you know how many steps are left to complete.

5. In the Style dialog box click **Next** to accept the default style (Professional), then click **Next** in the Title dialog box

6. In the Heading Fields dialog box click in the **Date text box** and change the date to **6/1/2003**; click in the **From text box** and type your own name; click in the **Subject text box** and type **Sales Department Summer Outing**; then click **Next**

7. In the Recipient dialog box click in the **To text box** and type **All Sales Reps**; click in the **CC text box** and type **Sue Ellen Monteiro**; then click **Next**

8. Click **Next** two more times to accept the defaults in the Closing Fields and Header/Footer dialog boxes, then click **Finish**
The memo appears in the document window, as shown in Figure A-16, ready for you to customize it further.

9. If the Office Assistant opens, click **Cancel** to close it

FIGURE A-14: Templates dialog box

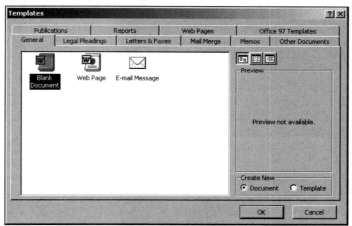

FIGURE A-15: Memo Wizard dialog box

This area shows your progress as you create the memo

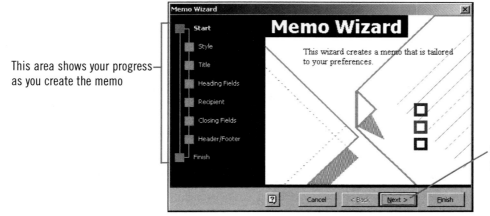

Click the Next > button to move to the next dialog box

FIGURE A-16: Completed memo ready for customization

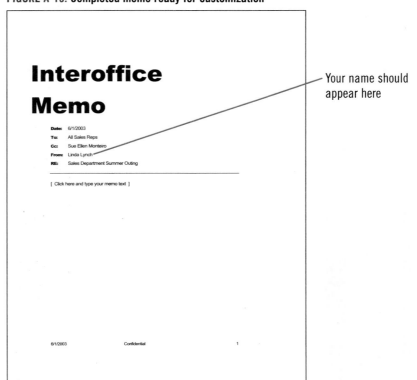

Your name should appear here

Office XP

Exiting an Office Program

When you complete all the work you want to accomplish in a given session, you can save and print your document, then close and exit the program. ✏️ You're ready to save and close your memo and exit Word because your day at Outdoor Designs is finished.

Steps

1. **Click the Save button 🖫 on the Standard toolbar**
   The Save As dialog box opens. If you have not saved the current document before, clicking the Save button opens the Save As dialog box. If you have already saved the document, clicking the Save button simply updates the saved document with any changes you have made since the last save.

2. **Navigate to the drive and folder where your Project Files are located, then type Summer Outing Memo in the File name text box**
   Compare your screen with Figure A-17.

3. **Click Save**
   The Save As dialog box closes.

4. **Click File on the menu bar, click Print, then click Print in the Print dialog box**
   A copy of the document prints.

QuickTip

You can also close a file by clicking the Close button in the top-right corner of the document window.

5. **Click File on the menu bar, then click Close**
   The memo closes. If you had made changes to the file since you saved it, a dialog box would have opened, prompting you to save the changes. (You can save changes to a document at any time by clicking File on the menu bar, then clicking Save, or by clicking the Save button 🖫 on the Standard toolbar.)

QuickTip

You can also exit a program by clicking the program window's close button at the right end of the title bar.

6. **Click File on the menu bar, then click Exit, as shown in Figure A-18**
   The Word program closes.

FIGURE A-17: Save As dialog box

Current drive or folder

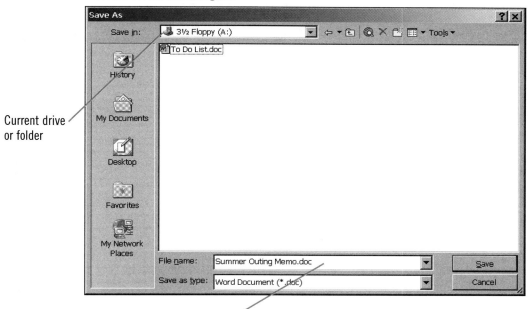

Filename

FIGURE A-18: Exiting a program

Step 6

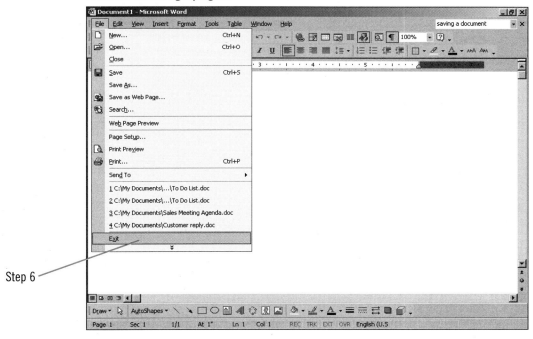

Practice

▶ Concepts Review

Label each of the elements shown in Figure A-19.

FIGURE A-19

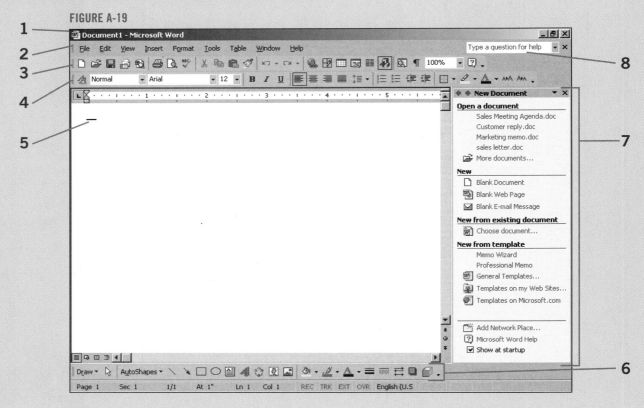

Match each of the following programs with the task for which it is most useful.

9. **Excel**   **a.** Manipulate and analyze spreadsheet data

10. **Access**   **b.** Schedule appointments, maintain to do lists, store contact information, and send e-mail

11. **Word**   **c.** Create slides for presentations and online demonstrations

12. **Outlook**   **d.** Create printed documents, such as memos and letters, and Web pages

13. **PowerPoint**   **e.** Organize databases of information

Select the best answer from the list of choices.

14. The phrase "Microsoft Office is a suite of programs" means that:
  a. Microsoft Office consists of one program that contains many features.
  b. The programs in Office function independently but work together when needed.
  c. You cannot use one Office program unless all the programs are open.
  d. The programs in Office must be installed on a network.

15. Word is used primarily to:
  a. Calculate loan payments and track expenses.
  b. Create text-based documents such as letters, memos, and reports.
  c. Track phone numbers and addresses.
  d. Maintain spreadsheet information.

16. In the New Office Document dialog box, you can:
  a. Start a new Excel spreadsheet.
  b. Start a new Word document.
  c. Start a new PowerPoint presentation.
  d. All of the above

17. To restore the configuration of the menus and toolbars in an Office application to their original state, you can:
  a. Press F1.
  b. Click the Save button on the Standard toolbar.
  c. Open the Customize dialog box, click the Options tab, then click Reset my usage data.
  d. Double-click the Status bar at the bottom of an Office application window.

18. To save an Office document as a Web page, you can:
  a. Click Web Page in the Save as type list box within the Save As dialog box.
  b. Click Rich Text Format in the Save as type list box within the Save As dialog box.
  c. Click Help on the menu bar, then click Show the Office Assistant.
  d. You can't save Office documents as Web pages.

19. The Formatting toolbar, located just below the Standard toolbar in most Office programs, contains buttons that help you:
  a. Get help from the Help system.
  b. Perform the most common tasks in an application, such as opening, saving, and printing a document.
  c. Draw artwork and work with graphical elements.
  d. Enhance the look of your document.

20. A wizard is a(n):
  a. Animated Office Assistant character.
  b. Shortcut file that is available only in Microsoft Word.
  c. Series of dialog boxes that guides you through completing a task or creating a document.
  d. Help file that teaches you about different Office programs.

▶ Skills Review

1. Understand Office XP Professional.
a. Review the programs and tools in the Office XP Professional suite.
b. How many applications are included with Office XP Professional? What are their names?
c. Which Office application would you use to create a term paper? A sales chart? An e-mail message?

2. Start an Office program.
a. Click the Start button.
b. Point to Programs, then click Microsoft Word.
c. Identify the elements of a typical Office application.
d. Where are the toolbars located? How would you minimize an Office application? How would you restore the application window? What is the purpose of the task pane?

3. Use menus, toolbars, and the task pane.
a. Open a new, blank document in the Word document window.
b. Use the Date and Time command on the Insert menu to insert the current date and time at the top of the document (select the second date and time format).
c. Press Enter twice, then type the following schedule, pressing Enter at the end of each line:
   10:00 a.m. Meet with Sales Director
   11:00 a.m. Write sales memo
   12:00 a.m. Lunch with Tina!
   2:00 p.m. Gather express packages
   3:00 p.m. Photocopy sales reports
d. Delete the last line in the schedule, then click the Undo button on the Standard toolbar to restore it.
e. Type your name at the bottom of the schedule.

4. Save, print, and close a file.
a. Open the Save As dialog box.
b. Name the current document *My Work Schedule*.
c. Navigate to the drive and folder where your Project Files are located.
d. Save the document.
e. Print the document by using a button on the Standard toolbar.
f. Close the document.

5. Use Help.
   a. Click Help on the menu bar, then click Show the Office Assistant.
   b. Type **How do I Print?**, then click Search.
   c. Click the Print a document option button.
   d. Maximize the right pane if you have trouble seeing the Help text.
   e. Read the topics in the window, clicking any additional topics that interest you.
   f. When you are finished, close the Help window.
   g. Click the What's This? command on the Help menu, then click the Open button 🗁 on the Standard toolbar.
   h. After reading the ScreenTip, click anywhere on the screen.
   i. Right-click the Office Assistant icon, then click Hide.

6. Create a new file with a wizard.
   a. Click File on the menu bar, then click New.
   b. Click General Templates in the New from template section of the task pane.
   c. Click the Letters & Faxes tab, click Letter Wizard, and then click OK.
   d. Click Send one letter in the Office Assistant dialog box.
   e. Click Next to accept the default letter format.
   f. Type **Jon Crump** in the Recipient's name text box, then press Tab.
   g. Type the following address in the Delivery address text box, then click Next:
      555 Green Tree Ave.
      North Bend, WA 98555
   h. Click Next to accept the default settings in the Other Elements tab.
   i. Type your name and address in the Sender's name and Return address text boxes.
   j. Type **Outdoor Designs** in the Company text box, then click Finish.
   k. Click Cancel in the Office Assistant dialog box to close the wizard.
   l. Delete the paragraph beginning with "Type your letter here."
   m. Insert the text **Welcome to the company!** in the letter.
   n. Save the letter as *Wizard Greeting Letter*, then print it.

7. Exit an Office program.
   a. Close the *Wizard Greeting Letter* document.
   b. Exit Word.

▶ Independent Challenge 1

Sue Ellen Monteiro has asked you to prepare a simple list of the do-it-yourself kits that Outdoor Designs sells, for inclusion in marketing letters, product brochures, and employee training. Use Word to prepare the list now and print a copy with your name at the top of it.

a. Start Microsoft Word and open a new, blank document.

b. Insert the current date at the top of the document.

c. Type **Outdoor Designs Kits** and your name below the date.

d. Enter a blank line, then type the following kit names, pressing Enter after each line:
Cascade Ski Sack
Coastal Parafoil Kite
Puget Sound Delta Kite
Olympic Rain Tent
Tent Vestibule
Franklin's Diamond
Columbia Gorge Runner

e. Insert the following kit names between the first and second kit names (i.e. between Cascade Ski Sack and Coastal Parafoil Kite):
The Green Flyer
Sonic Boomer Stunt Kite

f. Save the document using the filename *Kit Names*, print a copy, then close the document and exit Word.

▶ Independent Challenge 2

Throughout this unit, you used Microsoft Word to learn about many features that are common to all Office programs, including screen elements such as toolbars. Use what you have learned to explore another Office program and see the similarities for yourself.

a. Start Microsoft Excel.

b. Compare the Excel program screen with what you know of the Word program screen. The grid-like structure of the Excel worksheet window is different from the blank document screen of Word, but many of the screen elements, such as scroll bars, commands, and buttons, are the same.

c. Experiment with entering text in this worksheet window by typing your name, then pressing [Enter].

d. Below your name, type the following numbers, one number per cell. (*Hint*: A cell is formed by the intersection of rows and columns in a worksheet. To store data in a cell, you press [Enter].)

25
50
75
100

e. The menus and toolbars in Excel have much in common with the menus and toolbars in Word. Click the Save button now to open the Save As dialog box, then save your workbook using the filename *Excel Practice*. Compare your screen with Figure A-20.

f. Click the Print button on the Standard toolbar to print the worksheet.

g. Experiment with additional menu and toolbar commands, then exit Excel.

FIGURE A-20

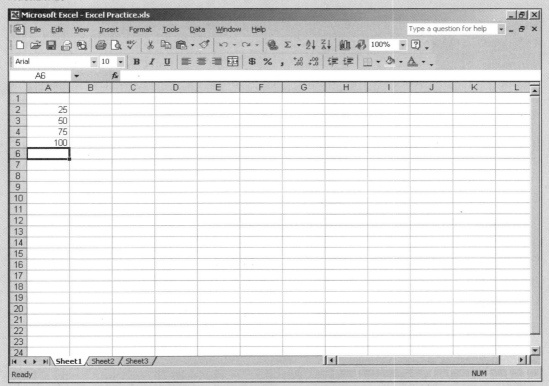

Independent Challenge 3

Increase your familiarity with Office documents by creating a letter using the Contemporary Document template in Word. The Contemporary Document template is very similar to the Letter Wizard that you have already used, but it does not step you through the process of creating a document using dialog boxes. Instead, you customize the letter by replacing selected text items with your own letter content. Use the Contemporary Document template to create a brief letter to Outdoor Designs employee Louisa Mendez reminding her that her sales report is due.

a. Start Word.

b. Click File on the menu bar, then click New.

c. Click General Templates in the New from template section of the task pane.

d. Click the Letters & Faxes tab, click Contemporary Letter, and then click OK.

e. Type the following address in the upper-right corner of the letter:
Outdoor Designs
1820 Big Timber Drive
Seattle, WA 98555

f. Change the company name at the top of the letter to **Outdoor Designs**.

g. In the recipients address field, type the following:
Luisa Mendez
555 Sunnyvale Lane
Denver, CO 80555

h. Change the greeting to Dear Madam.

i. Delete the instructions in the letter, and type the following text in its place:
Send in your sales report data immediately.

j. Type your name at the bottom of the letter, and delete the job title section.

k. Save the letter as *Template Sales Letter*, print a copy, then close the document and exit Word.

Independent Challenge 4

Microsoft offers a wealth of guidance on the World Wide Web for getting the most from Microsoft Office. This information will be useful to you as you start your new job at Outdoor Designs. Use the Office on the Web command now to visit the Microsoft Office Assistance Center and research one or more Office applications. Copy one or two paragraphs of text from the Web site to your own Word document so that you can remember the information.

a. Start Microsoft Word.

b. Open the Help menu, then click Office on the Web.

c. If necessary, connect to the Internet. When you are connected to the Microsoft Office Assistance Center (you may need to first specify your country on the Microsoft Office Worldwide page), examine the Web site to see what type of information is being offered about Office applications.

d. Click a link with information related to Microsoft Word or another Office application. (*Hint*: The Working with Documents link often contains information about creating Word documents.)

e. Open an article about some aspect of creating documents, then select two or three paragraphs of text and press Ctrl+C to copy it to the clipboard. (For example, open the article entitled "Create Party Invitations, Envelopes, and Labels with Word 2002".)

f. Click the Word document icon on the task bar to restore the Word application, then press Ctrl+V to paste the information from the Office Web site into your document.

g. Type your name at the top of the Word document, then save the document using the filename *Office Product Information*.

h. Print the document and then close it. When you are finished, disconnect from the Internet, then exit Word.

► Visual Workshop

Use the skills you have learned in this unit to create the document shown in Figure A-21. (*Hint*: It was created using a wizard in the Memos tab of the Templates dialog box.) Type your own name in the From field. When you have finished, save the document as *Germany Memo*, then print a copy.

FIGURE A-21

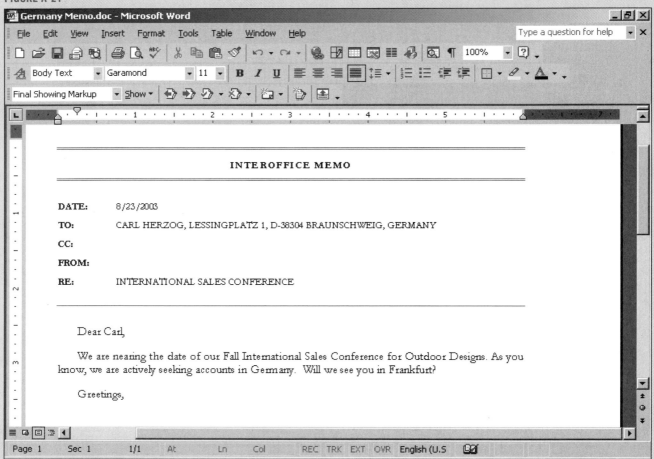

Creating
a Document

- ► **Plan a document**
- ► **Create a new document from an existing file**
- ► **Enter text in a document**
- ► **Edit a document**
- ► **Move and copy text**
- ► **Find and replace text**
- ► **Check spelling and grammar**
- ► **Preview and print a document**

You can create professional looking documents using Microsoft Word 2002, the word processor that comes with Microsoft Office. In this unit, you will learn some basic skills to help you create, edit, and print a document. You'll also learn how to use Word to find and replace text, check your spelling and grammar, and print a document. ◄━━ Sue Ellen Monteiro, the sales manager for Outdoor Designs, asks you to finish a memo to the sales representatives that she started. The memo needs to remind the sales reps that their monthly sales reports are due and inform them of the location for the January sales meeting.

Word 2002

Planning a Document

Before you begin to create any document, even a simple memo, you should outline its content and plan how you want it to look. You should consider who will read your document and what type of presentation will get your message across most clearly. As you grow more experienced in Word, you may not need to write out a plan for each simple document, but you should always review these steps to make sure you've covered the important elements. ✐ Before you begin working on your memo to the sales representatives, you plan what you want to accomplish and how to accomplish it. Figure A-1 shows a sample plan.

Details

► **Determine the document's purpose and content**
You have three goals for your memo. You need to remind the sales representatives to send in their monthly sales reports on time and to communicate that the location of the January sales meeting is set for Scottsdale, Arizona. You also want to introduce yourself to them as the new summer intern, and describe some of your job responsibilities.

► **Determine the document's length**
You decide to keep the memo short, to keep the representatives interested and to make sure they obtain the information they need quickly.

► **Determine the document's format and formatting**
A standard business memo format is an appropriate format to convey the information. Your short and simple memo doesn't need a lot of formatting to make it attractive and readable.

► **Determine the document's organization**
You'll include the typical "To:" and "From:" lines at the top of the memo, followed by the main content, a closing, and your name. You will also CC: Sue Ellen on the memo.

► **Determine how to create the document—from scratch or with a template**
The templates and wizards provided in Word can help you create many types of documents, including memos. Sue Ellen already created part of the memo using a Memo template. She has asked you to finish it and send it to the reps from you. You will open the file that she started, save it with a new name, and add additional text to it.

1. Purpose and Content

    Remind reps that sales reports are due next week.

    Introduce myself and tell them that I'm responsible for processing their

    commission checks.

    Communicate location and dates of the January sales meeting and product training

    sessions.

2. Format and formatting

    Standard business memo format. Keep formatting simple.

3. Organization

    Include "To:" and "From:" lines at the top of memo, followed by main

    content, a closing, and my name.

4. Length

    Keep it short - 1 page.

5. How to create

    Add to Sue Ellen's memo.

Word 2002

Word 2002

Creating a New Document from an Existing File

You can create a new document in several ways in Microsoft Word. You can use the Blank Document command on the New Document task pane to create a new, blank document and then type your text into it. You can also use a template or wizard to start a particular kind of document such as a memo or fax cover sheet. If you want to base your new document on existing material, such as a letter or report that is similar to a new one you want to create, you can open a copy of the existing document and save it with a new name by using the Choose document command on the New Document task pane. Creating a new file in this way keeps the original file intact in case you want to use it again, while saving you the trouble of creating the document from scratch. Sue Ellen gives you her partially completed memo, which includes some of the information about the Sales Meeting. You'll open a copy of her document and then save it with a different name.

Trouble?

If the New Document task pane is not open, click File on the menu bar, then click New to open it.

QuickTip

To quickly return to the last location you displayed, click the Back button ⇐ on the toolbar in the New from Existing Document dialog box.

1. Click the **Start button** ▣Start on the taskbar, point to **Programs**, then click **Microsoft Word**
   Your screen should look similar to Figure A-2.

2. Click **Choose document** in the New from existing document section in the New Document task pane
   The New from Existing Document dialog box opens.

3. Click the **Look in list arrow**, then click the drive and folder where your Project Files are located
   All the Word files in the selected folder, including WD A-1, appear in the list of files. See Figure A-3.

4. Double-click **WD A-1**
   After a moment, the memo document opens in the document window and the task pane closes, giving you more room to work. The title bar shows the temporary file name Document2.

5. Click the **Save button** 🖫 on the Standard toolbar
   The Save As dialog box opens.

6. Click the **Look in list arrow**, navigate to the drive and folder where your Project Files are located, select the text **Professional Memo** in the File name box, type **Sales Rep Memo**, then click **OK**
   Word saves the new file, Sales Rep Memo, to the drive and folder you specified. The title bar changes to reflect the new name. The file WD A-1 remains closed and intact.

7. Click **View** on the menu bar, point to **Toolbars**, click **Customize**, click the **Options tab**, verify that the Show Standard and Formatting toolbars on two rows check box contains a check mark, click the **Reset my usage data button**, click **Yes**, then click **Close**
   Displaying the Standard and Formatting toolbars on two rows gives you access to more buttons than having them just on one row. Clicking the reset my usage data button sets the toolbars to their default configuration.

QuickTip

The Show/Hide ¶ button is a toggle button. Clicking it once turns it on to show formatting marks, clicking it again turns it off, to hide the formatting marks.

8. Click the **Show/Hide ¶ button** ¶ on the Standard toolbar
   Your screen now displays formatting marks. Dots appear between words to indicate spaces, and a ¶ appears at the end of paragraph returns. Showing formatting marks makes it easier to identify unintended spaces, paragraph returns, and other punctuation errors in a document. Compare your screen with Figure A-4.

FIGURE A-2: Word window with New Document task pane open

Choose document command

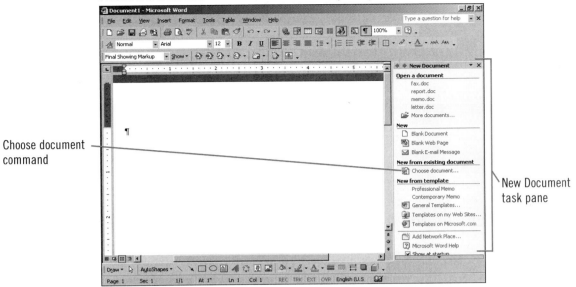

New Document task pane

FIGURE A-3: New from Existing Document dialog box

Project Files

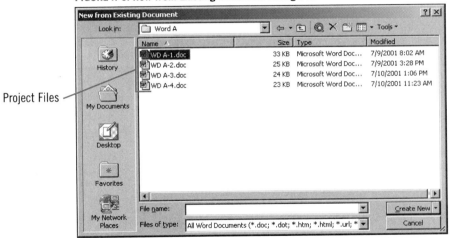

FIGURE A-4: Word program window with an unsaved copy of file WD A-1 open

Show/Hide ¶ button

Paragraph marks indicate the end of paragraphs

Dots between words indicate spaces

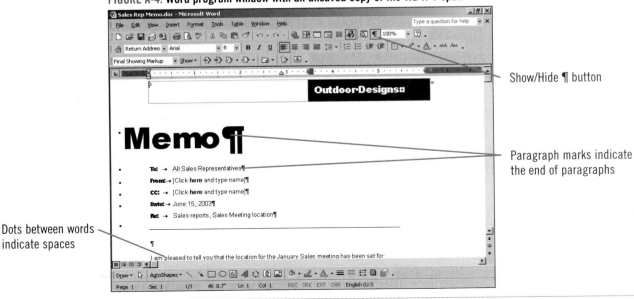

Word 2002

Entering Text in a Document

The first step in creating a document is to **enter**, or type, text that is the content of your document in the Word document window. Before you get started, it's a good idea to make sure you are viewing the document in a way that's suitable for entering and editing text. A **view** is the way in which Word displays the document you are working on. Word provides you with many different views. For instance, **Print Layout view** shows all elements of the printed page and is the view that's best for seeing how the document will look when printed. For entering and editing text, it's better to use **Normal view**, which hides some of the page elements so that you can focus on writing and editing. Sue Ellen's memo already contains some text describing the location of the sales meeting. You will enter text above this existing text to remind the reps to turn in their sales reports. You will also introduce yourself and describe your responsibilities.

1. Click **View** on the menu bar, then click **Normal**

2. Click anywhere in the text **Click here and type name** in the CC: line of the memo
   "Click here and type name" is a **placeholder**, temporary text that prompts you to enter appropriate information in that location. When you click in the placeholder, the entire line becomes highlighted, or **selected**, as shown in Figure A-5. Any text you enter automatically replaces selected text.

3. Type **Sue Ellen Monteiro,** then press [↓] three times
   As soon as you started typing, the characters you typed replaced the placeholder text. The blinking, vertical line on the screen is the **insertion point**. The insertion point indicates where text will be inserted when you type.

4. Type **Greetings from the Seattle office!**, press [Enter], type **I look forward to working with you throughout the summer!**, then press [Enter]
   As you type, the existing text moves down to make room for the new text. When you press [Enter], the insertion point moves down one line and to the left margin.

5. Type **teh**, then press [Spacebar]
   Notice that even though you typed "teh" Word assumed that you meant to type "The" and automatically corrected it. This automatic correction capability is called **AutoCorrect**.

6. Type the following, but do not press [Enter] when you reach the right edge of your screen
   end of June is rapidly approaching. I have been asked by Sue Ellen Monteiro, our sales manager, to remind you that your monthly reports are due next week.
   At some point before the words "to remind you," the word you were typing moved down, or **wrapped** to the next line on the screen. This is known as **word wrap**, a feature that automatically pushes text to the next line when the insertion point meets the right margin.

QuickTip

The way your text wraps may not exactly match the figures in this book. Text wraps according to the printer driver your particular machine uses.

7. Press [Enter], then continue typing the rest of the memo, making sure to type the errors as shown (type "the" twice and don't correct the misspelled words)
   Please send them directly to me at the Seattle office. I am the new intern for the the Outdoor Designs Sales and Marketing groop, and I will be recording your sales data and processing your commission chevks.
   If you see red, wavy lines under the misspelled words on your screen, this indicates that automatic spell checking is turned on and these words have been flagged as possible misspellings. Green wavy lines indicate grammatical errors. See Figure A-6.

FIGURE A-5: Placeholder text selected

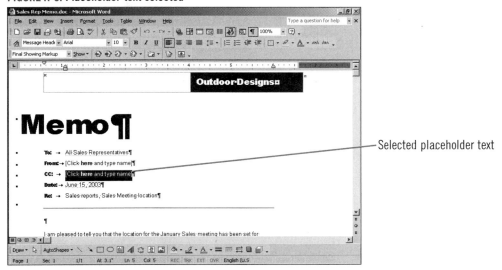

Selected placeholder text

FIGURE A-6: Memo with all text entered

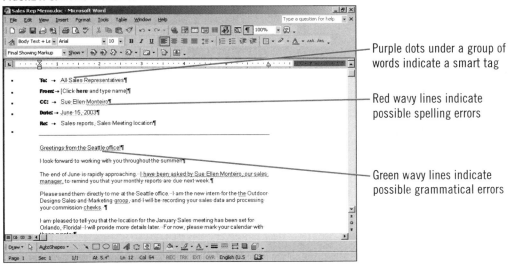

Purple dots under a group of words indicate a smart tag

Red wavy lines indicate possible spelling errors

Green wavy lines indicate possible grammatical errors

Word 2002

CLUES TO USE

Using AutoCorrect

The AutoCorrect feature makes corrections to certain words as you type. For example, if you type "comapny" instead of "company," as soon as you press the [Spacebar] Word corrects the misspelling. After Word makes the correction, a small blue bar appears ▬▬▬ under the corrected text. If you place the mouse pointer over this bar, the AutoCorrect options button appears. 🍪 ▾. Click the AutoCorrect Options button to display a list of options, as shown in Figure A-7, then click an option.

You can turn AutoCorrect on and off in the AutoCorrect dialog box. To open this dialog box, click Tools on the menu bar, then click AutoCorrect Options. You can turn any of the options on or off by clicking the check boxes. If you don't want the AutoCorrect Options buttons to show, deselect the Show AutoCorrect Options

buttons check box. If there is a word you mistype frequently, you can add it to the replacement list by typing it with the error in the Replace text box, then typing the correct version in the With text box.

FIGURE A-7: AutoCorrect Options Menu

The end of June is rapidly approaching. I have be
🍪 ▾ ger, to remind you that your monthly reports

↩ Undo Automatic Corrections

   Stop Auto-capitalizing First Letter of Sentences

   Stop Automatically Correcting "teh"

🍪 Control AutoCorrect Options...

AutoCorrect options button

Word 2002

Editing a Document

After you enter text in a Word document, you can **edit**, or modify, the text in several ways. To delete individual letters, you can press [Backspace] or [Delete]. You can also select a block of unwanted text entirely, then press [Delete] to delete the selection or type new text to replace it. To perform editing tasks, you need to move the insertion point around the document. You can do this by pointing and clicking, or you can use the keyboard. Table A-2 describes keys you can use to move the insertion point around the document. As you read the memo, you decide to make some changes. First you want to correct one of the misspellings.

1. Click between the letters **o** and **p** in the word "groop" in the fourth paragraph
The insertion point blinks between these two letters. You could also have pressed the [↑] and [→] keys to move the insertion point to this location.

Trouble?

If Word is in Overwrite mode, you cannot insert any text between letters; text you type deletes the characters to the right of the insertion point. You can tell that Word is in Overwrite mode if the letters "OVR" are highlighted on the status bar. To turn off Overwrite mode, press [Insert] or double-click OVR on the status bar.

2. Press [**Backspace**], then type **u**
When you pressed [Backspace], the "o" was deleted. Pressing [Backspace] deletes the character to the left of the insertion point. Pressing [Delete] deletes the character to the right of the insertion point. Notice that the red wavy lines are now gone from under the word, indicating that now it is spelled correctly.

3. Click to the left of the letter **O** in "Outdoor Designs" in the fourth paragraph
The insertion point blinks before the word "Outdoor."

4. Press and hold down [**Ctrl**] and [**Shift**] and press [→] twice to select the words "Outdoor Designs" and the blank space following them, then release the keys
"Outdoor Designs" is selected, as shown in Figure A-8.

QuickTip

To extend the selection only one character at a time, press only [Shift] while pressing [→] or [←].

5. Press [**Delete**]
The words "Outdoor Designs" are removed from the document. Notice that the text after the deleted words wraps back to fill the empty space.

6. Double-click the word **them** in the first line of the fourth paragraph
When you double-click a word, the entire word becomes selected.

7. Type **your reports**
The characters you type replace the selected text.

QuickTip

To undo just the most recent action more quickly, click the Undo button 🔄 instead of the button's list arrow.

8. Click the **Undo button list arrow** 🔄▾ on the Standard toolbar, then click **Typing "your reports"** (the first entry in the list) as shown in Figure A-9
The word "them" reappears in the document exactly how and where it was before you changed it. You can select as many actions from the Undo list as you want; the most recent action is listed first.

9. Click the **Save button** 💾 on the Standard toolbar

Using Click and Type

Click and Type is a feature that allows you to begin typing in almost any blank area of a document without pressing [Enter], [Tab], or [Spacebar] to move the insertion point to that location. Instead, you simply double-click where you want to begin typing. Click and Type is available only in Print Layout view and Web Layout view and only in areas that do not contain a bulleted or numbered list, a left or right indent, a picture with text

wrapping, or multiple columns. To see if this feature is available, point to the area where you'd like to type; if the pointer changes to I≡, Click and Type is available and you can double-click to start typing there. To disable this feature (or to turn it on if it has been disabled), click Tools on the menu bar, click Options, click the Edit tab, then click the Enable click and type check box to deselect it (or to select it to turn this feature on).

FIGURE A-8: Two words selected

Selected text

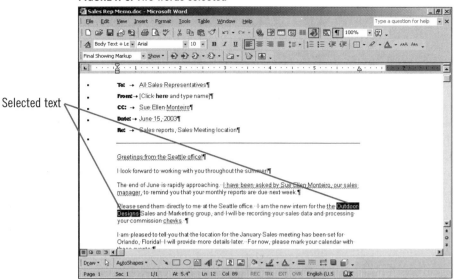

FIGURE A-9: Undo list

Undo button

Click top item to
undo last action

Undo button
list arrow

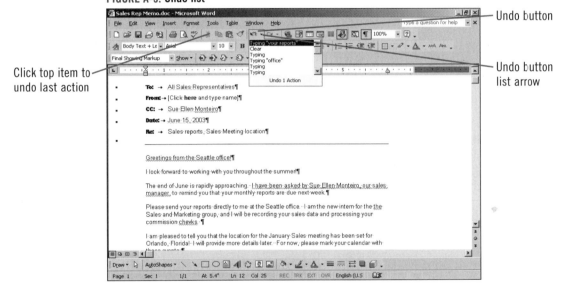

TABLE A-1: Useful keys for moving the insertion point around a document

keyboard key	moves insertion point	
[Backspace]	Back one space deleting previous character	
[↑],[↓]	Up or down one line	
[Ctrl] [←], [Ctrl] [→]	One word to the right or left	
[Home]	To the beginning of the line	
[End]	To the end of the line	
[Ctrl][Home]	To the beginning of the document	
[Ctrl][End]	To the end of the document	

Moving and Copying Text

You can move and copy text from one part of your document to another using the Cut, Copy, and Paste commands. You can **cut** (remove) or **copy** (duplicate) selected text from your document, place it on the **Windows Clipboard** (a temporary storage area in your computer's memory for cut and copied items), and then **paste** (insert) it in a new location. If you need to copy or move multiple items, you can use the **Office Clipboard**, which works like the Windows Clipboard but stores up to 24 items at a time and is available only in Office applications. You can also move or copy text using a technique called **drag and drop**, in which you select the text you want to move, then use the mouse to drag it to a new location. Items you drag and drop do not get copied to the Windows or Office Clipboard. While checking your memo, you decide that you want to move and copy text.

1. Click **View** on the menu bar, click **Task Pane**, click the **Zoom list arrow** on the Standard toolbar, click **Page Width**, click the **Other task panes arrow** on the task pane, then click **Clipboard**

The entire width of the memo text now fits on the screen, making it easier to work with the Clipboard task pane. At the moment, the Clipboard is empty.

2. Double-click **summer** at the end of the second paragraph to select it, then click the **Copy button** on the Standard toolbar

The text item "summer" is now copied to the Office Clipboard. See Figure A-10.

3. Click to the left of **intern** in the fourth paragraph, then click the **Paste button**

The copied text from the Clipboard is pasted into the document, and also remains on the Office Clipboard. If you clicked the Paste button again you would paste this same text again. Notice that a paste icon appears under the pasted text. This is the Paste Options button.

4. Click the **Paste Options button**

The Paste Options menu opens, and displays several options for applying formatting to the pasted text. By default, the pasted text maintains its original formatting, which in this situation is fine, since it matches the paragraph text.

5. Click outside the menu to close the Paste Options menu, position the mouse pointer to the left of the second paragraph until it changes to ⤢, then click

The entire line, including the paragraph mark, is selected. See Figure A-11. The area to the left of the left margin is the **selection bar**. When you position the mouse pointer in the selection bar, it changes to ⤢, which you use to select entire lines.

6. Click the **Cut button** on the Standard toolbar

The text is cut from the document and is now the first item in the Clipboard task pane.

7. Click to the left of **commission** in the third paragraph, click **summer** in the Clipboard task pane, then press **[Spacebar]**

8. Scroll to the end of the document, click the **paragraph mark** below the last paragraph, then click the first item in the Clipboard, which begins **I look forward**

The paragraph from the Clipboard is inserted in the new location.

9. Position the mouse pointer in the selection bar to the left of January 14-18 until it changes to ⤢, click, drag the selected text to the left of **I look forward to working with you throughout the summer**, then release the mouse button

As you drag, the pointer changes to ⤢, and an indicator line shows you where the text will be pasted. Notice that the dragged text did not appear as an item on the Clipboard. See Figure A-12.

FIGURE A-10: Text copied to the Office Clipboard

Selected text that was copied

Text copied to Clipboard

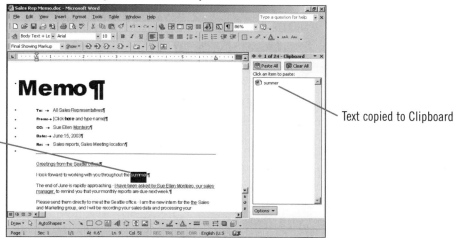

FIGURE A-11: Line of selected text

Entire line of text
selected

Selection bar area

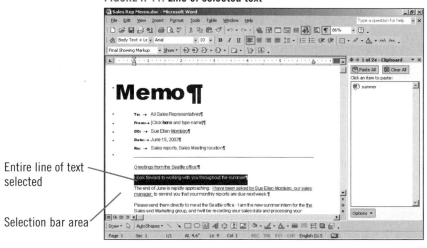

FIGURE A-12: Dragging text

Dragged text

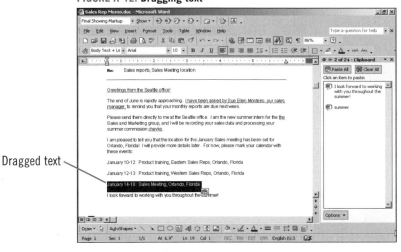

Activating the Office Clipboard

The Office Clipboard stores multiple items only if the Office Clipboard is active. Opening the Clipboard task pane automatically makes it active. If you want to activate the Office Clipboard without showing the task pane, click Options on the Clipboard task pane, then click Collect without showing Office Clipboard. If the Office Clipboard is not active, then you can only copy one item at a time, as with the Windows Clipboard.

Word 2002

Finding and Replacing Text

The **Replace command** helps you quickly and easily substitute a new word or phrase for one or more occurrences of a particular word or phrase in a document. First you tell Word the text to search for, then you tell Word what you want to replace it with. You can replace every occurrence of the text in one action or you can review each occurrence and choose to replace or keep the text. ✐ You have just learned that the location of the January Sales meeting has changed from Orlando, Florida to Scottsdale, Arizona. You need to update this in the memo. You decide to use the Replace command to speed up the process.

1. **Click View on the menu bar, click Task Pane, click the Zoom list arrow on the Standard toolbar, then click 100%**
   The task pane closes and the memo appears on screen at a zoom level of 100%.

2. **Press [Ctrl][Home], click Edit on the menu bar, then click Replace**
   The insertion point moves to the beginning of the document, and the Find and Replace dialog box opens.

3. **Type Orlando, Florida in the Find what text box, press [Tab], then type Scottsdale, Arizona in the Replace with text box**
   Compare your screen with Figure A-13.

4. **Click Find Next, then drag the dialog box out of the way if necessary**
   Word searches the document from the insertion point and selects the first instance of "Orlando, Florida." See Figure A-14.

5. **Click Replace**
   Word replaces the first instance of "Orlando, Florida" with "Scottsdale, Arizona," and then moves to the next instance of "Orlando, Florida." You do not want to replace this occurrence, because the Eastern reps are still going to hold their product training session in Orlando.

QuickTip

Clicking More in the Find and Replace dialog box expands the dialog box to let you further customize the Find and Replace commands, such as matching the case or format of a word or phrase.

6. **Click Find Next**
   Word leaves the second instance of "Orlando, Florida" unchanged and locates the next occurrence of it.

7. **Click Replace**
   Word replaces the third instance with "Scottsdale, Arizona" and then locates the fourth instance of "Orlando, Florida."

8. **Click Replace**
   An alert box opens, telling you that Word has finished searching the document.

9. **Click OK to close the alert box, click Close in the Find and Replace dialog box, then save your changes to the document**

FIGURE A-13: Find and Replace dialog box

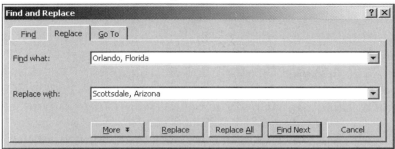

FIGURE A-14: First occurence of find what text

First instance
of found word
is highlighted

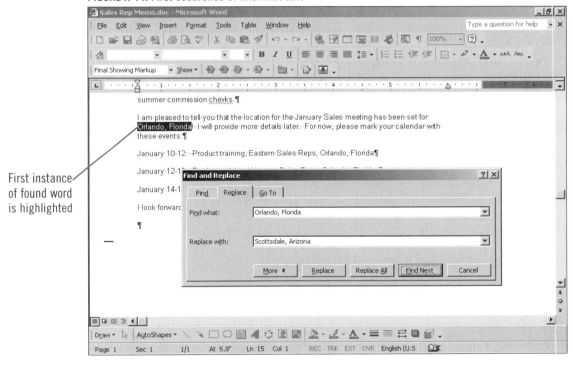

Using the Find command

The Find command on the Edit menu opens the Find and Replace dialog box with the Find tab on top. It is similar to the Replace command, but searches for text without replacing it. The Find command is useful when you want to locate a particular word or phrase in a document. To use the Find command, type the word or phrase you're looking for in the Find what text box, then click Find Next. If the word or phrase is found, Word scrolls to its location and it is selected. To search for the next occurrence of the word or phrase in the document, click Find Next again.

Checking Spelling and Grammar

Word provides tools to help you make sure that your documents are free of spelling and grammatical errors. Word's AutoCorrect feature corrects your errors as you type them, but Word is not able to correct all mistakes in this way. Word identifies possible misspelled words by underlining them in red wavy lines. Word identifies possible grammatical errors such as passive voice by underlining them in green wavy lines. If you right-click the flagged misspelled words or grammatical errors, a pop-up menu opens, displaying a list of possible correctly spelled or phrased alternatives. You can also run the Spelling and Grammar Checker to open the Spelling and Grammar dialog box. Words underlined in purple dots are not misspelled; these are identified as smart tags. Smart tags are items that Word has identified as a particular type of data, such as a name, address, or phone number, and upon which you can perform a variety of actions without having to open another Office application. ✐ You decide to use Word's Spelling and Grammar checking tools to ensure that your memo is free of errors.

1. Click **Tools** on the menu bar, click **Spelling and Grammar** to open the Spelling and Grammar dialog box, then verify that there is a check box in the Check Grammar check box

2. Right-click the word chevks in the third paragraph
   A pop-up menu opens, displaying a list of possible alternatives to the misspelled word, along with other options. See Figure A-15.

3. Click **checks**
   The correctly spelled word "checks" replaces the misspelled word.

QuickTip

If the correct spelling of the word does not appear in the list, you can type it in the top section of the dialog box.

4. Press **[Ctrl][Home]**, click the **Spelling and Grammar button** ▧ on the Standard toolbar, then verify that the **Check grammar check box** contains a check mark
   The first possible error identified is Sue Ellen's last name, "Monteiro," as shown in Figure A-16. This is not an error. You need to choose one of the buttons in the dialog box. You can accept the suggested spelling if one is offered by clicking Change or Change All (if more than one spelling is suggested, first highlight the spelling you want to use). You can ignore the error by clicking Ignore or Ignore All. You can add the word to the dictionary so that Word no longer flags it as an error by clicking Add. You can highlight a correction and then add the entry to AutoCorrect, so that this misspelling will be corrected as you type.

QuickTip

You can add words to AutoCorrect by clicking Tools on the menu bar, clicking AutoCorrect, then clicking the AutoCorrect tab.

5. Click **Ignore All**
   The Spelling Checker will skip every instance of this word as it continues checking the document. Word moves to the next possible error, the first sentence of your memo, which is flagged as a sentence fragment. You don't want to change this, but you do want Word to identify future sentence fragments.

Trouble?

If you did not type the intentional errors as instructed in the Entering Text in a Document lesson, or if you made unintentional errors, follow the prompts in the dialog box, correcting errors as appropriate; then skip to Step 8.

6. Click **Ignore Once**
   The green wavy line is removed from the screen under the first sentence, and Word moves to the next possible error. The next error identified is a possible grammatical error. Word suggests an alternate construction for the phrase in the passive voice in the second paragraph.

7. Click **Change**
   The sentence is changed in the document, and the next possible error is identified. The word "the" appears twice in a row.

8. Click **Delete**
   A message box appears, informing you that the spelling and grammar check is complete.

9. Click **OK**, then save your changes to the document

FIGURE A-15: Spelling shortcut menu with possible correctly spelled alternatives

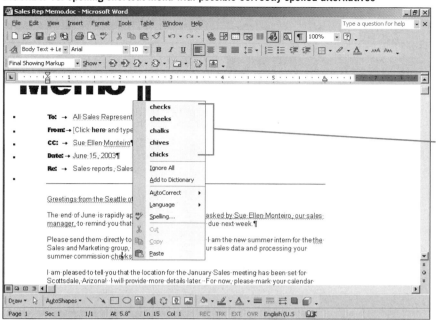

Possible correctly spelled alternatives

FIGURE A-16: Spelling and Grammer dialog box with spelling error identified

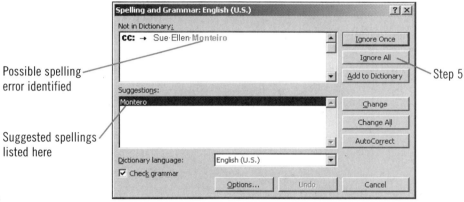

Possible spelling error identified

Suggested spellings listed here

Step 5

Using smart tags

Words in your document underlined with purple dots are called smart tags. Smart tags are items that Word has identified as a particular data type, such as a name, address, or phone number, and upon which you can perform a variety of actions without having to open another Office application. If you position the mouse over the purple dotted line, the Smart Tag Actions button appears. Click this button to view a list of commands you can perform on that smart tag. See Figure A-17. For instance, if the smart tag is a name, the menu will contain options for sending mail, scheduling a meeting, opening a contact, adding it to contacts, or inserting an address. You can also specify that the

smart tag be removed or open the Smart Tag Options tab on the AutoCorrect dialog box, which provides you with options for using smart tags.

FIGURE A-17: Smart Tag Options shortcut menu

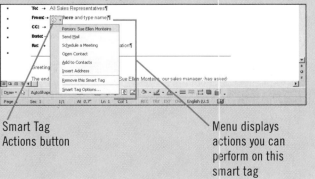

Smart Tag Actions button

Menu displays actions you can perform on this smart tag

Word 2002

Previewing and Printing a Document

When you are finished creating and editing a document, you are ready to print it. Before printing, it's a good idea to view your document in **Print Preview**, which shows the document exactly as it will appear on the printed page. Use Print Preview to check page margins and your document's overall appearance. There are many other ways to view a document in Word. See Table A-2 for a description of the other views. ✐ Before you print the memo, you want to make sure it looks exactly as you want. Then you can close the document and exit Word.

Steps

QuickTip

The Multiple Pages button ▓ on the Print Preview toolbar lets you see up to 24 pages of a document at a time.

1. Click the Print Preview button 🔍 on the Standard toolbar

The Print Preview window opens, showing the memo as it will appear when printed. See Figure A-18. You can use the mouse pointer to zoom in on your document.

2. Move the mouse pointer 🔍 over the top part of the memo, then click

The document enlarges to 100% in the Print Preview window with the top part of the memo displayed, and the pointer changes to 🔍.

3. Click the Magnifier button 🔍 on the toolbar

The pointer changes to a I, indicating that you can now edit text in this window.

4. Click anywhere in the text Click here and type name in the From: line, type your name, then click 🔍 again

QuickTip

To print the document without opening the Print dialog box, click the Print button 🖨 on the Standard toolbar. This will print the document according to the current settings in the Print dialog box.

5. Click Close on the Print Preview toolbar, click File on the menu bar, then click Print

The Print dialog box opens, as shown in Figure A-19. The Print dialog box lets you specify your printing settings, such as the range of pages you want to print (if you don't want to print an entire document), the number of copies you want to print, and print scaling (which you use to fit your document on a specified number of pages). You can also configure the settings of the default printer by clicking the Properties button and changing the settings in the Properties dialog box.

6. Click OK

The Print dialog box closes. After a few moments the letter emerges from your printer. Compare your letter to Figure A-20.

7. Save your changes to the document, click File on the menu bar, then click Exit

The Sales Rep Memo file is saved, and the document and Word both close.

TABLE A-2: Ways to view a document

View	How it displays a document	Used For
Normal	Does not show all of page elements	Typing and editing text
Web Layout	As it would appear as Web page	Creating a Web page
Print Layout	Shows all elements of the printed page	Previewing the layout of printed page
Outline	Shows only the headings in a document	Reviewing the structure of the content
Full Screen	Removes toolbars and scrollbars	Maximizing workspace
Document Map	Shows only headings	Navigating a document
Web Page Preview	Shows document in a Web browser	Previewing a Web page
Print Preview	Shows multiple pages at reduced size	Previewing a printed document

FIGURE A-18: Print Preview window

Magnifier button

One page button

Print Preview toolbar

Multiple pages button

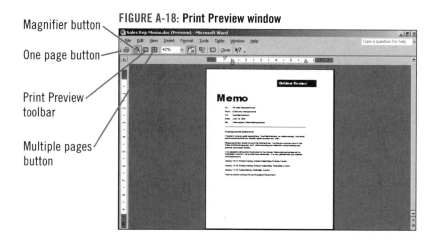

FIGURE A-19: Print dialog box

Your printer is probably different

Choose which pages to print in the Print range section

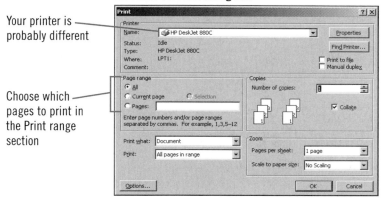

Figure A-20: Final printed memo

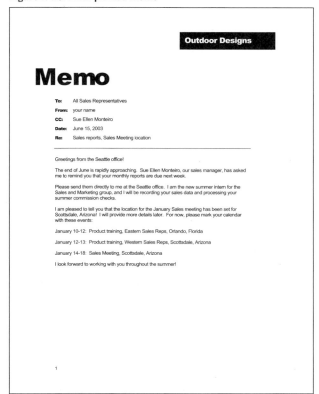

Practice

► Concepts Review

Label the Word window elements shown in Figure A-21.

FIGURE A-21

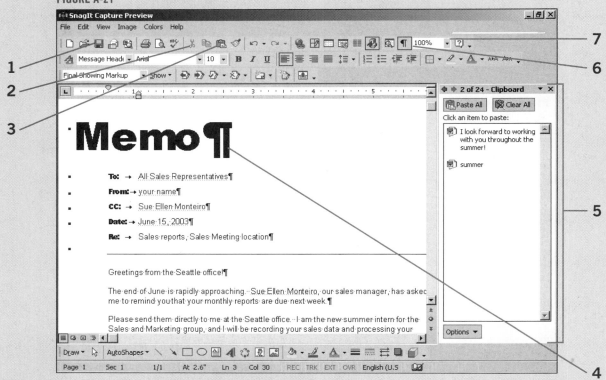

Match each of the toolbar buttons with its effect.

8. ☐
9. ↺
10. 🖺
11. ✎
12. ¶

a. Checks the spelling and grammar in the document
b. Reverses your last action
c. Shows/hides paragraph marks
d. Copies the selected text to the Clipboard
e. Saves the current document to disk

Select the best answer from the list of choices.

13. **Which of the following techniques do you use to create a new document based on an existing file?**
    a. Click the Blank Document command on the New Documents task pane.
    b. Click the Choose Document command on the New Documents task pane.
    c. Click File on the menu bar, then click New.
    d. Click a template from the General Templates area of the New Document task pane.

14. **Which of the following key combinations moves the insertion point to the beginning of a document?**
    a. [Ctrl][Home]
    b. [Alt][Tab]
    c. [Home]
    d. [Page Up]

15. **Which of these techniques cannot be used to move text from one location to another in Word?**
    a. The Cut and Paste buttons on the toolbar
    b. The Cut and Paste commands on the Edit menu
    c. The drag and drop technique
    d. The [Del] and [Ins] keys

16. **Purple dots under a word or phrase indicate that the word or phrase is:**
    a. Incorrectly spelled.
    b. A grammatically incorrect sentence.
    c. A smart tag.
    d. A word that has been automatically corrected.

17. **The feature that automatically fixes spelling errors as you type is:**
    a. AutoCorrect.
    b. Spell checker.
    c. Thesaurus.
    d. Smart tag.

18. **Which view is most useful for viewing and editing text in a document?**
    a. Normal view
    b. Print layout view
    c. Page layout view
    d. Print preview

▶ Skills Review

1. **Create a new document from an existing file.**
    a. Start Microsoft Word and verify that the New Document task pane is open. If Word is open and the New Document task pane is not open, click File on the menu bar, then click New.
    b. Open a copy of the file WD A-2 from the drive and folder where your Student Files are located by using a link in the New Document task pane.
    c. Save the new document as *Meeting Confirmation*.
    d. Identify as many elements in the document window as you can without referring to the lesson.

2. Enter text in a document.

   a. Verify that formatting marks are visible on your screen. (If they are not, use the Show/Hide button to make them appear.)

   b. Move the insertion point to the paragraph marker two lines below the greeting in the letter.

   c. Type the following text: **It was great speaking with you this morning. We are very happy that you have chosen the Red Rock Conference Center to host your senior management summer strategy meeting.**

   d. Press [Enter], then use the arrow keys to move the insertion point to the end of the document.

   e. Replace the placeholder text Your Name below the closing with your name.

   f. Save your changes to the document.

3. Edit a document.

   a. Select the text It was great speaking with you in the first paragraph, then type **Thanks for your phone call.**

   b. Delete the word summer in the first paragraph.

   c. Just before the word I that begins the third paragraph, type **Pursuant to our discussion,**

   d. Using the keyboard, select the text a flip chart or.

   e. Delete the selected phrase.

   f. Undo the change using a button on the Standard toolbar.

   g. Save your changes to the document.

4. Move and copy text.

   a. Open the task pane, then choose the setting on the Zoom list that lets you view the entire width of the page.

   b. Open the Clipboard task pane.

   c. Select the word conference in the third paragraph, then copy it to the Clipboard.

   d. In the second paragraph, select the sentence We look forward to your stay.

   e. Click the Cut button, then press [Backspace] to delete the extra paragraph mark.

   f. Click before the word table in the second paragraph, then click the conference item in the Clipboard task pane.

   g. Scroll to the end of the letter, click the paragraph mark one line above Sincerely, then paste the text We look forward to your stay.

   h. Use the mouse to select the paragraph beginning with A one-third deposit, then drag the paragraph to the left of the text All the details of your stay at the beginning of the third paragraph. (Note: Do NOT select the paragraph mark at the end of the selected sentence.)

   i. Click to the right of June 1 in the third paragraph, then press [Enter] twice.

   j. Delete two of the blank lines between the last two paragraphs.

   k. Close the Clipboard task pane, then set the zoom to 100% using the Zoom list arrow.

   l. Save your changes.

5. Find and Replace text.

   a. Move the insertion point to the beginning of the letter, to the left of Red Rock Conference Center in the letterhead.

   b. Use the Replace command to replace all instances of the word Edison with Galileo.

   c. Close the Find and Replace dialog box.

6. Check Spelling and Grammar.

   a. Correct the spelling of the misspelled word equippd by right clicking and choosing the correct spelling from the shortcut menu.

   b. Move the insertion point to the beginning of the document.

   c. Open the Spelling and Grammar dialog box

d. Correct all the spelling and grammatical errors that Word identifies, then close the alert box that opens when the spelling and grammar check is complete.

e. Save your changes.

7. Preview and print a document.

a. View the document in Print Preview.

b. Zoom in on the bottom part of the letter using the Magnifying glass pointer.

c. Click the Magnifier button on the Print Preview toolbar button.

d. Double-click the word "Sincerely" to select it, then type **Best regards**.

e. Close the Print Preview window.

f. Save your changes.

g. Print the document, then compare it to Figure A-22.

h. Close the document and exit Word.

FIGURE A-22

► Independent Challenge 1

As the national sales manager for Little Guy Toys, Inc., you are in charge of organizing the company's summer sales conference. You need to prepare a letter inviting the sales managers and field sales representatives to the conference. The conference will take place at the Palm Grove Inn and Conference Center in Fort Lauderdale, Florida on August 15, 2003. The meetings will run from 10:00 a.m. until 5:00 p.m. After the meetings, there will be an awards ceremony and banquet, featuring motivational speaker Cecil Huntington. In the letter, you need to provide the date and location information and request that the attendees confirm their travel plans with you within the next three weeks.

a. Open the file WD A-3, and save it as *Sales Meeting Letter*.

b. Delete the recipient Name, Address, and City, State, or Postal Code placeholders so that one copy can be sent to all conference attendees.

c. Delete the placeholder text START TYPING YOUR LETTER HERE, then write a short letter inviting everyone to the conference; include all information listed in the paragraph describing this exercise. Make sure you tell the recipients to confirm their travel plans with you by July 21.

d. You suddenly learn that the Palm Grove Inn and Conference Center will not be able to accommodate the meeting. Fortunately, you are able to make a reservation at the Coconut Resort and Conference Center, also in Fort Lauderdale. Replace all instances of Palm Grove Inn and Conference Center with Coconut Resort.

e. At the bottom of the page, delete the placeholder text Your Name and replace it with your name.

f. After you enter all the text, check the spelling and grammar.

g. Save your changes.

h. Use Print Preview to see how the printed letter will look. When you're finished, print a copy, sign it, then close the document.

▶ Independent Challenge 2

You provide office help to Sam Kosta, who operates a small charter fishing boat company in Gloucester, Massachusetts. He wants to exhibit his services at a trade show in Pennsylvania in hopes of attracting more customers for the summer. He asked you to write a letter of inquiry to the coordinator of the trade show, which is held each spring in Allentown, Pennsylvania. He wants you to find out the dates of the trade show, the cost of a small booth, how many people attend, and who the typical exhibitors are. In addition, he wants you to request any general literature distributed for the show, such as hotel information, past experiences, airline discounts, and so on. The letter should fit on one page.

a. Open the file WD A-4, and save it as *Exhibitor Inquiry*.

b. Replace the recipient name and address placeholder text with the following name and address: Sandra Lynch, Coordinator, Allentown Fishing Show, 4599 Elm Street, Allentown, PA 18101.

c. Write a short letter to the trade show coordinator, asking Sam's questions as described in the introductory paragraph for this exercise. Replace the placeholder text at the bottom of the letter with your name.

d. Check the spelling and grammar.

e. Save your changes.

f. Use Print Preview to see how the printed letter will look. When you're finished, print a copy of the letter, then close the document.

▶ Independent Challenge 3

You are the Vice President of Sales for a pet products company called Cats 'n' Dogs. You have contracted with Quality Recruiters, an executive search firm in Toronto, Canada to find candidates to fill the position of national sales manager in Canada. You need to write Joan Day, your recruiter at the search firm, a letter, summarizing the type of candidates you would like to interview.

a. Start Word and a new, blank document.

b. Begin the letter with today's date.

c. Enter the recipient's name and address as follows: Joan Day, Senior Executive Recruiter, Quality Recruiters, 4400 Edgar Road, Montreal H4Z 1Z2 Canada.

d. In the body of the letter, thank Joan for her help on the phone and indicate that you are following up to confirm the type of candidates you would like to see for the Canadian national sales manager position. Specify that you would like to see candidates with at least five years experience in sales management, preferably in the retail market. Also state that all candidates must be willing to travel 60% of the time and be fluent in both English and French. Be sure to include salary information for the position, and whether the company will include a relocation package. Include your name in the closing of the letter.

e. Check the spelling and grammar in your letter.

f. Save the document as *Recruiter Letter*.

g. Use Print Preview to verify the layout of the letter.

h. Print the letter, then close it.

 # Independent Challenge 4

You've won a scholarship to continue your studies in a foreign country. The field of study can be anything you want—for instance a language, a historical subject, dramatic arts, music, or anything else you are interested in. You can pick a school anywhere in the world that teaches your chosen subject. You first need to decide an area of study that you are interested in. You then need to do some research on the Internet to find a school that offers a course in your desired area of study. Once you've completed your research, you then need to write a letter to the scholarship foundation, describing the course of study you have chosen and providing details on location, cost, and time frame.

a. Log on to the Internet, go to a search engine site such as AltaVista (www.altavista.com) or www.google.com and search for courses of study in the country of your choice.

b. Once you've identified the course or courses you wish to take, jot down the following information on a piece of paper: name and address of the school, name of the course, duration of the course, cost of the course (using the currency of your chosen country).

c. Once you've gathered your research, start Word, click General Templates in the New Document task pane, click the Letters and Faxes tab, then double-click the Elegant Letter icon to open a new document based on this template.

d. Click the company name placeholder, type **From the Desk of**, then add your name.

e. Scroll to the bottom of the page, click each of the placeholders in turn, and enter a fictitious address, phone number, and fax number.

f. Replace the recipient address placeholder with the name and address of the scholarship foundation contact: Lauren Waters, Executive Director, The Independent Study Foundation, 4433 Snake Hill Road, Boise, ID 83706.

g. Replace the text Sir or Madam in the salutation with Ms. Waters.

h. Select the two lines acting as a placeholder in the body of the letter (but not the paragraph mark), delete them, then type a three paragraph letter. In the first paragraph, describe the course you have chosen, explain why you want to take it, and note when applications are due. In the second paragraph, describe the school where you will take the course and provide the address. In the third paragraph, provide the cost of the course and the date when payment is due if you are accepted.

i. Add your name at the end of the letter.

j. Check the spelling and grammar of this letter.

k. Save the document as *Study Abroad Letter*.

l. Preview and print the document, then close it and exit Word.

Visual Workshop

Use the Professional Memo template to create the document shown in Figure A-23. (*Hint*: Click General Templates in the New Document task pane, click the Memo tab, then double click Professional Memo.) Replace the placeholder text with the text shown. Add your name in the From line of the memo. When you finish, save the memo as *Company Picnic*, and then print it.

FIGURE A-23

Red Bird Publishing

Memo

To: All Employees

From: Your name

Date: June 1, 2003

Re: Company Picnic

You know what they say about all work and no play

Mark your calendar for Friday, July 25 for the company summer picnic! Shut down your laptop and hop on the bus for a day of fun in the sun at Huntington Beach!

Bring your bathing suit, a beach towel, and some sunscreen. Join in a volleyball competition or just lounge on the sand and enjoy the water. Enjoy an old-fashioned lunch of barbecued chicken, ribs, or veggie burgers!

We have chartered three buses for this event. The office will shut down promptly at 11:00 and the last bus will leave from the lobby at 11:30. The buses will return to the office at 5:00.

We look forward to seeing you there!

Enhancing
a Document

Objectives

► **Change font type and size**
► **Change font color, style, and effects**
► **Change alignment and line spacing**
► **Change margin settings**
► **Set tabs and indents**
► **Add bulleted and numbered lists**
► **Apply and modify styles**
► **Insert manual page breaks**

In addition to letters and memos, you can use Word to prepare brochures, flyers, and newsletters. To make all these documents effective, you can use Word to **format,** or enhance, the way the document looks. In this unit, you will use several methods to change the way characters and paragraphs look. You will also learn how to control where pages begin and end in a multiple-page document. Dean Holmes, marketing manager for Outdoor Designs, gives you a product information sheet on the Alpine Ski Sack Kit, the company's newest product, and asks you to format it so that it is readable and attractive. Sales representatives will refer to the product information sheet to promote this kit when they call stores that carry their products. The more clearly the sheet is formatted, the easier it will be for the sales representatives to find information when they need it.

Word 2002

Changing Font Type and Size

Choosing an appropriate font is the first step in formatting your document effectively. A **font** is a set of characters in a particular design. You can also change the **font size** so that text is larger or smaller. The unit for measuring font size is points. A **point** is 1/72 of an inch, so the common font size of 12, for example, is 1/6 of an inch tall. You can also change the way selected words look by changing the **font style** by applying bold, underline, or italic formatting. Table B-1 shows some examples of common fonts with varying font sizes and font styles. You can access many commands related to fonts from the Formatting toolbar. You can also use the Font command on the Format menu to open the Font dialog box. To format existing text, you must first select it. To apply formatting to text as you type, select the formatting options you want, then start typing. All the text in the product information sheet is the same font type (Times New Roman) and size (12 point). You decide to change the title's font type and increase the size so it stands out from the rest of the document.

1. Start Word, then click **Choose document** in the New Document task pane
   The New from Existing Document dialog box opens.

Trouble?

If you are not in Normal View, click the Normal View button ▤ on the Standard toolbar.

2. Click the **Look in list arrow**, navigate to the drive and folder where your Project Files are located, click **WD B-1**, then click **Create New**
   The unformatted product information sheet opens in Normal view.

3. Click the **Save button** 🖫 on the Standard toolbar, navigate to the drive and folder where your Project Files are located, type **Ski Sack Sheet** in the File name box, then click **Save**
   Word saves a copy of the file with a new name in the same location as your Project Files.

4. If necessary, click the **Show/Hide ¶ button** ¶ on the Standard toolbar to display formatting marks

QuickTip

Remember that you can select an entire line by placing the pointer in the selection bar until the pointer changes to ⟋, then clicking.

5. Select **Outdoor Designs** and **New Product Information Sheet**, the first two lines of the document
   The lines are selected; now you can format them.

6. Click the **Font list arrow** on the Formatting toolbar until you see **Arial** (you might have to scroll down to find it)
   See Figure B-1.

QuickTip

To use a button or list arrow that is not visible, click the Toolbar Options arrow ⟩⟩ on the right end of the appropriate toolbar, click Add or Remove buttons, click the name of the toolbar, click the button you need, then click outside the list to close it.

7. Click **Arial**
   The selected text changes to the Arial font; "Arial" appears in the Font list box and will remain there as long as the insertion point remains in any text with the Arial font type.

8. Click the **Font Size list arrow** on the Formatting toolbar, click **18**, then click anywhere in the document window to deselect the text
   The font size of the selected text increases to 18. See Figure B-2. Depending on where you clicked to deselect the text, the Font and Font Size list boxes may display different information than what is shown in the figure.

9. Click the **Save button** 🖫 on the Standard toolbar
   The formatting changes are saved to disk.

FIGURE B-1: Font list open with Arial selected

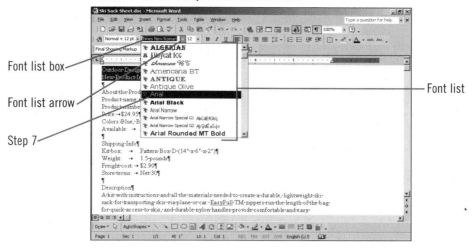

Font list box

Font list arrow

Step 7

Font list

FIGURE B-2: Selected text formatted with 18-point Arial

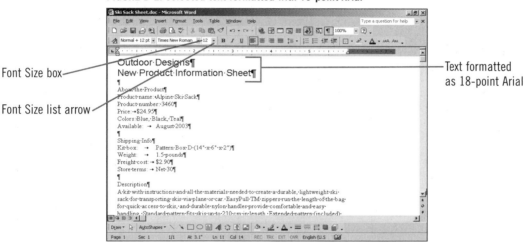

Font Size box

Font Size list arrow

Text formatted
as 18-point Arial

TABLE B-1: Font type, size, and style samples

font formats	samples
Font	Times New Roman, **Impact**, **Broadway**, CASTELLAR, *Freestyle Script*, **Rockwell**
Size	eight point, twelve point, fourteen point, eighteen point
Style	**Bold**, *italic*, underline, ***bold italic***, dotted underline

Understanding fonts

Font creation, or **fontography**, is an old business. In ancient times, scribes concerned with the uniformity of letters and symbols wrote in standard forms so future generations could easily understand their writing. Some of today's fonts are descended from these earlier type styles; others were developed in modern times. Before you can use fonts on a computer, they must be installed. The Windows operating system comes with several TrueType fonts, such as Arial and Times New Roman, installed. **TrueType fonts** are fonts that look the same on your screen as they do on your printed page. The symbol that appears in the Font list identifies which fonts are TrueType fonts. Your system might include other fonts supplied by the manufacturer of your printer or another company. To see which fonts are installed on your system, click the Font list arrow on the Formatting toolbar and scroll through the list.

Word 2002

Changing Font Color, Style, and Effects

Sometimes you want to emphasize certain words, phrases, or lines of text to convey their importance. To add emphasis, you can use font styles, such as **bold** (darker type), *italic* (slanted type), and <u>underline</u>. You can also make certain words stand out by changing the color of the font. Or, you can apply **font effects**, special enhancements such as small caps, shadow, and superscript that you can apply to selected text. To save time, you can use the Format Painter button to copy the formatting of selected text to other text. ✎ You continue to format the Ski Sack Kit sheet by applying font styles, colors, and effects to certain words.

Steps

1. Select **Outdoor Designs**, the first line of text, click the **Bold button B** on the Formatting toolbar, click the **Font Color list arrow A·**, then click the **Blue square** in the second row, as shown in Figure B-3
   The first line of the document now appears in blue. The Font Color button now shows a blue stripe on it, indicating that this is the current color. Clicking the Font Color button (not the list arrow) applies the current color to selected text. Clicking the Font Color list arrow lets you choose a different color to apply to selected text.

QuickTip

You can also use the keyboard shortcuts [Ctrl][B], [Ctrl][I], and [Ctrl][U] to format selected text in boldface, italic, and underline, respectively.

2. Select **Product name:** in the fourth line of text, click the **Bold button B** on the Formatting toolbar, then click the **Italic button I** on the Formatting toolbar
   The selected text is now formatted in bold and italic.

3. Double-click the **Format Painter button ✎** on the Standard toolbar
   The pointer changes to ✎I, indicating that you can apply the formatting of the selected text to any text you select next. Because you double-clicked the format painter button, you can apply the selected formatting multiple times, until you click another button or press [Esc]. Clicking this button once lets you apply the selected formatting once.

4. Select **Product number:** in the fifth line
   The bold and italic formatting is applied to the selected text.

QuickTip

Use different styles, colors and effects selectively. Too many different colors and styles can make your document look busy and distracting, so that nothing stands out.

5. Select **Price:** in the sixth line, select **Colors:** in the seventh line, then select **Available:** in the eighth line

6. Select **Kit box:**, **Weight:**, **Freight cost:**, and **Store terms:** below the Shipping Info heading, then press **[Esc]**
   The pointer changes back to I, as shown in Figure B-4.

7. Click the **down scroll arrow** until the paragraph under the heading Description is visible, select the letters **TM** after the word "EasyPull" in line 2, click **Format** on the menu bar, then click **Font**
   The Font dialog box opens, with the Font tab in front, as shown in Figure B-5. You can use this dialog box to apply special font effects.

8. Click the **Superscript check box** in the Effects section, then click **OK**
   "TM" now appears slightly raised above the word "EasyPull" as a trademark symbol.

9. Press **[Ctrl][End]**, select **Profitable Craft Merchandising** under Kit Promotions, click the **Italic button I**, then save your changes to the document
   The magazine title now is italicized.

FIGURE B-3: Font Color menu with blue square selected

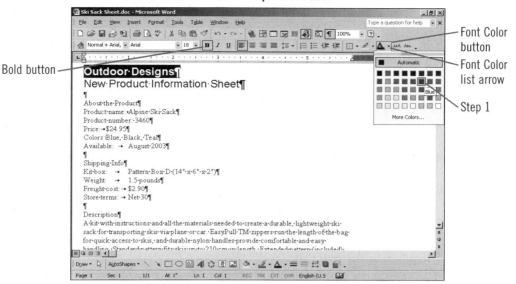

Bold button

Font Color button

Font Color list arrow

Step 1

FIGURE B-4: Bold and italic formatting applied using the Format Painter button

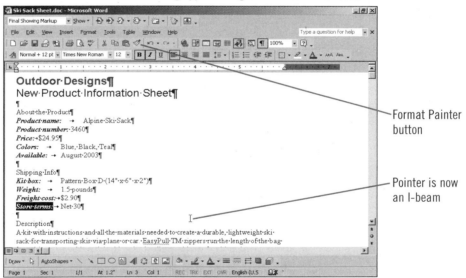

Format Painter button

Pointer is now an I-beam

FIGURE B-5: Font dialog box with the Font tab in front

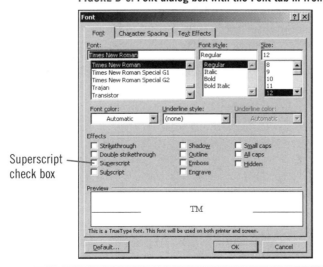

Superscript check box

Changing Alignment and Line Spacing

The amount of space between the edge of the page and your document text is called the **margin**. You can change the **alignment**, or position of text in relation to a document's margins, with the alignment buttons on the toolbar. For example, titles are often centered, headings left-aligned, and paragraphs **justified** (aligned equally between the left and right margins). You can also adjust the line spacing between lines using the Paragraph dialog box. ✒ All of the text in the Ski Sack information sheet is aligned along the left margin. You decide to center the title and justify the paragraph below the Description heading. You also need to increase the amount of spacing between the lines in the Description paragraph.

1. Press **[Ctrl][Home]**, then select the first two lines, **Outdoor Designs** and **New Product Information Sheet**
   The first two lines are selected.

2. Click the **Center button** 🔳 on the Formatting toolbar, then click anywhere away from the selected text
   The text is centered between the two margins and the text is deselected. See Figure B-6.

3. Scroll down until you see the paragraph under the heading **Description**, then click anywhere in the paragraph
   Although you need to select text to change character formats such as font size or font style, you can change most paragraph formatting, such as alignment, just by positioning the insertion point anywhere in the paragraph.

4. Click the **Justify button** 🔳 on the Formatting toolbar
   The Description paragraph's alignment changes to **justified**, which means it is aligned at both margins. When you select Justified alignment, Word adds or reduces the space between each word so that the text is aligned along both the right and left margins. This is different from **center**-aligning text, which does not adjust spacing but merely places the text equally between the margins.

5. Click **Format** on the menu bar, then click **Paragraph**
   The Paragraph dialog box opens with the Indents and Spacing tab in front, as shown in Figure B-7. You can use this dialog box to make extensive paragraph formatting changes in addition to those available on the Formatting toolbar, such as changing the space between lines and controlling line and page breaks.

6. Click the **Line spacing list arrow**, click **1.5 lines**, then click **OK**
   The paragraph is now both justified and has 1½ lines of space between each line, making it easier to read. Compare your screen with Figure B-8.

FIGURE B-6: Title centered

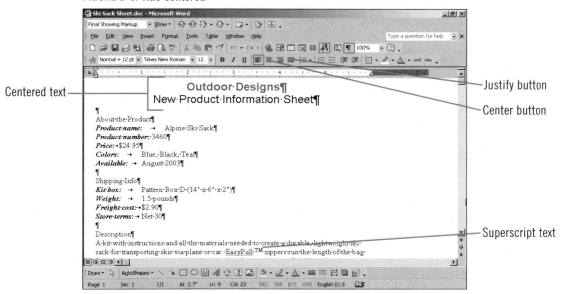

FIGURE B-7: Paragraph dialog box with Indents and Spacing tab in front

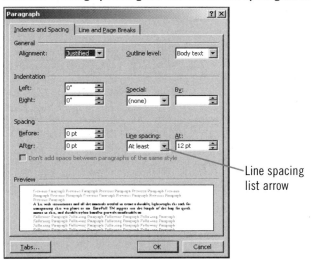

FIGURE B-8: Paragraph justified with 1.5 line spacing applied

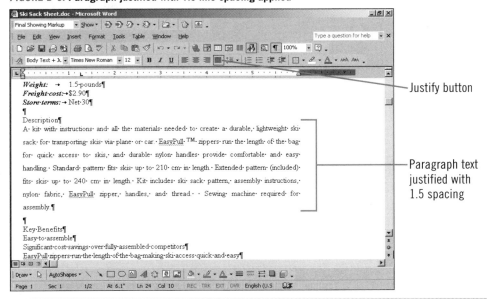

Changing Margin Settings

Word sets default page margins at 1" from the top and bottom of the page, and 1.25" from the left and right sides of the page. You can change the margin settings in Print Layout view, Print Preview, or any view using the Page Setup dialog box. When you change the margins, Word automatically adjusts line wrapping and **repaginates** (renumbers the pages of) your document. To evaluate what margin settings to use in a specific document, you need to switch to Print Layout view or Print Preview to see the actual margins on the page. You cannot see the margins in any other view. The margins on the Ski Sack product information sheet are the default margins. Style guidelines at Outdoor Designs mandate that all product information sheets should have one-inch margins around the whole document, so you need to change the margins in your document.

Steps

1. Click **File** on the menu bar, then click **Page Setup**
   The Page Setup dialog box opens with options for changing page formatting.

2. Click the **Margins tab** if it is not already in front
   See Figure B-9. The Margins tab contains margin text boxes, a Preview box, and a Default button (to restore default settings). The first margin text box, Top, is currently selected and does not need to be modified.

3. Press **[Tab]** twice
   The Left text box is selected. Pressing [Tab] moves the insertion point from one text box to the next.

4. Type 1 in the Left text box, then press **[Tab]**
   The Left text box shows 1 and the Right text box is selected. Word adds the inch symbol when you close the Page Setup dialog box. The Preview box shows the new left margin.

5. Type 1 in the Right text box, then click **OK**
   The Page Setup dialog box closes, and the left and right margins in the product information sheet change to one inch.

6. Click the **Print Layout View button** 📧 to the left of the horizontal scroll bar
   The view switches to Print Layout, and you can see the document margins. Use the ruler to verify that the left and right margins are one inch from the edges of the page. See Figure B-10.

7. Save your changes to the document

QuickTip

For mechanical reasons, most printers require at least a 1/4" margin around the page.

FIGURE B-9: Margins tab in the Page Setup dialog box

Margins tab —

Set margins here —

Preview box —

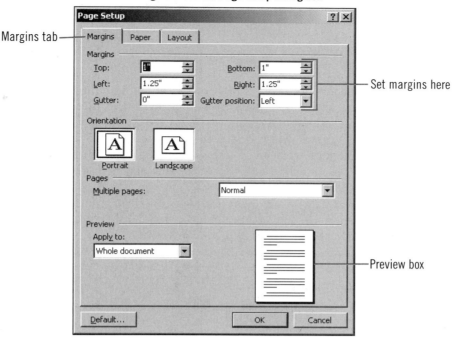

FIGURE B-10: Document in Print Layout view

1-inch margin —

Print Layout View button —

Normal View button —

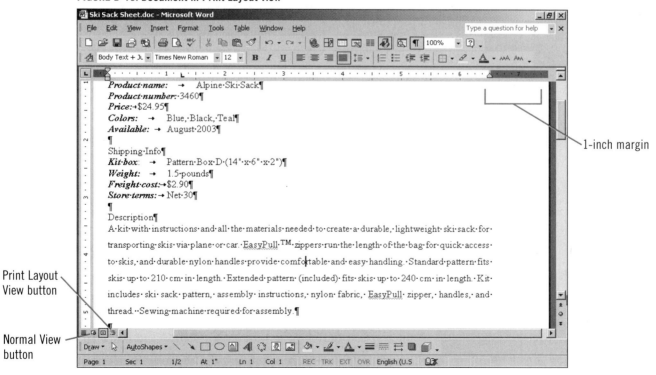

Setting Tabs and Indents

Word 2002

Tabs and indents are two important tools for positioning and aligning text to improve the appearance of a document. A **tab** is a set position where text following a tab character is aligned. An **indent** is a set amount of space between the edge of a paragraph and the right or left margin. The ruler makes it easy to set **tab stops** (locations the insertion point moves to when you press [Tab]) and indents, and to see immediately how they affect your document. The default ruler is marked in inches, and it contains symbols for left margins, right margins, indents, and tab stops. There is a tab character following each colon in the product information sheet, but the tab stops are not all set at the same position. Also, the first item under the Kit Promotions heading contains two lines, and would look neater if the second line were aligned under the first word after the tab. You decide to use the ruler to change the first tab stop for all lines in the document. You also want to indent the second line of the first paragraph under "Kit Promotions."

1. Press [Ctrl][Home]
The insertion point moves to the beginning of the document.

QuickTip

Press [Ctrl][A] to select all the text in the document quickly.

2. Click **Edit** on the menu bar, then click **Select All**
The entire document is selected. Any formatting changes you make will now be applied to all lines and paragraphs in the document.

Trouble?

If you click the wrong place, make sure the text is selected, then either drag the tab to the correct position, or drag it off the ruler and try again.

3. Click the **1.25" mark** on the ruler, as shown in Figure B-11
As long as you hold the mouse button, a vertical line appears on the document so that you can see (and move) the location of the tab stop in the document. The text after existing tab characters in each line aligns at the new tab stop position. Any text without tabs is left unchanged.

4. Point to the tab stop you just set until the ScreenTip "Left Tab" appears
This lets you verify that you have set a left tab.

5. Scroll to the items under the **Kit Promotions** heading, then click anywhere in the line that begins **Advertising:**

6. Position the pointer over the **Left Indent marker** ◻, then drag the ◻ to the 1" mark on the ruler
The paragraph is indented to the 1-inch position. See Figure B-12. This formatting does not look right. You don't want to indent the entire paragraph from the left margin; you want only the second line of the paragraph to be indented, so that it appears to hang directly below the word "Profitable."

7. Click the **Undo button** ◻ on the Standard toolbar

QuickTip

You can close the ruler if you want to make more room for the document in the window by clicking View on the menu bar, then clicking Ruler.

8. Position the pointer over the **Hanging Indent marker** ◻ on the ruler, then click and hold ◻
Make sure the ScreenTip identifies the marker as Hanging Indent and not First Line Indent or Left Indent. A dotted vertical line appears.

9. Drag the ◻ to the right until the dotted line is flush with the **P** in **Profitable** and the Hanging Indent marker is on top of the tab marker, as shown in Figure B-13; then save your changes to the document
The second line of the paragraph now is indented under the word "Profitable." See Figure B-13. The first line in the paragraph is set off, or "hangs," from the lines of text that wrap below it. This is called a **hanging indent**. A **first line indent** is where only the first line indents. With a **right indent**, the paragraph is indented from the right margin.

FIGURE B-11: Setting a tab stop on the ruler

Step 3

Vertical line
indicates tab
position

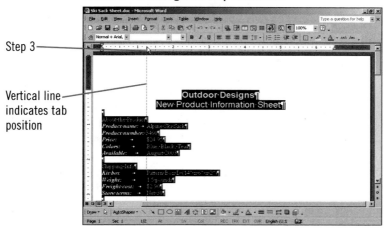

FIGURE B-12: Dragging to create a left indent

First Line indent
marker

Hanging indent
marker

Left indent marker

Both lines of paragraph
indented to 1-inch mark

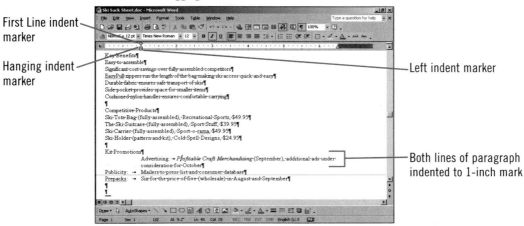

FIGURE B-13: Paragraph formatted with hanging indent

Hanging indent
marker

First line of
paragraph
"hangs" above
subsequent line

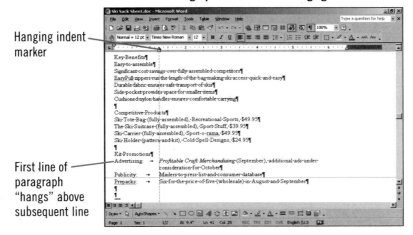

Setting a first line indent paragraph

You can also use the ruler to indent the first line of a paragraph. Select the paragraphs you want to indent, then drag the First Line Indent marker, shown in Figure B-12, to the indent position you want. As an alternative, you can click Format on the menu bar, click Paragraph to open the Paragraph dialog box, click the Special list arrow, click First line, then set the indent position in the By box.

Adding Bulleted and Numbered Lists

Microsoft Word provides many tools for organizing your text into a more orderly format. You can easily organize groups of related paragraphs into bulleted or numbered lists. A **bullet** is a small graphic—most often a dot—used to identify an item in a list. In a bulleted list, each paragraph is set off with a bullet, and the text is formatted with a hanging indent. Use a numbered list when you want to present items in a particular order. To create a list out of existing paragraphs, select the paragraphs you want to format into a list, then click the Numbering or Bullets button on the Formatting toolbar. If you want to use a bullet or numbering style that's different from the default, you can open the Bullets and Numbering Format dialog box and choose from several custom styles or create your own. ✒ You decide to add numbered and bulleted lists to the Ski Sack information sheet to make it easier to reference.

1. Click the **Normal View button** 🔲, then select the **four lines of text** under the heading **Competitive Products**

2. Click the **Numbering button** 📄 on the Formatting toolbar
   The items now appear sequentially numbered from 1 to 4, with the default numbering style applied. The first of each paragraph is indented, and as you can see by looking at the ruler, a tab and hanging indent are set.

3. Click **Format** on the menu bar, click **Bullets and Numbering**, then click the **Numbered tab** if necessary
   The numbered tab of the Bullets and Numbering dialog box presents you with eight different numbered list styles from which you can choose. See Figure B-14.

4. Click the third option in the top row, then click **OK**
   Each number in the list now has a parenthesis after it.

5. Click at the end of the fourth item in the list, then press **[Enter]**
   The number 5, followed by a parenthesis, is inserted automatically and formatted like the item above it.

6. Type **Ski Caddy (fully assembled), Bags Unlimited, $24.95**

7. Select the six lines of text under the heading Key Benefits, then click the **Bullets button** 📄 on the Formatting toolbar
   The items are now indented, with each item preceded by a round bullet, the default style.

8. Click **Format** on the menu bar, click **Bullets and Numbering**, click the third style in the second row, click **OK,** then click anywhere to deselect the text
   The style of the bullets changes to the arrowhead style, as shown in Figure B-15.

FIGURE B-14: Numbered tab of Bullets and Numbering dialog box

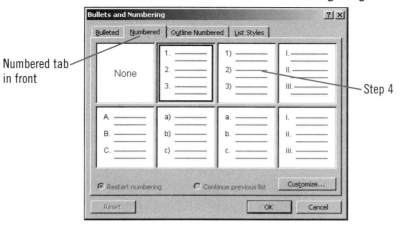

Numbered tab in front

Step 4

FIGURE B-15: Ski Sack Sheet with bulleted and numbered lists

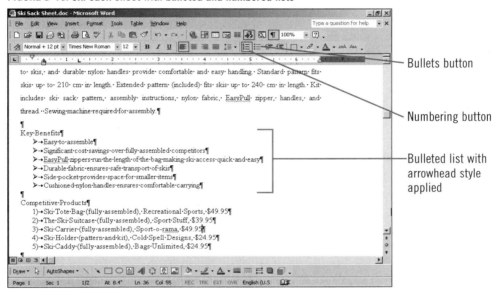

Bullets button

Numbering button

Bulleted list with arrowhead style applied

CLUES TO USE

Using AutoFormat

The AutoFormat feature in Word formats certain elements of your documents, such as numbered lists, bulleted lists and fractions, automatically. For instance, if you type "1)" then press [Enter], Word automatically inserts "2)" on the next line. You can reject an AutoFormatting action by clicking the AutoCorrect Options button 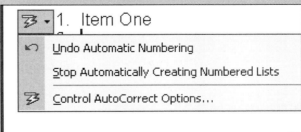 that appears after the action occurs. In the AutoCorrect Options list that opens, click one of the options to undo the action. See Figure B-16. In this example, you would click Undo Automatic Numbering to undo the change, or click Stop Automatically Creating Numbered Lists to prevent Word from making this AutoFormatting change in the future. You can control which features are formatted automatically by using the AutoCorrect dialog box. To do this, click Tools on

the menu bar, then click AutoCorrect Options to open the AutoCorrect dialog box. When options on the AutoFormat tab or the AutoFormat as You Type tab are selected, Word automatically formats the selected options as you type. By default, AutoFormat is turned on. To turn off AutoFormat, deselect the check boxes in the AutoFormat tab, then click OK.

FIGURE B-16: AutoFormat Options shortcut menu

Word 2002

Applying and Modifying Styles

When you find yourself making the same formatting changes to text over and over again, you can save time by applying a paragraph **style**, or set of predefined formatting characteristics for characters or paragraphs. Word comes with several built-in styles that are included in every Word document. For instance, the Normal style is the default paragraph style for any blank, new Word document, and the Heading 1 style is the default paragraph style for first-level headings. To apply a style, you first position the insertion point anywhere in the paragraph you want to format and then choose the style you want from the Styles and Formatting task pane. You can modify the built-in styles, or you can create your own using the Styles and Formatting task pane. You decide to format the headings in the Ski Sack product information sheet so they stand out from the rest of the text. By applying the Heading 1 style to the headings and then modifying the style to suit your preferences, you can accomplish this task quickly.

Steps

1. Click **Format** on the menu bar, then click **Styles and Formatting**

   The Styles and Formatting task pane opens, showing a variety of predefined formatting styles you can apply to selected text. The style names in the list are shown with their corresponding formatting so that you can see what changes you are applying. The list of items in the Pick formatting to apply list includes all of the formatting in your document, as well as predefined styles.

2. Click the **Show list arrow** at the bottom of the task pane, then click **Available styles**

   The list of items changes to show only Word's built-in styles.

3. Press **[Ctrl][Home]**, then click anywhere in the heading **About the Product**

4. Click **Heading 1** in the Pick formatting to apply list in the task pane

   The About the Product text is now formatted with the Heading 1 style, which is 16-point Arial boldface. See Figure B-17. You can see that using a style requires fewer steps than making each formatting change individually.

QuickTip

You can also apply a style by clicking the Style down arrow in the Formatting toolbar, then clicking a style in the list.

5. Repeat Step 4 to apply the Heading 1 style to the headings **Shipping Info**, **Description**, **Key Benefits**, **Competitive Products**, and **Kit Promotions**

6. Position the mouse pointer over the right edge of Heading 1 in the task pane, click the **down arrow** that appears, then click **Modify**

   The Modify Style dialog box opens. Any changes you make here will affect all the text in this document that is formatted with the Heading 1 style.

7. Click **Format**, then click **Border**

   The Borders and Shading dialog box opens, with the Borders tab in front.

8. Click the **Box option** in the Setting section, then click **OK**

   The Modify Style box shows a preview of what the modified Heading will look like, as shown in Figure B-18.

9. Click **OK** to close the Modify Style dialog box, click **View** on the menu bar, then click **Task Pane**

   The headings are all reformatted with a box border around them, and the task pane closes.

FIGURE B-17: Heading 1 Style applied to text

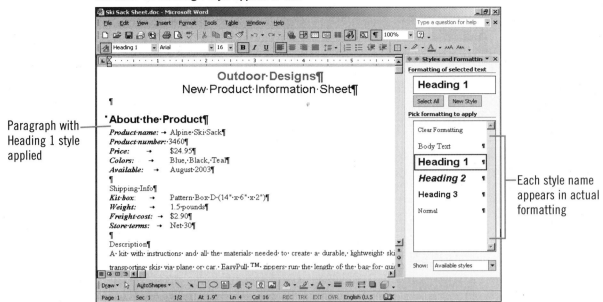

Paragraph with Heading 1 style applied

Each style name appears in actual formatting

FIGURE B-18: Modify Style dialog box showing a preview of the modified style

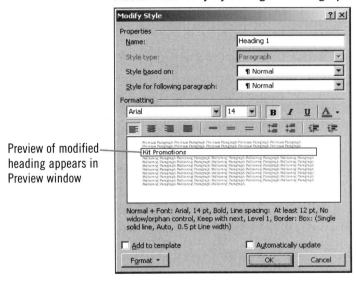

Preview of modified heading appears in Preview window

Modifying a style by example

You don't have to use the Modify Style dialog box to modify a style. You can also modify a style by changing the format of some sample text and then updating the style to match the selection in the Styles and Formatting task pane. To do this, modify the formatting of some text that is formatted in the style you want to modify. While the text is still selected, open the Styles and Formatting task pane, position the pointer over the style you want to update, click the down arrow on the right end of the style name button to open the pop-up menu, then click Update to Match Selection, as shown in Figure B-19.

FIGURE B-19: Style pop-up menu

Inserting Manual Page Breaks

Word automatically wraps text in a document to the next page when the last line of the current page is full. If you want text to go on to the next page before the current page is full, you can also manually insert a **page break** using the Break command on the Insert menu. Before you print a document that has several pages you should preview it with the Print Preview command to determine whether you need to insert manual page breaks. ✏ The Ski Sack information sheet breaks to a second page at an awkward place. You decide to add a page break to make the document easier to read.

1. Click at the beginning of the heading **Key Benefits**, click **Insert** on the menu bar, then click **Break**
   The Break dialog box opens.

QuickTip

You can remove a manual page break by deleting the dotted line for the page break just as you would a character of text, using either the [Backspace] key or the [Delete] key.

2. Make sure the **Page break option button** is selected, then click **OK**
   A manual page break is inserted into the document before the Description heading, as shown in Figure B-20. In Normal view, a dotted line across the page marks a page break, and the words "Page Break" in the middle of the line indicate a manual page break.

3. Click at the beginning of the heading **Kit Promotions**, then press **[Ctrl][Enter]**
   This keyboard shortcut is a quick way to insert a manual page break. The document is now three pages, with the Kit Promotional section on the third page.

4. Click the **Print Preview button** 🔍 on the Standard toolbar

5. Click the **Multiple Pages button** ▦ on the Print Preview toolbar, point to the third icon in the first row of the palette and wait until the ScreenTip reads "**1 × 3 Pages**," then click
   The three pages of the document appear side by side in Print Preview. See Figure B-21.

6. Click **Close** on the Print Preview toolbar, click the **page break above Kit Promotions**, then press **[Delete]**
   The document is now only two pages long.

7. Press **[Ctrl][End]**, press **[Enter]** twice, type your name, then click the **Save button** 💾 on the Standard toolbar

8. Click **File** on the menu bar, click **Print**, click **OK**, then click the **Close button** on the Word program window
   The document prints on two pages, as shown in Figure B-22, and then both the Ski Sack Sheet document and Word close.

Using widow and orphan control

A **widow** is the last line of a paragraph that appears by itself on top of a page. An **orphan** is the first line of a paragraph that appears by itself on the bottom of a page. You can prevent these unattractive elements from occurring by using the Paragraph dialog box (click Format on the menu bar, then click Paragraph).

Click the Line and Page Breaks tab, then click the Widow/Orphan control check box to add a check mark. With these settings, Word automatically increases the length of a page by one line to prevent a widow, and forces a page break one line sooner to prevent an orphan where necessary.

FIGURE B-20: Page break inserted in the document

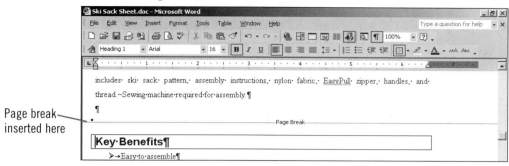

Page break inserted here

FIGURE B-21: Three-page Ski Sack Sheet in Print Preview

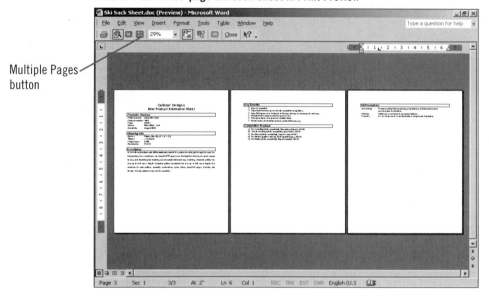

Multiple Pages button

FIGURE B-22: Completed Ski Sack Sheet document

Outdoor Designs
New Product Information Sheet

About the Product

Product name: Alpine Ski Sack
Product number: 3460
Price: $24.95
Colors: Blue, Black, Teal
Available: August 2003

Shipping Info

Kit box: Pattern Box D (14" x 6" x 2")
Weight: 1.5 pounds
Freight cost: $2.90
Store terms: Net 30

Description

A kit with instructions and all the materials needed to create a durable, lightweight ski sack for transporting skis via plane or car. EasyPull ™ zippers run the length of the bag for quick access to skis, and durable nylon handles provide comfortable and easy handling. Standard pattern fits skis up to 210 cm in length. Extended pattern (included) fits skis up to 240 cm in length. Kit includes ski sack pattern, assembly instructions, nylon fabric, EasyPull zipper, handles, and thread. Sewing machine required for assembly.

Key Benefits

➢ Easy to assemble
➢ Significant cost savings over fully assembled competitors
➢ EasyPull zippers run the length of the bag making ski access quick and easy
➢ Durable fabric ensures safe transport of skis
➢ Side pocket provides space for smaller items
➢ Cushioned nylon handles ensures comfortable carrying

Competitive Products

1) Ski Tote Bag (fully assembled), Recreational Sports, $49.95
2) The Ski Suitcase (fully assembled), Sport Stuff, $39.95
3) Ski Carrier (fully assembled), Sport-o-rama, $49.95
4) Ski Holder (pattern and kit), Cold Spell Designs, $24.95
5) Ski Caddy (fully assembled), Bags Unlimited, $24.95

Kit Promotions

Advertising: *Profitable Craft Merchandising* (September), additional ads under consideration for October
Publicity: Mailers to press list and consumer database
Prepacks: Six for the price of five (wholesale) in August and September

Your name

Practice

► Concepts Review

Label the Word window elements shown in Figure B-23.

FIGURE B-23

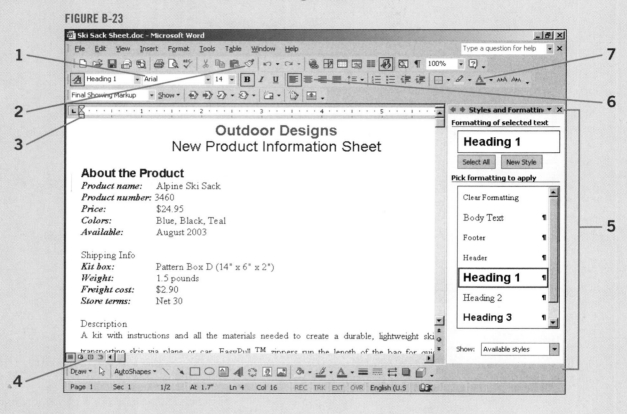

Match each toolbar button with the effect it creates.

8. 🖌
9. 🅰
10. 🛆
11. ▤
12. ▭

a. Copies formatting from one text selection and applies it to another
b. Justifies the current paragraph
c. Creates a left indent
d. Creates an indent that hangs over text below
e. Changes font color

Select the best answer from the list of choices.

13. **Font size is measured in:**
    a. pixels.
    b. points.
    c. TrueType.
    d. Centimeters.

14. **The amount of space between the edge of the page and your document text is called the:**
    a. alignment.
    b. margin.
    c. tab.
    d. hanging indent.

15. **If the alignment of text in a paragraph is justified, what is true about the text?**
    a. It is aligned at the right margin.
    b. It is aligned at the left margin.
    c. It is aligned at the center of the page.
    d. It is aligned at both the right and left margins.

16. **Which of these dialog boxes would you use to change line spacing from single spacing to double spacing?**
    a. Paragraph dialog box
    b. Font dialog box
    c. Page Setup dialog box
    d. AutoFormat dialog box

17. **What are the default page margin settings in Word?**
    a. 1.25" all around the document
    b. 1" all around the document
    c. 1.5" for the top and bottom margins, 2" for the left and right margins
    d. 1" for the top and bottom margins, 1.25" for the left and right margins

18. **If you want to reject an AutoFormatting action, what do you do?**
    a. Click Format on the menu bar, then click Reject AutoFormat.
    b. Click the AutoFormat Options button, then click an option from the shortcut menu.
    c. Press [Ctrl][End].
    d. Click the Undo button.

19. **A set amount of space between the edge of a paragraph and the right or left margin is called a(n):**
    a. tab.
    b. tab stop.
    c. indent.
    d. style.

20. **How do you insert a manual page break in a document?**
    a. Click File on the menu bar, then click New.
    b. Click Insert on the menu bar, then click Break.
    c. Press [Ctrl][A].
    d. Press [Ctrl][Shift].

Skills Review

1. **Change font type and size.**
   a. Start Word, use the Choose document command on the task pane to open a copy of the file WD B-2 from the drive and folder where your Project Files are located, then save the new document as *Member Welcome Letter*.
   b. Select the entire document.
   c. Change the font type to Arial.
   d. Select the first four lines in the document, then change the font type to Metro (if Metro is not available, choose another font).
   e. Select the first line of the document, then change the font size to 18.
   f. Save your changes to the document.

2. **Change font color, style, and effects.**
   a. Select the first line, The Bay City Repertory Theatre, then change the font color to red (choose the red square in the third row).
   b. Format the selected text in bold.
   c. Use the Font dialog box to apply a shadow effect to the selected text.
   d. Scroll down until you see the heading Forster Theatre, then format this text in bold.
   e. Apply bold formatting to the heading Stephens Theatre a few lines below the Forster Theatre heading.
   f. Apply underline formatting to the words Play and Dates in the line below Forster Theatre.
   g. Format the text Romeo and Juliet in the line below Forster Theatre in italic.
   h. Use the Format Painter button to apply italic formatting to the three other play titles below Romeo and Juliet. Use the Format Painter button to apply italic formatting to the two play titles below the Stephens Theatre heading.
   i. Save your changes.

3. **Change alignment and line spacing.**
   a. Center the first four lines of the document.
   b. Apply double space paragraph formatting to the four lines of text, beginning with the text Tickets to all six productions and ending with the text Invitations to members-only events near the top of the page.
   c. Save your changes.

4. **Change margin settings.**
   a. Use the Page Setup dialog box to change the top margin setting to .8 inches.
   b. Change the bottom margin setting to .8 inches.
   c. Switch to Print Layout view.
   d. Use the ruler to verify the new margin setting at the top of the page.
   e. Return to Normal view.
   f. Save your settings.

5. **Set tabs and indents.**
   a. Place the insertion point at the beginning of the word Play in the line below the Forster Theatre heading, press and hold [Shift], then press [↓] 10 times to select all the play listings.
   b. Set a tab at the 3" mark on the ruler.
   c. Indent the selected text to the ½ inch mark on the ruler.
   d. Scroll to the top of the page, then select the four lines of text beginning with Tickets to six productions through Invitations to members-only events.
   e. Indent this selected text to the ½ inch mark on the ruler.
   f. Save your changes.

6. Add bulleted and numbered lists.

   a. Apply bullet formatting to the four lines of selected text, choosing the diamond style bullets of the Bullets and Numbering dialog box.

   b. Scroll down until you see the line that begins Fill out the Exchange Ticket form, then select this line and the two lines after it.

   c. Format these three paragraphs as a numbered list.

   d. Use the Bullets and Numbering dialog box to change the style of the number to 1) 2) 3) (a number followed by a parenthesis).

   e. Save your changes.

7. Apply and modify styles.

   a. Open the Styles and Formatting task pane, and make sure that Available styles is selected in the Show list box.

   b. Scroll to the top of the document, then apply the Heading 1 style to the heading Productions for the 2003-2004 Season heading.

   c. Apply the Heading 1 style to the following headings in the document: Excellent Seats, Invitations to Special Events, and Discounted Ticket Rates.

   d. Modify the Heading 1 style to bold italic with a shadow effect.

   e. Close the Styles and Formatting task pane, then save your changes.

8. Insert manual page breaks.

   a. Insert a page break before the heading Excellent Seats using a menu command.

   b. Insert a page break before the heading Discounted Ticket Rates using a keyboard combination.

   c. View the document in Print Preview mode.

   d. Use the Multiple Pages button on the Print Preview toolbar to view all three pages of the document.

   e. Close the Print Preview toolbar.

   f. Delete the page break before the heading Discounted Rates.

   g. Scroll to the end of the document, then replace the text Matthew Marshall with your name.

   h. Save your changes.

   i. Preview and print the document, compare your document with Figure B-24, then exit Word.

FIGURE B-24

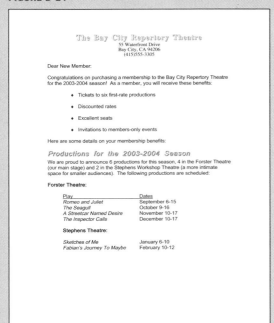

▶ Independent Challenge 1

You are the Sales Coordinator for Little Guy Toys, Inc. The National Sales Manager has given you an unformatted version of the agenda for the January Sales Conference and asked you to format it.

a. Use the Choose document command on the New Document task pane to open a copy of the file WD B-3 from the drive and folder where your Project Files are located, then save the new document as *Sales Meeting Agenda*.

b. Center-align the first six lines of the document (from Little Guy Toys through the Fax number).

c. Format the first line in Impact 14 point. Format the company address, phone and fax numbers in Arial 8 point.

d. Format the remaining lines of the document in Arial 10 point.

e. Center-align the line August 15, 2003 and the line Coconut Resort, Fort Lauderdale, Florida.

f. Apply bold formatting to each presenter name in the document, then apply italic formatting to all job titles.

g. Select the text from 9:00 to the end of the document, then insert a tab stop at the 1.5 inch mark on the ruler.

h. Create a hanging indents for the 11:00, 1:00 and 3:15 time slots so that the second line wraps under the tab stop position (1").

i. Apply the Heading 1 style to the text Sales Meeting Agenda.

j. Modify the Heading 1 style so that it is center-aligned (*Hint*: In the Modify Style dialog box, click Format, click Paragraph, then choose Centered from the Alignment list.)

k. Type your name at the end of the document, then center-align it.

l. Save your changes, then print the document.

▶ Independent Challenge 2

Sam Kosta, the owner of a charter fishing boat company, wants to create an information sheet describing his fishing tours. He has written down some information about his tours including a description and pricing information and asked you to format it for him. He has also written a form letter to potential customers that he wants to send out with the information sheet.

a. Use the Choose document command on the New Document task pane to open a copy of the file WD B-4 from the drive and folder where your Project Files are located, then save the new document as *Tour Information Sheet*.

b. Separate the letter from the information sheet by inserting a page break after the letter so that the information sheet is on a second page.

c. Format the Big Tuna name, address, phone, and fax numbers at the top of the letter using any font type, style, and effects you like to make it look like professional letterhead. Center-align it. Then copy this formatting to the company name and address at the top of the second page.

d. Format the text of the letter using a font style that you like.

e. On page 2, apply Heading 1 and Heading 2 styles to the headings in the information sheet to make it easy to read and orderly.

f. Modify the Heading 1 style, making a formatting change that you think improves the appearance of this style for the document.

g. On page 2, format the text under the headings using a font of your choice.

h. Format the list of items under About the Boats as a bulleted list using any bullet style you want.

i. Apply bold, superscript formatting to the asterisk at the end of the Day trip line at the bottom of page 2 and also to the asterisk (∗) at the beginning of the last line.

j. Format the last line of the information sheet choosing a font type and style that makes it appear smaller than the information in the body of the document.

k. Insert a tab stop so that the three items under the Fishing Guide heading line up with each other. You can insert the tab stop anywhere you think is appropriate.

l. Type your name at the end of the information sheet.

m. Save your changes, preview, and then print the letter and information sheet.

▶ Independent Challenge 3

Edward Wills is the owner of the Eucalyptus Inn in Sydney, Australia. He has decided to offer guests one free night at his inn if they stay for three nights. He has typed the information for a certificate in Word and has given it to you to format.

a. Use the Choose document command on the New Document task pane to open a copy of the file WD B-5 from the drive and folder where your Project Files are located, then save the new document as *Certificate*.

b. Using the skills you learned in this unit, format the certificate using fonts, types, sizes, styles, and effects that you think are appropriate. Use your creativity to produce a great-looking document.

c. Format some of the text on the certificate as a bulleted list, choosing whatever style you like.

d. Adjust the top and bottom margins to a different measurement, and change the paper orientation to Landscape.

e. Type your name somewhere on the certificate.

f. Save your changes, print the certificate, then close the document.

Independent Challenge 4

You are a member of a group that is taking a trip to a foreign city. Your group can be any type of group you want—a family gathering, a sports team, a choral group, or whatever you like. The city you choose is also up to you. Your role in this group is to create a restaurant directory for your other participants to use while traveling. You first need to do some research on the Internet. Once you've completed your research, you need to write a letter to the other members of your group and refer to the restaurant directory.

a. Log on to the Internet, then visit a search engine site such as AltaVista (www.altavista.com) or Google (www.google.com) and search for restaurants in the city of your choice.

b. Jot down on a piece of paper the names, addresses, and phone numbers of six different restaurants, two of which are low priced, two of which are moderately priced, and two of which are expensive. For each restaurant, write a brief description of the type of cuisine served there.

c. Start Word, start a new, blank document, type your name and address on the top of the page, center-align it, and format it using font types, styles, and effects you think look good.

d. Write a letter to the other members of your group telling them that you have enclosed a restaurant guide you created for the upcoming trip.

e. Left-align the body of the letter, and format the body text, using a font you like.

f. Insert a page break after your letter closing.

g. Type **Restaurant Guide** at the top of page 2 and format it in whatever font you like.

h. On page 2, type three headings: **Low Priced**, **Moderately Priced**, and **Expensive**, then apply the Heading 1 style to each one. Under each heading, type the name of two restaurants, including their address and phone number and a description of the type of cuisine. Use your best judgment in formatting this information so that it is clear and consistent, using font styles, indents, paragraph spacing, or bulleted or numbered lists that make sense and are appropriate. Make sure the guide fits entirely on one page.

i. Save the document as *Restaurant Guide*, then print it.

Visual Workshop

Use the Choose document command in the New Document task pane to open a copy of the file WD B-6 from the drive and folder where your Project Files are located, then save the new document as *Juice Menu*. Format the document so it appears as shown in Figure B-25. Modify the Heading 1 style so that it matches the red headings on the menu page. (*Hint*: Format one of the headings as Impress BT 14 point, underlined, center-aligned, and red; click the arrow on the right side of the Heading 1 item in the task pane, then click Update to match selection.) Even if you can't match every font type and size exactly, try to format your document so it looks as much like the one shown as possible.

FIGURE B-25

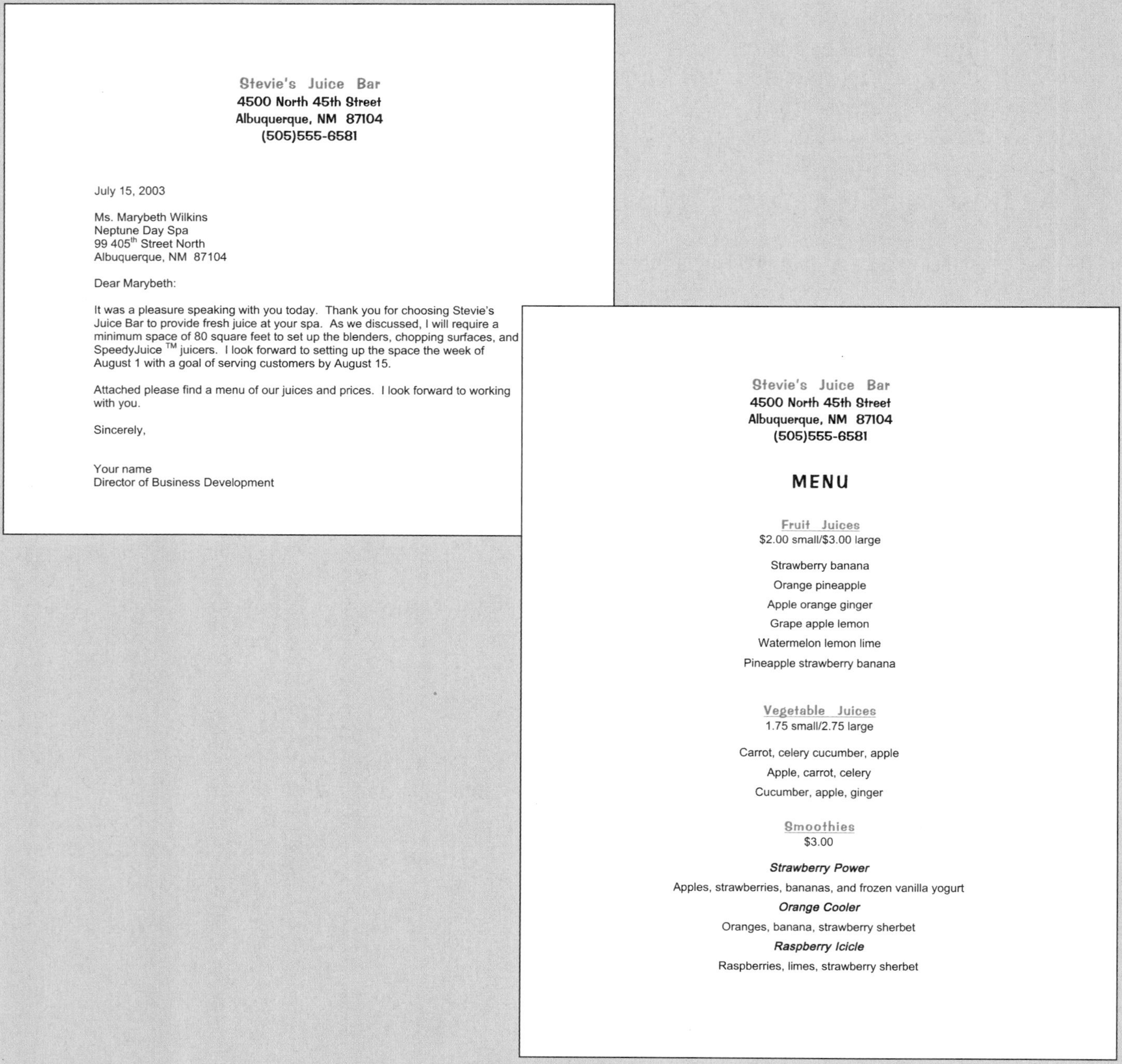

Stevie's Juice Bar
4500 North 45th Street
Albuquerque, NM 87104
(505)555-6581

July 15, 2003

Ms. Marybeth Wilkins
Neptune Day Spa
99 405th Street North
Albuquerque, NM 87104

Dear Marybeth:

It was a pleasure speaking with you today. Thank you for choosing Stevie's Juice Bar to provide fresh juice at your spa. As we discussed, I will require a minimum space of 80 square feet to set up the blenders, chopping surfaces, and SpeedyJuice ™ juicers. I look forward to setting up the space the week of August 1 with a goal of serving customers by August 15.

Attached please find a menu of our juices and prices. I look forward to working with you.

Sincerely,

Your name
Director of Business Development

Stevie's Juice Bar
4500 North 45th Street
Albuquerque, NM 87104
(505)555-6581

MENU

Fruit Juices
$2.00 small/$3.00 large

Strawberry banana

Orange pineapple

Apple orange ginger

Grape apple lemon

Watermelon lemon lime

Pineapple strawberry banana

Vegetable Juices
1.75 small/2.75 large

Carrot, celery cucumber, apple

Apple, carrot, celery

Cucumber, apple, ginger

Smoothies
$3.00

Strawberry Power
Apples, strawberries, bananas, and frozen vanilla yogurt
Orange Cooler
Oranges, banana, strawberry sherbet
Raspberry Icicle
Raspberries, limes, strawberry sherbet

Adding

Special Elements to a Document

Objectives

- ► **Create a table**
- ► **Insert and delete columns and rows**
- ► **Format a table**
- ► **Insert WordArt**
- ► **Add clip art**
- ► **Insert a footnote**
- ► **Insert a header or footer**
- ► **Add borders and shading**

In this unit, you will learn a combination of skills for making a document more attractive and informative. If you need to present information in a rows and columns format, you can insert a table. If you want to add visual interest to your document, or illustrate specific points, you can add graphic elements. Word also lets you easily add footnotes. If your document contains multiple pages, you may also want to include page numbers and other information at the top or bottom of each page; Word makes it easy to insert headers and footers that contain this information and appear on every page of your document. Dean Holmes, marketing manager for Outdoor Designs, has asked you to finish a flyer he's been working on to promote the company's line of kite packs. You'll insert a table to organize the details on each kite pack, and you'll add borders, shading, and graphic elements to give the flyer visual appeal. You'll also document some of the information in the flyer with a footnote, and you'll insert a header and footer.

Word 2002

Creating a Table

Not all information in a document is best presented in a running flow of text. Sometimes, it's more effective to present information in a tabular format. A **table** is made up of rows and columns, and can contain both text and graphics. You can insert a table using the Insert Table button on the Standard toolbar or the Insert Table command on the Table menu. When you first create a table, you specify the number of rows and columns you want in the table, but you can add and delete them as you modify the table.   Dean gives you a file containing both the flyer's text and suggestions he typed. He suggests that you begin by inserting a table into the flyer to organize the information about all of the different Kite Packs.

1. **Start Word, use the Choose document command on the New Document task pane to open a copy of the file WD C-1 from the drive and folder where your Project Files are located, then save the new document as Kite Flyer**
   The promotional flyer opens in Print Layout view. This view is most useful when you want to see how text, graphics, and other special elements will be positioned on the printed page. To separate his notes to you from the flyer text, Dean enclosed them in double angle brackets, such as "<<Insert Clip Art>>."

2. **Make sure formatting marks are showing by clicking the Show/Hide ¶ button ▮ on the Standard toolbar if necessary**

3. **Scroll down, position the insertion point to the left of the text <<Insert Table>> until it changes to a ⇗ , click to select the line of text, then press [Delete]**
   This is where you will insert the table.

4. **Click the Insert Table button ▦ on the Standard toolbar**
   A grid opens below the button.

5. **Click and drag to create a 5 × 4 table, as shown in Figure C-1**
   After you release the mouse button, a table with five rows and four columns appears below the first paragraph of text in the document. The insertion point is in the first cell. A **cell** is the intersection of a row and a column.

6. **Type Item Number, then press [Tab]**
   Pressing [Tab] moves the insertion point to the next cell, either to the right of the current cell or to the beginning of the next row if it is at the end of the row. Pressing [Enter] inserts a paragraph mark in the current cell, moving the insertion point down a line, but not to the next cell. The mark in each cell is an **end-of-cell mark**. Text you type is inserted to the left of the end-of-cell mark. The marks to the right of the ends of the rows are **end-of-row marks**.

QuickTip

You can also move to a different cell by clicking the cell you want to move to or by using the arrow keys to navigate.

7. **Type Name, press [Tab], type Skill Level, press [Tab], type Optimum Flying Weather, then press [Tab]**
   Notice that the text "Optimum Flying Weather" wrapped to a second line in the cell because it could not fit on one line. Notice also that after you typed the last column heading, "Optimum Flying Weather," pressing [Tab] moved the insertion point to the first cell in the second row.

Trouble?

If you accidentally pressed [Tab] after the last entry, a new row was added. Click the Undo button ▭ to delete the new row.

8. **Type the following text in the table, pressing [Tab] after each entry to move to the next cell, but do not press [Tab] after the last entry, then save your changes**

501	Coastal Parafoil	Beginner	Gentle winds
502	Puget Sound Delta	Beginner	Gentle winds or rain
601	Columbia Gorge Runner	Advanced	Strong winds
701	Green Flyer	Advanced	Strong winds

   Compare your screen to Figure C-2. Don't worry if some of the text in your table wraps differently from the figure; this will vary depending on your monitor and printer settings.

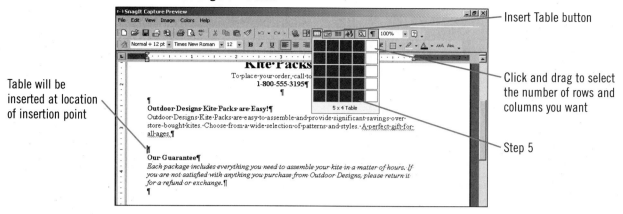

FIGURE C-1: Inserting a 5 × 4 table

Insert Table button

Click and drag to select the number of rows and columns you want

Table will be inserted at location of insertion point

Step 5

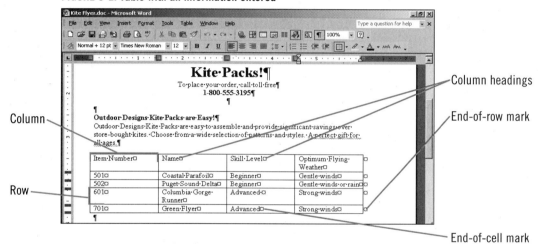

FIGURE C-2: Table with all information entered

Column headings

End-of-row mark

Column

Row

End-of-cell mark

CLUES TO USE

Creating multiple columns

Another way to organize text is to create multiple columns. By default, the text you enter in a blank document is formatted in a single column. If you want to increase the amount of text on a page and add white space to improve readability, you can format your text in multiple columns, like a newspaper. To present all or part of the text in your document in multiple columns, click Format on the menu bar, then click Columns. The Columns dialog box opens, as shown in Figure C-3. Here you set the number of columns, the width of each column, and the space between columns. To apply the multiple columns format to the entire document, choose Whole document in the Apply to list box at the bottom of the dialog box. To apply the multiple columns to just part of the document, click at the point in your document where you want the multiple columns to start, open the Columns dialog box, then choose This point forward in the Apply to list box. Then, to format the rest of the document as a single column, place the insertion point where you want the multiple columns to end, open

the Columns dialog box again, choose one column, then click This point forward in the Apply to list box. You can also create multiple columns by selecting the text you want to reformat, clicking the Columns button on the Standard toolbar, then dragging to select the number of columns you want.

FIGURE C-3: Columns dialog box

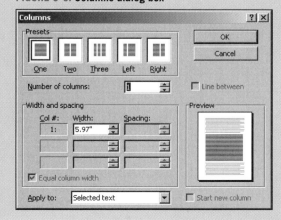

Inserting and Deleting Columns and Rows

After you create a table, you might need to add or delete rows or columns. To add a new row to the end of your table, you can simply click in the last cell in your table, then press [Tab]. You can also use the Insert Rows and Insert Columns buttons on the Standard toolbar, or the Insert command on the Table menu. To delete a row or column, you select it, click Table on the menu bar, click Delete, then click the name of the item you want to delete. ✐ You realize you need to add two new rows for two new products, and that you forgot to include the prices of the kites in the table. You need to add two rows and a column to include this information. You also need to delete one of the kite packs that has been discontinued.

1. Click the last cell in the table, press **[Tab]**, then enter the following information in the new row, pressing **[Tab]** after each entry except for the last one

   702   Sonic Boomer   Advanced   Strong winds

2. Position the mouse pointer over **the top of the column of end-of-row marks outside the right edge of the table** so that the pointer changes to ↓ , then click to select all of the end-of-row marks
   Compare your screen to Figure C-4. Notice that the Insert Columns button 🔳 has replaced the Insert Table button 🔲 on the Standard toolbar.

3. Click the **Insert Columns button** 🔳
   A new column is inserted as the last column in the table.

4. Click in the first cell of the new column, type **Price**, then press **[↓]**
   Pressing the arrow keys also moves the insertion point.

5. Enter the prices in the last column as shown below, pressing **[↓]** to move to each cell

   $19.95 $22.95 $24.95 $39.95 $49.95

6. Click in any cell in the row containing information about item number 502, click **Table** on the menu bar, point to **Delete**, then click **Rows**
   The entire row is deleted, and the rest of the rows move up to close up the space.

7. Point to the **selection bar** for the fourth row (that begins with 701) until the pointer changes to 𝄞 , then click to select the row

8. Click the **Insert Rows button** 🔳 on the Formatting toolbar

9. Type the following information in the new row, then save your changes:

   602   Cascade Diver   Advanced   Strong winds $39.95
   Your screen should look similar to Figure C-5.

FIGURE C-4: Selecting the end-of-row marks

Insert Columns button has replaced the Insert Table button on toolbar

End-of-row marks are selected

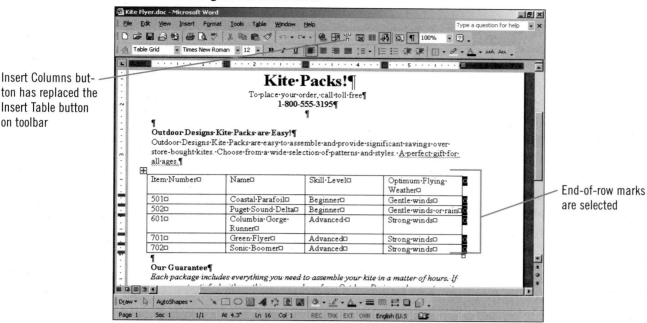

FIGURE C-5: Table with columns and rows added and a row deleted

Column added

Row deleted

Row added

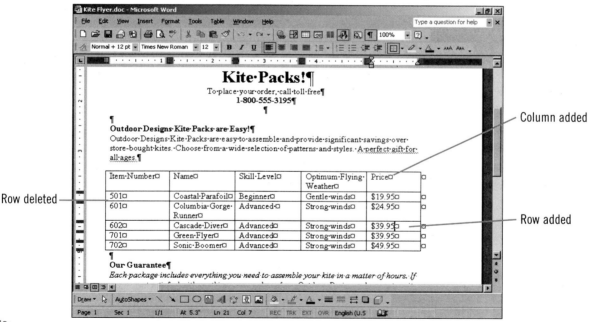

CLUES TO USE

Creating a table with the Draw Table button

You can also use the Draw Table button [pencil icon] on the Tables and Borders toolbar to create a table. To do this, first open the Tables and Borders toolbar if necessary by clicking the Tables and Borders button [icon] on the Standard toolbar. Click [pencil icon] on the Tables and Borders toolbar, then drag in a diagonal motion to create the outside border of the table. To create columns, drag vertically from the top border down to create the columns, and drag horizontally from the outside border across to create rows. If you make a mistake and need to delete rows or columns, click the Eraser button [icon] on the Tables and Borders toolbar, then drag through the unwanted columns or rows to delete them.

Word 2002

Formatting Tables

After you create a table you can format it manually by changing the font styles, and adding borders and shading. You can save time by using the Table AutoFormat command to format your table with a preset combination of formatting choices. Table AutoFormat includes 45 professionally designed formats from which to choose. You can customize the way AutoFormat formats your table by selecting options in the Table AutoFormat dialog box. You can also improve the appearance of your table by adjusting column widths. To widen a column, position the pointer between two columns until it changes to a ◄‖► then drag to the left or right. Now that the information in your table is complete, you decide to format the table using Table AutoFormat.

Steps

1. With the insertion point still in the table, click **Table** on the menu bar, then click **Table AutoFormat**

   The Table AutoFormat dialog box opens. The Preview box displays a sample of the AutoFormat that is currently selected in the list.

2. In the Table styles list, click **Table Colorful 2**

   The Preview box changes to display the Table Colorful 2 AutoFormat.

3. In the Apply special formats to section, click the **First column check box** to deselect it, then click the **Last column check box** to deselect it

   The Table Colorful 2 AutoFormat treats the first column and last column differently from the body of the table because in some tables, the first column contains row headings and the last column contains totals. Your table contains data in both the first and last columns, however, so you don't want these columns to have special formatting. Compare your screen to Figure C-6.

4. Click **Apply**

   The Table AutoFormat dialog box closes, and the table in your document is formatted with the selected AutoFormat.

5. Position the mouse pointer between the **Item Number** column and the **Name** column so the pointer changes to ◄‖►, drag the pointer to the left so it is over the letter **m** in the word Number, then release the mouse pointer

   The width of the column to the left of the mouse pointer expands, so that all entries in the "Name" column now fit on one line, and the column heading "Item Number" is now on two lines.

6. Position the mouse pointer between the **Optimum Flying Weather** column and the **Price** column so that the pointer changes to ◄‖►, then double-click

   The width of the Optimum Flying Weather column expands, increasing the amount of space between the data in the last two columns. Double-clicking the vertical gridline adjusts the width of a column automatically.

7. Position the mouse pointer in the **selection bar for the column headings row** so that the pointer changes to ⌐, then click

   The row is selected.

8. Click the **Center button** ≡ on the Standard toolbar, then click in the document away from the table text

   The column headings are centered, and the table text is deselected.

9. Save your changes to the document

   Compare your screen to Figure C-7.

FIGURE C-6: Table AutoFormat dialog box

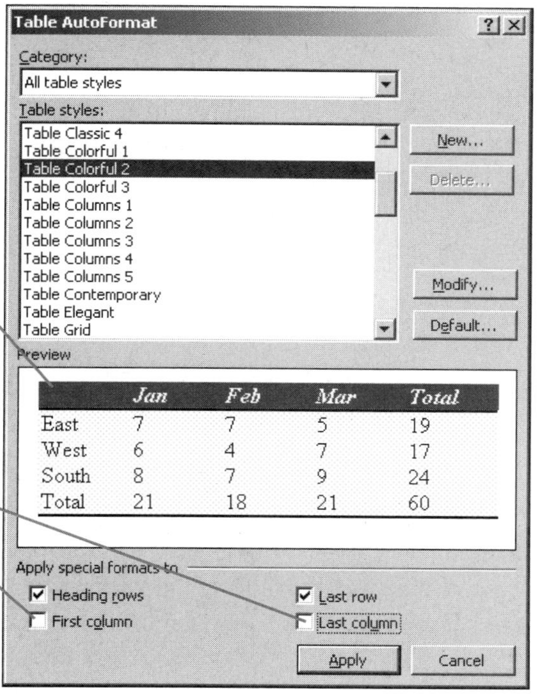

Preview of currently selected table style appears here

Step 3

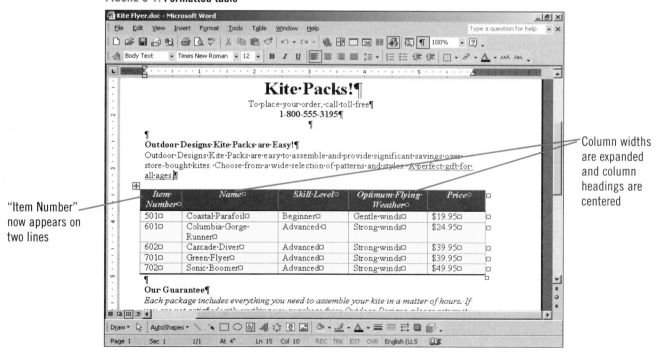

FIGURE C-7: Formatted table

"Item Number" now appears on two lines

Column widths are expanded and column headings are centered

Word 2002

Inserting WordArt

You can insert several types of artistic elements into your documents. One type is **WordArt**, stylized text with sophisticated text formatting features. A piece of WordArt text is an **object**, which means you can move and resize it as a single unit. As Dean suggested, you want to use WordArt to add the name of the company to the kite flyer.

Steps

1. Press **[Ctrl][Home]**, select **<<Insert Company Name as WordArt>>**, then press **[Delete]**
   Dean's suggestion is removed from the document, and the insertion point is on the blank line at the top of the flyer.

Trouble?

If the Drawing toolbar is not visible, click the Drawing button on the Standard toolbar.

2. Click the **Insert WordArt button** on the Drawing toolbar
   The WordArt Gallery dialog box opens. This dialog box lets you choose from a variety of WordArt styles.

3. Click the WordArt style in the first row and the third column, as shown in Figure C-8, then click **OK**
   The Edit WordArt Text dialog box opens, as shown in Figure C-9. Here you type or edit the text of your WordArt object, and make any desired changes to the font and font size. The text you type will replace the text "Your Text Here."

4. Type **Outdoor Designs**, click the **Font Size list arrow**, click **32**, then click **OK**
   The WordArt object appears in the document at the location of the insertion point.

5. Click the **WordArt object**
   Selection handles appear around the object, and the WordArt toolbar opens. **Selection handles** are small squares that appear when an object is selected, indicating that you can move or resize the object. When a WordArt object is selected, the WordArt toolbar opens, so that you can make editing and formatting changes.

Trouble?

If the WordArt toolbar doesn't open when you click the WordArt object, you can open it by clicking View on the menu bar, pointing to Toolbars, then clicking WordArt.

6. Click the **Format WordArt button** on the WordArt toolbar, click the **Color list arrow** in the Fill section, click the **dark red square** in the second row, first column, then click **OK**

7. Click the **WordArt Shape button** on the WordArt toolbar, then click the **Wave 2 shape** in the third row, sixth column

QuickTip

To edit the WordArt object, double-click it or click Edit Text on the WordArt toolbar.

8. With the WordArt object selected, click the **Center button**

9. Position the mouse pointer over the **lower-left selection handle** so that it changes to ↙, drag the handle down and to the left approximately ½" as shown in Figure C-10, then click outside the object

FIGURE C-8: WordArt Gallery

Step 3

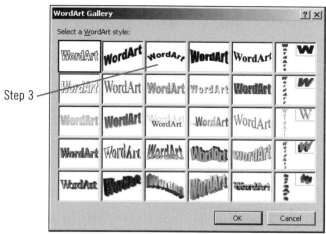

FIGURE C-9: Edit WordArt Text dialog box

Font list arrow

Text you type
replaces this text

Font size list arrow

FIGURE C-10: WordArt in document

Lower left selection
handle

WordArt Shape button

Format WordArt
button

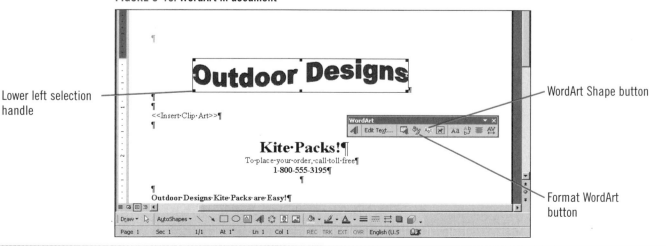

Word 2002

Adding Clip Art

You can insert many different types of graphics into your documents to help illustrate a point or enhance the overall visual appeal. You can insert images from files stored on disk or downloaded from the Web, and you can even draw your own images using the tools on the Drawing toolbar. You also have access to hundreds of ready-made images, or **clip art**, through the **Clip Organizer**, a program shared by all Microsoft Office applications. The Clip Organizer is a catalog of clip art, animations, videos, and photographs, all of which are called **clips**. The clips can be located in various places on your hard drive, or on the Office Media Content CD, or on a Web site that Microsoft maintains that contains additional clip art, and the Clip Organizer makes it easy to manage them all from one location. You access the Clip Organizer through the Insert Clip Art task pane. Dean suggested that you add clip art to the kite flyer to enhance its visual appeal.

1. Select the text **<<Insert Clip Art>>**, then press **[Delete]**

QuickTip

If the Add Clips to Organizer dialog box appears, click Later.

2. Click **Insert** on the menu bar, point to **Picture**, then click **Clip Art**
   The Insert Clip Art task pane opens.

3. Click in the **Search text box**, type **kite**, then click **Search**
   The task pane displays thumbnail previews of all available images that are associated with the word "kite."

Trouble?

Your selection of clip art might differ. If the image shown in the figure does not appear in the Search Results area, click Insert on the menu bar, point to Picture, click From File, navigate to the drive and folder where your Project Files are located, click Kite.wmf, click OK, then skip to Step 6.

4. Click the **kite image** shown in Figure C-11, then close the task pane
   The image appears in the document.

5. Click the **kite image**
   In order to work with a clip-art image you must first select it, just as you do WordArt and other objects.

6. Drag the **top-right-corner selection handle** down and to the left until the image is approximately 1" wide
   The image is resized. Notice that this image is left-aligned at the insertion point. By default, clip images are formatted to be **inline with text**, so that they can be moved and aligned just like a text selection.

QuickTip

To change the formatting of an image from inline with text to a **floating picture**, so you can position it more precisely on the page, click Picture on the Format menu, click the Layout tab, then click a different wrapping style.

7. Click the **Center button** on the Standard toolbar, then click outside the image
   The kite image is now centered in the document and deselected. Compare your screen with Figure C-12.

8. Save your changes to the document

FIGURE C-11: Insert Clip Art task pane with kite results

Step 4

FIGURE C-12: Kite flyer with Clip Art image centered on page

Center button

Kite is now centered in document

Inserting pictures, sounds, and videos

The Clip Organizer gives you access to much more than images. You can also search for photographs, movies, animations, and sounds. To do this, click the Results should be list arrow in the task pane, click the media type that you want to find, then click Search. You can also use the Clip Organizer to search for clips on Design Gallery Live, a special Web site maintained by Microsoft that contains regularly updated collections of clips. To access Design Gallery Live, click Clips Online in the Insert Clip Art task pane. Enter your search information in the Search area, click Go, preview the results such as the ones shown in Figure C-13, click any clip to see a larger view if you wish, and then click the download button below any clip to download it. The Clip Organizer downloads the clip to the appropriate folder on your hard disk.

FIGURE C-13: Design Gallery Live search results

Word 2002

Inserting a Footnote

If your document contains references to other source material, you might want to add footnotes or endnotes. A **footnote** is a note or citation that appears at the bottom of a document page. An **endnote** is a note or citation that appears at the end of a document and is used when you don't want to interrupt the flow of text. Both footnotes and endnotes contain two linked parts: the **reference mark** (usually a number or symbol) in a document and the corresponding note text. Dean wants to make sure that readers understand that the prices do not include taxes or shipping costs. He asks you to insert a footnote clarifying this.

Steps

1. **Scroll down so you can see the table, then click directly after the word Price in the table**
   The insertion point should be just before the end-of-cell mark.

2. **Click Insert on the menu bar, point to Reference, then click Footnote**
   The Footnote and Endnote dialog box opens, as shown in Figure C-14. By default, the Footnotes option button is selected.

3. **Type * in the Custom mark text box**
   In documents with more than one footnote, you can use the AutoNumber option to have Word automatically number the footnotes or endnotes and adjust the numbering whenever you insert or delete notes. You're inserting only one footnote in the flyer, however, so you'll use a mark instead.

QuickTip

To choose from a variety of custom marks, click the Symbol button to open the Symbol dialog box and choose from the symbols available.

4. **Click Insert**
   The Footnote and Endnote dialog box closes and the insertion point moves to the bottom of the page in the footnote area, where you'll enter your footnote text. The asterisk is inserted as a **footnote reference mark** next to the word "Price" in the table.

5. **Type Prices do not include taxes or shipping costs.**
   The footnote text appears in the footnote area, with a small leading asterisk.

QuickTip

To delete a footnote from a document, select the footnote reference mark in the body of the text and delete it. The corresponding footnote is deleted and any remaining footnotes are renumbered automatically.

6. **Select the footnote text, then click the Italic button _I_ on the Formatting toolbar**
   The footnote style changes to italic. This will further distinguish the footnote from the rest of the flyer and ensure that it doesn't distract the reader from the main text.

7. **Click the Font Size list arrow on the Formatting toolbar, click 8, then click anywhere in the document window**
   The point size is reduced to 8 points, as shown in Figure C-15, and the text is deselected. Footnote text appears only in Print Layout view and in Print Preview, but you can click Footnotes on the View menu in any view to view and edit the footnote text.

8. **Save your changes to the document**

FIGURE C-14: Footnote and Endnote dialog box

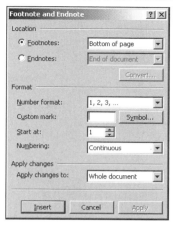

FIGURE C-15: Completed footnote

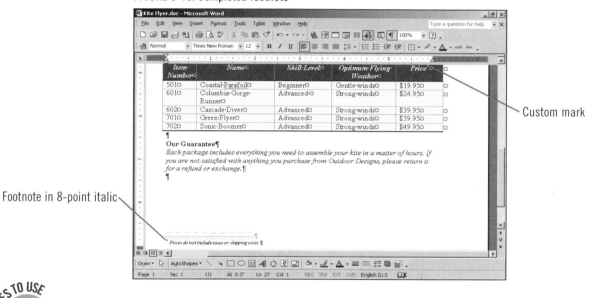

Custom mark

Footnote in 8-point italic

Working with lengthy documents

In a lengthy document, it can be difficult for readers to find the information they need. You can make the document easier to navigate by inserting one or more reference tables: a table of contents, an index, a table of figures, or a table of authorities. You can insert a **table of contents** (a list of the headings in your document), an **index** (a list of key words and terms and their page location), a **table of figures** (a list of the figures in a document and their location), and a **table of authorities** (a list of references in a legal document, such as cases or statutes, and their page location). Word's Index and Tables dialog box automates the creation and formatting of tables so they are updated whenever you make changes to the document. Depending on the type of table you insert, first you might need to specify the headings or terms in your document that you want

to include. To create a reference table, click Insert on the menu bar, click Reference, click Index and Tables, then click the appropriate tab, as shown in Figure C-16.

FIGURE C-16: Index and Tables dialog box

Unit C

Word 2002

Inserting a Header or Footer

You might want to add certain text, such as page numbers, the date, your name, or the filename, to the top or the bottom of every page in a document. A **header** is text that appears just below the top margin of every page, and a **footer** is text that appears just above the bottom margin of every page. ✏ Dean wants to review the flyer and provide feedback before you print the flyer, so you decide to add a header clarifying that this is a first draft.

Steps 1234

1. **Click View on the menu bar, then click Header and Footer**
   The insertion point moves to the header area at the top of the document, and the Header and Footer toolbar opens, as shown in Figure C-17. The text you enter in the Header area appears at the top of every page in a document. You can format header and footer text in the same way you format regular text.

2. **Type Outdoor Designs Confidential, Draft 1.0 in the header field, click the Center button ≡ on the Formatting toolbar, select the text, then click the Italic button 𝐼**
   The header text is centered at the top of the page and italicized.

3. **Click the Switch Between Header and Footer button ▤ on the Header and Footer toolbar**
   The document scrolls down automatically, and the insertion point appears in the Footer area.

4. **Type your name, followed by a comma (,) then press [Spacebar]**
   Now you can insert the current date, so Dean will know when the information was last updated.

5. **Click the Insert Date button ▤ on the Header and Footer toolbar**
   The current date appears in the footer. The date will be updated automatically each time you open the document.

QuickTip

If the Filename AutoText entry is not available, type "Kite Flyer".

6. **Press [Tab] twice to move to the right margin, type Filename:, press [Spacebar], click Insert AutoText on the Header and Footer toolbar, point to Header/Footer, then click Filename**
   The filename appears in the footer. If you save the document under a new name, the footer will reflect the new filename.

QuickTip

To edit a header or footer in Normal view, you can click the Header and Footer command on the View menu, and the header area will open. In Print Layout view, you can simply double-click the header or footer area.

7. **Click Close on the Header and Footer toolbar**
   The document appears in Print Layout view, a view that lets you see the Headers and Footers on the page. You can also see Headers and Footers in Print Preview. You cannot see the Headers and Footers in Normal view.

8. **Click the Normal View button ▤ to the left of the horizontal scroll bar, then save your changes**
   Notice that you cannot see the header and footer in this view. They are visible only in Print Preview and Print Layout view, but you can access them from any view by clicking the View menu and then clicking Header and Footer.

FIGURE C-17: Header area

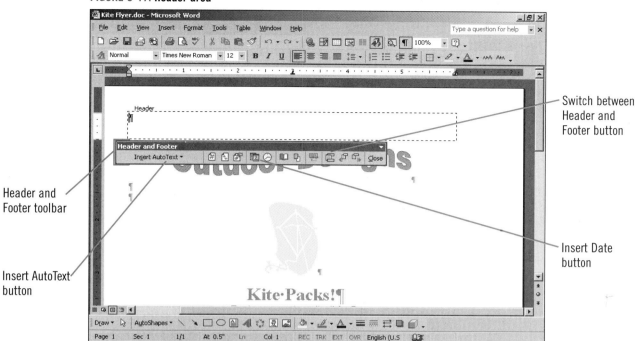

Switch between Header and Footer button

Header and Footer toolbar

Insert Date button

Insert AutoText button

CLUES TO USE

Working with headers and footers in a multipage document

In a multipage document, the first page often does not need a header or footer. For example, because the first page of a report might be a title page with your name, the date, and so on, you wouldn't want a header or footer containing this information. To eliminate the header and footer on the first page, click File on the menu bar, click Page Setup, then click the Layout tab. Click the Different first page check box to add a check mark, as shown in Figure C-18. If you want to add a different header or footer to the first page, click anywhere in the first page of the document, open the Header or Footer field, then type the new text. You can also create different headers or footers for odd- and even-numbered pages. For example, you might want the title and filename of a long, bound document to appear on all the odd-numbered pages, and the page number and date to appear on all the even-numbered pages. On the Layout tab in the Page Setup dialog box, click the Different Odd and Even check box to add a check mark, then insert the appropriate text in the header or footer areas of any odd or even page.

FIGURE C-18: Page Setup dialog box

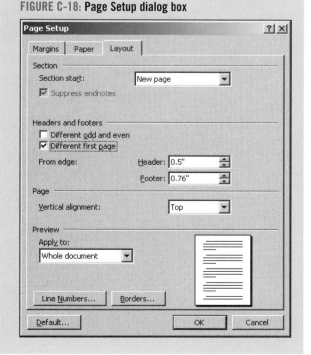

Adding Borders and Shading

You can add borders and shading around words, paragraphs, or entire pages to enhance a document. Shading a block of text can help set it apart from the main document, and adding a border around selected text can add visual interest. The easiest way to add a simple border is to select the text around which you want to add a border, click the Border button list arrow on the Standard toolbar, then select the border style you want to use. You can add a line at the top, bottom, left, or right edges of the selected text, or outline the selected text with a border. You can create more elaborate borders and add shading to selected text by using the Borders and Shading dialog box. ✒ You decide to add a border and shading to the "Our Guarantee" paragraph at the bottom of the page to set it off from the rest of the document.

1. Scroll down, then select the heading **Our Guarantee** and the paragraph below it

2. Click **Format** on the menu bar, click **Borders and Shading**, then click the **Shading tab**

3. Click the **third box in the top row** of the fill section (Gray-10%), as shown in Figure C-19
   The Preview area shows how the text will appear with the Gray 10% shading.

4. Click the **Borders tab**, then click the **Box style** in the Setting section
   The Preview area now shows what the paragraph will look like with the gray shading and box border applied. Notice the buttons in the Preview window. You can use these buttons to apply a border along any edge or through the middle of selected text.

5. Scroll down in the Style list , click the **double line style**, then click **OK**
   The Our Guarantee heading and paragraph now appear with shading and a double line border.

6. Select the text **Our Guarantee**, then click the **Center button** 🖺

7. Click the **Print Preview button** 🔍 on the Standard toolbar
   A preview of how the printed document will look appears in the Print Preview window. The document fits nicely on one page, so there's no need to make any additional changes.

8. Click the **Close** on the Print Preview toolbar, save your changes, then click the **Print button** 🖨 on the Standard toolbar
   The final copy of the kite flyer prints, as shown in Figure C-20.

9. Click **File** on the menu bar, then click **Exit**
   The Kite Flyer document and the Word program close.

FIGURE C-19: Shading tab in Borders and Shading dialog box

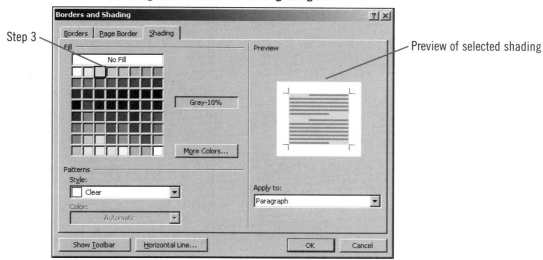

Step 3

Preview of selected shading

FIGURE C-20: Printout of completed Kite Flyer

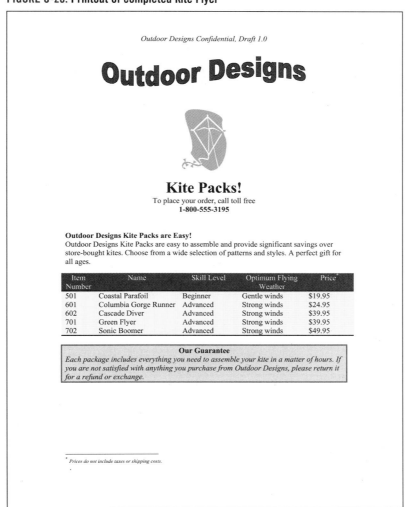

Practice

► Concepts Review

Label the Word window elements shown in Figure C-21.

FIGURE C-21

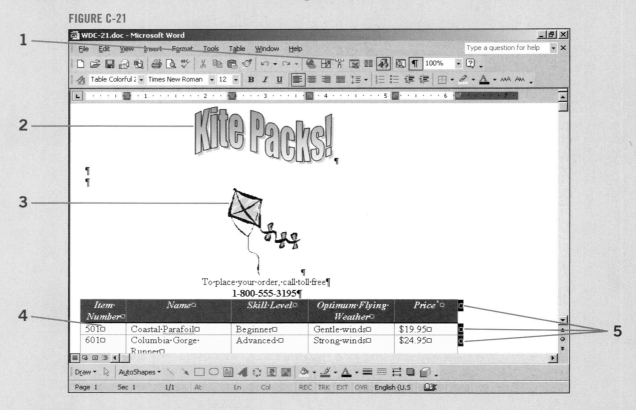

Match each toolbar button with its effect.

6.
7.
8.
9.
10.
11.

a. Inserts a new row in a table
b. Inserts new WordArt
c. Inserts a new column in a table
d. Inserts a new table
e. Opens Format WordArt dialog box
f. Applies a shape to selected WordArt

Select the best answer from the list of choices.

12. Which of the following can you place in a cell of a table?
   a. Text
   b. Graphics
   c. WordArt
   d. All of the above

13. **Which of the following actions does NOT move the insertion point to a new cell?**
    a. Pressing [Enter]
    b. Pressing [Tab]
    c. Pressing [↓]
    d. Pressing [→]

14. **Which of the following procedures does NOT insert a new row?**
    a. Pressing [Tab] at the end of the last row
    b. Selecting a row, then pressing [Enter]
    c. Selecting a row, then clicking the Insert Rows button
    d. Selecting a row, clicking Table on the menu bar, clicking Insert, then clicking Rows Above

15. **Which of the following procedures does NOT adjust the width of a column?**
    a. Double-clicking the ↔‖↔ when positioned between column headings
    b. Dragging the pointer ↔‖↔ when it is positioned between two columns
    c. Double-clicking the pointer ⇗ when it is positioned on the left side of a row
    d. Dragging the pointer ↔‖↔ when it is on the right edge of a table

16. **In which of the following views do the header and footer appear in the document?**
    a. Normal view
    b. Print Layout view
    c. Page Layout view
    d. Web Layout view

17. **What is the name of the repository of clip art, animations, and photographs that all Office applications share?**
    a. Clip Gallery
    b. Media Library
    c. Media Gallery
    d. Clip Organizer

18. **When you insert a row in a table using the Insert Rows button on the Standard toolbar, the new row appears:**
    a. Below the insertion point.
    b. Above the insertion point.
    c. As the last row in the table.
    d. As the first row of the table.

19. **The Table AutoFormat command allows you to:**
    a. Automatically change column widths in a table.
    b. Design your own format for a table.
    c. Choose a predesigned format for a table.
    d. Modify the number of rows and columns in a table.

▶ Skills Review

1. **Create a table.**
   a. Start Microsoft Word, use the Choose document command on the New Document task pane to open a copy of the file WD C-2 from the drive and folder where your Project Files are located, then save the new document as *Special Offer*.
   b. Place the insertion point to the left of the paragraph mark below the first paragraph of text.
   c. Insert a table that is five rows long and three columns wide.

d. Enter the data shown in Table C-1 into the table you created. Use [Tab], the arrow keys, and the mouse to place the insertion point in each cell.

e. Save your changes to the document.

2. **Insert and delete columns and rows.**

   a. Click to the left of the end-of-row mark at the end of the last row.

   b. Insert a new row as the last row in the table.

   c. Insert the following information in cells in the new row:

   11 or more

   50%

   1500' of 50-lb. Line

   d. Select the last column in the table.

   e. Insert a column.

   f. Insert the information from Table C-2 into the new column.

   g. Save your changes.

3. **Format a table.**

   a. With the insertion point still in the table, open the Table AutoFormat dialog box.

   b. Click Table Grid 8 in the Table styles list.

   c. Clear the Last row and the Last column check boxes.

   d. Click Apply.

   e. Drag the first column divider approximately ½" to the left so the column is just wide enough for the "11 or more" entry, but the column heading No. of Kites Ordered remains on two lines.

   f. Double-click the second column-divider line.

   g. Double-click as necessary the third column-divider line so the "overnight for additional cost" entry appears on a second line and the last entry, in the Shipping column, appears on one line.

   h. Save your changes.

4. **Insert WordArt.**

   a. Place the insertion point in the blank line between Outdoor Designs and the first paragraph at the top of the document.

   b. Click the Insert WordArt button on the Drawing toolbar.

   c. Select the WordArt style in the third row and the fifth column, then click OK.

   d. Type **Go Fly a Kite Sale**, change the font size to 32, then click OK.

   e. Select the WordArt object, click the Format WordArt button on the WordArt toolbar, click the Color tab, click the Color list arrow in the Fill area, click the red square (first column, third row), then click OK.

   f. Click the WordArt shape button, then click the Double Wave 1 shape (third row, seventh column).

   g. Center the WordArt object, then save your changes.

5. **Insert clip art.**

   a. Place the insertion point to the left of the Outdoor Designs Special Offer heading.

   b. Open the Insert Clip Art task pane.

   c. Type **sun** in the Search text box, then click Search.

   d. Click an image of the sun. (If no sun images appear in the Results section of the task pane, type another search word of your choosing that relates to nature or health, then insert one of the resulting images.)

   e. Close the Insert ClipArt task pane.

   f. Select the image, then drag the lower-right resize handle so the image is approximately ½" square, just a little bit bigger than the O in Outdoor Designs.

TABLE C-1

No. of Kites Ordered	Discount	Extra Line
1	10%	None
2-4	20%	500' of 30-lb. Line
5-7	30%	1000' of 30-lb. Line
8-10	40%	1500' of 30-lb. Line

TABLE C-2

Shipping Available
2-day for additional cost
2-day for additional cost
2-day at no additional cost; overnight for additional cost
2-day at no additional cost; overnight for additional cost
Overnight at no additional cost

g. Select the clip art, click the Copy button, click to the right of Special Offer, then click the Paste button.

h. Save your changes.

6. **Insert footnotes.**

   a. Place the insertion point after the period at the end of the second sentence in the paragraph at the top of the document, which ends with the text for everyone in the family.

   b. Click Insert on the menu bar, click Reference, then click Footnote.

   c. Click the Custom mark option button, then type an asterisk (*) in the Custom mark text box.

   d. Close the Footnote and Endnote dialog box.

   e. Type **Sale applies only to selected Kite Kits**.

   f. Select the footnote text.

   g. Format the footnote as Times New Roman 8-point italic.

   h. Compare your document to Figure C-22, then save your changes.

FIGURE C-22

7. **Insert headers and footers.**

   a. Click View on the menu bar, then click Header and Footer.

   b. Click the Switch Between Header and Footer button on the Header and Footer toolbar.

   c. Type your name, press [Spacebar], type **updated on**, then press [Spacebar].

   d. Click the Insert Date button on the Header and Footer toolbar.

   e. Press [Tab] twice, click Insert AutoText on the Header and Footer toolbar, point to Header/Footer, then click Filename. (If this AutoText entry is not available, choose a different AutoText entry from the list or type **Filename: Special Offer.doc**.)

   f. Format the footer in Times Roman 8-point italic.

   g. Close the Header and Footer toolbar.

8. **Add borders and shading**

   a. Select the first line of the document, Outdoor Designs Special Offer.

   b. Click Format on the menu bar, click Borders and Shading, then click the Borders tab.

   c. Click the bottom edge of the diagram in the Preview window to insert a horizontal border, then click OK.

   d. Scroll down, select the entire line of text To place your order, call toll free 1-800-555-3195, open the Borders and Shading dialog box, then click the Shadow style in the Setting area.

   e. Click the Shading tab, click the Gray 10% square in the Fill area (third square, first row) then click OK.

   f. Add your name to the bottom of the document below the Our Guarantee paragraph, then print one copy of the document.

   g. Save your changes, close the document, then exit Word.

▶ Independent Challenge 1

Joel, the owner of The Steak Pit, recently discovered that the other three steak restaurants in town charge much more for the same steak, potato, and garden salad meal than The Steak Pit does. Because Joel is going to have new menus printed for The Steak Pit, he wants to compare his prices with those of other local restaurants. He asks you to create a simple quick reference sheet that he can use to compare the information he has gathered. He asks you to put all the information in table format, with separate columns for the restaurant name, location, steak size, and price.

   a. Open a copy of the file WD C-3 from the drive and folder where your Project Files are located, then save the new document as *Price Comparisons*.

b. Modify the WordArt object at the top of the document by choosing a new font, a new shape, and a new Fill color for the font.

c. Replace the text <<Insert table>> with a 4 × 4 table.

d. Enter the information shown in Table C-3 into the table one row at a time.

e. Use the AutoFormat to format the table appropriately.

f. Insert a footnote saying that The Grill has been open only three months.

g. Insert one or more clip art images above the table.

h. Add a footer that contains your name.

i. Save your changes.

j. Print a copy of the document, then close it.

TABLE C-3

Restaurant	Location	Steak Size	Price
Jimmy's	Waterfront	12 oz.	$22.95
The Grill	Mall	8 oz.	$18.75
The Bull House	Town Square	10 oz.	$19.95

▶ Independent Challenge 2

Jordan Rowley in the Human Resources Department at Little Guy Toys, Inc. has asked you to prepare a flyer for the annual Company Picnic on August 15, 2003. The picnic will take place at Clearwater Beach from 11:00 AM until 5:00 PM. The company will provide lobster and chicken dinners for adults, hot dogs and hamburgers for children, and build-your-own ice cream sundaes for all. Attendees can spend the day swimming, wind surfing, and playing volleyball. Other activities include a team sand castle building contest and a children's treasure hunt.

a. Prepare a one-page document based on the information supplied.

b. Create WordArt using the text Company Picnic, choosing a WordArt design that you like from the WordArt Gallery and formatting it appropriately.

c. Include a table containing the information shown in Table C-4.

TABLE C-4

Activity	Time	Location
Buses depart	10:30	Lobby
Lunch	12:00-1:30	Clearwater Beach Pavilion
Volleyball Tournament	2:00-3:30	Beach Area 1
Sand Castle Contest	3:00	Beach Area 2
Wind Surfing	2:00-4:00	Beach Area 3
Kids Treasure Hunt	2:00	Meet at Beach House

d. Format the table using a Table AutoFormat that appeals to you.

e. Insert two pieces of clip art that appropriately illustrate the planned activities.

f. Insert a center-aligned footer that contains your name, then save the file as *Company Picnic Flyer*.

g. Print the flyer.

▶ Independent Challenge 3

You have been hired as the coordinator at the Sunset Spa to create personalized schedules for each customer. You need to complete a schedule for a customer named Linda Russell who is booked for a day of treatments.

a. Open a copy of the file WD C-4 from the drive and folder where your Project Files are located, then save the new document as *Spa Schedule*.

b. At the end of the document, insert a table containing the information shown in Table C-5.

c. Format the table using a Table AutoFormat that you like.

d. Add two more rows to the table to add two more time slots. Make up treatments and rooms for each.

TABLE C-5

Time	Treatment	Room
9:30-10:30	Aromatherapy facial	Lavender Room
10:45-12:00	Deep tissue massage	Rosemary Room
12:00	Spa lunch	Dining Room
1:00-2:00	Sea Salt body scrub	Ocean Mist Room
2:00-3:00	Hydrotherapy bath	Gentle Breezes Room

e. Create WordArt out of the text The Sunset Spa at the top of the page. Change the WordArt shape and the color of the WordArt.

f. Insert two pieces of appropriate clip art in the document.

g. Using your best judgment, apply borders and shading to at least one part of the document.

h. Insert a footnote in an appropriate place, using a custom mark of your choosing, that says all cell phones must be turned off at all times in the spa. Format it appropriately.

i. Insert a footer that contains your name, right-aligned.

j. Save your changes, print a copy of the flyer, then close the document.

 Independent Challenge 4

You and your friends or family have decided to take a three-day trip to a city of your choice in Europe. You are in charge of coordinating the activities for the group while you are in the city. You will first need to do some research on the Internet about your chosen city. Once you've completed your research, you then need to write a letter to the other members of your group that contains a table showing your planned activities.

a. Log on to the Internet, go to a search engine site such as Google (www.google.com) or AltaVista (www.altavista.com) and research cultural events, activities, and historical landmarks for that city.

b. Start Word, start a new, blank document, then type your name and address at the top of the page.

c. Apply WordArt formatting to your name in a design of your choosing.

d. Write a letter to the other members of your group telling them that you've completed the research about your chosen city and have put together a table of suggested activities. Include your name in the closing.

e. Insert a table with at least four columns and four rows; type the following column headings: Date, Historical Landmark, Cultural Exhibit, Activity. Fill in the information in the rows based on your research.

f. Format the table using an AutoFormat of your choosing.

g. Insert two pieces of clip art that appropriately illustrate your chosen city.

h. Save the document as *City Guide*, print it, then close the file.

► Visual Workshop

Create the document shown in Figure C-23 and save it as *Scuba Flyer*. Add your name to the end of the document.

FIGURE C-23

The Union Health and Fitness Center
1500 Mako Way
La Jolla, CA 92093
(858)555-9874

Discover Scuba

The Union Health and Fitness Center is pleased to offer Scuba lessons[*] beginning September 1. Certified PADI[**] instructors will teach all classes, and state-of-the-art Scuba equipment will be provided. See the table below for a description of each class level and sign up today!

Class Level	Description	Time to complete	Cost
Skin Diver	For beginners. Cost includes lesson, gear, and shallow water beach dive.	3.5 hours	$69.00
Open Water Diver Course	Earn your PADI open water diving certificate. Cost includes all class materials and equipment for 5 dives.	25 hours	$200.00
Advanced Open Water Diver course	For certified divers who want to learn navigation, night diving, and deep diving skills.	20 hours	$300.00

Experience the thrill of the undersea world

---
[*] Advance reservations and medical release forms required.
[**] Professional Association of Diving Instructors

Creating
and Enhancing a Worksheet

Objectives

- ► **Navigate a workbook**
- ► **Enter numbers and labels**
- ► **Change column width and row height**
- ► **Use formulas**
- ► **Edit a worksheet**
- ► **Change alignment and number format**
- ► **Change font type and font style and add borders**
- ► **Save a worksheet as a Web page**
- ► **Preview and print a worksheet**

In this unit, you will learn how to create and work with an Excel worksheet. A **worksheet** is an electronic spreadsheet, consisting of rows and columns, that performs numeric calculations. You can use a worksheet for many purposes, such as analyzing data, calculating a loan payment, or organizing and displaying your data in a chart. A **workbook** is the kind of file you create in Excel; it can contain one or more worksheets. ⟋ To help the sales representatives track their product orders, Sue Ellen Monteiro, the sales manager for Outdoor Designs, asks you to build a worksheet to record orders as they arrive from the sales representatives. You will also enter the order information, modify the worksheet so it is easy to use, and print the final product for Sue Ellen's review.

Excel 2002

Navigating a Workbook

Many workbooks you create in Excel will use only one worksheet, with the other sheets remaining blank. You will recognize many of the toolbar buttons and menu commands because of the shared interface among the Office programs. Unlike a Word document, however, an Excel worksheet is divided into a grid of rows and columns. Figure A-1 identifies some important elements in the Excel workbook window. ✐━━ In order to start working on the product order worksheet, you need to start Excel, familiarize yourself with the workbook window, and save a blank workbook.

Steps 123 4

QuickTip
If this is the first time you are using Excel, click the Start using Microsoft Excel option button in the Welcome to Microsoft Excel dialog box, then close the Office Assistant.

1. Click the Start button on the taskbar, point to Programs, then click Microsoft Excel

A blank workbook opens, as shown in Figure A-1. Excel contains elements that are in every Microsoft Office program, including a menu bar, toolbars, a workspace (the workbook window), scroll bars, a status indicator, program window and workbook window sizing buttons, and a control menu box. When you first start Excel, the New Workbook task pane is also open, presenting you with options for starting a new or opening an existing workbook. In new workbooks, the **cell** in the upper-left corner of the first worksheet (called Sheet1) is the **active cell**, the cell where data you enter will be inserted. This cell is referred to as "A1," the cell where column A and row 1 intersect.

2. Click View on the menu bar, point to Toolbars, click Customize, click the Options tab if necessary, click the Show Standard and Formatting toolbars on two rows check box to add a check mark if necessary, click the Reset my usage data button, click Yes in the message box, then click Close

These steps place the Standard and Formatting toolbars on two rows (if they were not already) and ensure that your screen will look like the ones presented in the Excel part of this book.

QuickTip
You can get help in Excel by clicking the Microsoft Excel Help button 🔲 on the Standard toolbar or by clicking a command on the Help menu.

3. Click the Close button in the task pane, then click cell B1

The task pane closes, and cell B1 becomes the active cell. (Note also how the mouse pointer changes to a cross ✚ when it is positioned over the workbook window.) Table A-1 lists several methods for selecting worksheet cells with the mouse or keyboard. The **name box** shows the name of the currently selected cell, and the **formula bar** shows the contents of the cell (it is currently empty).

4. Press [←]

Cell A1 is now the active cell. You can also move to and select a cell by clicking it, by using the arrow keys, or by pressing [Tab] (to move one cell to the right) or [Shift]+[Tab] (to move one cell to the left), or by pressing [Enter] (to move one cell down).

5. Press [→] three times to move to cell D1

6. Scroll down until you see row 65, and then click cell H65

7. Click sheet tab Sheet2

Sheet2 becomes the active sheet, as shown in Figure A-2. To move among the sheets in a workbook, you click the sheet tab of the sheet you want to move to. By default, a blank workbook contains three blank worksheets, but you can add or remove as many as you need, and you can rename and rearrange them.

QuickTip
A blank worksheet contains 65,536 rows and 256 columns; however, it is unlikely you would ever fill an entire worksheet with data. When working on a large project, it is usually more convenient to use several worksheets within a workbook to organize your data.

8. Click the Sheet1 sheet tab to return to this worksheet, then press [Ctrl][Home]

This keyboard shortcut returns you to cell A1.

9. Click the Save button 🔲 on the Standard toolbar, navigate to the drive and folder where your Project Files are located, then save the file as Product Order 6-30

FIGURE A-1: Excel worksheet window with important elements labeled (toolbars on one row)

Column headers

Name box

Formula bar

Row headers

Rows

Sheet tab

Task Pane

Columns

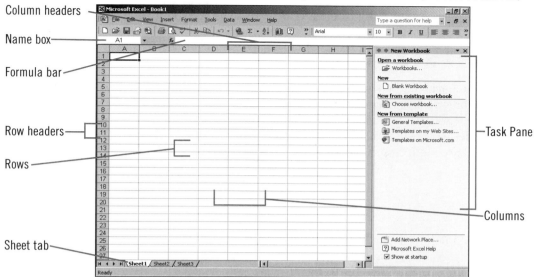

FIGURE A-2: Moving among worksheets in a workbook (toolbars on two rows)

Active sheet

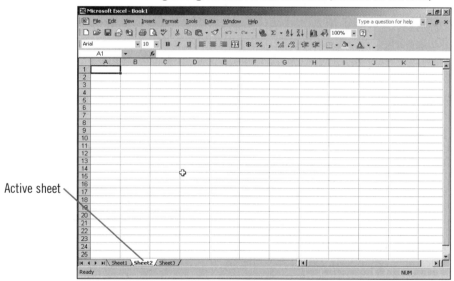

TABLE A-1: Methods for selecting worksheet cells

to select	with the mouse	with the keyboard
A cell	Click the cell	Use arrow keys
A row	Click the row header	Select a cell in the row, then press [Shift][Spacebar]
A column	Click the column header	Select a cell in the column, then press [Ctrl][Spacebar]
A group of cells	Drag across the cells	Press [Shift], then use arrow keys
A worksheet	Click the Select All button above row 1	Press [Ctrl][A]

Entering Numbers and Labels

You enter numbers and labels into a worksheet by typing data in cells. You must select a cell before you can enter data in it. 🖉 You decide to practice entering numbers and labels into the worksheet by entering a product order from a sales representative. The completed product order will serve as an internal tracking sheet that the Outdoor Designs accounting department will use to process the order.

Steps 1234

1. **In cell A1 type Outdoor Designs Product Order**
   As you type, the text appears in cell A1 and in the Formula bar, as shown in Figure A-3. The text you typed is a label, data that serves as a description instead of a calculation. Labels can extend into neighboring cells that don't contain data, so the text "Outdoor Designs Product Order" extends into cells B1 and C1, but it is contained only in cell A1.

2. **Press [Enter]**
   Pressing [Enter] causes Excel to accept your entry and activate the next cell in the column.

3. **Press [↓] to move to cell A3**
   Cell A3 is selected and "A3" appears in the name box, identifying your current location. You can use the arrow keys to accept an entry and move to the next cell in the direction of the arrow key. However, when you are entering data in multiple columns, it is easier to press [Enter] after the last column because this moves you to the first column, as you will see in Step 4.

4. **Type these four lines, remembering to press [Enter] after each line**
   Sales rep: Kimberly Ullom
   Store: Mountain Air, North Bend, WA
   Order date: June 30, 2003
   Terms: Payment 30 days after receipt (Net 30)

QuickTip

Pressing [Tab] is the same as pressing [→] in the worksheet. You might find that using [Tab] is more convenient for entering multiple columns of data.

5. **Press [Enter] until cell A8 is the active cell, then type the following text in columns A through D of rows 8 and 9, pressing [Tab] to move to the next cell in a row, and pressing [Enter] at the end of each row**

Kit num	Kit name	Price	Quantity
#401	Cascade Ski Sack	19.95	5

   Pressing [Enter] at the end of a row of data activates the first cell in the row below the data, rather than activating the next cell in the current column. When you typed "19.95" in cell C9, the text in cell B9 was cut off. When text is wider than a cell, it spills into the adjacent cell unless that cell has data in it. (But the data hasn't been deleted, it is just not visible now.) You'll widen the necessary cells later to display the data again.

6. **Beginning with cell A10, continue typing the following data in the worksheet; remember to press [Tab] to move one cell to the right and [Enter] to move to the next row**

#501	Coastal Parafoil Kite	22.95	1
#502	Puget Sound Delta Kite	24.95	2
#801	Olympic Rain Tent	79.95	2
#802	Tent Vestibule	19.95	1

   The text is entered in the worksheet, as shown in Figure A-4.

7. **Click the Save button 🖫 on the Standard toolbar**

FIGURE A-3: Worksheet text in Formula bar and in neighboring cells

Name box displays name of selected cell

Formula bar displays contents of selected cells

Cell A1

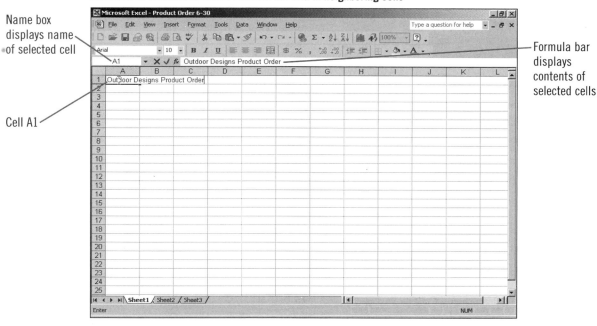

FIGURE A-4: Worksheet after entering product order data

Data that extends beyond the width of a column is hidden because cells to the right contain data; you'll fix this later

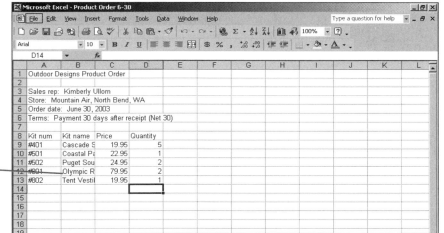

Using data entry keys

As you enter data in your worksheets, you can use some keyboard keys to work more effectively. Pressing [Caps Lock] configures your keyboard to enter text labels in all uppercase characters. Pressing [Num Lock] configures the keys on the numeric keypad to insert numbers and mathematical operators. If you enter lengthy data in Excel, [Num Lock] can speed the process significantly.

Changing Column Width and Row Height

You can adjust column widths and row heights by dragging the column or row borders with the mouse or by using the Format menu. Dragging with the mouse is a quick and easy method when it's not necessary to achieve an exact width or height.　　　　You need to adjust the column width and row height in the Product Order 6-30 worksheet to make the information in the worksheet more readable.

Steps

1. Position the pointer on the column line between columns **B** and **C** in the column header area so the pointer changes to +‖+, as shown in Figure A-5

QuickTip

You can also change column width and row height using the Format menu. To change the column width, click Format on the menu bar, point to Column, click Width, then type the desired width (in characters). To change the row height, click Format on the menu bar, point to Row, click Height, then type the desired height (in points).

2. Double-click the **column line**
   The width of column B is automatically widened to fit the longest cell in the column, using a feature called **AutoFit**.

3. Click the number **7** to the left of row 7
   The row is selected. The number 7 is the **row header** for row 7. Selecting a row header or a **column header**, such as the letter above column C, lets you make changes to an entire row or column at once. To select a row header or column header, you simply click the row number or column letter.

4. Position the pointer on the row line between rows **7** and **8** in the row header area
   The pointer changes to ═╪═. Each row's height is automatically adjusted to be at least as large as the largest font in the row, so you need to change the row height only if you want to increase or decrease its size.

Trouble?

If you cannot resize the row height to exactly 21.00 points, make it as close to this measurement as possible.

5. Click the **row line** and slowly drag the pointer down until you see **Height: 21.75 (29 pixels)** in the ScreenTip, as shown in Figure A-6, then release the mouse button
   The height of row 7 changes from 12 to 21.75 points.

FIGURE A-5: Changing the column width in the worksheet

Pointer on column border

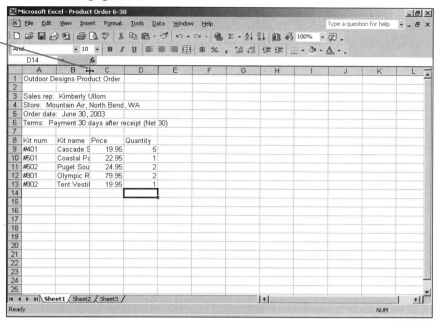

FIGURE A-6: Changing the row height in the worksheet

Current row height in points (and pixels)

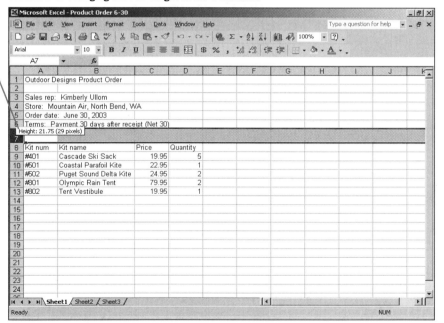

Excel 2002

Using Formulas

To perform a calculation in the worksheet, you enter a formula in a cell. A **formula** is an equation that calculates a new value from existing values. Formulas can contain numbers, mathematical operators (+ for addition, – for minus, and so on), cell references (A1, E42), and **functions** (commonly used formulas that come preprogrammed with Excel). Table A-2 lists some mathematical operators you can use in a formula, in the order in which Excel evaluates them in a formula that contains multiple operators. Formulas can be copied and moved just like other data in a worksheet—a process that is streamlined by the use of **Smart Tags**, tiny formatting icons that automatically appear in the worksheet and present you with choices for formatting the data you have copied. (Smart Tags are a new feature of Office XP and appear in other Office XP applications as well.) The product order worksheet should provide subtotals for each item ordered. You want to create a formula to calculate these subtotals.

1. **Click cell E8, type Subtotal, then press [↓]**

2. **Type =**
   The equal sign (=) indicates that you're about to enter a formula in cell E9. Everything you enter in a cell after the equal sign, including any numbers, mathematical operators, cell references, or functions, is included in the formula.

3. **Press [←] twice to move to cell C9**
   Cell C9, which appears as a **cell reference** in the formula, is selected, meaning that the value in cell C9 will be used when the formula is calculated. The formula is displayed in both the Formula bar and in cell E9.

4. **Type * (an asterisk), then click cell D9**
   When the formula is calculated, the product price in cell C9 is multiplied by the quantity in cell D9.

5. **Press [Enter], then press [↑]**
   The result of the formula (99.75) appears in cell E9. Notice that although the formula's result appears in cell E9, the formula itself appears in the Formula bar.

6. **Press [↓], type =C10*D10, then press [Enter]**
   You can type cell references as well as pressing the arrow keys or clicking to insert them.

7. **Press [↑] to move to cell E10**
   You can copy a formula from one cell into cells that appear below it or to its right by clicking and dragging the **Fill handle** (the small black square in the lower corner of a selected cell) on the selected cell. When you move the pointer over a Fill handle, the pointer changes to **+**.

8. **Click the Fill handle for cell E10, drag down to cell E13, then release the mouse button**
   The subtotal formula is replicated in cells E10 through E13, and the subtotal for each product appears. In addition, Excel displays a **Smart Tag** in the worksheet that lets you select what will be copied—the entire contents of the cells, just the formatting, or just the data.

9. **Click the Smart Tag, then click Copy Cells**
   This default option copies the complete contents of the cells (with formatting), as shown in Figure A-7. The Smart Tag remains visible until you make additional edits on your worksheet.

QuickTip
If you want your worksheet to display formulas instead of their results in cells, click Tools on the menu bar, click Options, click the View tab, click the Formulas check box to add a checkmark, then click OK.

FIGURE A-7: The results of using the Fill box to copy the subtotal formula into cells E10 through E13

Equal sign indicates a formula

Results of this formula appear in cell E10

Outline indicates new row size as you drag the pointer

Smart Tag

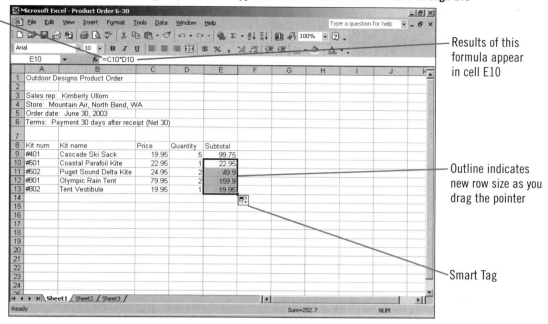

TABLE A-2: Useful mathematical operators (in order of evaluation)

operator	description	example	result
( )	Parentheses	(3+6)*3	27
^	Exponent	10^2	100
*	Multiplication	7*5	35
/	Division	20/4	5
+	Addition	5+5	10
–	Subtraction	12–8	4

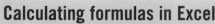

Calculating formulas in Excel

When you enter a formula that contains more than one mathematical operator, standard algebraic rules are followed to determine which calculation is performed first. First, the calculations within parentheses are evaluated. Then, the rules dictate that exponential calculations be performed first, multiplication and division calculations second, and addition and subtraction calculations last. If there is more than one calculation in the same category, they are evaluated from left to right.

Excel 2002

Editing a Worksheet

You can edit cells in a worksheet in several ways. You can revise a single cell by clicking it and editing its contents in the Formula bar. You can cut, copy, and paste blocks of cells using the Edit menu or the toolbar. You can also move cells using the drag and drop method. Mountain Air increased its order for Coastal Parafoil kites and extended the payment grace period. You edit the product order worksheet to reflect these changes.

Steps

1. **Select cell D10, type 3, then press [Enter]**
   The number in cell D10 changes from 1 to 3, and the formula in cell E10 is recalculated when you press [Enter], so the subtotal changes from 22.95 to 68.85.

2. **Click cell A6**
   The cell is selected, and the label "Terms: Payment 30 days after receipt (Net 30)" appears in the Formula bar. If you begin typing in a cell that contains data without first selecting any data, the complete contents of the cell are replaced by what you type.

3. **Position the mouse over the formula bar, select the first 3 in the label, type 6, select the second 3 in the Formula bar, then type 6**
   The number 3 is replaced when you type the new number, 6. When you select text, new text replaces selected text as you type. The Formula bar now contains the label "Terms: Payment 60 days after receipt (Net 60)."

4. **Press [Enter]**
   The updated label appears in the worksheet in cell A6.

5. **Select row 7 in the worksheet by clicking the row header for row 7**
   When you insert a new row into the worksheet, it is inserted above the one that is selected.

6. **Click Insert on the menu bar, then click Rows**
   A new row is added to the worksheet, and the rows below it are renumbered. By default, new rows are created using the format of the row above, but you don't need to keep this formatting. A Smart Tag appears next to the inserted row so that you can adjust the automatic formatting applied to the row if you want.

7. **Click the Smart Tag, then click Format Same As Below**

8. **Select row 3, position the pointer over the bottom of the row so it changes to ⬚, drag row 3 down until row 7 is selected and the ScreenTip reads 7:7, then release the mouse button**
   The contents of row 3 move to row 7. The contents of row 3 are now empty.

9. **Right-click the row header for row 3, click Delete on the pop-up menu, then click the Save button 💾 on the Standard toolbar**
   This eliminates the empty row, as shown in Figure A-8, and saves your changes to the worksheet.

QuickTip

You can use the Find and Replace commands to find or change any type of data, such as a word, phrase, value, or formula, automatically to data you specify throughout one or more worksheets, by clicking Edit on the menu bar, then clicking Find or Replace.

Trouble?

If you realize that you made a mistake after pressing [Enter], click the Undo button ↺ on the Standard toolbar to return the cell contents to their previous state.

Trouble?

If you select a cell, row or column and then press [Delete], only the contents of the selection are deleted. You must click Delete on the Edit menu or the pop-up menu to delete the actual cell, row, or column.

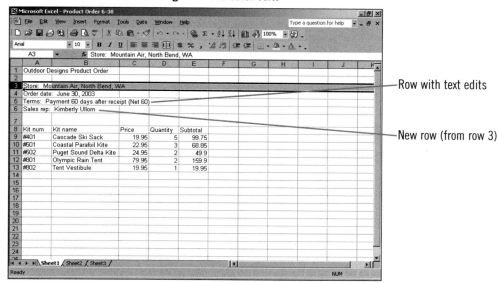

Row with text edits

New row (from row 3)

Understanding relative and absolute cell references

By default, cell references in a worksheet are relative—that is, when you copy a formula, the cell references change to refer to cells relative to the new location. For example, a formula in cell D5 that reads "=B5*C5" changes to "=B6*C6" when you copy the formula down one row. This makes reusing formulas easy and convenient. However, there may be times when you want a cell reference to always refer to a specific cell, no matter where in the worksheet you copy the formula. For example, cell C5 might contain a value by which you want to multiply every cell in column B. In these situations, you use an absolute cell reference. To indicate an absolute cell reference, you type a dollar sign ($) before the part of the address you want to remain absolute. For example, if you want the entire cell address to be absolute, as in the example discussed here, you would type "C5" (you could also type "$C5" or "C$5" if you wanted only the row or column to remain absolute, but the rest of the cell reference to change according to the new location

of the formula). See Figure A-9. Note that when you move a formula, the cell references remain absolute.

FIGURE A-9: Copying an absolute cell reference

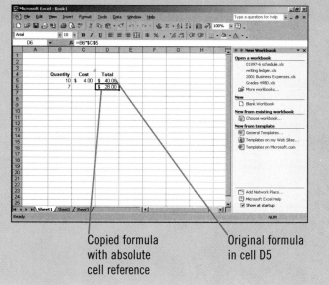

Copied formula with absolute cell reference

Original formula in cell D5

Excel 2002

Changing Alignment and Number Format

When you first enter data in a cell, labels are left-aligned and values are right-aligned by default, but you can change the alignment any time. You can also format numbers to appear in one of several standard formats, including currency, percent, and date. Changing alignment and number format can improve the look of your worksheet and make it easier to read. ➤ You use the formatting options to improve the appearance of the product order worksheet.

Steps

1. **Select row 8 in the worksheet, then click the Center button ▦ on the Formatting toolbar**
   Each label in row 8 is centered in its cell. There are three choices for aligning cell data using the Formatting toolbar: right, center, or left.

2. **Select cells D9 through D13**

3. **Click Format on the menu bar, click Cells, then click the Alignment tab**
   You can use the Format Cells dialog box to change a variety of cell attributes. You can change how numbers are formatted in the Number tab. You can change font type, size, and other font attributes in the Font tab. You can add borders, patterns, and shading to cells in the Border and Patterns tabs. You can also protect a worksheet so users cannot make inadvertent changes, by locking cells or hiding formulas in the Protection tab. The Alignment tab contains a greater variety of alignment options than the Formatting toolbar, as shown in Figure A-10.

4. **Click the Horizontal drop-down list box, click Center, then click OK**
   The contents of the five cells in the column are centered.

5. **Select cells A1 through E1**
   The cell containing the title "Outdoor Designs Product Order" and the four blank cells to the right of it are selected.

   > **QuickTip**
   > To deselect selected cells, click anywhere in the worksheet window.

6. **Click the Merge and Center button ▦ on the Formatting toolbar**
   The worksheet title is centered across the five selected cells. (Note that the cell reference of the title is still A1, however.)

7. **Select cells A9 through A13, then click ▦**
   The contents of the five cells are centered.

8. **Select cells C9 through C13, then click the Currency Style button ⑀ on the Formatting toolbar**
   The five cells in the Price column are formatted as currency (dollars and cents).

   > **QuickTip**
   > You can also press [F4] to repeat the last edit or formatting change you made.

9. **Select cells E9 through E13, click ⑀, then click the Save button ⊟ on the Standard toolbar**
   The five cells in the Subtotal column are formatted as currency, as shown in Figure A-11, and your changes to the worksheet are saved to disk.

FIGURE A-10: Format Cells dialog box

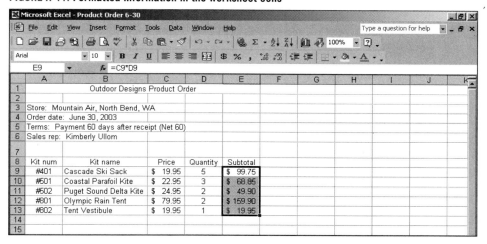

Click to format numbers

Click to change alignment

Click to change font type

Click to add borders to cells

Click to protect cells from inadvertent edits

Click to add patterns and shading to cells

FIGURE A-11: Formatted information in the worksheet cells

Kit num	Kit name	Price	Quantity	Subtotal
#401	Cascade Ski Sack	$ 19.95	5	$ 99.75
#501	Coastal Parafoil Kite	$ 22.95	3	$ 68.85
#502	Puget Sound Delta Kite	$ 24.95	2	$ 49.90
#801	Olympic Rain Tent	$ 79.95	2	$ 159.90
#802	Tent Vestibule	$ 19.95	1	$ 19.95

Outdoor Designs Product Order

Store: Mountain Air, North Bend, WA
Order date: June 30, 2003
Terms: Payment 60 days after receipt (Net 60)
Sales rep: Kimberly Ullom

Changing the number format

You can format numbers in several ways. The Formatting toolbar has toolbar buttons for common number formats such as the Currency Style button [$], the Percent Style button [%], and the Comma Style button [,]. Other useful number formats include Date, which lets you format a number using several date formats; Time, which formats numbers in various time formats; Fraction, which formats numbers as fractions; and Exponential, which formats numbers in scientific notation. To change the number format in cells, select the cell(s) to change, click the Cells command on the Format menu, then click the Number tab.

Changing Font and Font Style and Adding Borders

You can change the font and font style of text in the Excel worksheet and add borders and shading to make important information stand out. The Border and Patterns tabs in the Format Cells dialog box help you take advantage of the unique rectangular design of worksheet cells to create impressive formatting effects. You can format individual cells or a **range**, a selection of two or more cells. ✎ You decide to make font formatting changes and add border and patterns in the worksheet to enhance the product order worksheet.

Steps

> **QuickTip**
>
> You can also use the Font tab in the Format Cells dialog box to make font formatting changes.

1. Select cell **A1**, then click the **Bold button** **B** and the **Italic button** **I** on the Formatting toolbar
   The formatting of the title "Outdoor Designs Product Order" changes to bold and italic.

2. Click the **Font Size list arrow** on the Formatting toolbar, click **16**, click the **Font list arrow**, scroll down, then click **Times New Roman**
   The title size and font changes to 16-point Times New Roman. Notice how the row height increases to accommodate the new font.

> **QuickTip**
>
> The AutoFormat command on the Format menu combines several formatting operations in one command and can effectively format a range of cells in several different styles.

3. Select row **8** in the worksheet, then click **B**
   The formatting of all the cells in the row changes to bold.

4. Select cell **A3**, click cell **A3** again and drag to cell **D6** to select all the cells in between, then release the mouse button
   The range of cells four cells wide and four cells long is selected. A range can also be referred to using a colon, such as "A3:D6" for the current selection. Now you can add a border around the entire range.

5. Click **Format** on the menu bar, click **Cells**, then click the **Border tab**
   You can use the Border tab of the Format Cells dialog box to add or change borders, line styles, and color formatting options.

> **QuickTip**
>
> The Borders button ▦▾ on the Formatting toolbar also allows you to format the borders around cells. On the Borders palette is a Draw Borders button which lets you manually click the cells to which you want to add borders.

6. Click the **Double line style** in the Style list box (the last item in the second column), as shown in Figure A-12, click the **Outline button** in the Presets area, then click **OK**
   The Format Cells dialog box closes, and a double line border appears around the block of selected cells. (The double border may not be completely visible while the cells are selected, however.)

7. Select the range **A8:E13** (a block of cells five cells wide and six cells long), click **Format** on the menu bar, then click **Cells**
   The Border tab opens because this is the last tab you worked with in the Format Cells dialog box.

> **QuickTip**
>
> If you want to create a colored border, first click the Color list arrow in the Border tab of the Format Cells dialog box, click a color, then specify the line style and border type.

8. Click the **Outline** and **Inside buttons** in the Presets area, make sure that the last line style option in the first column is selected, click **OK**, then click anywhere outside of the selection to deselect the cells
   A single line border appears around each cell in the selection. Notice that this border is solid black, while the normal cell borders shown on the worksheet are light gray. Solid black indicates that the border will be printed by the printer.

9. Save your changes to the workbook

FIGURE A-12: Adding a border to a selection

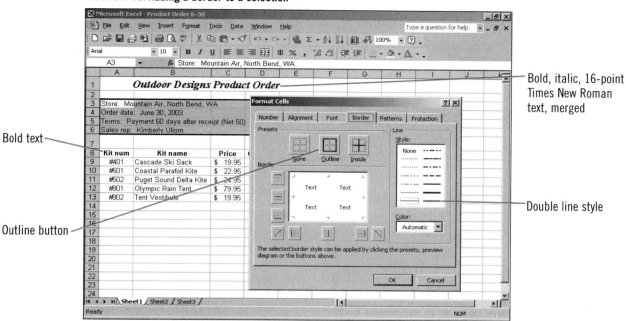

Bold text

Outline button

Bold, italic, 16-point
Times New Roman
text, merged

Double line style

Adding shading to cells

You can fill one or more worksheet cells with shading or a shaded pattern using the Patterns tab on the Format Cells dialog box. Patterns and Shading work like other types of formatting: first you select the cells you want to format, then you click the formatting options you want in the Patterns tab of the Format Cells dialog box. Select the shading color, then click the Pattern list arrow, as shown in Figure A-13, to apply different shading patterns to your selection. If you do not apply a pattern, the cell will be filled only with the color you chose.

FIGURE A-13: Patterns tab in the Format Cells dialog box

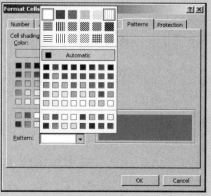

Saving a Worksheet as a Web Page

Web pages are becoming an important mechanism for sharing many different types of data, including Excel worksheets. Excel 2002 lets you save your spreadsheet in HTML (Hypertext Markup Language) format, so that it can be routed electronically or posted on the Web for easy access. The Save As Web Page command on the File menu facilitates this process. After you save a Web page using Excel, you can view it by using the default Web browser on your system, such as Netscape Navigator or Microsoft Internet Explorer. Save the product order worksheet now as a Web page.

Steps

1. Click File on the menu bar, then click Save as Web Page

The Save As dialog box opens, as shown in Figure A-14. This dialog box is similar to the standard Save As dialog box in Office applications, except that it allows you to save just the current worksheet as a Web page (by clicking the Selection: Sheet option button), permits your Web page to be interactive (by clicking the Add interactivity check box), and gives you advanced options for creating HTML documents (by clicking the Publish button).

2. Click the Selection: Sheet option button

This option directs Excel to include only the current worksheet in the HTML document.

QuickTip

You can click Change Title in the Save As dialog box to enter a title for the HTML document, which will appear above the document when it is viewed in a Web browser.

3. Click the Add interactivity check box

By selecting Add interactivity, you direct Excel to make the Web page respond to user input and calculate formulas. If this check box is not selected, the worksheet will appear as a **static Web page**, meaning that it can be viewed but not used by the user. (A common use for static Web pages is presenting a table of information that users will not modify, such as tax tables or price lists.)

4. Double-click in the File name text box, then type Web Order Form 6-30

The filename for your Web page does not need to match the Excel filename of your workbook, although it can be the same if you wish. You're changing the name here so that your coworkers can easily identify the Web page.

5. Click Save

Excel saves the Web page on your hard disk using the name Web Order Form 6-30.htm. (Excel saves this file as a separate document, then your worksheet reappears.) You can now e-mail the new .htm file to a coworker using Microsoft Outlook, copy the file to the Web, or view the file using a Web browser on your system. Figure A-15 shows what the Web page looks like in Internet Explorer, a Web browser program. As you can see, the Web page contains a toolbar with many Excel commands and features, and the data you entered looks much as it did in Microsoft Excel. Since you added interactivity to the worksheet, the Subtotal formulas will also be recalculated if you change the values in the Price or Quantity columns.

FIGURE A-14: The Save as Web Page command opens this Save As dialog box

Click here to include just the current worksheet in your Web page

Click here to give your Web page a title

Use advanced HTML document options

Click here to add interactive features

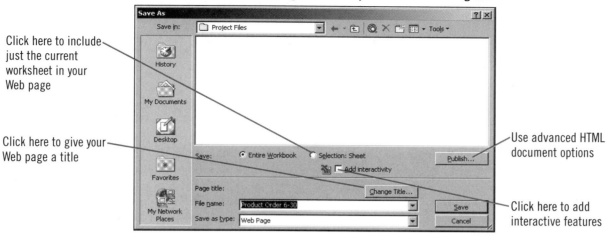

FIGURE A-15: The product order worksheet in HTML format, as it appears in the Internet Explorer browser

Internet Explorer title bar and tools

Product order worksheet in HTML format

Limited-use Excel toolbar

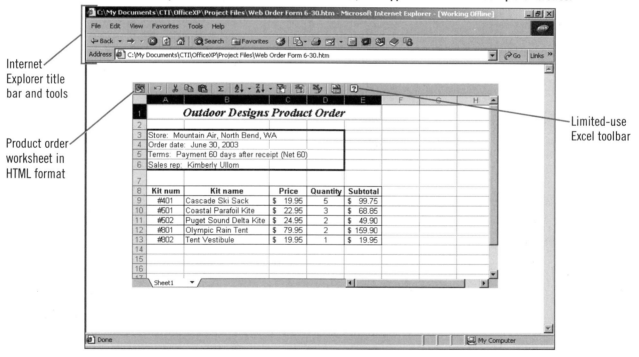

Excel 2002

Previewing and Printing a Worksheet

When you finish working with a worksheet and have saved your work, you are ready to print it. It is important to save your work before printing so that if you experience technical problems while printing, you do not lose your work. Print Preview is a useful prelude to printing; it allows you to examine your document as it will appear when printed, up close in "zoom" mode so you can detect any layout problems that would prove undesirable in a final printed copy. After you preview your document, printing an actual copy is as simple as clicking the Print command on the File menu. ➤ You have finished working with the Product Order 6-30 workbook, so you are ready to preview and print the product order worksheet now.

QuickTip

When you use color in your worksheets, your document appears in the Print Preview window in color only if you have a color printer. If you do not have a color printer, your document appears in black and white.

QuickTip

Use the Page Setup command on the File menu to change page margins, paper orientation, and other printing options.

QuickTip

If you want to print one copy of the entire worksheet without changing any settings, you can also click the Print button 🖨 on the Standard toolbar.

QuickTip

As an alternative to Print Preview, you can verify the page breaks in your worksheet by clicking the Page Break Preview command on the View menu. You can adjust where page breaks are located by dragging them with the mouse. When you're finished, click Normal on the View menu.

1. Click **File** on the menu bar, then click **Print Preview**
   The Print Preview window opens, and the Product Order 6-30 worksheet looks as it will on the printed page. Several command buttons that control the Print Preview window's operation appear across the top of the window.

2. Move the mouse pointer over the document page
   The pointer changes to the **zoom pointer** 🔍 , which you can use to examine parts of the document more closely.

3. Click the title of the worksheet with the zoom pointer
   The worksheet enlarges to full size in the Print Preview window, as shown in Figure A-16. After you zoom in on an area of the worksheet, you can click anywhere in the document to return to full page view.

4. Click anywhere in the document, then click **Close** on the Print Preview toolbar
   The Print Preview window closes, and the product order worksheet reappears in Normal view.

5. Click **File** on the menu bar, then click **Print**
   The Print dialog box opens. You use this dialog box to specify the printer you want to use, the range to print (the selected cells, the selected worksheet, specific pages in the worksheet, or the whole workbook), and the number of copies you want to print.

6. Verify that your printer is on and connected to your computer
   If you have questions, ask your instructor or technical support person for help.

7. Click **OK**
   The Print dialog box closes and the worksheet prints.

8. Click the **Save button** 💾 on the Standard toolbar

9. Click the program window **Close button**
   The Product Order 6-30 worksheet and the Excel program both close.

FIGURE A-16: Worksheet in Print Preview

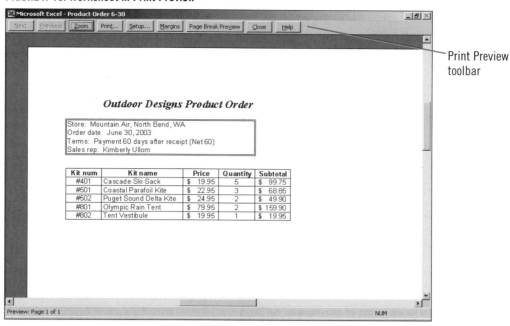

Print Preview toolbar

Adding headers and footers

Before you print your worksheet, you might want to add page numbers, the current date, or some other text to the top or bottom of each page. You can add this information to your worksheet using the Header and Footer command on the View menu. A standard header or footer in the worksheet is one line long and can contain standard or customized information. Figure A-17 shows a header that contains the filename and a footer that contains the page number and the total number of pages. You won't see headers and footers in the worksheet window, but you can examine them in Print Preview.

FIGURE A-17: Headers and Footers tab of Page Setup dialog box

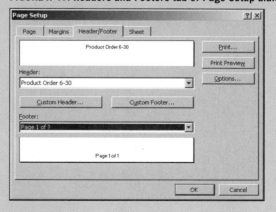

Practice

► Concepts Review

Label each worksheet element shown in Figure A-18.

FIGURE A-18

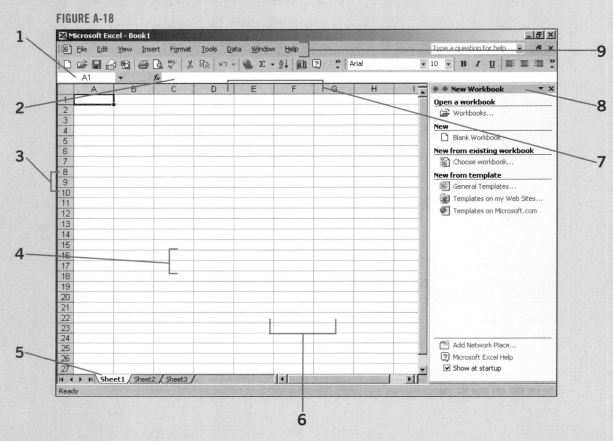

Match the formulas with the result that Excel computes.

10. (2 + 6) * 3   a. 3.5
11. 7 ^ 3   b. 24
12. 3 * 20 / 25   c. 1.005859
13. 15 - 8 / 2   d. 11
14. (15 − 8) / 2   e. 2.4
15. 1 + 2 * 3 / 4 ^ 5   f. 343

Select the best answer from the list of choices.

16. The name of the cell located in column B and row 2 is:
  a. 1A.   **c.** 2B.
  b. A1.   **d.** B2.

17. How do you select an entire column in the worksheet?
  a. Click the row number to the left of the column.   **c.** Press [Esc].
  b. Click the column letter at the top of the column.   **d.** Press [Shift][Tab].

18. Cell borders are added with which Excel menu command?
  a. Format, Cells   **c.** Edit, Paste
  b. Format, Style   **d.** Edit, Fill

19. Which button is used to merge and center text in a group of cells?
  a. $\boxed{\Sigma}$ **c.** $\boxed{\text{🛅} \cdot}$
  b. $\boxed{\text{🔳}}$ **d.** $\boxed{^{+.0}_{.00}}$

20. To delete a row in the worksheet, which technique would you use?
  a. Select the row, then press [Del].
  b. Select the row, then click Edit, Clear, All.
  c. Highlight any cell in the row, then click Edit, Delete, Entire Row.
  d. Highlight any cell in the row, then click Edit, Cut.

21. To create a Web page, or HTML document, from your Excel worksheet, which command would you choose?
  a. File, Save As   **c.** File, Web Page Preview
  b. File, Save As Web Page   **d.** File, Print Preview

▶ ## Skills Review

1. Navigate a workbook.
  a. Start Microsoft Excel.
  b. Identify the program window elements using Figure A-1 as a reference.
  c. Click cell H10, click cell Z95, click Sheet3, click Sheet1, then press [Ctrl][Home].

2. Enter numbers and labels.
  a. Type the following information starting in cell A1, pressing [Enter] and [Tab] as indicated, to create a shipping ticket.
    Outdoor Designs Shipping Ticket [Enter]
    Ship to: [Enter]
    Grandma's Kites [Enter]
    21 Huron Road [Enter]
    Cavour, SD 55555 [Enter]
    Date: July 30, 2003 [Enter]
    Kit num [Tab] Quantity [Tab] Kit name [Tab] Price [Enter]
    #401 [Tab] 2 [Tab] Cascade Mobile Sack [Tab] 19.95 [Enter]
    #501 [Tab] 2[Tab] Coastal Parafoil Kite[Tab] 22.95 [Enter]
    #503 [Tab] 3 [Tab] Franklin's Diamond [Tab] 19.95 [Enter]
    #701 [Tab] 2 [Tab] Sonic Boomer Stunt Kite [Tab] 49.95 [Enter]
    #801 [Tab] 1 [Tab] Olympic Rain Tent [Tab] 79.95 [Enter]
  b. Enter your name in cell C2.
  c. Save the workbook as *Shipping Ticket 7-30*.

3. **Adjust column width and row height.**

   a. Position the pointer on the column line between columns C and D, then double-click the column line.

   b. Position the pointer on the row line between rows 7 and 8.

   c. Drag the pointer down so the row is about 23 points high, then release the mouse button.

4. **Use Formulas.**

   a. Click cell E7, type **Item Total**, then press [Enter].

   b. Enter a formula in cell E8 that multiplies the value of cell B8 and the value of cell D8.

   c. Use the Fill handle to copy the formula you entered in cell E8 to cells E9 through E12.

5. **Edit worksheet data.**

   a. Select cell D8, then click the Formula bar.

   b. Change 19.95 in the Formula bar to 29.99, then press [Enter].

   c. Select rows 8 and 9 (which contain information about items #401 and #501), and drag them to rows 13 and 14.

   d. Select rows 8 and 9 (which are now blank), click Edit on the toolbar, then click Delete.

   e. Select row 7, then click Rows on the Insert menu.

6. **Change the alignment and number format.**

   a. Select row 8, then center the data in the row.

   b. Merge and center cells A1 through E1.

   c. Center the range A9:B13 and column C.

   d. Change the number format of the data in the Price and Item Total columns to currency using the Currency Style button on the Formatting toolbar.

7. **Change the font and font style and add borders.**

   a. Select cell A1, format it with underline formatting, then change the font to Century Schoolbook (or a font of your choice if this font is not available) and the font size to 16 point.

   b. Select the range A3:B6, open the Format Cells dialog box, then click the Border tab.

   c. Click the thickest line style (the sixth style in the second column), click the Outline button, then click OK. Compare your screen to Figure A-19.

   d. Save your changes to the worksheet.

8. **Save a worksheet as a Web page.**

   a. Click File on the menu bar, then click Save as Web Page.

   b. Click the Selection: Sheet option button and the Add interactivity check box.

   c. Save the file as *Web Shipping Ticket*.

   d. Open the Web page in your Web browser, view it, then close the Web page and your Web browser.

9. **Preview and Print a worksheet.**

   a. Click View on the menu bar, then click Header and Footer.

   b. Click the Footer list arrow, click Page 1 of ?, then click OK.

   c. View the worksheet in Print Preview and verify the contents.

   d. Click the Close button on the Print Preview toolbar.

   e. Save and print the worksheet, then exit Excel.

FIGURE A-19

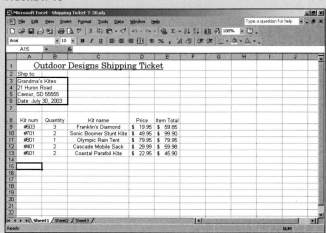

Independent Challenge 1

At Canada in Print, a Canadian book and stationary company, you must provide the Sales and Marketing Department with a monthly order summary. The summary includes the order number, account name, order date, order total, and payment. You also provide a monthly sales total and indicate what percentage of the year's sales to date the month's orders represent.

  a. Open a new workbook, then enter the title **March Order Summary** in cell A1.

  b. Enter the following information, starting in cell A3.

Order#	Account	Date	Total	Paid
300	Canada Books	3/5/2003	2500	0
301	Songs and Such	3/10/2003	950	950
302	Ontario Cards	3/7/2003	3005	0
303	Cards-n-More	3/25/2003	7261	2000
304	Alberta Notion	3/14/2003	800	800
	Monthly Total			
	Percent of year to date		.09	

  c. Widen or narrow each column as necessary so that the data in each column fits comfortably.

  d. Drag rows 9 and 10, which contain the Monthly Total and Percent of year to date information, down to rows 10 and 11. Reduce the row height of row 9, which is now blank, to 6.00.

  e. Enter a formula in cell D10 that adds the figures in the Total column. Then change the amount in cell D4 from 2500 to 1700.

  f. Center the order numbers in cells A4 through A8.

  g. Format the numbers in D4 through E8 with commas and zero decimal places. Format cell D10 for Currency with no decimal places and format cell D11 as Percent with no decimal places.

  h. Center the title across columns A through E. Change the font to 18-point bold Arial Narrow. Change the labels in cells B10 and B11 to bold Arial Narrow as well.

  i. Add a border line at the top and bottom of the column labels in cells A3 through E3. Choose the second line style in the second column, and change the line color to green. Add the same type of line above cells A10 through E10 and below cells A11 through E11.

  j. Insert a new row above row 2, then enter your name the new row. Center it across columns A through E, and format it in the font and font style of your choice.

  k. Save the workbook as *March Order Summary*, preview it, then print it.

  l. Close the workbook.

Excel 2002

▶ Independent Challenge 2

You help the lead accountant at The Green Thumb Company prepare a monthly expense summary from information in the company's general accounting journal. Create a worksheet that displays and totals the business expenses in the following table, using a formula to calculate the total expense. After you create the worksheet, enter the title **The Green Thumb Company: October Expenses** at the top, and format it in Green type using the Times New Roman font in 14-point size. Include your name near the top of the worksheet, as shown in Figure A-20. Save the workbook as *October Expenses*, then print a copy and close the workbook.

October Expenses	Cost
Office Rent and Insurance	$16,637.00
Contracted Work Expenses	$5,400.00
Postage and Express Mail	$1147.71
Books and Research Materials	$837.65
Misc.	$652.90
Journals/Online Charges	$639.40
Taxes and Fees	$2,482.00
Phone	$3,765.32
Travel	$3,252.11

FIGURE A-20

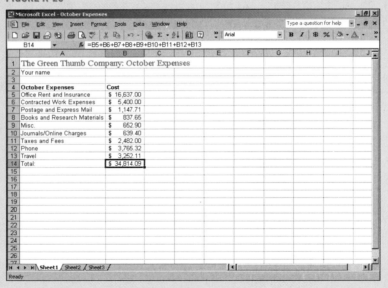

▶ Independent Challenge 3

The company you work for, New England Bail and Wire, is slowly upgrading its accounting and business systems, despite the objections of Franklin Leatherbag, the company president, who has never really trusted computers. Write a short, two-page essay for Mr. Leatherbag that introduces the Excel program as a potential tool for increasing productivity in the company. Highlight at least three useful features of Excel that you have learned in this unit. Write the essay using Microsoft Word, type your name at the bottom, save the document as *Excel Features*, print a copy, then exit Word.

 Independent Challenge 4

The travel director of the cruise ship company that you work for is leaving tomorrow for a whirlwind scouting trip to Anchorage, Seattle, Portland, and San Francisco. She has asked you to find out about local weather conditions. Use the World Wide Web to gather forecast information for these cities, then create an Excel worksheet to list the temperatures expected.

  a. Open a new Excel workbook, and save it as *Weather Info*.

  b. Log on to the Internet, go to the AltaVista search engine at **www.altavista.com**, and enter the search text **world weather forecast**. Click one of the links that provides free weather information for U.S. cities.

  c. Locate the five-day forecast for each of the cities your travel director is heading to, and enter each five-day forecast in the Excel worksheet in a row that begins with the name of the city.

  d. At the end of each row, create a column named Average that contains a formula that calculates the average temperature during the five-day period you have selected. (*Hint*: To determine an average, add all of the values, then divide by the number of values.)

  e. Add a meaningful title to the top of the worksheet, add your name to the row below the title, then format the contents of the worksheet in an attractive way.

  f. Save your changes, preview the worksheet, and print it. When you're finished, close your browser and log off from the Internet, then close the workbook and exit Excel.

► Visual Workshop

Create the regional sales report shown in Figure A-21 using the commands, formulas, and techniques you learned in this unit. Save the workbook as *Regional Sales Analysis* on your Project Disk, enter your name in cell A13, preview the worksheet, then print a copy.

FIGURE A-21

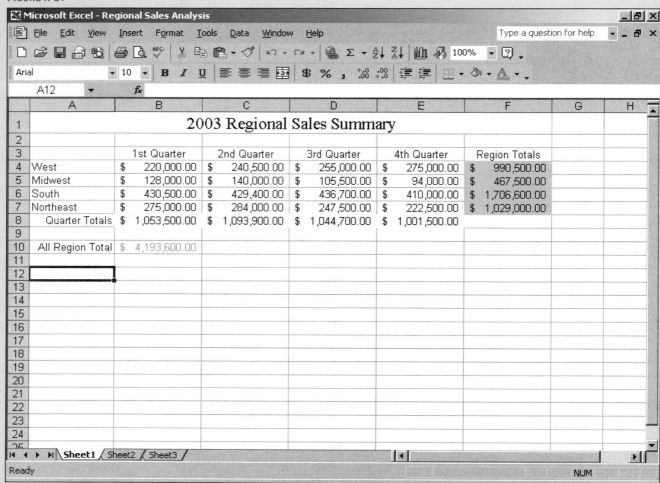

Working
with Excel Functions

Objectives

- ► **Understand functions**
- ► **Use the SUM function**
- ► **Use date and time functions**
- ► **Use statistical functions**
- ► **Use financial functions**
- ► **Sort rows**
- ► **Filter data and print**

In this unit you learn about **functions**, prewritten formulas that you can use instead of typing all the parts to a formula. When you use a function, usually all you have to do is enter the appropriate values or cell references. Excel comes with hundreds of functions, which you can use for simple calculations, such as addition and averaging, and for more complex calculations, such as calculating loan payments or finding the standard deviation of a selection of database entries. ✎— Dean Holmes, marketing manager for Outdoor Designs, has asked you to help him update the product order sheet. You'll use functions to finalize the worksheet so that it provides meaningful sales and account data for the Marketing and Accounting Departments. When you finish, you'll print a copy of the document for the Order Processing Department.

Understanding Functions

Each Excel function has a name that you usually see in all capital letters. The SUM function, for example, adds values, the ROUND function rounds a number to a specified number of digits, and so on. There are four parts to every function: an equal sign, the function name, a set of parentheses, and arguments separated by commas and enclosed in parentheses. **Arguments** are information a function needs to perform a task and can be values (such as 100 or .02) or cell references (such as B3 or A9:G16). Figure B-1 shows the anatomy of the Excel function named AVERAGE, which calculates the average of a set of numbers contained in cells in a worksheet. The AVERAGE function accepts values from one or more cells, referred to as a **reference** or a **range reference**, as arguments. ✎ Dean asks you to open the Outdoor Designs product order worksheet and prepare to add functions to it by familiarizing yourself with the variety of functions available.

1. Start Excel, then in the New Workbook task pane click **Choose workbook** in the New from existing workbook section
The New from Existing Workbook dialog box opens. This dialog box lets you create a new workbook based on an existing one without modifying an existing workbook.

QuickTip

If the New Workbook task pane is not open, click File on the menu bar, click Open, click the drive and folder that contain your Project Files, click the filename EX B-1, click Open, then skip to Step 3.

2. Click the **Look in list arrow**, navigate to the drive and folder where your Project Files are stored, click the filename **XL B-1**, then click **Create New**

QuickTip

You can also create a new workbook based on an existing one by opening the existing Excel workbook, clicking File on the menu bar, then clicking Save As and saving the workbook under a new name.

3. Click **File** on the menu bar, click **Save As**, make sure the Save in list box displays the drive and folder containing your Project Files and the filename in the File name text box is selected, type **Mountain Air Order**, then click **Save**
The worksheet is saved with a new name.

4. Click any cell, then click the **Insert Function button** 🔲 to the left of the Formula bar
The Insert Function dialog box opens, which allows you to select and insert functions from a list of predesigned choices. (You can also type the information that makes up a function directly in the Formula bar, but you have to know the function name and the necessary arguments.) At the top of the Insert Function dialog box is a Search for a function box that lets you type a function name, business problem, or related word, then click Go. If Excel recognizes part of the phrase you entered, it will list the related functions. Functions are also organized by category in the Or select a category drop-down list box, and functions in the current category are listed alphabetically in the Select a function list box at the bottom of the dialog box. Table B-1 describes some of the most commonly used categories.

QuickTip

The Search for a function box is a new feature of Excel 2002, designed to give you quick access to the functions you need—even if you've forgotten their names.

5. Type **calculate monthly payments** in the Search for a function box, then click **Go**
Excel displays the PMT (Payment), IPMT (Interest Payment), and NPER (Number of Periods) functions in the list box. The drop-down list box now contains the text "Recommended" because you have used Excel's Search for a function box for a function recommendation. See Figure B-2.

6. Click the **Or select a category list arrow**, then click **Statistical**
The Select a function list box lists Excel's statistical functions in alphabetical order.

QuickTip

If you click Help on this function link at the bottom of the Insert Function dialog box, Excel opens a very useful window containing information about how the current function is used.

7. Click **AVERAGE** in the Select a function list
The section at the bottom of the dialog box displays the name of the currently selected function, its arguments, and a brief description of the function's purpose.

8. Click **All** in the Function category list, scroll through and read the list of function names, then click **Cancel**
The All category lists all functions available in Excel, regardless of category.

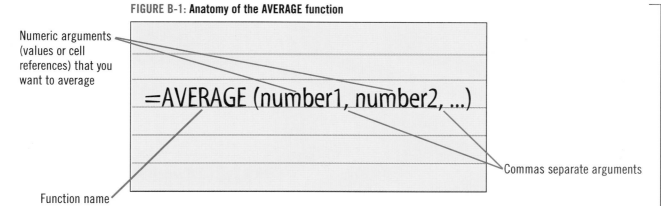

FIGURE B-1: Anatomy of the AVERAGE function

Numeric arguments (values or cell references) that you want to average

=AVERAGE (number1, number2, ...)

Commas separate arguments

Function name

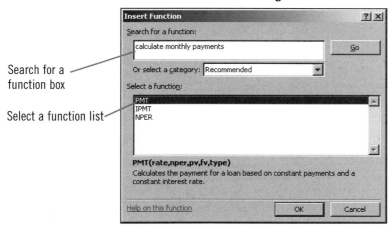

FIGURE B-2: Insert Function dialog box

Search for a function box

Select a function list

TABLE B-1: Categories of some common worksheet functions

category	used for
Date & Time	Calculations involving dates and times
Financial	Loan payments, appreciation, and depreciation
Information	Determining the type of data stored within a cell
Logical	Calculations that produce the result TRUE or FALSE
Lookup & Reference	Finding values in lists or tables or finding references for cells
Math & Trig	Simple and complex mathematical calculations
Statistical	Average, sum, variance, and standard deviation calculations
Text	Comparing, converting, and reformatting text strings in cells

CLUES TO USE

Planning to use functions

Using functions in a worksheet requires planning in advance, because many arguments used in functions come from worksheet cells. Because you can include worksheet ranges as arguments, you should organize your rows and columns when building a worksheet so you can select and include them in functions. Before you start creating formulas from scratch, you need to determine what results you want from your worksheet data and examine the list of Excel functions in the Help system to see if any functions are available for your calculations. You can also use many Excel functions in building databases in Access.

Using the SUM Function

The most frequently used worksheet function, **SUM**, totals all numbers and cell references included as function arguments. Table B-2 lists other commonly used mathematical functions. To use the SUM function in a formula, click the AutoSum button on the Standard toolbar, then edit the function arguments in the Formula bar. The AutoSum feature uses the SUM function, but is a distinct tool in Excel. You are now ready to enhance your Outdoor Designs worksheet with functions. The product order worksheet would not be complete without the total dollar amount and the total number of items to be shipped. Use the SUM function to total the Quantity and Subtotal columns.

1. Click cell **C14**, click the **Align Right button** on the Formatting toolbar, click the **Bold button** on the Formatting toolbar, type **Totals**, then press **[Tab]**
The label "Totals" is entered in cell C14 with the specified formatting.

2. Click the **Insert Function button**
The Insert Function dialog box opens.

3. Click the **Or Select a category list arrow**, click **Math & Trig**, then scroll down in the Select a function list and click **SUM**
The section below the function list displays the arguments for the SUM function and a brief description.

4. Click **OK**
The Insert Function dialog box closes, and the Function Arguments dialog box opens, as shown in Figure B-3. The arguments (D9:D13) are already entered in the Number1 text box.

5. Make sure the Number1 range reference is **D9:D13**, then click **OK**
You can use a colon to indicate a range of values, or a **range reference**. The formula calculates the sum of cells D9 through D13 and displays the result, 13, in cell D14.

6. Click cell **E14**, then click the **AutoSum button** Σ on the Standard toolbar
AutoSum offers a quicker method for calculating sums in consecutive cells, and for performing other simple calculations, including Average, Count, and Max. See Table B-2 for a description. When you use AutoSum, Excel selects a range in the worksheet to add using the SUM function; you can either accept the selection by pressing [Enter] or change it by dragging to select a different range. The cells in the range E9:E13 (see Figure B-4) are selected in the worksheet and appear in the cell and in the Formula bar. These are the cells you want to sum.

7. Press **[Enter]**
The formula calculates and displays the result, $398.35, in cell E14. Notice that the currency style was applied to cell E14 to match the style in the SUM range reference.

8. Click cell **D14**, then click the **Center button** on the Formatting toolbar

9. Click the **Save button** on the Standard toolbar

Trouble?
If your range reference is not D9:D13, click in the Number1 text box, delete the current value, then type the correct reference.

QuickTip
To choose a different function available through the AutoSum button, click the AutoSum button list arrow, then click the function you want to use, or click More Functions to open the Insert Function dialog box.

FIGURE B-3: **Using the SUM function to calculate a column total**

Formula in menu bar

Sum dialog box

Formula result

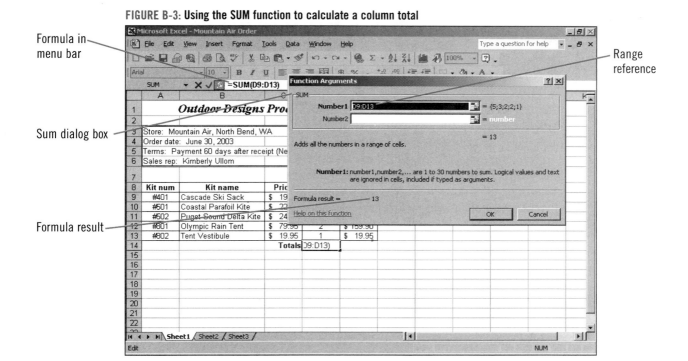

Range reference

FIGURE B-4: **Using the AutoSum button to calculate a column total**

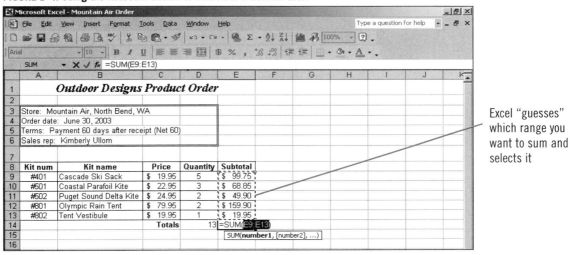

Excel "guesses" which range you want to sum and selects it

TABLE B-2: **Commonly used mathematical functions available through the AutoSum button**

function	description
AVERAGE(argument)	Calculates the average value of the arguments
COUNT(argument)	Calculates the number of values in the argument list
MAX(argument)	Calculates the largest value in the argument list
MIN(argument)	Calculates the smallest value in the argument list
SUM(argument)	Calculates the sum of the arguments

Unit B
Excel 2002

Using Date and Time Functions

The Excel date and time functions let you display the current date and/or time in your worksheet and can help you calculate the time between important events. Some date and time functions return recognizable text values that you can display "as is" in your worksheets; other date and time functions return special numeric values called **serial numbers**, which require special formatting. ▰▰▰ Dean asks you to add a formula to the product order worksheet that calculates payment due dates for the store placing the order. Use the NOW function to enter the current date in the worksheet, and use the Format Cells dialog box to format the date's style. You also want to enter a formula that uses the current date to calculate when a payment is due.

Steps

1. **Click cell A16, type Ship date:, then press [Tab]**
   The label "Ship date:" appears in cell A16, and cell B16 is selected.

QuickTip

Function names are not case sensitive. When typing function names, you can use uppercase or lowercase letters.

2. **Type =NOW( ), then press [Enter]**
   You have typed the NOW function in cell B16 instead of using the Insert Function dialog box. You did not enter any arguments within the parentheses because this function does not require any. The results of this function, the current date and time, appear in the cell.

3. **Select cell B16, click Format on the menu bar, then click Cells**
   The Number tab in the Format Cells dialog box opens, as shown in Figure B-5. You can change the way the date and time are displayed by using the Number tab in the Format Cells dialog box.

4. **Click the Date category if necessary, click March 14, 2001 in the Type list if necessary, then click OK**
   The Format Cells dialog box closes, and today's date appears in cell B16, with the month spelled out, followed by the day and year.

5. **Click cell A17, type Pmt due:, then press [Tab]**
   The label "Pmt due:" is entered in cell A17, and cell B17 is selected. In this cell, you'll enter a formula that calculates the day when full payment is due from the store, assuming a 60-day payment grace period.

6. **Type =, press [↑] to select cell B16, type +60, then press [Enter]**
   The payment due date appears in cell B17, as shown in Figure B-6. The payment due date is calculated by adding 60 days (net 60) to the current date. The number of days in each month is considered in the calculation.

7. **Save your changes to the workbook**

FIGURE B-5: Changing the date format

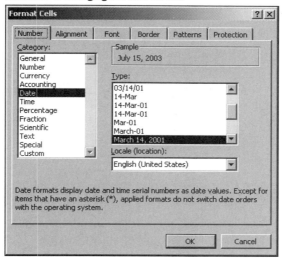

FIGURE B-6: Product order worksheet after date calculations

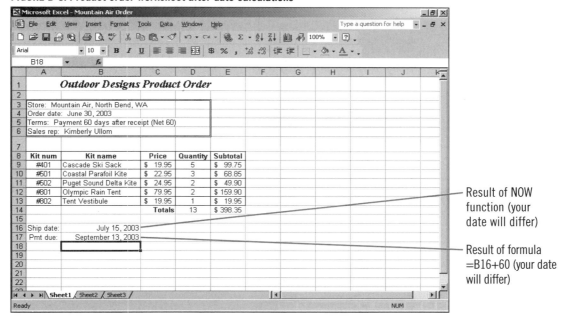

Result of NOW function (your date will differ)

Result of formula =B16+60 (your date will differ)

How dates are calculated using serial numbers

When you enter a date in a worksheet cell, the date appears in a familiar format (such as August 11, 2003) but it is actually stored as a **serial number** that represents the number of days since January 1, 1900. Dates are stored as serial numbers so they can be used in calculations. For example, in this lesson you added 60 days to the current date. To Excel, the formula in cell B17 in Figure B-6 is really =36995+60. Memorizing how serial numbers work is not the most important thing to learn about Excel, but it does provide some context for how Excel performs date computations. Occasionally in online Help, you see serial numbers described as date and time codes. Don't be confused; serial numbers and date and time codes are the same thing.

Using Statistical Functions

Excel 2002

Excel's statistical functions let you assemble, classify, and tabulate numeric data in your worksheet. ✐ Dean wants to know the average amount for each item in the product order, so you decide to use the Average function to add this information.

Steps 1234

1. **Click cell A19, type Avg order:, then press [Tab]**
   The label "Avg order:" appears in cell A19, and cell B19 is selected.

2. **Click the Insert Function button fx**
   The Insert Function dialog box opens.

3. **Click the Or select a category list arrow, click Statistical, click AVERAGE in the Select a function list, read the description, then click OK**
   The Insert Function dialog box closes, and the Function Arguments dialog box opens.

4. **Click the Reduce button** in the Number1 text box, as shown in Figure B-7
   The dialog box changes size and moves out of the way. Now you can use the pointer to select the range on which to calculate an average.

QuickTip
You can include one function as an argument in another function if its result is compatible. For example, the formula =SUM(5,SQRT(9)) adds the number 5 to the square root (SQRT) of 9 and displays the result (8).

5. **Select the range E9:E13 (the Subtotal column), press [Enter], then click OK**
   The range E9:E13 is an argument in the AVERAGE function in the Formula bar. The result, $79.67, is displayed in cell B19, as shown in Figure B-8.

6. **Click the Save button** on the Standard toolbar

FIGURE B-7: Reducing the size of the AVERAGE dialog box

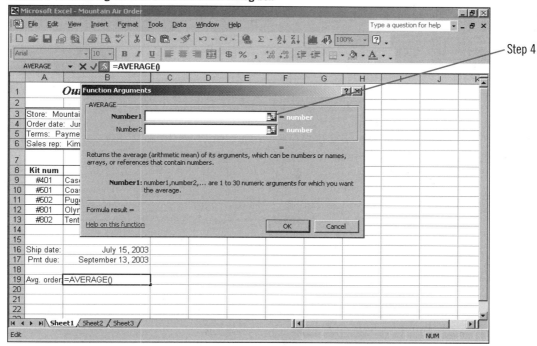

FIGURE B-8: Product order worksheet with AVERAGE function

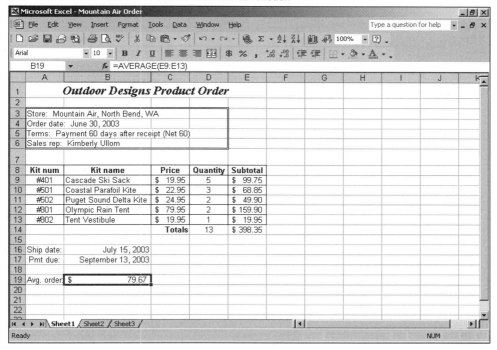

Mathematical functions

Another useful category of functions that produces values as results are the mathematical functions. These functions perform many mathematical and trigonometric calculations found on a standard scientific calculator, including ABS (absolute value), COS (cosine), LOG (logarithm), and SQRT (square root). Most mathematical functions take a single number as an argument and produce a single number as a result. For more information about using the mathematical functions, search for "ABS", "COS", "LOG", and "SQRT" in Help.

B

Excel 2002

Using Financial Functions

The Excel financial functions help you calculate loan payments, appreciation, and depreciation using worksheet data. 　　　 Outdoor Designs extends credit to approved wholesale customers who want to pay for their purchases over a 12-month period. Use the PMT function to determine what the monthly payment would be if the Mountain Air store chose to finance its outstanding balance.

Steps 1 2 3 4

1. Click cell **A20**, type **12 pmts:**, then press **[Tab]**
   The label "12 pmts:" is entered in cell A20, and cell B20 is selected.

2. Click the **Insert Function button** 🔣

3. Click the **Or select a category list arrow**, click **Financial**, scroll down the Select a function list, click **PMT**, then click **OK**
   The Insert Function dialog box closes, and the PMT dialog box opens. The PMT function determines the periodic payment for a loan based on the interest rate charged, the payment term (number of payments), and the principal loan amount. As with all functions, you can specify the function arguments as numbers or cell references. The arguments are Rate (the interest rate), Nper (the number of payments), and Pv (present value of the loan, or the principal).

4. Type **10%/12** in the Rate text box, then press **[Tab]**
   The rate is 10%, and the rate is calculated over a 12-month period.

5. Type **12** in the Nper text box, then press **[Tab]**
   There are 12 payments in the loan term.

6. Type **-E14** in the Pv text box
   You can enter a cell reference or an amount in the Pv text box. The Function Argument dialog box is shown in Figure B-9. Pv represents the amount of the loan at the beginning of the loan period. Money that is paid out, such as a loan payment, is represented by a negative number, represented by a minus sign (−). Money that you receive, such as a deposit, is represented as a positive number. The FV and Type arguments are optional for the PMT function and you don't need them for this worksheet. FV sets the future value of the investment when the loan term is over. The default value is 0, which means that when the loan is paid off it has a cash value of $0. The Type argument identifies when you make your payment. A value of 1 means that you pay at the beginning of the month, and a value of 0 means that you pay at the end of the month (0 is the default). Interestingly, the time of payment influences how much you pay.

Trouble?

If your result is a negative number, you did not enter the Pv amount as a negative value. Click cell B20, then edit the formula in the Formula bar so it is =PMT(10%/12,12,-E14).

7. Click **OK**
   The result, $35.02, appears in cell B20, as shown in Figure B-10. Mountain Air will pay this amount monthly for 12 months if it chooses to finance its purchase.

8. Save your changes to the workbook

FIGURE B-9: Completed PMT dialog box

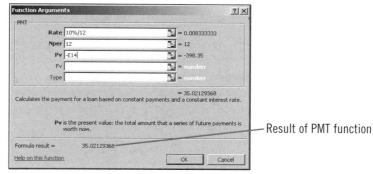

Result of PMT function

FIGURE B-10: Product order worksheet with PMT function

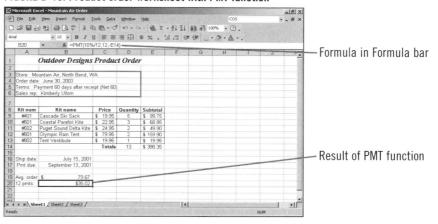

Formula in Formula bar

Result of PMT function

CLUES TO USE

Using Excel templates on the Web

Microsoft Corporation provides access to several preformatted Excel templates on the Web for dozens of common office forms, such as billing statements, invoices, and purchase orders. Many people use the Excel financial functions, like the Pmt function you have experimented with here. You can use these templates by clicking New on the File menu, then clicking the Templates on Microsoft.com link in the task pane and answering the questions that the Microsoft Office Update Web site asks you about your country of origin, business interests, and so on. Figure B-11 shows a Billing Statement template downloaded from the Web that you can use to quickly bill customers for the goods or services provided (it's similar to the product order sheet you've been creating in this unit). You can use this template as it is, or change it by using the same techniques you would use if you created the worksheet yourself. Can you find the financial functions that are used in these templates?

FIGURE B-11: Template on the Microsoft Office Update Web site

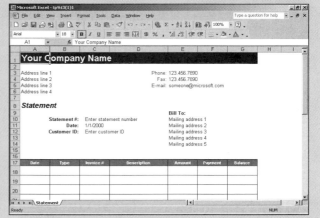

Excel 2002

Sorting Rows

In Excel there are many sort commands that allow you to sort rows in the worksheet by comparing values in one or more columns. You can sort rows alphabetically or numerically, and in ascending or descending order. You added all of the information that Dean requested to the product order worksheet. Use the Sort command to organize the information so the lowest-priced item is listed first and the highest-priced item is listed last.

1. Select rows **9** through **13**

QuickTip

If your selection includes headers (text that identifies the values in the columns), then click the Header row option button in the Sort dialog box so the headers will not be sorted.

2. Click **Data** on the menu bar, then click **Sort**

    The Sort dialog box opens. You can sort based on three columns in case some cells contain the same data, and each column can be sorted in ascending or descending order. Ascending order means that the letter A comes before the letter Z, and the number 1 comes before the number 9. Descending order means that the letter Z comes before the letter A, and the number 9 comes before the number 1. The Sort list arrow indicates that the values in Column A will be sorted in ascending order.

3. Click the **No header row option button**, if necessary, to select it

    You did not select the headers in the table. If you had, you could click this button to ensure that Excel did not sort the header row along with the other rows.

4. Click the **Sort by list arrow**, then click **Column C**

    You have selected Column C (Price) as your primary sort criterion, as shown in Figure B-12. You want to sort in ascending order by the data in this column.

QuickTip

You can sort the rows in your worksheet any number of times, depending on the order in which you want your information presented. To undo the results of a sort immediately after performing it, click the Undo button on the Standard toolbar.

5. Click **OK**

    The Sort dialog box closes, and the rows appear in ascending order, from the smallest value to the largest, as shown in Figure B-13. Note that there is a "tie" in the first two rows—they both have $19.95 listed in column C. The largest price is listed as $79.95, and resides in the last row.

6. Save your changes to the workbook

FIGURE B-12: Sort dialog box

FIGURE B-13: Order information sorted by kit price (column C)

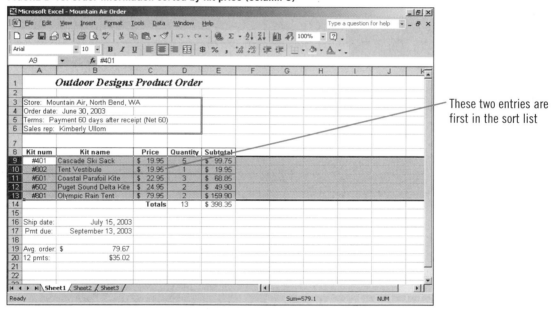

These two entries are first in the sort list

Sorting by more than one column

If more than one row contains the same value in the column you are sorting by, the sort results in a "tie." For example, the sort you practiced in this lesson resulted in a tie because both rows at the top contained the value $19.95 in column C. To break the tie, you can use the "Then by" list box in the Sort dialog box. A common use of multiple sort columns is sorting customers first by last name, and then by first name. You can use up to three columns to refine your sort in this way.

Excel 2002

Filtering Data and Printing

When your worksheet contains a large amount of data, you might need to filter the data to display only the data you need. You can apply a filter to only one worksheet column at a time by specifying the value that you want to see. A filter is different from a sort. A sort lists all of your data in a specified order, but a **filter** displays only the data you want to see. ✐ Dean wants you to filter the data so he can see only order lines that contain a kit price of $19.95. Then he asks you to print the worksheet.

1. Click cell **A8**

2. Click **Data** on the menu bar, point to **Filter**, then click **AutoFilter**
   List arrows appear in the column headings in row 8, as shown in Figure B-14. You can click any list arrow to display the list of available filters for that column. Excel creates filters for each of the values in the column, plus default filters to select all values, custom values, or the top 10 values. You can also customize a filter to find values using comparison operators and specific values.

3. Click the **Price list arrow**, then click **$19.95**
   Only the rows that contain a value of $19.95 in the price column appear, as shown in Figure B-15.

4. Turn on your printer, if necessary

5. Click the **Print button** 🖨 on the Standard toolbar
   After a few moments the worksheet emerges from your printer ready for Dean to review.

6. Click the **Price list arrow** again, then click **(All)**
   All of your worksheet data appears.

7. Click **Data** on the menu bar, point to **Filter**, then click **AutoFilter** to turn it off

8. Save your changes to the workbook

9. Click the **Close button** on the Excel program window
   The Mountain Air Order workbook and Excel both close.

FIGURE B-14: Worksheet with filter list arrows

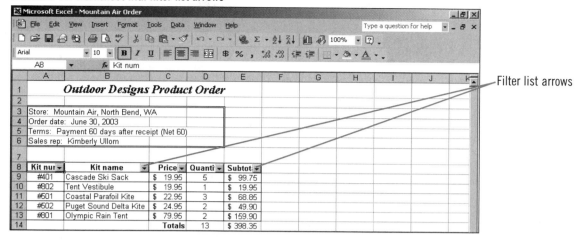

Filter list arrows

FIGURE B-15: Worksheet after applying filter

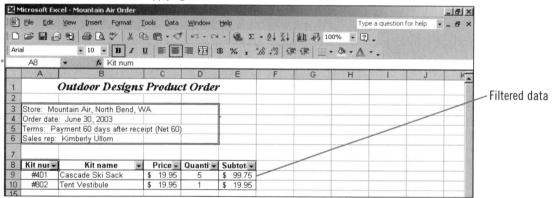

Filtered data

Customizing a filter

You can use any of the predefined filters to filter your worksheet data, but sometimes you might need to show filters that require calculations, such as customer records with a balance that is greater than the credit limit. To do this, click the (Custom...) option in the filter list, then use the Custom AutoFilter dialog box to enter your filter information. Click the list arrow to see the available choices. You can filter using comparison operations (greater than, equal to, etc.) against another value. Look up the word "filters" in Help to learn more about using custom filters.

Practice

► Concepts Review

Label each of the elements of the Excel worksheet window shown in Figure B-16.

FIGURE B-16

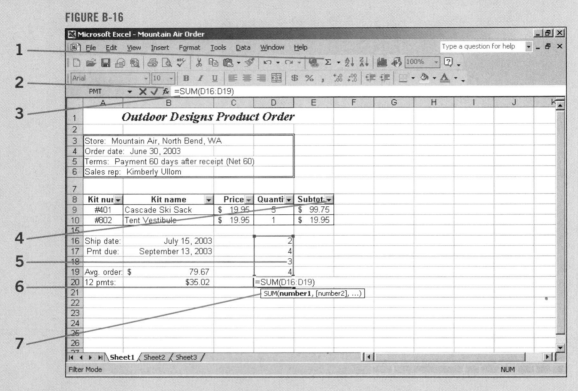

Match components of the formula =SUM(5,SQRT(9)) with their descriptions.

8. SUM
9. 5
10. SQRT(9)
11. =
12. ,

a. Number used as an argument in a function
b. Symbol that indicates that the following text is a formula
c. Function used as an argument in a function
d. Symbol used to separate arguments in functions
e. Function name

Select the best answer from the list of choices.

13. **Which toolbar button opens the Insert Function dialog box?**
    a. Σ
    b. A↓
    c. 📋 ▾
    d. *f*x

14. **Which answer best describes statistical functions?**
    a. Functions used for average, sum, variance, and standard deviation calculations
    b. Functions used for mathematical and trigonometric calculations
    c. Functions used for loan payments, appreciation, and depreciation calculations
    d. Functions involving date and time calculations

15. **Which answer best describes a function argument?**
    a. A number, cell reference, or expression that a function uses to perform a calculation
    b. The abbreviated name of the function
    c. The parentheses following the function name in the Formula bar
    d. The result of a function calculation

16. **What type of argument do you use with the NOW( ) function?**
    a. number1, number2, …
    b. A cell reference
    c. A cell range
    d. The NOW( ) function doesn't have any arguments.

17. **How would Excel evaluate the formula =SUM(2,SQRT(16))?**
    a. 2
    b. 4
    c. 6
    d. 8

18. **What does E9:E12 represent in the formula =SUM(E9:E12)?**
    a. The average of cells E9 and E12
    b. Two cell references
    c. A range of three cells
    d. A range of four cells

19. **What answer would Excel calculate for the formula =AVERAGE(2,5,14)?**
    a. 6
    b. 7
    c. 8
    d. 9

20. **An Excel filter allows you to:**
    a. Sort the rows in a worksheet alphabetically or numerically.
    b. Sort selected rows, using a second or third column to resolve "ties."
    c. Display rows that match a specific value in one of the column list boxes.
    d. Search for functions in the Insert Function dialog box.

▶ Skills Review

1. Understand functions.
   a. Start Excel.
   b. Use the Choose file command to open a copy of the file XL B-2 from the drive and folder where your Project Files are located.
   c. Save the new workbook as *April Sales*.

2. Use the SUM function.
   a. Click cell D15.
   b. Click the AutoSum button on the Standard toolbar.
   c. Change the range reference to cells D5:D13, then press [Enter].
   d. Save your changes to the workbook.

3. Use date and time functions.
   a. In cell F5, enter the formula that calculates the payment date considering a 45-day payment grace period.
   b. Use the Fill handle to copy the formula in cell F5 to cells F6:F13.
   c. Select the range E5:F13.
   d. Open Format Cells dialog box, then click the Number tab if necessary.
   e. Change the date format to display dates in the format Day-Month-Year, then click OK.

4. Use statistical functions.
   a. Click cell D17, then open the Insert Function dialog box.
   b. Use the AVERAGE function to determine the average order amount for the month.
   c. Enter cells D5:D13 as the Number1 range, then click OK.
   d. Save your changes to the workbook.

5. Use financial functions.
   a. Click cell G5, then insert a PMT function to calculate a loan payment.
   b. Enter 9%/12 as the rate, 12 as the term, -D5 as the principal amount, then click OK.
   c. Use the Fill handle to copy the formula into cells G6:G13.

6. Sort rows.
   a. Select rows 4 through 13.
   b. Click Data on the menu bar, then click Sort.
   c. Make sure the Header row option button is selected.
   d. Sort the rows first by Region, then by Amount.
   e. Verify the sorting order in rows 5 through 13. (The worksheet should be sorted by region first, and then the amounts should be sorted within each region.)

7. Filter data and print.
   a. Click cell A4.
   b. Click Data on the menu bar, point to Filter, then click AutoFilter.
   c. Click the Amount list arrow and the Custom option.
   d. Specify Amount values greater than 800 only.
   e. Enter your name in cell B2 of the worksheet.
   f. Print a copy of the filtered worksheet, then display all rows again.
   g. Turn off the AutoFilter feature.
   h. Save your changes, then exit Excel.

▶ Independent Challenge 1

The Jupiter Glass Works factory is reviewing its U.S. sales figures, and has asked you to create a worksheet that summarizes quarterly sales totals for each region. In addition, you have been asked to highlight the total sales, the average sales, and the best and worst selling regions.

   a. Start Excel, start a new workbook, and save it as *Regional Glass Sales*.

   b. Enter the label **Quarterly Sales Analysis** in cell A1.

   c. In cells B3, C3, D3, and E3, enter the labels **1st Quarter**, **2nd Quarter**, **3rd Quarter**, and **4th Quarter**, then widen the cells so that the labels fit comfortably.

   d. In cells A4, A5, A6, and A7, enter the labels **Northeast**, **South**, **Midwest**, and **West**, then widen Column A so that it matches the width of Columns B-E.

   e. In row 4, enter the following quarterly sales totals for the Northeast region: **$25,350**, **$28,400**, **$16,730**, **$19,340**. In row 5, enter the following quarterly sales for the South region: **$18,750**, **$24,000**, **$19,000**, **$21,345**. In row 6, enter the following quarterly sales for the Midwest region: **$56,300**, **$69,340**, **$52,400**, **$78,950**. In row 7, enter the following quarterly sales for the West region: **$34,500**, **$28,754**, **$9,650**, **$16,780**. Format cells B4:E8 with currency formatting.

   f. In cell B8, enter a formula that uses the SUM function to total the 1st Quarter sales in column B. Use the Fill tool to replicate the formula in cells C8:E8.

   g. In cell F4, enter a formula that uses the SUM function to compute the Northeast region sales total. Use the Fill tool to replicate the formula in cells F5:F7. Place the label Region Totals in cell F3, and the label Quarter Totals in cell A8.

   h. In cells A10, A11, and A12, enter the labels **Average quarter:**, **High quarter:**, and **Low quarter:**.

   i. In cell B10, use the AVERAGE function to compute the average quarterly sales total for the year. In cell B11, use the MAX function to compute the maximum (or highest) quarterly sales total for the year. In cell B12, use the MIN function to compute the minimum (or lowest) quarterly sales total for the year. Format cells B10:B12 with currency formatting.

   j. Save your changes, add your name to the top of the worksheet, print it, then close the workbook.

▶ Independent Challenge 2

The business supply company you work for, Rusty's Business World, has just received the raw sales data for the fourth quarter (October-December 2003). Rusty has asked you to examine the worksheet for sales trends, including the highest individual sale, the overall sales total, and the number of sales reps who logged sales transactions of over $1000 this quarter. Prepare this information now using the XL B-3 worksheet as your source for the raw sales data.

   a. Open the file XL B-3 from the drive and folder where your Project Files are stored, then save it as *Oct-Dec Paper Sales*.

   b. Use the AutoFilter command to start your analysis of the sales data.

   c. Use the Region column to locate the sales rep with the highest individual sale in the quarter, then type the person's name at the bottom of the worksheet.

   d. Use the Region header to determine the highest individual sales transaction in the quarter. Type this dollar amount at the bottom of the worksheet.

   e. Use the Sales header to display the number of transactions over $1000. Type the number of $1000-plus sales at the bottom of the worksheet.

   f. Click All in the Sales header, then use the Month header to determine the month with the largest number of sales transactions (not the biggest dollar amount). Type the month name at the bottom of the worksheet.

   g. Click All in the Month header, then place a SUM function at the bottom of the worksheet that computes the total value of all sales in column D.

h. Use the Description column to display only the sales transactions involving Paper, then use a SUM function to compute the total value of paper costs, and type the value at the bottom of the worksheet.

i. Remove the filter, then sort rows 6 through 40 using Sales Rep as the first sort column, Month as the second sort column, and Sales as the third sort column. Add your name to the top of the worksheet, save your changes, print the worksheet, then close the workbook.

▶ Independent Challenge 3

A local company that manufactures boots and outdoor footwear is marketing guided outdoor adventures—including helicopter skiing, orienteering, hang gliding, ballooning, trail riding, and backpacking. They have asked Outdoor Designs to join in partnership with them to plan and promote the tours, and you have been given the task of reviewing last year's trip data to determine the most popular trips, how long customers will need to save for the more expensive excursions, and other projections.

a. Open the file XL B-4 from the drive and folder where your Project Files are stored, then save it as *Outdoor Trips 2003*. See Figure B-17 for the layout of the project file you'll be using.

b. Use the SUM function to find the total number of trips taken each month. Also use the SUM function to enter a grand total on the worksheet.

c. Use the MAX function to identify the most popular trip, based on the totals you have calculated. Enter the label **Most Popular** next to the result, then type the name of the most popular trip.

d. Use the NPER function to find how long it will take to save $2350 for a balloon vacation in France if you save $175 per month in a savings account that earns 4.5% interest compounded monthly. Enter the label **Save $175/month for** on the worksheet next to the function. (Use online Help to learn about the NPER function. The Rate is 4.5%, the payment is how much you want to save each month [entered as a negative number, because it's cash going out], the present value is zero, and the future value is the amount you want to save.) Format the result using the accounting format, with one decimal place, and no symbol in the cell.

e. Use the PMT function to find the monthly payment if you borrowed the $2350 at a 10% annual rate with 12 months to repay. Enter the label **Monthly Payment** next to the result.

f. Insert a formula in the cell that calculates the projected number of trips in the year 2003, allowing for a 10% growth rate (use the formula =(B14*1.1). Use the fill tool to replicate the formula in cells C15:C19.

g. Add your name above the title at the top of the worksheet, save your changes, print the worksheet in landscape orientation, then close the workbook.

FIGURE B-15: The Outdoor Trips worksheet

Independent Challenge 4

Your long lost uncle just gave you $20,000, and you have decided to invest half of it in the stock market. The World Wide Web has many sites that make it easy to find information about the current prices of stocks. Before investing your money, you decide to investigate the purchase of three stocks: Intel Corporation, Sun Microsystems, Inc., and Microsoft Corporation. You decide to use the Web to find this information.

a. Open a new Excel workbook, and save it as *Stock Tracker*.

b. Log on to the Internet and use your browser to go to www.nasdaq.com.

c. Use the Nasdaq Stock Exchange site to find the most recent quote information for the following three stocks: Intel Corporation (symbol: intc), Sun Microsystems, Inc. (symbol: sunw), and Microsoft Corporation (symbol: msft).

d. Enter the following labels in row 3, starting in cell B3: **Today's High**, **Today's Low**, **Last Sale**, **Previous Close**, and **Net Change**.

e. Enter the following labels in column A, starting in cell A4: **Intel**, **Sun**, and **Microsoft**.

f. Change the width of columns A-F so that the largest labels fit comfortably.

g. Enter the values into the appropriate cells using the information you retrieved from the NASDAQ site.

h. Format the cells that contain dollar values to appear as currency with four decimal places.

i. Enter the label **Investment** and the label **Shares** on the worksheet. You will spend $3000 for Intel stock, $4000 for Sun stock, and $3000 for Microsoft stock. Enter these values into the Investment column, format them as currency, and then add formulas to the Shares column to show the number of shares you can purchase based on the last sale price.

j. Log off the Internet, and close your browser.

k. Save your changes, add your name below the title at the top of the worksheet, preview the worksheet, then print it.

l. Close the workbook and exit Excel.

Excel 2002

▶ Visual Workshop

Create the worksheet shown in Figure B-18 using commands and techniques you learned in this unit. Save the workbook as *Soccer Analysis*, add your name to the top of the worksheet, and print it.

FIGURE B-18

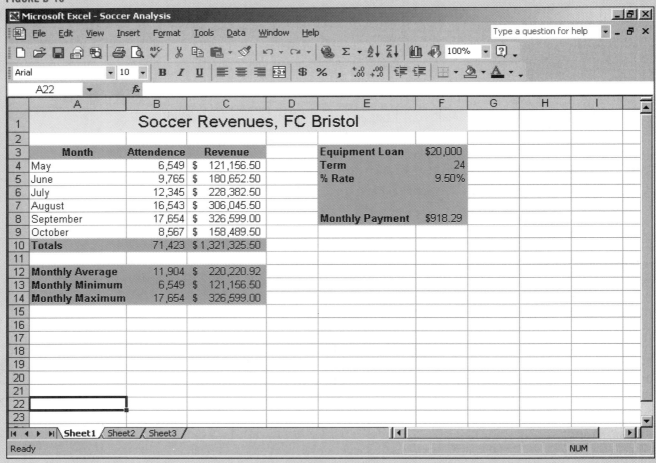

Unit C

Creating

Excel Charts

Objectives

- ► **Plan a chart**
- ► **Create a chart**
- ► **Move and resize a chart and chart objects**
- ► **Change the chart type**
- ► **Add axis labels and gridlines**
- ► **Change chart fonts and colors**
- ► **Enhance a chart**
- ► **Preview and print a chart**

In this unit, you learn how to create and work with charts. A **chart** is a visual representation of worksheet data. For example, a chart can present the number of kite kits sold in a month or the amount of water consumed each summer, in a format that is easy to understand and remember.
In this unit, you will create a chart for Dean Holmes, marketing manager for Outdoor Designs, to show the regional sales figures graphically for the first and second quarters of 2003. You'll also customize the chart, then print a final copy of the chart, which Dean can distribute to the sales and marketing group.

Planning a Chart

Excel 2002

Before you create a chart, you need to do some general planning, deciding what data you want to display, what kind of chart you want to use, and so on. To make sure the Outdoor Designs regional sales chart that Dean requested includes all necessary information in an effective format, you begin by planning it.

In planning a chart, it is important to:

► **Identify the purpose of the data**

What data are you including in the worksheet? How will the data fit in the report or memo you're creating? What data would you like to highlight with a chart? For example, the sales and marketing group will use the chart that you create for Dean to evaluate how business is growing and to determine which regions need special attention.

► **Design the worksheet so Excel will create the chart you want**

Group your data into logical rows and columns. As you'll learn in the next lesson, Excel uses the worksheet row and column labels to create labels and other identifiers for the chart. Review the chart terms and descriptions shown in Table C-1 to make sure that you understand them before moving on to the next lesson.

QuickTip

In addition to the chart types shown in Figure C-1, Excel provides 3-D versions of the area, bar, line, and pie charts, and similar variations for the other chart types.

► **Determine the chart type**

Consider the chart types shown in Figure C-1 and described in Table C-2. Which chart type will best represent the data you want to include? (The first five chart types are the most important to memorize.) Do you want to show one category of data or make comparisons between two categories? Several chart types are appropriate for the regional sales figures; however, Dean's preference for column charts might influence your final decision.

Now you're ready to choose the chart type you want, create the chart, and edit it. You'll start Excel and create your first chart in the next lesson.

TABLE C-1: Chart terms

term	definition
Gridlines	Horizontal and vertical lines connecting to the X-axis and Y-axis
Labels	Text describing data in the chart
Legend	Box explaining what the labels, colors, and patterns in the chart represent
X-axis	Horizontal line in a chart containing a series of related values from the worksheet
Y-axis	Vertical line in a chart containing a series of related values from the worksheet

TABLE C-2: Excel 2002 chart types and descriptions

chart type	description
Area	Shows relative importance of values over a period of time
Bar	Compares values across categories
Column	Compares values across categories
Line	Shows trends by category over time
Pie	Describes the relationship of parts to the whole
Radar	Shows changes in data or data frequency relative to a center point
XY (Scatter)	Shows the relationship between two kinds of related data
Doughnut	Presents data similarly to a pie chart
Surface	Shows trends in two values over time
Bubble	Compares three sets of values
Stock	Compares High, Low, and Close values
Cylinder	Like a stacked column chart with a cylindrical shape
Pyramid	Like a stacked column chart with a pyramid shape
Cone	Like a stacked column chart with a cone shape

FIGURE C-1: Excel 2002 chart types

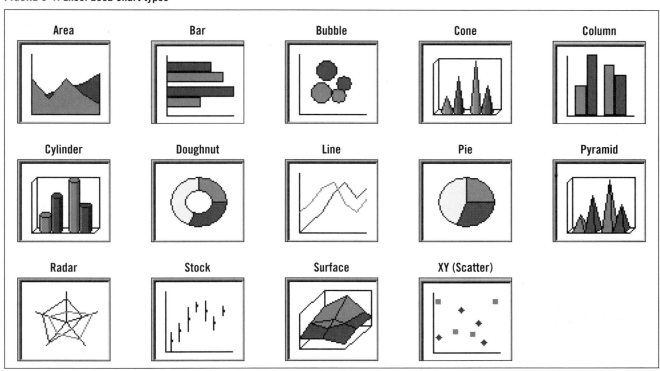

Excel 2002

Creating a Chart

Creating a chart in Excel is simple. You open a worksheet file, select the cells that contain the data you want to display in a chart, then use the Chart Wizard to create and format the chart. After you create a chart, if the worksheet data on which the chart is based changes, the chart automatically displays the new values. ✎ The worksheet that contains the data for the Outdoor Designs sales chart contains sales figures for the past two quarters for the four sales territories in the United States: Northeast, South, Midwest, and West. Dean provided a workbook containing the sales data, so you have everything you need to create the chart he requested.

Steps

1. Start Excel, use the Choose workbook command in the New Workbook task pane to open the file **XL C-1** from the drive and folder where your Project Files are located, then save it as **Sales Chart**

2. Select cells **A5** through **C9**
   The cell range A5:C9 is selected in the worksheet and will be used to create the chart. Notice that you selected the row and column labels, but not the column totals. For most charts, you should avoid including totals when selecting worksheet cells.

3. Click the **Chart Wizard button** 📊 on the Standard toolbar
   The first dialog box of the Chart Wizard opens, as shown in Figure C-3. You use the Chart Wizard to choose the type of chart you want to create, to select the data range (if you did not select it first), and to add a title, border, or gridlines to the chart. By default, Excel has selected the Column chart type and the Clustered Column sub type for your chart.

4. Click **Next**
   The second dialog box lets you choose the data to chart and whether the data will appear in rows or columns in the worksheet. The data in your chart is organized as a **series**, or a sequence of numbers that shows a trend. Displaying the series in columns is the default. A data series can be organized in rows or columns, depending on how you created your worksheet. You selected the correct series data before clicking the Chart Wizard button, so the data range is correct.

5. Click the **Columns option button** to select it if necessary, then click **Next**
   In the third Chart Wizard dialog box, you see a sample of your chart with the default settings. You can change the chart title, the way data appears in the chart, and other formatting options in this dialog box. Notice that the region names from the worksheet are on the chart's X-axis and that the sales amounts from the worksheet are on the chart's Y-axis. Sales data is graphically displayed in the chart; the blue and purple bars correspond to the first quarter and second quarter, respectively.

6. Click in the **Chart title text box**, then type **Regional Sales 2003**
   The title appears in the sample chart box, as shown in Figure C-3.

7. Click **Next**
   In the final Chart Wizard dialog box you assign the location for the chart. You can place it as an object in a new worksheet or in the current worksheet, which is the default option.

8. Click **Finish**, then click the **Save button** 💾 on the Standard toolbar
   Charts are saved as a part of the workbook file. The column chart appears in the current worksheet, as shown in Figure C-4. The chart is selected, as indicated by the selection handles around the chart. The Chart toolbar usually appears when a chart is selected, as it is now. Your Chart toolbar might appear in a different position from what is shown in Figure C-4; it might be docked or floating in the window, or it might not appear at all.

Trouble?

If you don't see the Chart title text box, click the Titles tab in the Chart Wizard dialog box.

QuickTip

To move a chart to another sheet in a workbook, click the chart to select it, click the Cut button ✂ on the Standard toolbar, click the destination sheet tab, then click the Paste button 📋.

FIGURE C-2: Using the Chart Wizard to create a chart

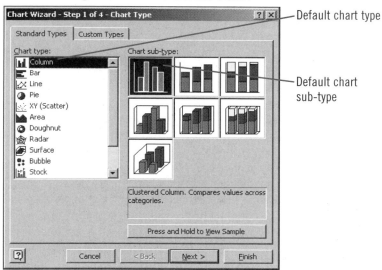

Default chart type

Default chart sub-type

FIGURE C-3: Adding a title to the chart in the Chart Wizard dialog box

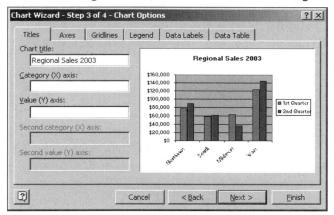

FIGURE C-4: Completed chart in the worksheet

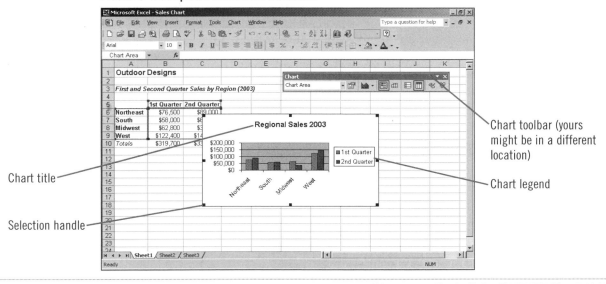

Chart toolbar (yours might be in a different location)

Chart legend

Chart title

Selection handle

Moving and Resizing a Chart and Chart Objects

You can move, resize, copy, and paste charts in a worksheet to achieve precise visual effects. Each chart has several components (known as **objects**) that you can modify independently of the rest of the chart. To move a chart object, you select it first, and then use the selection handles and the pointer to change its size or click and drag it to a new location. Occasionally you'll find that a chart object cannot be moved (such as the chart axis) or resized (such as the chart title); in these cases you'll need to be content with the location or size of the object. ✏️ Dean wants the chart to appear below the worksheet data. He also wants you to change the location of the legend.

Steps

1. If the chart is not selected, click anywhere inside the chart to select it

2. If the Chart toolbar is below the chart, drag the **Chart toolbar title bar** up to move the toolbar so it is above the chart, as shown in Figure C-5

3. Point to a blank area of the chart until the ScreenTip "Chart Area" appears, click and drag the **entire chart** down so that the top-left corner of the chart is aligned with the top-left corner of cell **A12**, then release the mouse button
   You moved the chart so all the worksheet data is visible.

4. Scroll down the worksheet so you can see cell **H28**

5. Position the pointer over the lower-right chart selection handle so it changes to ↘, click and drag the selection handle down so the chart's lower-right edge is aligned with the lower-right edge of cell **H28**, then release the mouse button
   The chart enlarges to the new dimensions. Figure C-5 shows the chart while you are resizing it. If you drag a corner selection handle, you increase or decrease a chart size proportionally. To increase or decrease only the height or width of a chart, you drag one of the side selection handles.

6. Scroll the worksheet up so you can see the chart legend and title, click the **legend** to select it, then drag it up to the position shown in Figure C-6
   The legend moves to its new location. Figure C-6 shows the legend while you are moving it.

7. Click outside the chart area in the worksheet to deselect the legend and the chart

8. Save your changes to the workbook

FIGURE C-5: **Resizing a chart**

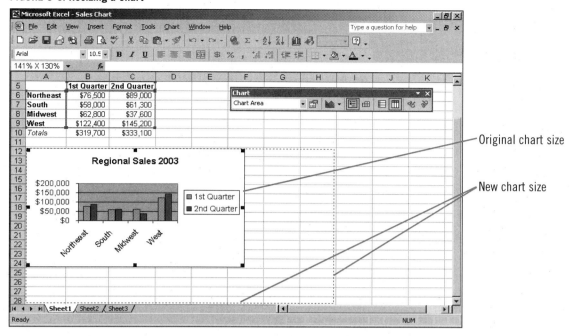

Original chart size

New chart size

FIGURE C-6: **Moving the legend**

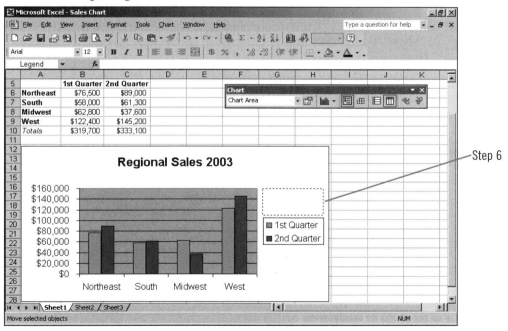

Step 6

Changing the Chart Type

You can change the chart type using the Chart toolbar or the Chart Type dialog box. In addition, you can display each chart type in one of several ways, depending on how you want to present the information. Table C-3 introduces you to the different toolbar buttons on the Chart toolbar. You decide to experiment with some different chart types to add flair to your presentation and present your data most effectively.

1. Click the **chart**

The Chart toolbar appears, and selection handles appear around the chart to indicate that it is selected.

2. Click the **Chart Type list arrow** on the Chart toolbar

Buttons for common chart types appear.

> **QuickTip**
>
> To choose from a complete collection of the chart types available in Excel, select the chart, click Chart on the menu bar, then click Chart Type to open the Chart Type dialog box.

3. Click the **3-D Column Chart button**, as shown in Figure C-7

The chart type changes to a 3-D column chart, as shown in Figure C-8. The first and second quarter sales figures appear as separate bars, so you can compare each quarter's results as well as the overall results. This chart emphasizes that each region experienced growth in sales except the Midwest region, whose sales declined by approximately 40%. The sales and marketing group will probably find this trend very interesting. You're not sure if this is what you want, so you decide to look at a different chart type.

> **Trouble?**
>
> The Chart Type button changes to display the last chart type you selected, but it always functions in the same way.

4. Click on the Chart toolbar, then click the **3-D Pie Chart button**

The chart changes to a 3-D pie chart, as shown in Figure C-9. This doesn't communicate the worksheet data clearly.

5. Click, then click

You like the 2-D Column chart type best for this chart.

6. Save your changes to the workbook

TABLE C-3: Chart toolbar buttons

icon	button name	description
	Format	Changes the properties of the currently selected chart object
	Chart Type	Changes the chart type
	Legend	Displays or hides the chart legend
	Data Table	Changes to chart data as values or as a chart
	By Row	Changes the chart to display worksheet data by rows
	By Column	Changes the chart to display worksheet data by columns
	Angle Text Downward	Changes selected text to read downward and diagonally
	Angle Text Upward	Changes selected text to read upward and diagonally

FIGURE C-7: Chart Type buttons

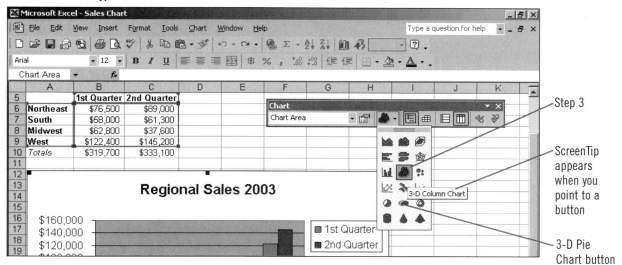

FIGURE C-8: 3-D Column chart of the worksheet data

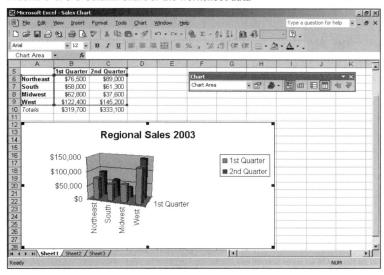

FIGURE C-9: 3-D Pie chart of the worksheet data

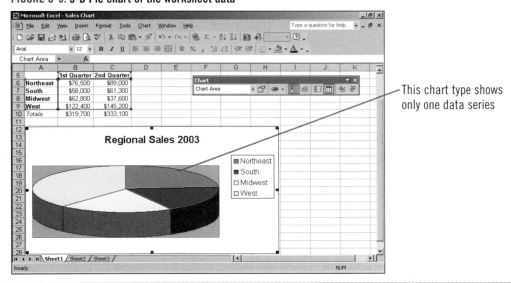

Excel 2002

Adding Axis Labels and Gridlines

Once you create a chart, you can customize it in a variety of ways using the Chart Options dialog box. You can add axis labels to clarify the chart data. You can also format each axis, add gridlines, change the placement of the chart legend, control label placement, and so on, modifying each chart element so that the overall effect is attractive and easy to understand. After you finish these customizations, you can move on to formatting the chart elements, which is a separate step. To clarify data in the regional sales chart, Dean asks you to add labels to the axes and add gridlines to the x-axis so the data is easier to read. These changes will also match the standard chart style used at Outdoor Designs.

1. **Click Chart on the menu bar, then click Chart Options**
   The Chart Options dialog box opens and displays tabs for changing the attributes of the title, axes, gridlines, legend, data labels, and data table.

2. **Click the Titles tab if necessary**
   The Titles tab lets you change the chart title and add labels for the chart axes.

QuickTip

Pressing [Tab] in a dialog box moves you among the text boxes, option buttons, and other elements in the dialog box.

3. **Type Region in the Category (X) axis text box, press [Tab], then type Amount in the Value (Y) axis text box**
   The new labels for the X- and Y-axes appear in the dialog box, as shown in Figure C-10. Note that the number of Y-axis grid lines has been reduced because the labels you added required space in the chart area.

4. **Click OK**
   The dialog box closes and the labels are added to the chart.

5. **Click Chart on the menu bar, click Chart Options, click the Gridlines tab, click the Major gridlines check box for the Category (X) axis, then click OK**
   Your chart now has gridlines for each axis. The Y-axis already has gridlines by default for this chart type.

6. **Deselect the chart by clicking anywhere outside the chart, then scroll down the worksheet if necessary to see the entire chart**
   The data in the chart is easy to read. See Figure C-11. You will enhance the appearance of the chart in the next lesson.

7. **Save your changes to the workbook**

FIGURE C-10: Adding labels to the chart axes in the Chart Options dialog box

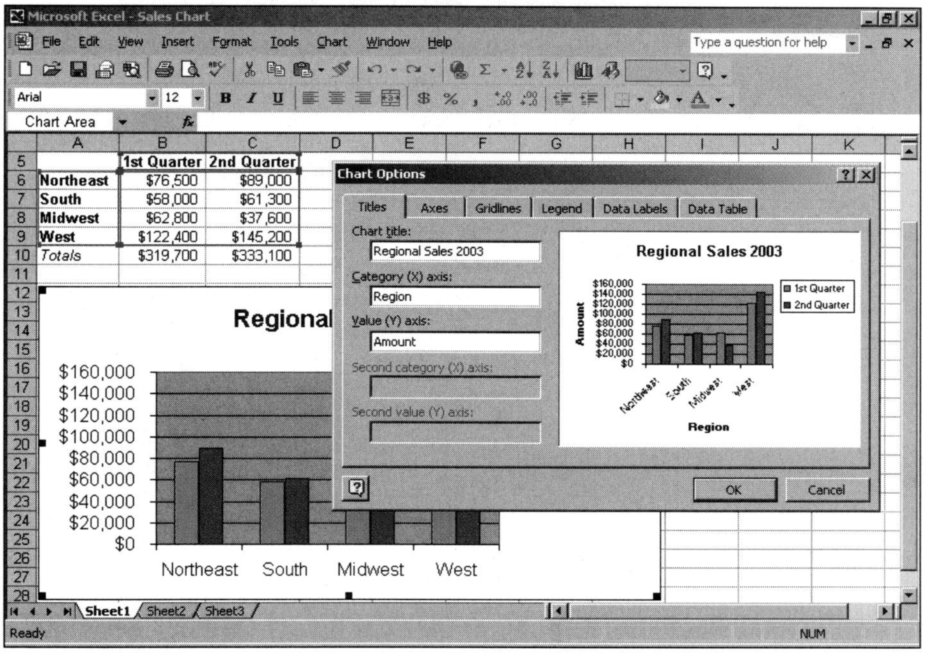

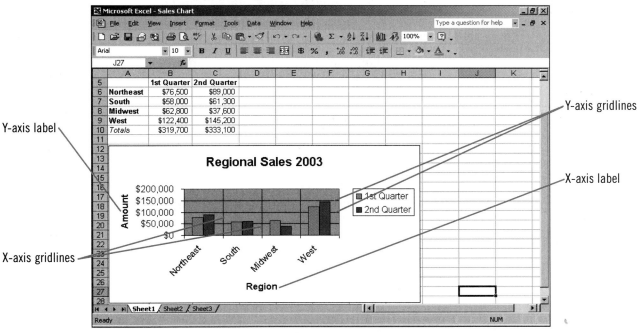

FIGURE C-11: Chart with major axis gridlines added

Excel 2002

Excel 2002

Changing Chart Fonts and Colors

You can also customize a chart by changing the font and style of chart text and the color and pattern of bars in the chart. Such customization makes your charts more readable, more effective, and better adapted to your specific needs. ✎━━ Outdoor Designs traditionally uses Times New Roman for the axis labels, so you want to change the fonts used in the chart. You also want to change the chart bar colors to blue and yellow to match the colors in next month's campaign.

Steps 1234

QuickTip

To open the Format Axis dialog box, you can also select any Y-axis label, then click the Format Axis button 🖳 on the Chart Toolbar. This button name changes depending on what is selected in the chart.

1. Right-click any **label** on the Y-axis (such as "50,000"), then click **Format Axis** on the pop-up menu
   The Format Axis dialog box opens. You can use this dialog box to change the patterns, scale, font, number style, or alignment of the Y-axis labels.

2. Click the **Font tab**, scroll down the Font list, click **Times New Roman**, then click **OK**
   The Format Axis dialog box closes, and the sales chart appears. The Y-axis labels change to Times New Roman font.

QuickTip

You can click the Font Size list arrow on the Formatting toolbar to change the font size of the Y-axis labels.

3. Click **one of the X-axis labels** (such as "Northeast"), click the **Font list arrow** on the Formatting toolbar, then click **Times New Roman** in the list
   The Formatting toolbar offers a quick way to make many formatting changes to chart objects. The X-axis labels change to the Times New Roman font.

QuickTip

Clicking a data point once selects the entire series; clicking it twice selects only that data point. Double-clicking opens the Format dialog box for the selected object.

4. Double-click **one of the 1st Quarter (blue) bars** in the chart
   The Patterns tab of the Format Data Series dialog box opens, as shown in Figure C-12. You can change the colors and patterns of the columns in your chart.

5. Click the **bright blue box** (the last box in the last row) in the Area color palette, then click **OK**
   The 1st Quarter bars and the 1st Quarter legend box change to bright blue.

6. Double-click **one of the 2nd Quarter (purple) bars** in the chart, click the **bright yellow box** (the third box in the last row), then click **OK**
   The 2nd Quarter bars and the 2nd Quarter legend box change to bright yellow.

7. Click anywhere outside the chart, then save your changes to the workbook
   Figure C-13 shows the completed chart. Notice that the Chart toolbar closes when the chart is not selected.

FIGURE C-12: Format Data Series dialog box

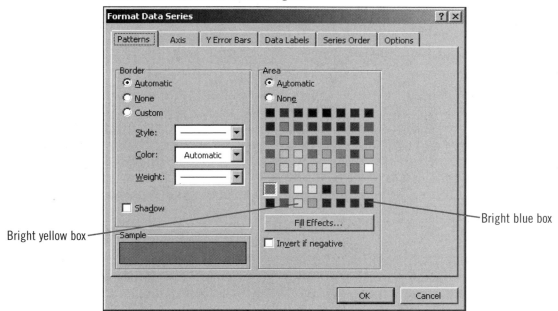

Bright yellow box

Bright blue box

FIGURE C-13: Chart with new labels and colors

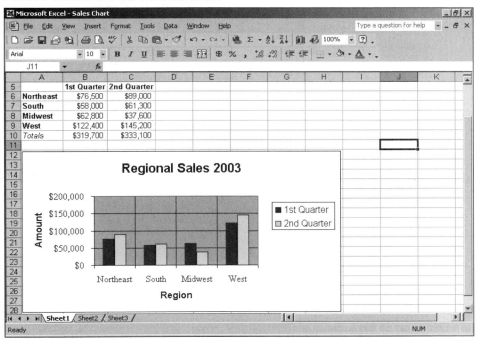

Enhancing a Chart

Excel 2002

There are many ways to change the appearance of a chart to increase its visual appeal and effectiveness. Dean asks you to change the chart background and format the title in a shadowed box to make the chart look more professional.

Trouble?

If Format Chart Area does not appear on the pop-up menu, right-click a different area of the chart, being careful to choose an area that does not contain a chart object.

1. **Right-click** anywhere in the chart area, click **Format Chart Area** on the pop-up menu, then click the **Patterns tab** if necessary
   The Format Chart Area dialog box opens. You can use this dialog box to change the chart background.

2. Click **Fill Effects**, then click the **Texture tab**
   The Texture tab of the Fill Effects dialog box lets you format the background with interesting textures. The section below the Texture list displays the name of the current Texture if one is selected.

3. Click the **Canvas box** (the second box in the fourth row), verify the name of the Texture in the section below the list, click **OK**, then click **OK** in the Format Chart Area dialog box
   The Fill Effects dialog box and the Format Chart Area dialog box both close, and the chart area appears with the new background, as shown in Figure C-14.

Trouble?

If the Chart toolbar covers the chart title, click the toolbar and drag it out of the way.

4. Click the **chart title**, then click the **Format Chart Title button** 🖼 on the Chart toolbar
   The Format Chart Title dialog box opens. You can use this dialog box to change the appearance of the title.

5. Click the **Font tab**, click the **Color list arrow**, click the **dark blue box** (the first box in the last row), then click **OK**
   The title changes to dark blue.

6. Click 🖼, click the **Patterns tab**, click the **Shadow check box** to add a check mark to it, then click **OK**
   The title appears with a white background and a shadow around the box.

7. Click anywhere outside the chart to deselect it, then save your changes to the workbook
   Your chart should look similar to Figure C-15.

FIGURE C-14: Chart with Canvas background

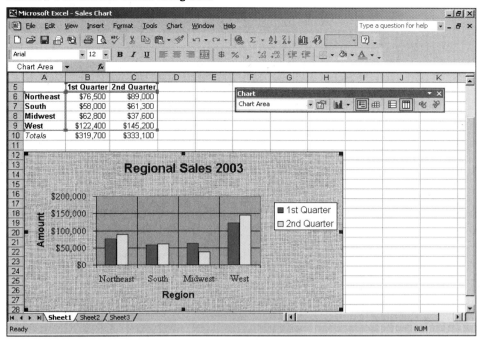

FIGURE C-15: Completed chart with new title style

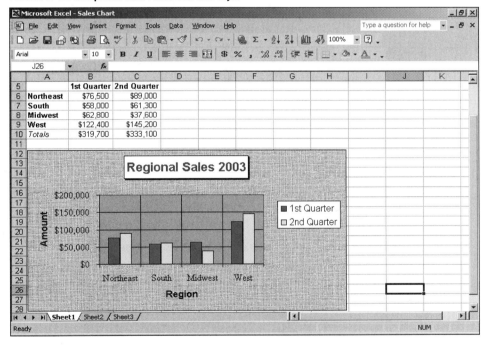

Adding enhancements to a chart

You can change a chart's appearance in many ways to make your chart more interesting and visually appealing. Make sure that you don't overdo it: a chart with too many colors or too many visual effects distracts your audience from the information you are trying to present. Make sure you use complementary colors. Remember, your primary goal when using charts is to communicate worksheet information effectively. In a business setting, you also want to look professional.

Excel 2002

Previewing and Printing a Chart

When you create a chart within a worksheet, you can print the chart by itself or with the data in the worksheet. To preview or print only the chart, click the Print Preview or Print button with the chart selected. To preview or print the chart with the worksheet, you first deselect the chart, then click the Print Preview or Print button. If you have a color printer attached to your system, your print preview will show any colors that are used in the chart. If you have a black and white printer, any chart colors will appear as grayscale, or as shades of gray. ✒ Dean is happy with your chart. He wants you to add a footer with the word "Confidential," today's date, and the page number to the bottom of the page before printing it. He asks you to preview the worksheet with the chart, then print a copy for distribution to the sales and marketing group.

1. **Make sure the chart is not selected, then click the Print Preview button 🔍 on the Standard toolbar**
   The worksheet appears in the Print Preview window in portrait orientation, which you can identify because the page is longer than it is wide. If your worksheet appears in landscape orientation, you probably forgot to deselect the chart.

Trouble?

If your worksheet appears in landscape orientation instead of portrait orientation, click the Portrait option button.

2. **Click Setup on the Print Preview toolbar**
   The Page tab appears. Using the Page tab, you can switch between portrait and landscape orientation, change the document scaling (reduction or enlargement percentage), and specify the paper type.

3. **Click the Header/Footer tab in the Page Setup dialog box**

4. **Click the Footer list arrow, then click the Confidential, <date>, Page 1 option in the list (or a similar option if this one is not available)**
   You can add a variety of built-in headers and footers to your worksheet to identify the date, filename, author, or page number of your workbook. Excel personalizes some of the information in the built-in headers and footers based on the registered user information entered when Excel is installed, so your choices may vary. You can customize a header or footer with your own information by clicking Custom Header or Custom Footer, then typing and using the buttons in the Header or Footer dialog box to insert and format the custom information.

5. **Click OK**
   The worksheet appears in Print Preview as it will appear on the page when printed. If you have a black-and-white printer your preview chart will appear in grayscale, as shown in Figure C-16, even though you formatted the chart using color.

6. **Use the Zoom pointer 🔍 to click the chart**
   Make sure the chart is correct, as shown in Figure C-17.

7. **Turn on your printer and make sure that it has paper**

8. **Click Print on the Print Preview toolbar, then click OK**
   The worksheet with the chart prints.

9. **Save your changes to the workbook, then click the program window Close button**
   The workbook and Excel close.

FIGURE C-16: Print Preview of worksheet

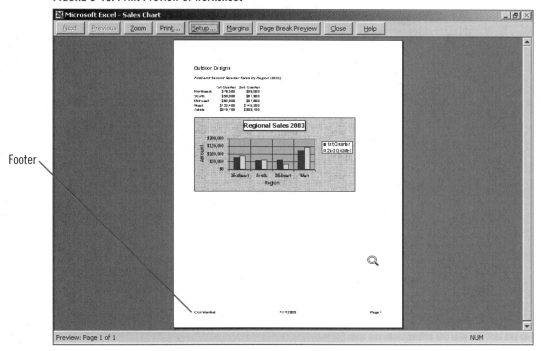

Footer

FIGURE C-17: Zooming the chart in Print Preview

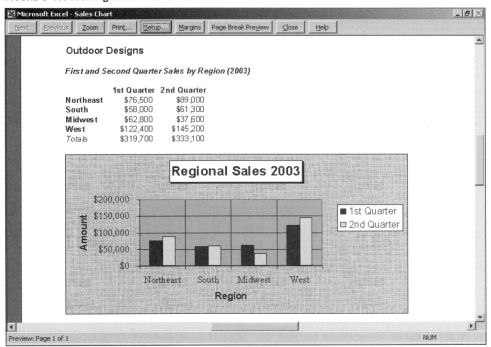

Practice

► Concepts Review

Label each element of the chart window shown in Figure C-18.

FIGURE C-18

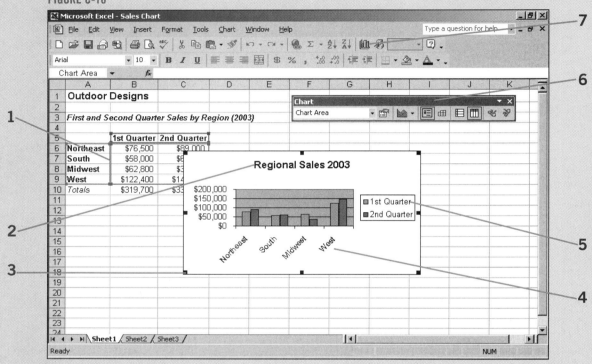

Match each chart type with its name.

8.   **a.** Pie Chart

9.   **b.** Line Chart

10.   **c.** Bar Chart

11.   **d.** Area Chart

12.   **e.** Radar Chart

13.   **f.** Column Chart

14.   **g.** Bubble Chart

15.   **h.** Stock Chart

Select the best answer from the choices listed.

16. **Before running the Chart Wizard to create a chart, you should:**
    a. Resize the chart using the selection handles.
    b. Select the rows and columns to be charted in the worksheet.
    c. Add Gridlines to the chart.
    d. Use the AVERAGE function.

17. **Which toolbar button do you click to create a new chart in a worksheet?**
    a. ▣   c. *fx*
    b. ✂   d. ▥

18. **Which command do you use to display the Chart toolbar?**
    a. Click Toolbars on the View menu, then click Chart
    b. Click Options on the Tools menu, then click the View tab
    c. Click ▥ on the Standard toolbar
    d. Click ↶ on the Standard toolbar

19. **Which definition best describes the X-axis in an Excel chart?**
    a. Horizontal and vertical lines that connect to the X-axis and Y-axis
    b. The vertical line that contains a series of related worksheet values
    c. The horizontal line that contains a series of related worksheet values
    d. A box that explains what the labels, colors, and patterns in the chart represent

20. **What is a good rule of thumb when formatting a chart?**
    a. Use as many patterns as possible to add interest to the chart.
    b. Use colors that are not complementary for readability.
    c. Make sure your chart type communicates your worksheet data effectively.
    d. Use colors that only print well on color printers.

21. **For which task do you use selection handles?**
    a. Resizing a chart object
    b. Moving a chart object
    c. Changing which chart object is selected
    d. Deleting a chart object

22. **What is the function of the ▥▾ button?**
    a. Changing the chart to display worksheet data by columns
    b. Changing the chart to display worksheet data by rows
    c. Hiding or displaying the legend
    d. Changing the chart type

23. **What button do you click in the Format Chart Area dialog box to change the texture of the chart background?**
    a. Fill Chart   c. Fill Chart Area
    b. Fill Effects   d. Fill Background

Skills Review

1. Plan a chart.
a. Use the Choose workbook command on the New Workbook task pane to open a copy of the file XL C-2 from the drive and folder where your Project Files are located.
b. Examine the worksheet data, and then consider what Excel chart types would best present this type of information.
c. Is the worksheet designed in such a way that it will be easy to create a chart? Would you recommend any modifications to the worksheet?

2. Create a chart.
a. Save the workbook as *Outdoor Trips Chart*.
b. Select cells A4 through C10, then click the Chart Wizard button on the Standard toolbar.
c. Specify the Bar Chart type in the Chart Type dialog box of the Chart Wizard.
d. Enter the title **Projected Trips** in the Chart Options step of the Chart Wizard dialog box.
e. Create the chart. The chart will look small and unfinished; you fix that in the steps below.

3. Move and resize a chart and chart objects.
a. Drag the chart so that the upper-left corner of the chart is aligned with the upper-left corner of cell A12.
b. Use the lower-right corner selection handle to drag the lower-right corner of the chart to align with the lower-right corner of cell G28.
c. Click and drag the legend to the upper-right corner of the chart area.

4. Change the chart type.
a. Display the Chart toolbar if necessary, then change the chart type to Pie Chart.
b. Change the chart type to Line Chart. (Use the ScreenTips to identify each chart button if necessary.)
c. Change the chart type to 3-D Bar Chart.
d. Change the chart type back to Bar Chart.
e. Save your changes.

5. Add axis labels and gridlines.
a. Change the font of the x-axis labels to Book Antiqua.
b. Change the font of the y-axis labels to Arial.
c. Use the Font Size list arrow on the Formatting toolbar to change the font size of the Y-axis labels to 9.
d. Open the Chart Options dialog box.
e. Click the Gridlines tab, then click the Major gridlines check box for the Value (Y) axis to clear it, click the Minor gridlines check boxes for both axes to place a check mark in them, then click OK.
f. Save your changes.

6. Change chart fonts and colors.
a. Click the chart title, then open the Format Chart Title dialog box.
b. Change the font to Times New Roman, and the font color to Sea Green.
c. Double-click one of the Totals '02 bars in the chart.
d. Change the color to Dark Green.
e. Double-click one of the Projected '03 bars in the chart.
f. Change the color to Light Green.
g. Save your changes.

7. Enhance a chart.
- **a.** Right-click the chart area, then open the Format Chart Area dialog box.
- **b.** Click the Patterns tab if necessary.
- **c.** Click the Fill Effects button, then click the Texture tab.
- **d.** Change the texture to Stationary.
- **e.** Open the Format Chart Title dialog box.
- **f.** Click the Shadow check box to add a check mark to it.
- **g.** Close the Format Chart Title dialog box.
- **h.** Save your changes.

8. Preview and print a chart.
- **a.** Add your name to the top of the worksheet.
- **b.** Select the chart, then open the Print Preview window.
- **c.** From Print Preview, open the Page Setup dialog box.
- **d.** Choose a built-in header that adds your name, the page number, and today's date.
- **e.** Close the Page Setup dialog box.
- **f.** Use the Zoom pointer to make sure that your chart and footer are correct on the page.
- **g.** Print the chart.
- **h.** Save your changes.
- **i.** Close the file, then exit Excel.

► Independent Challenge 1

Outdoor Designs is preparing an annual report with sales information from the past four quarters. Dean Holmes has asked you to prepare an area chart containing this information, which might be suitable for sending to the major accounts. Use the XL C-3 workbook to create an area chart, and experiment with other formats to see if you can highlight the information in even better ways.

- **a.** Open the file XL C-3 from the drive and folder where your Project Files are located, then save it as *Annual Sales Chart*.
- **b.** Create a stacked area chart of the data for the first four quarters of the year, using an appropriate chart title. (*Hint*: Click the Chart subtypes and look in the description below the subtypes for the name Stacked Area to find this chart.)
- **c.** Move the chart down in the worksheet, then enlarge it.
- **d.** Experiment with the following chart types: pie, doughnut, column, and pyramid. Would they be appropriate or inappropriate for the sales data? Why?
- **e.** Change back to the 3-D stacked area chart type.
- **f.** Change the font size of the labels for the values on the X- and Y-axes to 9 point.
- **g.** Change the chart area background to a solid color of your choice.
- **h.** Add a footer that contains your name to the chart.
- **i.** Save your changes, preview the chart, print it, then close the file.

Independent Challenge 2

The Maple Leaf Pet Hospital, located in Vancouver, British Columbia, is evaluating its July business. George St. Clair, the office manager, wants to know what percentage of time employees spend treating each type of animal. This information will be useful when it's time to hire additional staff. Use the XL C-4 workbook on your Project Disk to create a pie chart that shows what percentage of visits each type of animal accounts for in July. Also use the chart to settle a bet you have with George that pigs accounted for more than 10% of the total July business.

a. Use the Choose workbook command on the New Workbook task pane to open a copy of the file XL C-4 from the drive and folder where your Project Files are located, then save it as *Animal Visits Chart*.

b. Create a 3-D pie chart of the data with the title Services by Animal Type.

c. Move the chart over in the worksheet, then enlarge it.

d. Use the Data Labels tab of the Chart Options dialog box to add labels to each slice of the pie. After you close the Chart Options dialog box, click and drag individual data labels as necessary so the chart is easy to read.

e. Separate the Pigs pie slice from the pie chart. (*Hint*: You will need to click the Pigs pie slice to select it, then drag it up and away from the pie to "explode" it.)

f. Who wins the bet?

g. Add your name to the worksheet.

h. Save your changes, preview the worksheet with the chart, print it, then close the file.

 # Independent Challenge 3

An innovative new art gallery is conducting research to determine how many people viewed a recent exhibit featuring popular local artists. They want you to create an area chart that depicts the number of people who attended over a six-month period and includes a breakdown of men, women, and children (under age 10), and seniors (over age 65) who attended. The attendance data is stored in the XL C-5 worksheet; you just need to create the chart.

a. Use the Choose workbook command on the New Workbook task pane to open a copy of the file XL C-5 from the drive and folder where your Project Files are located, then save it as *Art Exhibit Chart*.

b. Create a stacked area chart of the data with the title Local Artist Show Attendance. How does this chart type meet the art gallery's needs?

c. Move the chart down in the worksheet, then enlarge it.

d. Change the title font to 20-point Times New Roman.

e. Add labels to the X- and Y-axes, named Month and Visitors, respectively.

f. Change the font size of the value labels on the X- and Y-axes to 10 point.

g. Change the chart background to an attractive texture.

h. Change the color of the chart title, then add a shadow box.

i. Add your name to the footer for the worksheet.

j. Save your changes, preview the chart, print the chart, then close the file.

Independent Challenge 4

When a movie is released, the studio pays close attention to its weekend gross amount as compared to its total gross. Sometimes the ratio of weekend gross to total gross indicates whether the movie is still popular. Use the World Wide Web to find information for last weekend's top grossing films. Then create an Excel chart to show the relationship between the weekend gross and the total gross of the top five film's revenues.

a. Start a blank Excel workbook, and save it as *Movie Box Office Chart* in the drive and folder where your Project Files are located.

b. Log on to the Internet and use your browser to go to www.altavista.com. Click the Arts & Entertainment link or search for a related Web site that provides movie box office information, such as www.ew.com.

c. Enter the movie name, weekend gross, and total gross for each movie listed. (You may also want to create a column containing the number of weeks a movie has been out, if that information is available.)

d. Create a chart for the five top grossing films. Choose an appropriate chart type for displaying the weekend gross versus the total gross.

e. Add an appropriate title and axis titles to the chart. Format the labels so they are easy to read.

f. Format the chart using the commands and techniques you learned in this unit.

g. Log off the Internet, and close your browser.

h. Add your name to the top of the worksheet.

i. Save your changes, preview the worksheet with the chart, print the worksheet, then close the file.

FIGURE C-19

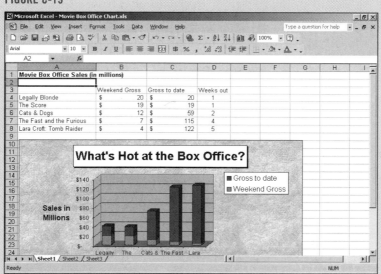

► Visual Workshop

Create the chart shown in Figure C-20 using the commands and techniques you learned in this unit. Save the workbook as *Candy Growth Chart* to the drive and folder where your Project Files are located. Add your name to the worksheet. Save your changes, preview the chart, print it, then close the file.

FIGURE C-20

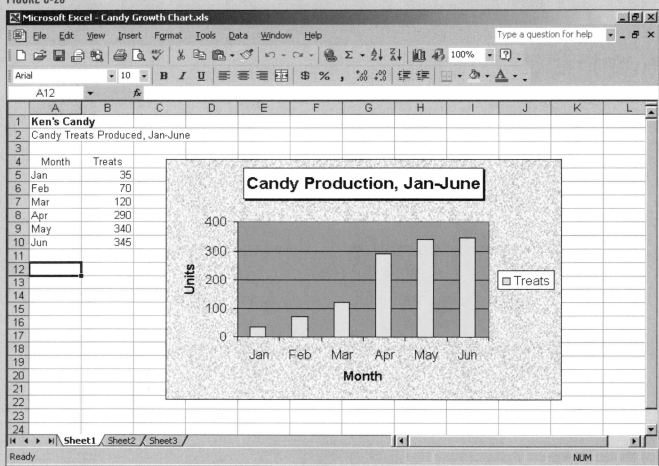

Creating

a Database

Objectives

- ▶ **Understand databases**
- ▶ **Create a database**
- ▶ **Design a table**
- ▶ **Modify a table**
- ▶ **Create a data entry form**
- ▶ **Enter data into a form**
- ▶ **Add and edit records**
- ▶ **Print a database and exit Access**

In this unit you learn about Microsoft Access 2002, the database program in Microsoft Office. A **database** is a collection of information organized in tables and stored electronically in a file. A database can contain information of any kind, from sales and financial records about your business, to lists of school friends and associates, and even the compact discs in your music collection. ➤ In this unit you'll help Elizabeth Fried, the database administrator for Outdoor Designs, use Access to create a database to help Outdoor Designs keep track of customers. After you create the database, you will create a data entry form and practice entering, editing, and manipulating data in it. You will then print the database and exit Access.

Understanding Databases

Database programs such as Access are powerful tools for both storing and retrieving information. Before you start using Access, you need to know some basic concepts about databases and database programs.  Elizabeth has assigned you the task of keeping track of each Outdoor Designs customer by creating a database with the customer's company name and contact information. Before you get started, you review some basic database concepts.

Details

Working with a database involves:

► ### Storing information in a database

Access stores information in **tables**, such as the sample table shown in Figure A-1, which contains information that a pet goods supplier, Sammy's Pet Supply, maintains about their pet store customers. Each row in the table is called a **record**, and contains all the information about a particular pet store. Records consist of **fields**, which contain information about one aspect of a particular record, such as an account number or company name. The column headings in the table are called **field names**. Because entering data in the rows and columns format of a table is tedious, you can create a form to make data entry easier. A **form** is a user-friendly window that contains text boxes and labels that let users easily input data, usually one record at a time. A form is based on a table. Figure A-2 shows a form that Sammy's Pet Supply might use to enter data about each pet store customer.

► ### Retrieving information from a database

Once a database is filled—or **populated**—with data, you can use Access queries or reports to retrieve the information in meaningful ways. A **query** extracts data from one or more tables in a database according to criteria that you set. For instance, in the pet store example, you could create a query that displays all the pet store customers in Texas. You can also create reports that print out selected information from the database. A **report** is a summary of information pulled from the information, specifically designed for printing.

► ### Working with relational databases

What makes Access so powerful is that it is a relational database. A **relational database** is a database that lets you store data in multiple tables that relate to each other. The benefit of this is that you can enter data once in individual tables and retrieve information from all or several of the tables as you need it. For instance, look at Figure A-3, which shows the structure of the Sammy's Pet Supply database. This database contains two tables; Customers and Customer Orders. Each table has mostly unique information, but they share Account Number as a common field. This common field is called the **primary key field**, which is a field that uniquely identifies a record among all other records in a database. Because the primary key field links the two tables, you could create a query that pulls out information from both tables. For instance, you could create a query that displays all the customers who live in Texas who placed orders greater than $5000 in the last three months.

FIGURE A-1: Sample database table containing records and fields

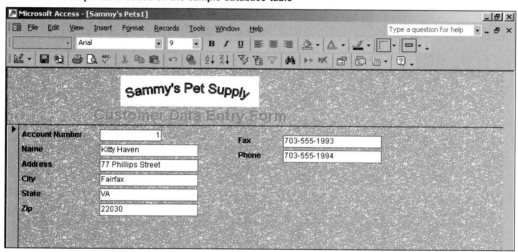

FIGURE A-2: Sample form based on the sample database table

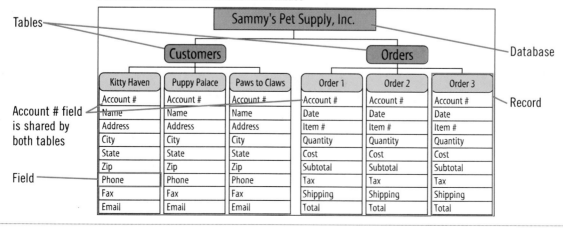

FIGURE A-3: Structure of relational database

Creating a Database

You start Access as you would any other Office application: by clicking the Start menu, pointing to Programs, then clicking Microsoft Access. When Access first opens, you see the Database toolbar and the New File task pane open in the Access window. You can use the New File task pane to open an existing database, to create a new database from scratch or based on an existing one, or to create a new database by using a template. To create a new database from scratch, you click the Blank Database command on the New File task pane, then save it to a location on your hard drive. After you save the database, the database window opens, where you choose from one of seven **database objects**, or program components that you can create and modify in Access to store, retrieve, and work with data. See Table A-1 for descriptions of each of the database objects available in Access. ✎ To start your work on the Outdoor Designs customer database, you need to start Access, open a blank database and save it, then open a new table.

1. Click the **Start button** on the taskbar, point to **Programs**, then click **Microsoft Access**
   Access starts and the program window opens, with the New File task pane on the right. See Figure A-4.

2. Click **Blank Database** in the New section of the New File task pane
   The File New Database dialog box opens, where you specify a name for your new database and the location where you want to save it. You must save a database before you can begin working in it.

3. Make sure the Look in box displays the drive and folder where your Project Files are stored, type **Outdoor Designs** in the File name box, then click **Create**
   The Outdoor Designs database window opens, as shown in Figure A-5. Currently, the Tables button is selected in the Objects list, and the right pane displays three choices for how to create a table: Create table in Design view lets you create and organize the fields before you begin entering data; Create table using wizard lets you start with a sample table and modify it to suit your needs; Create table by entering data lets you type data in a blank table and specify the fields as you work.

4. Double-click **Create table in Design view**
   The new table opens in Design view. Access includes many views for working with a database object. When creating a table, for example, you can switch between Design view and Datasheet view.

Trouble?
If your Table Properties sheet is open, click its Close button to close it.

5. Click the **Design view window Maximize button** if the table window does not fill the screen
   The Design view window now fills the screen, as shown in Figure A-6. You use this window to specify the fields you want in your table. The title bar displays the filename of the object you are creating (currently Table1) and the type of object you are creating (Table). Below the toolbar is a grid with the headings Field Name, Data Type, and Description. You use the grid area below the headings to specify the field names for your table, and other information you plan to enter about the data you intend to enter in the table.

Choosing the best Access file format

When you create a new database, Access saves it in Access 2000 format by default. Using Access 2000 as the default file format has the advantage of letting users of the previous version of Access view your database. You can tell which file format Access is using by looking at the title bar of the database window. If you are creating a complex database, however, and don't care whether users of previous versions of Access can view it or not, you might wish to change the file format to Access 2002. If you are working with a large database, saving it in Access 2002 format will improve performance. To change the file format, click Tools on the menu bar, click Options, click the Advanced tab, click the Default File Format list arrow, then click Access 2002.

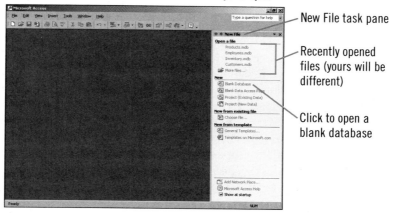

FIGURE A-4: Access window with New File task pane open

New File task pane

Recently opened files (yours will be different)

Click to open a blank database

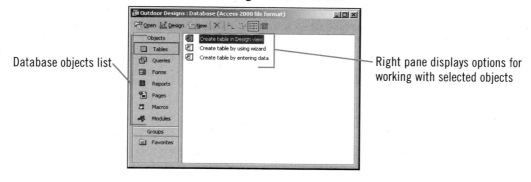

FIGURE A-5: Outdoor Designs database window

Database objects list

Right pane displays options for working with selected objects

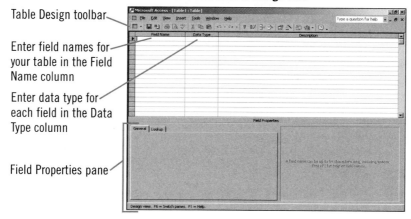

FIGURE A-6: Blank table in Design view

Table Design toolbar

Enter field names for your table in the Field Name column

Enter data type for each field in the Data Type column

Field Properties pane

TABLE A-1: Database objects available in Access

object	description
Table	A collection of data on a specific topic organized in rows (records) and columns (fields)
Query	A set of criteria specified to retrieve data from a database
Form	A window that lets you enter, edit, and display information in a database one record at a time
Report	A summary of database information designed specifically for printing
Page	A Web page that is linked to a database, for use when creating a form for a Web site
Macro	A set of actions that perform a task
Module	A set of procedures in Visual Basic that is stored together as one named unit

Designing a Table

Before you can begin entering data in a database table, you need to design the table, by specifying the kinds of information it will contain and the order in which the information should appear. You use Design view to design the structure of your table, and you can return to this view any time you need to make additional changes to the table's structure. To design a table, you need to specify a name for each field and its **data type** (such as text or currency). See Table A-2 for a description of data types you can use. You can also include a description for each field so that other users of the database will understand exactly what type of data they should enter in each field. Once you've entered your fields, you can set **field properties**, or specifications for what kind of data can be entered, for each field. Before saving your table, you should specify the primary key field, which Access needs to uniquely identify each record in the database. The order in which you enter fields in Design view determines the structure of the data entry form that Access creates; you can change the order of fields in a database table or in a form by rearranging them in Design view. You are ready to design the Customers table by entering field names and specifying the data type of each. You decide to designate Customer ID as the primary key field.

Steps

QuickTip

Field names can contain up to 64 characters, including letters, numbers, spaces, and some special characters.

1. **Make sure the insertion point is in the first field name cell, type Customer ID, then press [Tab]**
   Customer ID appears as the first field in the table, and the insertion point moves to the Data Type column. You use this column to specify what type of data the user will be able to type in the field.

2. **Click the Data Type list arrow, then click AutoNumber**
   The AutoNumber data type assigns a unique sequential number to each record in the database as you enter it.

3. **Click the Primary Key button ⬕ on the Table Design toolbar**
   A key icon appears to the left of the Customer ID field, identifying it as the primary key field for this table. The Customer ID field is a good field to use as the primary key field because the AutoNumber data type guarantees that each record is uniquely identified, even if some fields contain information that is identical to fields in other records. For instance, if you have two customers that share the same address, their Customer ID number will uniquely identify them.

QuickTip

To navigate in Design view, you can click the cell you want to move to, you can press [Tab] or [Enter] to move to the next cell or [Shift][Tab] to move to the previous cell, or you can use the arrow keys.

4. **Press [Enter] twice to move to the second field name cell, type Company, then press [Tab]**
   The default data type, Text, appears in the Data Type column, as shown in Figure A-7. If you don't specify a field type, the Text data type is assigned. This data type lets you enter text (such as names), numbers that don't require calculations (such as phone numbers), or combinations of text and numbers (such as street addresses). The Field Properties pane shows the default information for this field. For example, the **field size** is 50 characters (which you can increase up to 255 characters) and the user is not required to enter a value for this field.

5. **Click in the third field name cell, type First Name, press [Enter] three times to accept the Text data type and move to the fourth field name cell, type Last Name, then press [Enter] three times**

6. **Enter the remaining field names and data types using Figure A-8 as a guide, pressing [Tab] as needed to move to the next cell**

7. **Click the Save button ⬕ on the Table Design toolbar**
   The Save As dialog box opens, as shown in Figure A-9. Although you have already saved the Outdoor Designs database, each object you create within the database needs to be saved and named individually.

8. **Type Customers, then click OK**
   The table is saved with the name "Customers" as part of the Outdoor Designs database.

FIGURE A-7: Specifying field names and data types in Design view

Primary key field indicator

Field Properties pane displays information about selected field

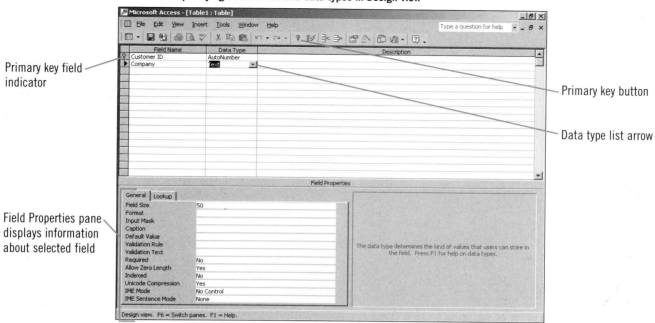

Primary key button

Data type list arrow

FIGURE A-8: Completed Customers table in Design view

Field Name	Data Type
Customer ID	AutoNumber
Company	Text
First Name	Text
Last Name	Text
Company or Department	Text
Billing Address	Text
City	Text
State Or Province	Text
Postal Code	Text
Country	Text
Contact Title	Text
Phone Number	Text
Fax Number	Text
Email Address	Text

FIGURE A-9: Save As dialog box

TABLE A-2: Common field data types

data type	description
Text	Text, numbers that don't require calculations, or a combination of text and numbers
Memo	Lengthy text (which can also contain numbers that don't require calculations)
Number	Numeric data to be used in calculations
Date/Time	Date and time values
Currency	Currency values and numeric data used in calculations
Yes/No	Fields that can contain only one of two values
AutoNumber	Unique sequential number that Access assigns to each new record; can't be edited

Modifying a Table

You can modify the structure of a table in Design view. You can add and delete fields, change data types, add **field descriptions** to help document the database by explaining the contents of a field, and change field properties. **Field properties** are specifications that dictate how field data is stored, handled, and displayed. You enter and edit information in the Field Properties pane by first selecting the field, then pressing [F6] to move to the Field Properties pane. ⬛ Elizabeth is pleased with the table, but she wants you to delete three fields, add two new fields, then change the field properties for four existing fields.

Steps

1. Click the **Company Or Department field row selector**, as shown in Figure A-10, right-click the selected row, then click **Delete Rows**

   When you delete a field, you lose all the data that is stored in that field. You have not entered any data in this database, so you can delete fields without losing any data.

2. Click the **Country field row selector**, right-click the selected row, click **Delete Rows**, click the **Contact Title field row selector**, right-click the selected row, then click **Delete Rows**

3. Click in the first blank field name cell below Email Address, type **Customer Since**, press **[Tab]**, click the **Data Type list arrow**, click **Date/Time**, press **[Tab]**, type **Date of first sale**, then press **[Tab]**

   You will use this field to track how long a customer has been with Outdoor Designs, based on the date of their first purchase.

4. Type **Active** in the next field name cell, press **[Tab]**, click the **Data Type list arrow**, click **Yes/No**, press **[Tab]**, then type **Yes if less than six months since last purchase; No if more than six months**

QuickTip

The Field Properties panel changes depending on which field is currently selected. Different data types have different field properties.

5. Click in the **State Or Province field name cell**, delete **Or Province**, press **[F6]** to move to the Field Properties panel, then type **2** in the Field Size text box

   You specified the field size as 2 because you want to record the states by their two-letter abbreviations. Because 2 is now specified for Field Size, users will not be able to enter more than two digits for this field. See Figure A-11.

QuickTip

To switch back to Design view from Datasheet view, click the Design button ▨ on the toolbar.

6. Click the **Save button** 🖫 on the Table Design toolbar, then click the **Datasheet View button** ▦

   Your screen should look like Figure A-12, with the Datasheet window open and maximized. In this view, you can see the field names you entered in Design view just below the toolbar. To see all the field names in the table, scroll to the right. Below the field names is a row of empty cells that you can populate with data. This first cell in this row is the field for the Customer ID, and contains the text (AutoNumber). The number will be generated automatically by Access as you complete each record. As you complete each row of data, a new row appears.

FIGURE A-10: Selecting a row to delete

Current field indicator

Step 1

Field row selectors

Enter explanation of field contents in Description column

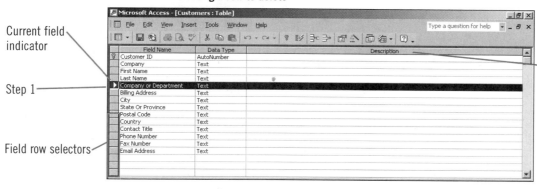

FIGURE A-11: Changing a field property

Edited field name

New fields added

Field size changed to 2

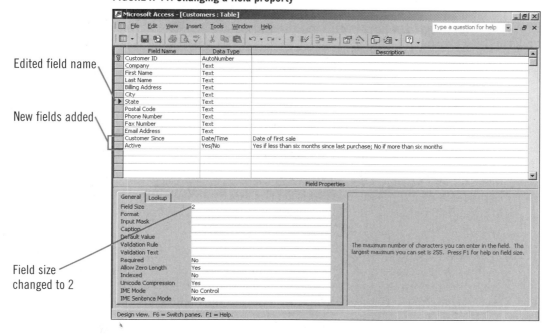

FIGURE A-12: Modified table in datasheet view

Customer ID field will be filled in automatically as records are entered

Field names appear as column headings

All other fields are blank

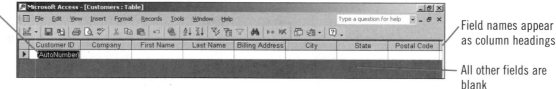

Access 2002

CLUES TO USE

Working in Datasheet view

Datasheet view is not ideal for entering data because it can be tedious and cause eyestrain to work in a rows-and-columns format where you see all the records at once. You also risk introducing errors into your database. The best view for entering large amounts of data is Form view, where you see just one record at a time. However, if you have to, you can insert records in Datasheet view by using the New Record command on the Insert menu or the New Record button on the toolbar. Datasheet view is most useful for those times when you want to see all the records at once, perhaps to compare them to each other for consistency. You can also use Datasheet view to quickly search for individual records, or sort records according to any criteria you set. To widen a column of cells so that you can read a field's entire contents, click a field in the column you want to adjust, click Format on the menu bar, click Column Width, then click Best Fit.

Access 2002

Creating a Data Entry Form

Though it is possible to enter information directly into the cells in Datasheet view, it's far easier to use a form to enter data. A form usually displays the fields for one record at a time, and contains **form controls**, which are devices for inputting data, such as text boxes, scroll bars, or check boxes. There are many ways to create a form. You can create a form using the Form Wizard to step you through the process, or you can design the form yourself in Design view. ✎ To complete the Customers table for the Outdoor Designs database, your colleagues will need to enter data for hundreds of customers. To make the process easier and minimize errors, you decide to create a data entry form by using the Form Wizard.

QuickTip
You can click the AutoForm button 🖼 on the Table Design or the Table Datasheet toolbar when a table is open to create a form automatically, based on the information in the table.

1. Click the **Close Window button** on the Datasheet window
   The datasheet window closes and the database window appears.

2. Click the **Forms button** in the Objects list in the database window, then double-click **Create form by using wizard**
   The Form Wizard dialog box opens, as shown in Figure A-13. Here you choose the database table on which the form is based and select the fields to include in the form.

3. Verify that **Table: Customers** is selected in the Table/Queries list box

4. Click the **Select All Fields button** >>
   All the fields from the Available Fields list box move into the Selected Fields list box. Because this form will be used to enter all the data into the Customers table, you want to use all the available fields.

5. Click **Next**
   Clicking Next accepts the current settings in the dialog box and moves you to the next dialog box in the Form Wizard. Clicking Back moves you to the previous dialog box, where you can make additional changes if you change your mind about an option.

6. Verify that **Columnar** is selected in the Layouts list, then click **Next**

7. Verify that **Standard** is selected in the Style list box, then click **Next**

8. Type **Customer Data Entry Form** in the What title do you want for your form text box, verify that the **Open the form to view or enter information option button** is selected, then click **Finish**
   Review all the elements of the form shown in Figure A-14. Form view displays records one at a time, with form controls for each field in the underlying table. A form control consists of a **field label**, which is the name of the field ("Company," for example), and the **field value text box**, into which users enter data. You will enter data into this form in the next lesson.

9. Click the **Save button** 🖫 on the Form Design toolbar

FIGURE A-13: Form Wizard dialog box

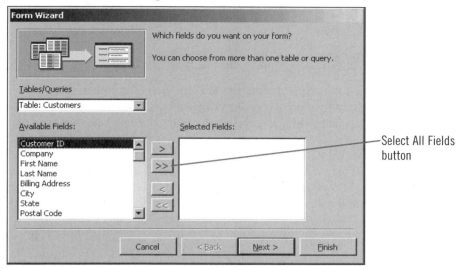

Select All Fields
button

FIGURE A-14: Customer Data Entry Form in the Form view window

Form name
appears here

Field names

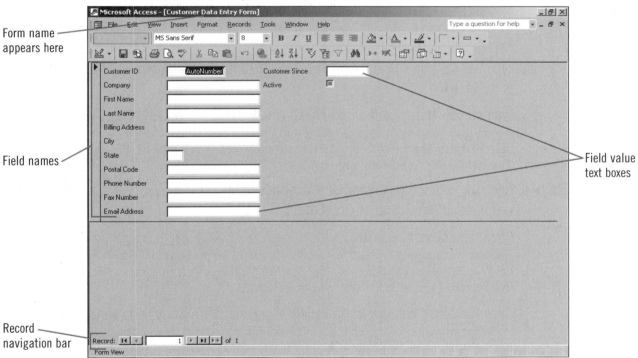

Field value
text boxes

Record
navigation bar

Entering Data into a Form

The best view for entering data is Form view. Working in Form view lets you concentrate on one record at a time, so that you can easily check the accuracy of your data as you enter it. To enter data for a particular field, you click in the field value text box, then type the appropriate data. To ensure that data is entered accurately, the field properties you set in Table Design view sometimes limit what you can enter in a form. For example, if you typed "Mass" in the state field, the form would only accept the first two letters, "Ma," because you set the Field Size for this field to 2.  It's a good idea to test a form after you create it, to make sure you can enter data easily and accurately. You are ready to test the form by entering a record in Form view for the company Cambridge Kite Supplies.

Steps

1. Press [Tab]

The insertion point moves to the Company field value text box. You didn't need to enter any data in the Customer ID field value text box because you assigned the AutoNumber data type for this field when you designed the table.

2. Type Cambridge Kite Supplies in the Company field

"Cambridge Kite Supplies" appears in the Company field. Notice that the Customer ID field value text box now contains the number 1. Access automatically assigned this number because this is the first record in the table.

> **QuickTip**
>
> To move to the previous field in a form, press [Shift][Tab]. To delete the contents of a selected field, press [Delete].

3. Press [Tab], type Stephen, press [Tab], type James, press [Tab], type 1437 Main Street, press [Tab], type Cambridge, press [Tab], type MA, then press [Tab]

The contact name, street address, city, and state are entered in the appropriate fields. See Figure A-15.

4. Type 02142, press [Tab], type 617-555-2323, press [Tab], type 617-555-2424, then press [Tab]

5. Type stevej@kites.com, press [Tab], type 6/31/96, then press [Tab]

An error message appears, indicating that the date you entered is not a valid one (June has only 30 days). This message appears because you set the data type for this field to Date/Time. This data type accepts only valid dates.

> **QuickTip**
>
> Pressing [F2] selects all the contents of a field value text box.

6. Click OK, click in the Customer Since field value text box, press [F2] to select all the text, type 6/30/96, then press [Enter]

7. Click the Active check box

A check mark appears in the box, indicating a yes response in the Active field. The Yes/No field can appear as either a check box or a Yes/No field, depending on the field property. The first record is complete, as shown in Figure A-16.

8. Click the Close Window button in the Customer Data Entry Form window

Data that you enter or edit in a form is automatically saved, so you can close the form without saving it first. The Customer Data Entry Form appears as an object on the Forms tab in the Outdoor Designs database window.

FIGURE A-15: Entering data in a field value text box

This field value was generated automatically

Record number indicates this is first record

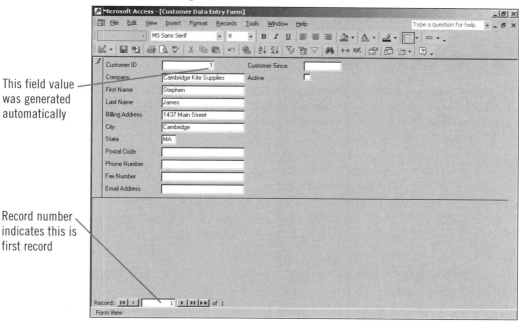

FIGURE A-16: Complete record entered in form

Selected field

Field name description appears on status bar to help user enter data correctly

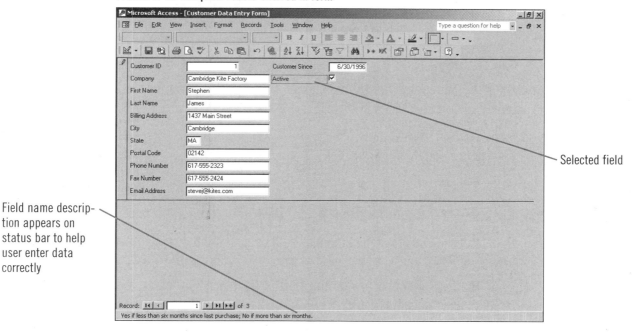

Adding and Editing Records

Almost inevitably, the data in a database needs correcting or revising. You also need to update your database from time to time by adding or deleting records. You can edit data or delete records in either Datasheet view or Form view. In either view, you edit fields by selecting the text in the field or field value text box, typing in the new entry, then pressing [Enter]. You add records using the New Record command on the Insert menu or the New Record button on the toolbar. In Datasheet view, you can add a record by clicking in the last field of the last record, then pressing [Tab]. You delete records using the Delete Record button on the toolbar. When your database contains more than one record, you can advance from one record to the next by using the record navigation buttons located just above the status bar. ➤ You need to add two more customers to the Customers table. You want to add the records using Form view, because it is the best view for data entry, and also make changes to two records.

1. **Click the Forms button in the Objects list, then double-click Customer Data Entry Form**
   The Customer Data Entry Form opens, as shown in Figure A-17. The record for Cambridge Kite Supplies is open and the number 1 appears in the Record indicator box at the bottom of the screen.

QuickTip

The New Record button is also located on the Record Navigation bar above the status bar.

2. **Click the New Record button ▸⁕ on the Formatting toolbar**
   A blank form for a new record opens, with the AutoNumber field value highlighted. The number 2 appears in the Record indicator box.

3. **Use the table below to complete the form for this record, then see Figure A-18**

Company	Mountain Air	Postal Code	98045
First Name	Lee	Phone Number	206-555-1541
Last Name	Allen	Fax Number	206-555-1542
Billing Address	40 Pond Street	Email Address	lee@air.com
City	Duvall	Customer Since	9/15/97
State	WA	Active	yes

4. **Click ▸⁕, then use the table below to complete the form for the third record**

Company	Butch's Outdoor Gear	Postal Code	94511
First Name	Butch	Phone Number	415-555-6222
Last Name	Panielo	Fax Number	415-555-6223
Billing Address	100 Bay View Ave.	Email Address	butch@outdoor.com
City	Bay City	Customer Since	5/20/99
State	CA	Active	yes

QuickTip

To edit a field value on a form, click in the field value text box, then press [F2].

5. **Click the First Record button ◄ on the Record Navigation bar**

6. **Double-click Supplies in the Company field value text box, type Factory, then press [Enter]**
   Cambridge Kite Supplies has changed its name to "Cambridge Kite Factory."

7. **Click the Next Record navigation button ▸ twice to display the record for Butch's Outdoor Gear, select 415-555-6223 in the Fax field value text box, then press [Delete]**

8. **Click in the Phone Number field value text box, press [F2] to select the phone number, right-click to open the pop-up menu, click Copy in the pop-up menu, click in the Fax field value text box, then click the Paste button 🖺**

9. **Close the Form view window, click the Tables button in the database window, then double-click Customers**
   The Customers table opens in Datasheet view. See Figure A-19.

FIGURE A-17: Customer Data Entry Form in Form view

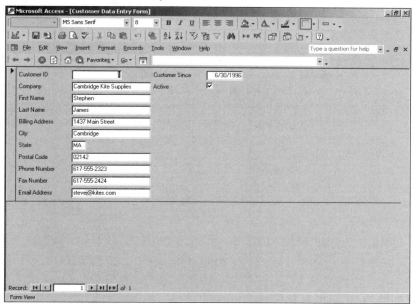

FIGURE A-18: Completed form for the second record

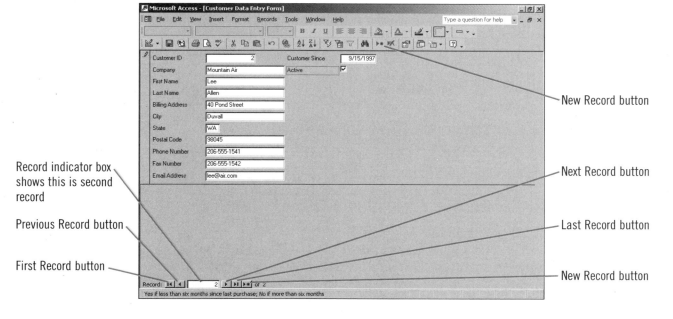

Record indicator box shows this is second record

Previous Record button

First Record button

New Record button

Next Record button

Last Record button

New Record button

FIGURE A-19: Three records in Datasheet view

Two new records

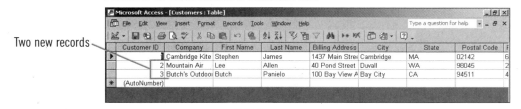

Printing a Database and Exiting Access

Entire databases are rarely printed because they often contain hundreds or even thousands of records; printing them all can be very time-consuming and impractical. However, printing one or more records for quick reference or mailing information is often useful. You decide to print the records in the Customer Data Entry Form to review your work with Elizabeth before you continue entering the remaining customers in the database.

Steps

1. Click the **Datasheet window Close button**, click the **Forms button** in the database window, then double-click **Customer Data Entry Form**
   The Customer Data Entry Form opens in Form view.

Trouble?

If the three records don't fit on one page, make sure that you are using one-inch margins and Portrait Orientation.

2. Click the **Print Preview button** on the Form View toolbar
   The Print Preview window opens, as shown in Figure A-20. By default, Access prints as many records as will fit per page. It turns out that all three records fit nicely on one page. In Print Preview, you can use the mouse pointer to zoom in or out on any part of the page.

3. Click the **Zoom button** on the Print Preview toolbar
   The page enlarges to fill the Print Preview window so you can get a better look at what will be printed. The pointer changes to 🔍 to indicate that the next time you click the page, the view will zoom out.

QuickTip

You can print the entire database, but not individual pages or records, from Print Preview. The Print command on the File menu lets you select specific pages for printing.

4. Verify that your printer is on and properly connected to your computer

5. Click the **Print button** on the Print Preview toolbar
   The page with the three records prints.

6. Click **Close** on the Print Preview toolbar
   You return to Form view.

7. Click the **Save button** on the Form View toolbar
   It is good practice to always save any changes you make during a working session before you exit Access.

8. Click **File** on the menu bar
   Clicking Close on this menu when a database object such as a table is open closes the object and keeps Access running. Clicking Exit closes all open objects and closes Access. See Figure A-21.

9. Click **Exit**
   The Outdoor Design database closes, and Access closes.

FIGURE A-20: Print Preview window

Zoom button

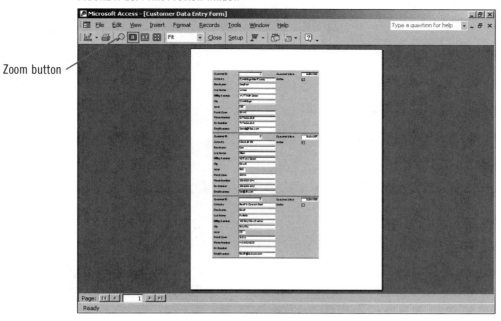

FIGURE A-21: File menu in Form view

Click Close to close open objects and keep Access running

Click Exit to close all open objects and exit Access

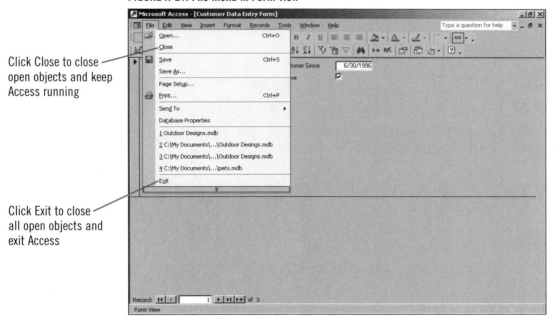

Practice

► Concepts Review

Label each of the elements of the Access window shown in Figure A-22.

FIGURE A-22

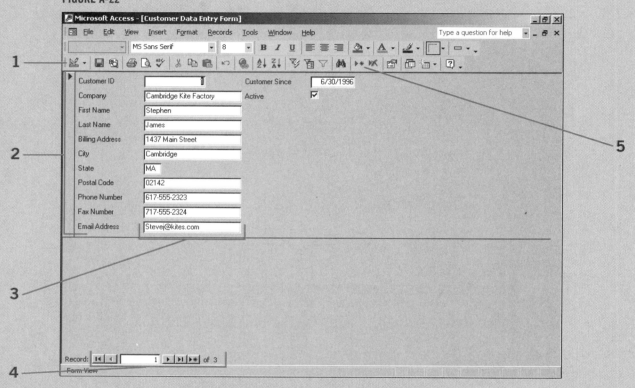

Match each of the terms with the statement that describes its function.

6. field control
7. field description
8. record
9. field properties
10. primary key field

a. Contains all the information about one person, business, or other entity
b. Makes sure each record in a database table is unique
c. Used for entering data on a form, such as a text box or check box
d. Provides useful information about a particular field for the person entering data in the field
e. Specifications for how data in a particular field is stored

Select the best answer from the list of choices.

11. What makes a relational database so powerful is that it:
   a. Lets you store information in multiple tables that are related to each other.
   b. Stores data electronically.
   c. Lets you sort information in ascending or descending order.
   d. Can store any kind of information.

12. The best view for entering data into a database is:
    a. Form view.
    b. Table design view.
    c. Datasheet view.
    d. Database view.

13. The best view for looking at all your records at once is:
    a. Database window.
    b. Datasheet view.
    c. Table design view.
    d. Form view.

14. To select all the contents of a field value text box on a form, press:
    a. [Tab].
    b. [F6].
    c. [Esc].
    d. [F2].

15. Which of the following is NOT a database object that is available in Access?
    a. Table
    b. Module
    c. Chart
    d. Macro

16. Which of the following methods is NOT used to insert a new record?
    a. Click in the last field of the last record in Datasheet view, then press [Tab].
    b. Click the New Record button on the toolbar.
    c. Choose the New Record command on the Insert menu.
    d. Click in any field value text box, then press [F6].

17. Which of the following activities is NOT possible to do in Design view?
    a. Set field properties
    b. Add fields
    c. Delete fields
    d. Enter data into a database

18. Which of the following activities is NOT possible to do in Form view?
    a. Add a record
    b. Delete a record
    c. Add a field
    d. Edit data in a field value text box

19. In a Form, which of the following methods does NOT advance you to the next field value text box?
    a. Clicking in the field value text box
    b. Pressing [Enter]
    c. Pressing [F2]
    d. Using the arrow keys

► Skills Review

1. **Create a database.**
   a. Start Access.
   b. Click Blank Database in the New File task pane.
   c. Save the database as *Evergreen Camping Supplies*.
   d. Double-click Create table in Design View.
   e. Maximize the window.

2. **Design a table.**
   a. Verify that the insertion point is in the first field name cell, type **Item Number**, press [Tab], click the Data Type list arrow, then click AutoNumber.
   b. Designate the Item Number field as the primary key field.
   c. Use the table to the right to enter the field names and data types for the remaining fields in the table:
   d. Save the table as *Evergreen Inventory*.

Field Name	Data Type
Department	Text
Item	Text
Color	Text
Size	Text
Model	Text
Price	Currency
Manufacturer	Text
Season	Date/Time
Data entered by	Text

3. Modify a table.

a. Add a new field to the end of the table called On-Hand with the data type Text.

b. Add a new field to the end of the table called Last Quantity Ordered with the data type Text.

c. Add a new field to the end of the table called Last Date Ordered with the data type Date/Time.

d. Delete the Season field.

e. Change the Field Size field property for the Size field to 20.

f. Save the changes to the table.

g. Change to Datasheet view.

4. Create a data entry form.

a. Click the Close Window button in the Datasheet View window.

b. Click the Forms button in the Objects list in the Database window.

c. Use the Form Wizard to create a data entry form based on the Evergreen Inventory table.

d. Add all the fields to the form, use the Columnar layout, choose the Ricepaper style, name the form Evergreen Inventory Data Entry Form, then finish creating the form by choosing to open it to view or enter information. See Figure A-23.

5. Enter data into a form.

a. Use the table below to enter data into the form:

Department	Camping
Item	Tent
Color	Hunter green
Size	8' x 10' x 6'
Model	Dome
Price	$229.0
Manufacturer	Henderson Tents
Data Entered by	Your name
On Hand	55
Last Quantity Ordered	100
Last Date Ordered	3/1/03

b. Add a new record. Use the table below to enter data for the second record:

Department	Camping
Item	Adult Sleeping Bag
Color	Black
Size	39" x 84"
Model	Zero Degree Snuggler
Price	$95.99
Manufacturer	Stargazer Sleeping Bags
Data Entered by	Your name
On Hand	42
Last Quantity Ordered	150
Last Date Ordered	5/20/03

FIGURE A-23

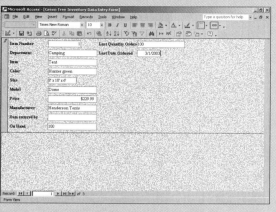

c. Insert a new record, then use the table below to enter data for the third record:

Department	Boating
Item	Inflatable Boat
Color	Red
Size	30" x 56"
Model	Two-person
Price	$39.99
Manufacturer	Marine Gear, Inc.
Data Entered by	Your name
On Hand	42
Last Quantity Ordered	75
Last Date Ordered	4/5/03

   d. Save your changes to the database.

6. **Add and edit records.**
   a. Verify that you are in Form view.
   b. Use the Record Navigation buttons to move to the first record.
   c. Select the Price field value.
   d. Type **279.99**.
   e. Press [Tab].
   f. Move to the last record.
   g. Change the Color field value to Blue.
   h. Save your changes to the database.

7. **Print a database and exit Access.**
   a. Click the Print Preview button.
   b. Verify that your fields and records look correct on both pages.
   c. Zoom in and out as needed to review the pages.
   d. Click the Print button.
   e. Click File on the menu bar.
   f. Close the form, saving changes if prompted.
   g. Exit Access.

 # Independent Challenge 1

You own and operate your own clothing company called TotWear, Inc. that makes handcrafted clothing for infants and toddlers. Up to now, you've been a one-person operation. But you recently expanded and hired several people to create a bigger inventory of your products. You decide to create a database to keep track of your products and monitor sales of each clothing item.

   a. Create a new, blank database, save the database as *TotWear*, and create a new table in Design view with the following fields and data types:

Field Name	Data Type	Field Name	Data Type
Product ID	AutoNumber	Quantity On Hand	Text
Item	Text	Unit Cost	Currency
Price	Currency	Washable	Yes/No
Size	Text	Data Entry by	Text
Material	Text		

b. Set the Product ID field as the Primary Key, then save the table as *Products*.

c. Create a form based on the Products table using a wizard, choosing the Columnar layout and a style you like. Save the form as *TotWear Products Form*. Add the following records to the form:

Item	Price	Size	Material	On Hand	Unit Cost	Washable?	Data Entered by
Bunny sleeper	$24.95	6 months	Cotton	37	$2.50	Yes	Your name
Denim dress	$29.95	3T	Denim	49	$5.75	Yes	Your name
Fleece poncho	$25.00	2T	Fleece	44	$8.25	Yes	Your name
Polar tunic	$21.00	3T	Fleece	22	$3.25	Yes	Your name
Capri pants	$19.95	3T	Cotton	25	$4.25	Yes	Your name

d. Print the database table in Form view, then close the database.

▶ Independent Challenge 2

As part of a long-term marketing strategy at the Sunset Spa, you decide to create a database of customers who have visited the spa for treatments. You will use the database to notify customers of special offers and events at the spa.

a. Create a new, blank database named *Sunset Spa* and create a new table in Design view that will track information about your customers and the types of services they have purchased at the spa.

b. Use Design view to design your table, adding at least 12 fields to it, only nine of which have the data type Text. Include at least one field each for the following data types: Date/Time, Yes/No, and AutoNumber.

c. Add the field Data Entry By that has a text data type.

d. Specify one of the fields as the primary key field.

e. Save the table as *Customers*, then create a form called *Customers*, based on the table, using the AutoForm button on the toolbar. (*Hint*: In the database window, make sure the Customers table is selected, click the AutoForm button to open the New Form dialog box, click AutoForm: Columnar, verify that the Customers table is selected as the data source, then click OK.)

f. Add five fictitious records to the database using Form view. Enter your name in the Data Entry By field value text box.

g. Print the database table, then close the database.

▶ Independent Challenge 3

As human resources manager for Little Guy Toys, you are responsible for tracking all employee records. You decide to create an electronic database of all full-time and part-time employees. This database will help you create reports for the president of the company.

a. Create a new, blank database named *Little Guy Toys* and create a new table in Design view using the fields and data types shown in the table to the right.

b. Choose one of the fields as the primary key, then save the table as *Employees*.

c. Add a field description to the Full time field that specifies that the user should enter Yes if the employee works more than 35 hours per week.

d. Use the Form Wizard to create a form based on the Employees table and use all the fields, the layout you think is best, the style of your choice, and the name *Employee Data Entry Form*.

Field Name	Data Type
Employee Number	AutoNumber
First Name	Text
Last Name	Text
Hire Date	Date/Time
Salary	Currency
Gender	Text
Full time?	Yes/No
Dept	Text

e. Add the following records to the database using Form view:

First Name	Last Name	Hire Date	Salary	Gender	Full time?	Dept
Sandra	Chan	4/22/01	52,000.00	F	Yes	Marketing
Cecil	Jose	5/7/98	30,000.00	M	No	Marketing
Carol	Brown	6/4/02	50,000.00	F	Yes	Products
Susan	Stillman	9/9/01	15,000.00	F	No	Legal
Anna	Hegenberger	5/10/02	37,500.00	F	Yes	Legal

f. Edit the first record to show your name instead of Sandra Chan's.

g. Print the table from Datasheet view, and then close the database.

 Independent Challenge 4

As manager of the Quick Stop Video Store, you keep track of all the movies that are for sale in the store. The owner of the store is from Australia and has decided to dedicate a room in his store to Australian videos. He has asked you to go online and do research on Australian films. He then wants you to create a database that provides information about each film. You will eventually use this database to track sales of these Australian videos for the store.

a. Log on to the Internet, go to a search engine site such as Google (www.google.com) or AltaVista (www.altavista.com) and research Australian videos. Find at least 10 that are of interest to you.

b. Start Access, create a new database named *Quick Stop Videos*, and then create a new table in Design view called *Australian Films* with the fields and data types shown in the table to the right:

c. Specify a primary key field for one of the fields.

d. Create a data entry form using a wizard. Choose an appropriate layout and style for the form. Save it as *Australian Films Form*.

e. Add records for eight Australian videos that you found on your search. Type your name in the Data Entry by field value text box.

f. Print the database from Form view and exit Access.

Field Name	Data Type
Category	Text
Director	Text
Movie Name	Text
Price	Currency
Release Year	Text
Starring	Text
Data Entry by	Text

Access 2002

► Visual Workshop

Create the database form shown below. (*Hint*: First create a new, blank database called *Comic Books*, then create a table called *Comics Inventory* that contains the fields shown in the form.) Use the form to add your name in the Title field. Save the form as *Comics Inventory Form*.

FIGURE A-24

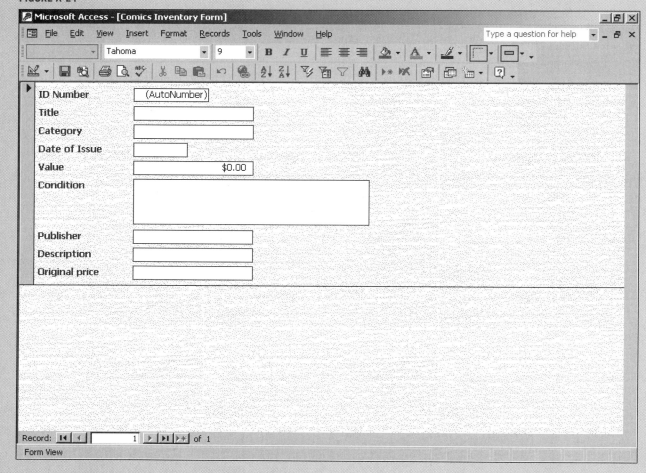

Working

with Forms and Data

Objectives

- ► **Open an existing database**
- ► **Modify a form's layout**
- ► **Format controls on a form**
- ► **Add a graphic to a form**
- ► **Filter a database**
- ► **Sort database records**
- ► **Create a query**
- ► **Protect a database**

Once you create a database, you can make entering data into it easier and more enjoyable by enhancing the appearance of forms. Once a database is populated with data, you can pull out the information you need by creating filters and queries and sorting the data in helpful ways. In this unit, you will learn how to open an existing database, and how to format a database form using fonts, styles, and graphic images. You will also learn how to search for information in a database by sorting data, using filters, and creating queries, as well as how to protect a database so that it cannot be modified without your permission.

Elizabeth Fried, the database administrator for Outdoor Designs, has put you in charge of customizing the Outdoor Designs database so that Sue Ellen Monteiro, the sales manager, can use it to track sales. You need to work with the database you created to answer some simple questions, improve the appearance of the data entry form, and add new fields to help employees who use it regularly. You also want to protect the database from unauthorized use.

Opening an Existing Database

Opening an existing database in Access is similar to opening a file in Word or Excel. To open an existing database, you can click the file on the Open a file list in the New File task pane, or you can click the More files command in the task pane and locate the drive and folder containing the database you want. If your computer is set up to display file extensions, you will notice that Access files have an .mdb extension. If you want to open an existing database and make changes to it while leaving the original file intact, you can use the Choose file command in the New File task pane to open a copy of the original file. The copy of the file that opens has the same file-name as the original file but ends with a number (e.g., "1") to distinguish it from the original file. ✏️ Elizabeth has asked you to make enhancements to the Customers form in the Outdoor Designs Sales Reps database. To get started, you decide to open the database and view the Customers table in both Datasheet view and Design view. Because you want to leave Elizabeth's original file intact, you will use the Choose File command to open a copy of the file.

1. **Start Access**

   The Access program window opens and displays the New File task pane on the right.

2. Click **Choose file** in the New File task pane, navigate to the drive and folder where your Project Files are located, click **Outdoor Designs Sales Reps**, then click **Create new**

   A copy of the original file opens. Notice that the database window title bar displays the filename "Outdoor Designs Sales Reps1", as shown in Figure B-1.

3. Click **Tables** in the Objects list if necessary, verify that the Customers table is selected, click **Open**, then maximize the **Customers: Table window**

   The Customers table opens in Datasheet view, as shown in Figure B-2. You can see that this table contains 12 records.

4. Click the **Design View button** 📐 on the Table Datasheet toolbar

   The Table opens in Design view. Notice that the CUSTOMERID field is the primary key field in this table.

5. Click the **Customers Table Close Window button**, click **Forms** in the Objects list, click **Customers** in the database window, then click **Open**

   The Customers form opens in Form view. You can see that it is a very plain looking form.

6. Click the **Design View button** 📐 on the Form View toolbar, then maximize the form window if necessary

   The Customers form appears in the maximized Design view window, as shown in Figure B-3. You use this view to make modifications to a form's layout. You can see that there are grid lines as well as two rulers in this view, one across the top of the window (the **horizontal ruler**) and one along the left side of the window (the **vertical ruler**). You use these rulers and grid lines to help place field labels, field value text boxes, and other controls or graphics on the form.

FIGURE B-1: Outdoor Designs Sales Reps database window

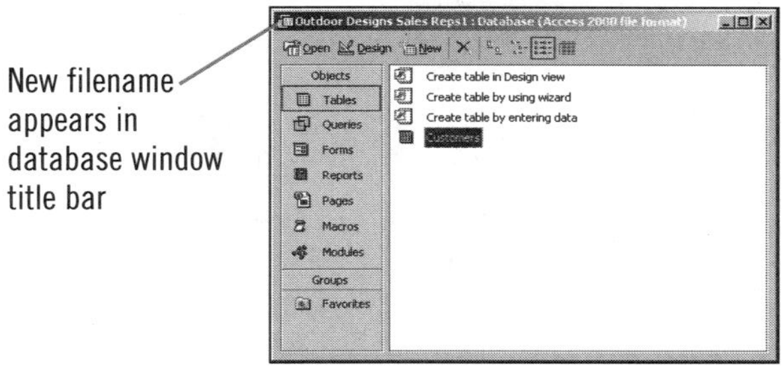
New filename appears in database window title bar
Outdoor Designs Sales Reps1 : Database (Access 2000 file format)
Objects
Tables
Queries
Forms
Reports
Pages
Macros
Modules
Groups
Favorites
Create table in Design view
Create table by using wizard
Create table by entering data
Customers

FIGURE B-2: Customers Table window in Datasheet view

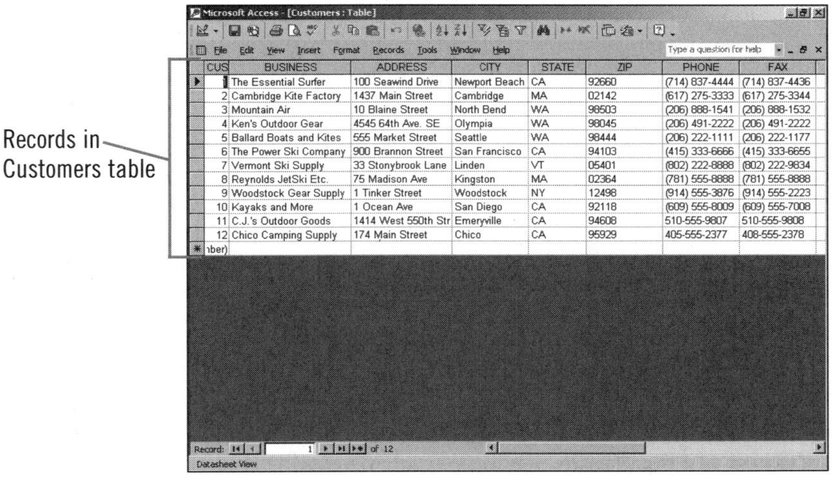
Records in Customers table
Microsoft Access - [Customers : Table]
CUS BUSINESS ADDRESS CITY STATE ZIP PHONE FAX
1 The Essential Surfer 100 Seawind Drive Newport Beach CA 92660 (714) 837-4444 (714) 837-4436
2 Cambridge Kite Factory 1437 Main Street Cambridge MA 02142 (617) 275-3333 (617) 275-3344
3 Mountain Air 10 Blaine Street North Bend WA 98503 (206) 888-1541 (206) 888-1532
4 Ken's Outdoor Gear 4545 64th Ave. SE Olympia WA 98045 (206) 491-2222 (206) 491-2222
5 Ballard Boats and Kites 555 Market Street Seattle WA 98444 (206) 222-1111 (206) 222-1177
6 The Power Ski Company 900 Brannon Street San Francisco CA 94103 (415) 333-6666 (415) 333-6655
7 Vermont Ski Supply 33 Stonybrook Lane Linden VT 05401 (802) 222-8888 (802) 222-9834
8 Reynolds JetSki Etc. 75 Madison Ave Kingston MA 02364 (781) 555-8888 (781) 555-8888
9 Woodstock Gear Supply 1 Tinker Street Woodstock NY 12498 (914) 555-3876 (914) 555-2223
10 Kayaks and More 1 Ocean Ave San Diego CA 92118 (609) 555-8009 (609) 555-7008
11 C.J.'s Outdoor Goods 1414 West 550th Str Emeryville CA 94608 510-555-9807 510-555-9808
12 Chico Camping Supply 174 Main Street Chico CA 95929 405-555-2377 408-555-2378
Record: 1 of 12
Datasheet View

FIGURE B-3: Customers form in Design view

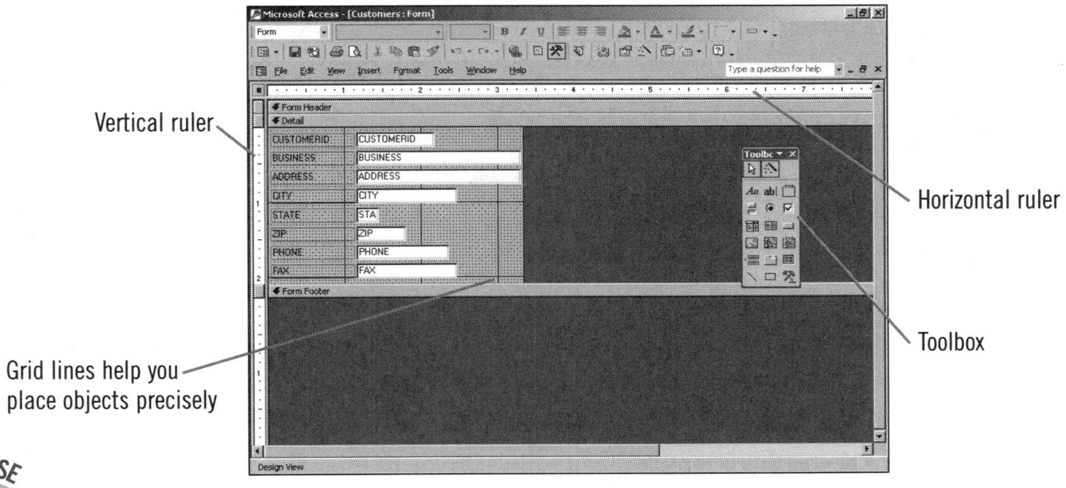
Vertical ruler
Horizontal ruler
Toolbox
Grid lines help you place objects precisely
Microsoft Access - [Customers : Form]
Form Header
Detail
CUSTOMERID
BUSINESS
ADDRESS
CITY
STATE
ZIP
PHONE
FAX
Form Footer
Design View

CLUES TO USE

Opening more than one database file at a time

If you have worked with other Office programs, you may expect to be able to work with many open database files at a time. In programs such as Microsoft Word or Excel, for example, you can switch between one or more open files by using buttons on the taskbar or through the Window menu on the menu bar. In Access, however, you can work with only one database file at a time. If you are working in one database file and then open a different database, the first file automatically closes. To work with more than one database at a time, you need to start Access again for each database you want to open. However, because Access is a relational database, you should design each database with all the tables, forms, and so on, that you need so you don't have to work with more than one database file at the same time.

Modifying a Form's Layout

Just as you can modify other Office files such as Excel workbooks and Word documents, you can edit forms and other database objects you create in Access. To modify an Access object, rather than the data in the database, you work in Design view. In Design view you can modify the layout of forms and other objects by moving, adding, or deleting controls. You add controls using the **field list**, which you can open using the Field List button on the Form Design toolbar. There are three types of controls you can use in a form: bound, unbound, and calculated. A **bound control** has a table or query as its information source. An **unbound control** is a control that is created in the form and has no connection to data in a table. Labels, titles, and graphics are all examples of unbound controls. A **calculated control** uses a mathematical equation from the form as its data source, which may include a bound control. For instance, a calculated control might calculate the total of two or more other bound controls. You can make visual changes to the form using the Format tab of an object's property sheet. The **property sheet** is a window that lets you view or change the selected object's properties. ◄ The Customers form does not contain the Sales field or the Rep field from the Customers table. You want to add these two fields as controls to your form, and then rearrange other controls to improve the layout, so it will be easier to enter data in the form.

1. Position the pointer on the right edge of the form, then, when it changes to ↔, drag the edge to the 6" mark on the horizontal ruler, as shown in Figure B-4
   The form is now wider and can accommodate the two additional fields you want to add.

2. Click the **Field List button** 🔲 on the Form Design toolbar
   The field list opens.

3. Scroll down the field list, then click and drag **REP** to the intersection of the 4" mark on the horizontal ruler and the 1" mark on the vertical ruler, as shown in Figure B-5
   By dragging the field name from the field list, you add both the bound control (the field value text box) and the unbound control (the field label) for the REP field to the form.

4. Drag **SALES** from the Field list to just below the REP field at the intersection of the 4" mark on the horizontal ruler and the 1½" mark on the vertical ruler, then click the **Field List Close button**

5. Click the **CUSTOMERID field value text box**
   Both the CUSTOMERID field value text box and the CUSTOMERID field label are selected, because clicking a field value text box also selects its accompanying field label. Notice that small squares, called **handles**, appear around both controls indicating that they are selected. You use handles to resize or move the selected control.

6. Place the pointer on the upper-right edge of the CustomerID field value text box so that the pointer changes to 🖐, then drag the text box so that its right edge is flush with the grid line at the 5" mark on the horizontal ruler

7. Press and hold [Shift], click the **REP field value text box**, click the **SALES field value text box**, release [Shift], click **Format** on the menu bar, point to **Align**, then click **Right**
   This right-aligns the CUSTOMERID, SALES, and REP fields with respect to each other.

8. Double-click the **CUSTOMERID field label**, to open the property sheet, click the **Format tab** if necessary, double-click **CUSTOMERID** in the Caption text box, type **Customer ID Number**, click the **Property Sheet close button**, then compare your screen to Figure B-6

9. Click the **Form View button** 🔲 on the Form Design toolbar, then review the modified form

QuickTip

To delete a control, select the control then press [Delete]. Deleting a control in Design view does not delete the field from the table, only from the form. To add the control back to the form, open the field list and drag the control to a location on the form.

QuickTip

The Align commands on the Format menu and the Align toolbar buttons work differently. The menu commands align controls with respect to each other on the form. The toolbar buttons align text within the text boxes.

FIGURE B-4: Widening the form

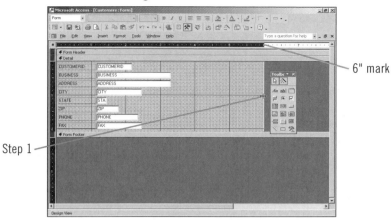

6" mark

Step 1

FIGURE B-5: Dragging a field from the field list

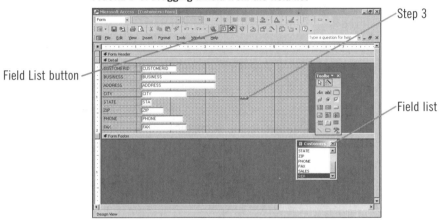

Step 3

Field List button

Field list

FIGURE B-6: Modified form in Design view

Repositioned and edited field label and field value text box

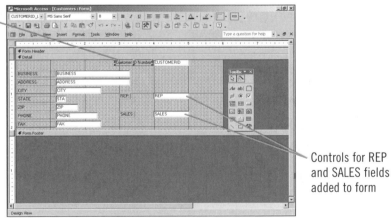

Controls for REP and SALES fields added to form

CLUES TO USE

Parts of the form

A form is divided into three sections: Form Header, Detail, and Form Footer. Each section is identified by a bar, which contains the section name and an arrow pointing to the section. The Form Header appears at the top of each form and can contain additional information, such as a company title or logo. The Detail section displays the field labels and data for each record. The Form Footer appears at the bottom of each form and can contain totals, instructions, or command buttons. You can resize a section by dragging the top edge of the section's bar up or down.

Formatting Controls on a Form

You can make formatting enhancements to a form by changing the font type and the style of labels and field values, adding borders and special effects, and adding labels. The Formatting (Form/Report) toolbar contains buttons for many common formatting changes, such as changing a label's border, font style, font size, color, and adding special effects. Those formatting options not available on the toolbar must be changed through the control's property sheet. To make this form simple to use as well as attractive for the sales representatives, you decide to change font size and color of the field labels, and to add a title label to identify the form.

Steps 1 2 3 4

1. Click the **Design View button** on the Form View toolbar, click the **Customer ID Number field label**, click the **Font/Fore Color list arrow** on the Formatting toolbar, click the **red square** (first column, third row), then click the **Bold button**

   The Customer ID Number field label is red and bold, and stands out from the other field labels. However, it no longer fits in the field label text box because of the bold formatting.

2. Position the pointer over the left edge of the Customer Number field label box so that it changes to ↔, then drag the edge to the left until all the text fits

QuickTip

Clicking a field label selects only the label; it does not select its associated field value text box.

3. Click the **BUSINESS field label**, press and hold [Shift], click the **ADDRESS field label**, click the **CITY field label**, click the **STATE field label**, click the **ZIP field label**, click the **PHONE field label**, click the **FAX field label**, click the **REP field label**, click the **SALES field label**, then release [Shift]

   Selection handles appear around all the field labels you selected.

4. Click the **Font/Fore Color button list arrow** on the Formatting toolbar, click the **blue square** (sixth column, second row), then click the **Bold button**

   All the field labels you selected now appear in blue and bold. See Figure B-7.

5. Click the **SALES field value text box**, click the **Line/Border Width button list arrow** on the Formatting toolbar, click **Line/Border Width 3**, click the **Special Effect button list arrow**, then click the **Special Effect: Shadowed button**

6. Position the pointer on the **top edge of the Detail bar** so that the pointer changes to ✚, then drag the edge down to the ½" mark on the vertical ruler

   The Form Header section opens. You can place additional information in this area.

Trouble?

If the Toolbox is not open on your screen, click the Toolbox button on the toolbar.

7. Click the **Label button** on the Toolbox, when the pointer changes to ⁺A click in the top-left corner of the Form Header section and drag down to the bottom of the Form Header section and over to the 5" mark on the horizontal ruler, then release the mouse button

   A label text box now fills the Form Header area.

QuickTip

Since blue was the last color you used, the Font/Fore Color button is set to blue.

8. Type **Outdoor Designs Customer Entry Form** in the label text box, press **[Enter]** to select the label control, click ▲, click the **Font Size list arrow** on the Formatting toolbar, click **18,** then click the **Center button**

   The label is formatted in blue, 18-point, MS Sans Serif font, as shown in Figure B-8.

9. Click the **Form View button** on the Form Design toolbar

   Your screen should look similar to Figure B-9.

FIGURE B-7: Form with font color changes and resized control

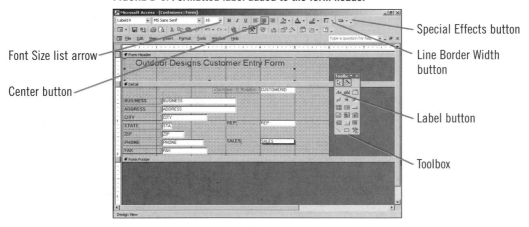

Font/Fore Color button

Selected field labels with blue color applied

FIGURE B-8: Formatted label added to the form header

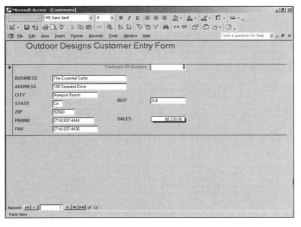

Special Effects button

Font Size list arrow

Line Border Width button

Center button

Label button

Toolbox

FIGURE B-9: Modified Customers Form in Form view

Changing tab order

When you set up a form, the order in which you will advance when you press [Tab] to enter data into the form is determined by the order of the fields in the table that the form is based on. If you want to change this for any reason, open the form in Design view, then click View on the menu bar to open the Tab Order dialog box. Drag the field selectors to reorder the listed fields, then click OK.

Adding a Graphic to a Form

You can add graphic images such as logos, clip art, or photos to a form to personalize it or make it more appealing. There are two ways to add an image: you can add one either as a bound image or as an unbound image. A **bound image** is a picture or object that is stored in a table as part of an individual record, and therefore changes with each record. For instance, a photo of a person that is stored as part of an employee record in an employee database is an example of a bound image. An **unbound image** is not tied to a data source, and stays the same for each record. For instance, a company logo added to a form header is an example of an unbound image; it stays the same for every record. To add an unbound image to a form, you use the Image button on the Toolbox. You decide to add an image of a tree as an unbound image to the Outdoor Designs database form to give the database an outdoor theme. You want to add the image in the Header section, below the label you created.

1. Click the **Design View button** 🔲 on the Form View toolbar
   The form appears in Design view.

2. Click the **Image button** 🔲 on the Toolbox, then, when the pointer changes to ⁺🖼, click in the Form Header area just below the **C** in "Customer Entry Form"
   The Insert Picture dialog box opens. You use this dialog box to locate and insert the image file you want.

3. Click the **Look in list arrow**, navigate to the drive and folder where your Project Files are located, click **tree.jpg**, then click **OK**
   An image of a tree is inserted below the Form Heading label, as shown in Figure B-10. Notice that the bottom edge of the Form Header area has dropped down to the 1½" mark on the ruler, to make room for the picture.

4. Point to the bottom edge of the Form Header section, then, when the pointer changes to ╪, drag the edge up to the 1" mark on the vertical ruler
   The top edge of the Detail area is now closer to the tree image, improving the look of the form.

5. Click the **Form View button** 🔲 on the Form Design toolbar
   Compare your screen to Figure B-11.

6. Click the **Save button** 🔲 on the Form View toolbar, click **File** on the menu bar, then click **Close**
   The form closes, and you return to the database window.

FIGURE B-10: Inserted image in form in Design view

Inserted image →

Form Header area expanded to make room for image →

Image button →

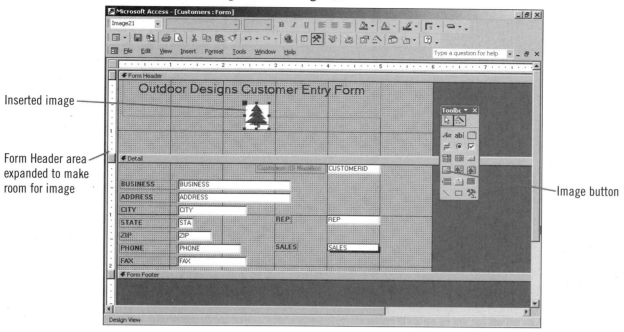

FIGURE B-11: Form with graphic image in Form view

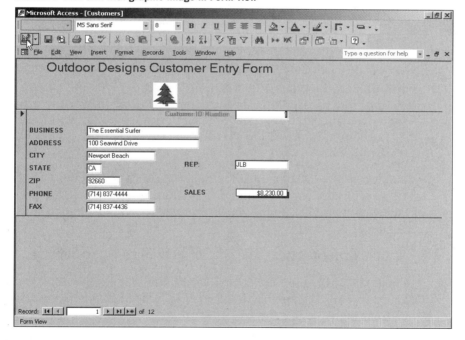

Adding a bound image to a form

If you want to add a bound image to a form, you first need to add a field to the underlying table that will contain the image, so that you can populate this field with an appropriate image for each record. To do this, open the table, switch to Table Design view, then insert a new field that has the data type OLE Object. Close the table, then open the form in Design view

and drag the new image field from the Field list to the Details section of the form. Next, switch to Form view, open a record, click the Object frame to select it, click Insert on the menu bar, click Object, click the Create from File option button in the Insert Object dialog box, click Browse, select the image file you want to insert, then click OK.

Access 2002

Filtering a Database

A **filter** organizes the records in a database to display only those records that meet certain criteria. For example, you might want to filter a database to see only the records for customers who live in Chicago, or those for customers who made a purchase within the past six months. **Criteria** are conditions or qualifications that must be met for a record to be displayed. The simplest way to filter a table is to select a field that matches your criterion, then use the Filter By Selection command to display those records that match the selection. If you want to specify more than one criterion for your filter, you use the Advanced Filter/Sort command on the Records menu to open the Filter window where you specify your criteria. A filter cannot be saved as an object, but you can save it as part of the table or form you are working on, and reapply it next time. You can also print the results of a filter or save a filter as a query. Sue Ellen has asked you to determine which California-based companies purchased at least $5000 worth of Outdoor Designs products. You decide to create a filter to display records that meet these criteria.

Steps

1. Click **Tables** in the Objects list, click the **Customers** table, click **Open**, then maximize the datasheet window if necessary
   The Customers table appears in the maximized Datasheet view.

2. Click in the **State field** of the first record (for the Essential Surfer), click **Records** on the menu bar, point to **Filter**, then click **Filter by Selection**
   Five records containing CA in the state field appear in the Datasheet window, as shown in Figure B-12.

3. Click the **Remove Filter button** on the Table Datasheet toolbar
   The filter is removed, and all the records in the table appear.

4. Click **Records** on the menu bar, point to **Filter**, click **Advanced Filter/Sort** to open the Filter window, then click the **Clear Grid button** on the Filter/Sort toolbar
   It's a good idea to clear the grid of any preexisting criteria before you apply a filter. The Filter window contains a top and a bottom pane. The top pane displays the Customers Table field list. The bottom pane contains the **filter design grid**, where you specify fields and their criteria for the filter.

5. Scroll down the Customers Table field list, then double-click **SALES**
   The Sales field is copied to the first column of the filter design grid in the lower pane. Double-clicking a field in the field list automatically copies it to the first available column in the filter grid.

6. Click the **Criteria cell** in the Sales column, then type **>5000**

7. Double-click **STATE** in the field list, type **CA** in the State Criteria cell, then press **[Enter]**
   Compare your screen to Figure B-13. Access adds quotation marks "CA" to distinguish this text from values.

8. Click the **Apply Filter button** on the Filter/Sort toolbar to apply the filter and view the filtered records in the Datasheet window, then drag the horizontal scroll box if necessary to view the Sales field
   The Essential Surfer, with purchases of $8230, and Chico Camping Supply, with purchases of $5890, are the only two records matching the filter. Compare your screen to Figure B-14.

9. Click the **Remove Filter button** on the Table Datasheet toolbar, click the **Customers Table Close Window button**, then click **Yes** to save your changes

Results of Filter by Selection

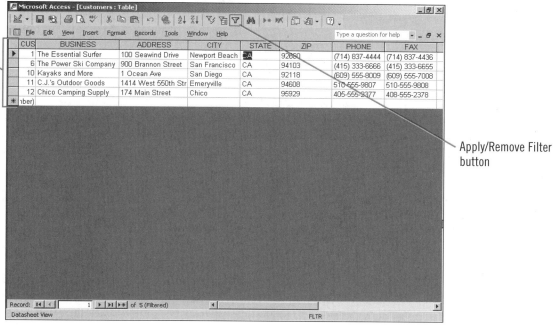

Apply/Remove Filter button

FIGURE B-13: Filter grid with criteria specified

Field List

Clear Grid button

Criteria set to show stores in CA with sales greater than $5000

Design grid

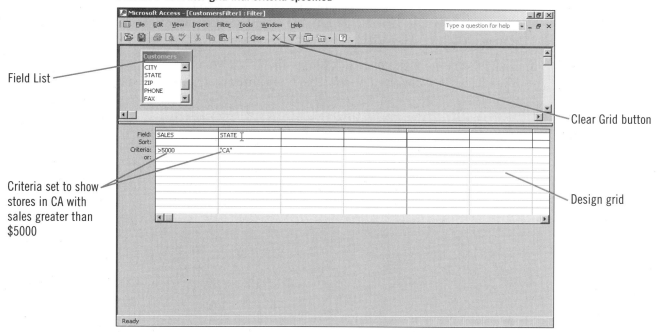

FIGURE B-14: Filtered table in Datasheet view

Only records that meet the criteria set in the Design grid appear

Access 2002

Sorting Database Records

You can rearrange, or **sort**, the records in your database in alphabetical or numerical order. When you sort your database, you need to specify the primary field for the sort. For example, in a customer database you would sort records by the BUSINESS, ZIP, or SALES field. You also must specify whether to sort the database in ascending order (alphabetically from A to Z or numerically from 0–9) or descending order (alphabetically from Z to A or numerically from 9–0). Unlike a filter, which only shows you the records that match your filter criteria, all the records in the database are displayed when you use the Sort command; they are simply reorganized. ✎ You want to sort the database alphabetically by company name to match other records in the Outdoor Designs.

1. **Open the Customers table**

2. **Click in any record in the BUSINESS field on the datasheet**
   The insertion point appears in the BUSINESS field. You can sort on a field either by selecting the entire column or by simply clicking any record in the field. At the moment, the datasheet is sorted in ascending order by Customer ID, as shown in Figure B-15.

3. **Click the Sort Ascending button 🔼 on the Table Datasheet toolbar**
   The records are now sorted in alphabetical order by business name, as shown in Figure B-16.

4. **Scroll to the right if necessary, click the SALES field, then click the Sort Descending button 🔽 on the Table Datasheet toolbar**
   The records are now sorted in descending order by sales amounts, as shown in Figure B-17. You see that Reynolds JetSki has had the highest sales this year, with $8900 in sales.

5. **Click File on the menu bar, click Close, then click No**
   Your changes are not saved, so the table is organized as it was before you sorted the records.

Sorting on more than one field

Sometimes you want to sort your records using more than one field. For example, you might wish to sort primarily by state, but also by customer name, so that within each state, the records are alphabetized. To sort on more than one field, click Records on the menu bar, point to Filter, click Advanced Filter/Sort on the submenu. Double-click the fields by which you want to sort in the field list so that they are copied to the field columns in the filter design grid, set the sort criteria in the Sort cells, then click the Apply Filter button on the toolbar.

FIGURE B-15: Datasheet sorted in ascending order by CustomerID

Records sorted in ascending order by CustomerID field

Sort Ascending button

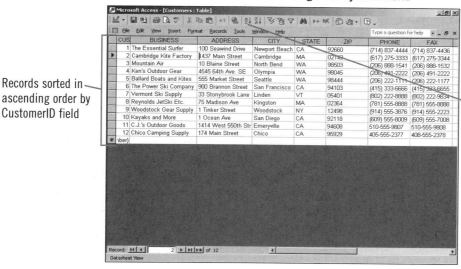

FIGURE B-16: Records sorted alphabetically by business name

Sort field

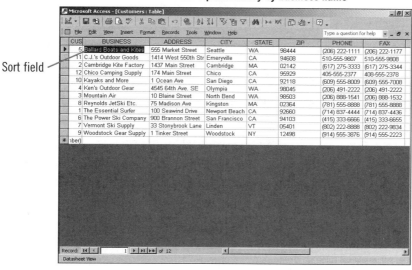

FIGURE B-17: Records sorted in descending order by Sales

Sort Descending button

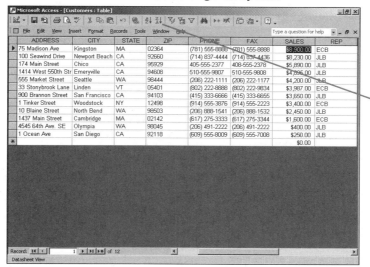

Creating a Query

A **query** is a database object that extracts data from one or more tables in a database according to criteria that you set. You can use a query to pull together information from several tables. Queries are similar to filters, but more powerful. A query lets you display only the fields you have specified, unlike a filter, which shows all of the table's fields. A query can also be saved as an object; a filter cannot. Records resulting from a query look like a table but are merely a view based on the query. The most commonly used query is the **select query**, in which records are collected and viewed, and can be modified later. ✏️ You want to design a simple query to create a list of customers in alphabetical order with their sales rep. You also want to create a query that shows the customers assigned to each sales representative.

Steps 1 2 3 4

1. **Click Queries in the Objects list, click New, click Design View, then click OK**
   The Show Table dialog box opens in the Select Query window, as shown in Figure B-18. The Customers table is the only available table, and it is selected by default.

2. **Click Add, click Close, then maximize the Query1: Select Query window**
   The Query design grid looks similar to the Filter/Sort design grid. You first add the fields you want to display in the query results by double-clicking them in the field list to copy them to the first available column in the design grid. Then you specify the criteria and a sort order for each field in the design grid area.

3. **Double-click BUSINESS in the field list, then double-click REP in the field list**
   The Business field appears in the first column of the design grid and the REP field appears in the second column of the design grid.

4. **Click in the Sort cell in the BUSINESS column, click the Sort list arrow, then click Ascending**
   This sorts the query in ascending order by business name.

5. **Click the Datasheet View button 🔲 on the Query Design toolbar**
   The results of this simple query appear, showing the Business and Rep fields with all the records in alphabetical order, as shown in Figure B-19.

QuickTip
Fields will appear in the order you place them in the design grid. You can insert new fields between existing ones and move fields by dragging the columns.

6. **Click the Design View button 🔽 on the Query Datasheet toolbar, click the Criteria cell in the REP column, type ECB, then press [Enter]**
   You have created a query to show only those customers who are assigned to Elizabeth Baxter, Rep ECB. See Figure B-20.

7. **Click 🔲, view the results, click the Save button 🔲, type Elizabeth's Customers in the Query name Save As text box, then click OK**

QuickTip
You can print the results of a query at any time by clicking the Print button on the toolbar.

8. **Click 🔽, double-click ECB in the Criteria cell for the REP field, type JLB, click 🔲, view the results, click File on the menu bar, click Save As, type Jon's Customers, then click OK**
   Now you have created a query for the other sales representative by simply modifying the criteria in the REP column and saving the revised query with a new name.

9. **Click the Print button 🖨 on the Query Datasheet toolbar, click File on the menu bar, then click Close**
   Both queries are saved as objects in the database file and appear in the database window. If records are added to the database, you can open these queries to see the updated information for each sales representative.

FIGURE B-18: Select Query window

Available tables you can add to the query are listed here

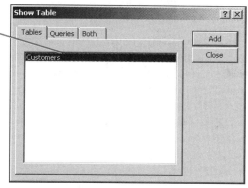

FIGURE B-19: Query results

Fields specified in query

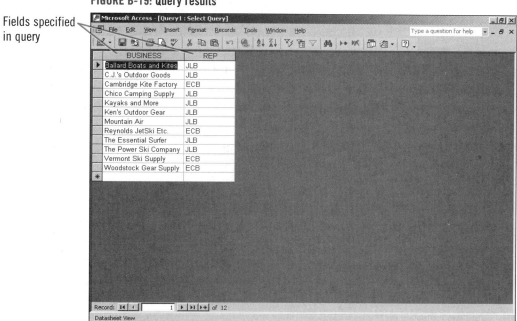

FIGURE B-20: Query design grid with criteria

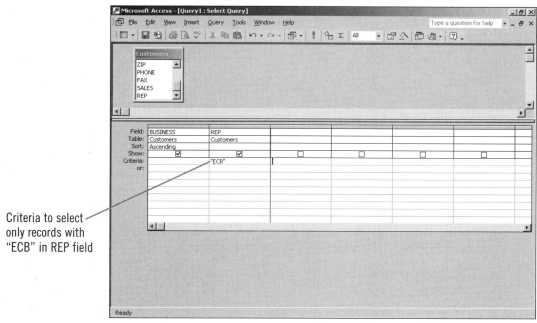

Criteria to select only records with "ECB" in REP field

Access 2002

Protecting a Database

You can protect a database from unauthorized viewing or modification by setting a password and by encrypting the database file. Setting a **password** means that to open the database file users must enter the correct characters in a dialog box. **Encrypting** further protects a database by compacting and scrambling the database file if it is opened by a utility program or other program in an attempt to bypass the password. **Decrypting** a database reverses the encryption process. ✎ To create a password-protected database, you must open it in **exclusive mode**, which means that no other users (on a network, for example) have access to it while it's open. Because this database contains sensitive data, Elizabeth wants you to password protect and encrypt the database.

Steps 1 2 3 4

1. Click **File** on the menu bar, click **Close**, click **File** on the menu bar, click **Open**, click the **Look in list arrow**, navigate to the drive and folder where your Project Files are located, click **Outdoor Designs Sales Reps1**, click the **Open list arrow**, then click **Open Exclusive**

   The Outdoor Designs database opens and, because you have exclusive rights to it, you are able to set a database password.

2. Click **Tools** on the menu bar, point to **Security**, then click **Set Database Password**

   The Set Database Password dialog box opens, as shown in Figure B-21, where you can enter and verify a password.

QuickTip

Asterisks, not characters, appear in the Password and Verify text boxes to further protect your password. Therefore, you must be careful when typing your password because you cannot verify your typing on the screen.

3. Type **OHIOstate**, press **[Tab]**, type **OHIOstate** again, then click **OK**

   Passwords are case-sensitive, so you must pay attention to capitalization when you enter and verify the password.

4. Click **File** on the menu bar, then click **Close**

   You can't encrypt or decrypt a database when it is open. In a **multiuser environment**, which permits more than one person to modify the same set of data at the same time, all users need to close the database before it can be encrypted.

5. Click **Tools** on the menu bar, point to **Security**, then click **Encrypt/Decrypt Database**

   The Encrypt/Decrypt Database dialog box opens, displaying the database files in this drive and folder location.

6. Click **Outdoor Designs Sales Reps1** as shown in Figure B-22, then click **OK**

   Because a password is required to get back into the database, the Password Required dialog box opens.

7. Type **OHIOstate**, then press **[Enter]**

   The Encrypt Database As dialog box opens, prompting you to enter a new filename for the encrypted database. If you specify the name of the database file that you chose to encrypt, the original file is automatically replaced with the encrypted version. That way, if an error occurs, the original file isn't deleted.

QuickTip

If you choose an encrypted file in the Encrypt/Decrypt Database dialog box, Access decrypts the file instead of encrypting it.

8. Click **Outdoor Designs Sales Reps1** in the File list box, click **Save**, then click **Yes** when prompted to replace the existing file

   The database has a password and is also encrypted. To decrypt the file, you would click Tools on the menu bar, point to Security, then click Encrypt/Decrypt.

9. Type **OHIOstate** in the dialog box, click **File** on the menu bar, then click **Exit**

FIGURE B-21: Set Database Password dialog box

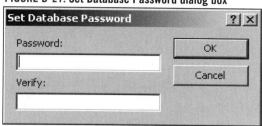

FIGURE B-22: Encrypt/Decrypt Database dialog box

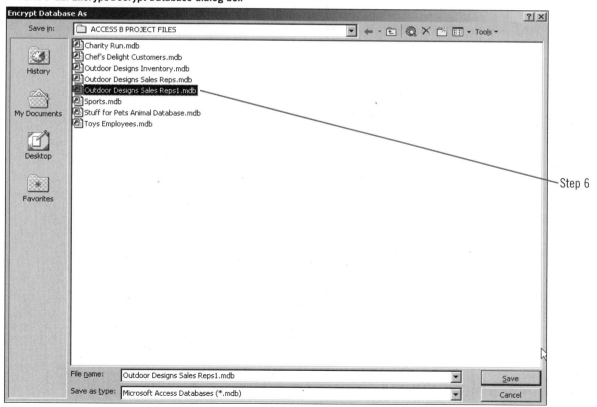

Practice

▶ Concepts Review

Label each of the elements of the Access window shown in Figure B-23.

FIGURE B-23

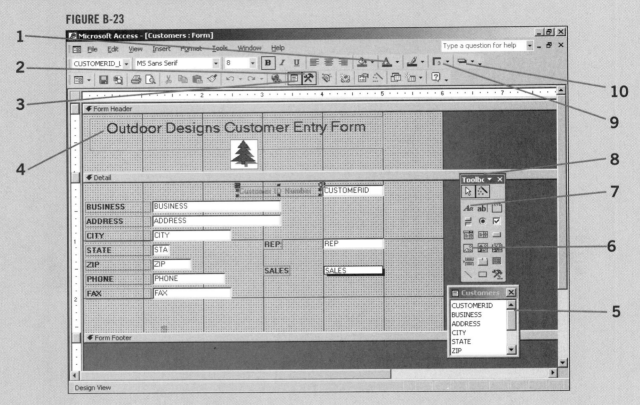

Match each of the buttons with its description.

11. Datasheet View   a.
12. Sort Descending   b.
13. Apply Filter   c.
14. Design View   d.
15. Clear Grid   e.
16. Field List   f.
17. Sort Ascending   g.

Select the best answer from the list of choices.

18. To create a text label on a form, you should:
   a. Drag a label text box, then type text into it.
   b. Click anywhere on the form, then start typing.
   c. Press [Ctrl][Enter], then start typing.
   d. Double-click anywhere on the form, then start typing.

19. Which of the following cannot be saved as an object in Access?
   a. A query
   b. A filter
   c. A table
   d. A form

20. In order to be able to set a password you must:
   a. Open the database in Exclusive Mode.
   b. Have a special code.
   c. Close all open applications.
   d. Encrypt the database.

21. If a database table has a state field, the best way to get a quick view of all customers who live in Florida is to:
   a. Use a filter to display Florida customers.
   b. Sort the database by state.
   c. Create a form with the state field.
   d. Search for California in the state field.

22. A control that is created in a form and has no connection to data in the underlying table is called a(n):
   a. Bound control.
   b. Unbound control.
   c. Calculated control.
   d. Property control.

23. A control that has a table or query as its information source is called a(n):
   a. Bound control.
   b. Unbound control.
   c. Calculated control.
   d. Property control.

24. A window that lets you view or make changes to a selected object is called the:
   a. Field list.
   b. Toolbox.
   c. Property Sheet.
   d. Design grid.

Skills Review

1. Open an existing database.
a. Start Access.
b. Use the Choose file command on the New File task pane to open a copy of the Outdoor Designs Inventory database file from the drive and folder where your Project Files are located.

2. Modify a form's layout.
a. Open the form Inventory Form in Form view, maximize the window, then switch to Design view.
b. Widen the Inventory form to 6".
c. Open the field list, then add the REORDER DATE field to the form, positioning it to the right of the ITEM NUMBER field at the 4" mark on the horizontal ruler.
d. Add the ON-HAND field and position it just below REORDER DATE on the form.
e. Use the [Shift] key to select the REORDER DATE field and the ON-HAND field, then right-align these fields.
f. Drag the Detail section down to create a 1½" vertical space in the Form Header area.
g. Create a label text box in the Form Header area that extends from the 1" mark on the vertical ruler down to the 1.5" mark on the vertical ruler, and over to the 5.5" mark on the horizontal ruler, then type **Inventory**.
h. Press [Enter] to select the label, then format the label in 24-point green (fourth column, second row of the palette). Center-align the label. You will use the space above the label to insert a graphic.

3. Format controls on a form.
a. Change the font color of the ITEM NUMBER field label and the ON-HAND field label to blue, then apply bold formatting.
b. Change the font color of all the remaining field labels on the form to green bold. If necessary, resize any field label text boxes so that all the text fits.
c. Change the font size of the ON-HAND field value text box to 12-point, then resize the control so that the data fits inside it.
d. Add a border around the ON-HAND field value text box using the Line Width 2 style, click the Special Effect button list arrow, then click the Shadowed style.

4. Add a graphic to a form.
a. Click the Image button on the toolbox.
b. Click in the Form Header area, above the Inventory label, then insert the file *logo1.jpg* from the drive and folder where your Project Files are located.
c. Reposition the graphic so that it is centered above the Inventory label.
d. View the form in Form view. Your form should look similar to Figure B-24.
e. Type your name in the DATA ENTRY BY field value text box for the first record, then print and save the form.

FIGURE B-24

5. Filter a database.

   a. Open the Inventory table in Datasheet view.

   b. Click in the DEPARTMENT field of the first record (Camping), click Records on the menu bar, point to Filter, then click Filter by Selection to display all the items from the Camping department.

   c. Click the Remove Filter button on the Table/Datasheet toolbar.

   d. Click Records on the menu bar, point to Filter, click Advanced Filter/Sort, then clear the grid of any preexisting criteria.

   e. Create a filter to find all items whose price is more than $25.00 using the criteria >25.00.

   f. Apply the filter, view the results, and print the datasheet showing your filtered results.

   g. Click the Remove Filter button, then create a new filter that finds all items of which there are fewer than 15 on hand (*Hint*: use the less than sign [<] in the filter grid).

   h. Apply the filter, view the results, then print the datasheet showing your filtered results.

   i. Click the Remove Filter button on the Table/Datasheet toolbar.

6. Sort database records.

   a. Click any record in the PRICE field in the datasheet.

   b. Sort the database by PRICE in descending order, then print the datasheet.

   c. Sort the database by DEPARTMENT in ascending order, then print the datasheet.

   d. Sort the database by REORDER DATE in descending order, then print the datasheet.

   e. Close the table datasheet without saving the changes.

7. Create a simple query.

   a. Click Queries in the Objects list.

   b. Create a new query in Design view.

   c. Add the Inventory table to the Query design grid, then close the Show Table dialog box.

   d. Add the ITEM, ITEM NUMBER, PRICE, and DATA ENTRY BY fields, in that order, to the Query design grid.

   e. Specify that the query results should be sorted by PRICE in ascending order.

   f. View the datasheet to see the query results.

   g. Save the query as *Items with Prices in Ascending Order*.

   h. Add the DEPARTMENT field to the Query design grid.

   i. Add a criterion to display only those items in the Camping department (*Hint*: In the Criteria cell for Camping, type **=camping**).

   j. View the results in Datasheet view.

   k. Type your name in the DATA ENTRY BY field for the first record.

   l. Print the results using the Print button on the Query Datasheet toolbar.

   m. Save the query as *Camping Department Items with Prices*.

8. Protect a database.

   a. Close the current database.

   b. Open the *Outdoor Designs Inventory* database in Open Exclusive Mode.

   c. Open the Set Database Password dialog box and set the password to **Smokey**.

   d. Verify the password, then close the database.

   e. Encrypt the Outdoor Designs Inventory database, then save it using the same filename.

   f. Close the database.

   g. Exit Access.

► Independent Challenge 1

In preparation for a Stuff for Pets marketing meeting, you need to create lists that update the marketing managers on the sales of each animal. You also need to enhance the Animals data entry form, which currently does not contain all the fields from the table and is difficult to use.

    a. Start Access, then use the Choose file command to open a copy of the file Stuff for Pets Animal Database from the drive and folder where your Project Files are located.

    b. Open the Animals form.

    c. Increase the width of the form so that it is 5.5" wide.

    d. Move the ID TAG NUMBER field value text box and label to the upper-right corner of the Details section, on the same level as the Category control.

    e. Add the RETAIL PRICE field to the form so that it is positioned just below the ID TAG NUMBER field.

    f. Format the field labels for all the controls in the Detail area in blue bold. Format the ID TAG NUMBER field label in red bold.

    g. Add a label to the Form Header area with the text Animals Database. Insert the image file logo2.jpg from your Project Files folder above the field label and position it so that it is centered.

    h. View the Form in Form view, type your name in the DATA ENTRY BY field value text box for the first record, then print the form.

    i. Close the form, then open the Animals table.

    j. Sort the database in descending order on the RETAIL PRICE field.

    k. Use the Filter by Selection command to find all the records for dogs.

    l. Create a query to find all the pets whose retail price is more than $100.00. Include the ID TAG NUMBER, CATEGORY, BREED, and RETAIL PRICE fields in the query. Save the query as *High-Priced Pets*.

    m. Print the results of the query using the Print button on the Query Datasheet toolbar.

    n. Protect the database from unauthorized users by setting a password. Type **Cleo** as the password.

    o. Save the database, then exit Access.

► Independent Challenge 2

You run a cooking school called Chef's Delight, based in Vancouver, Canada. You recently purchased a large quantity of rice cookers and woks for cooking Chinese food. You decide to use the customer database to create a listing of all the students who have taken a course from you in Chinese cooking, and write them a letter informing them of your available products.

    a. Use the Choose file command in the task pane to open a copy of the file Chef's Delight Customers from the drive and folder where your Project Files are located.

    b. Open the Customers table, then use the Filter by Selection command to show customers who have taken a course in Chinese Cooking. Type your name in the DATA ENTRY BY field for the first filtered record, then print the datasheet.

    c. Create a query that shows all the customers who have taken the Chinese cooking class showing the FIRST, LAST, CLASS TAKEN, and DATA ENTRY BY fields. Save the query with the name *Chinese Cooking Students*.

    d. Create a new form for the Customers table using a wizard, choosing any style you want. Save the form as *Customer Data Entry Form*.

    e. Format the form in Design view using fonts, colors, and border styles and modifying the layout as you see fit to make it visually appealing.

    f. Add the label **Chef's Delight** in the form header. Format the label using a font size, style, and color you like.

    g. Print the first three records in Form view.

    h. Save your changes, then exit Access.

► Independent Challenge 3

As human resources manager for Little Guy Toys, you need to work with the data in your employee database to prepare for an upcoming meeting. You need to identify employees who have been with the company for 3 years, 5 years, and 10 years so you can present each with a Service Appreciation gift at your upcoming company meeting. You also decide to create a data entry form so that adding information for new hires will be easier for your assistant.

a. Use the Choose file command to open a copy of the file Toys Employees from the drive and folder where your Project Files are located.

b. Open the Employees table, then sort the table in ascending order by the HIRE DATE field, type your name in the DATA ENTRY BY field of the first record, then print the datasheet.

c. Create a query using Design view that shows all the employees hired earlier than 9/1/93 and the fields for FIRST NAME, LAST NAME, HIRE DATE, and DEPARTMENT. Save this Query as *10 Year Service Awards*.

d. Create another query based on the 10 Year Service Awards query that shows employees who were hired before 9/1/98 and after 9/1/93. (In the Criteria Cell, type **>9/1/93** and **<9/1/98**). Save this query as *5 Year Service Awards*.

e. Create a third query based on the 5 Year Service Awards that shows employees who were hired before 9/1/2000 and after 9/1/98.Save this query as *3 Year Service Awards*. Close the query.

f. Open and view the *Employee Data Entry* form in Form view. Then, open the form in Design view and make modifications to make it more visually appealing using any fonts, font sizes and colors that you feel are appropriate. Make any changes to the layout of the controls that you feel would make the form easier to use.

g. Add the label **Little Guy Toys Employees** to the Form Header area and format it so that it stands out.

h. Print the first three records in the form.

i. Save the file.

j. This is a sensitive file; protect the database using the password **BOSTON**.

k. Close the database, then exit Access.

 # Independent Challenge 4

You want to develop a database to keep track of your favorite films. The Internet has many Web pages that offer synopses of films available on video.

a. Log on to the Internet, go to a search engine site such as Google (www.google.com) or AltaVista (www.altavista.com) and research information about five of your favorite recently released films. Print the results of your search.

b. Research information on ten of your favorite films that were released in the last ten years. Print the results of your search.

c. Start Access, then use the Choose File command to open a copy of the database file Films from the drive and folder where your Project Files are located.

d. Modify the Films table to add a Yes/No field for whether you would see the film again.

e. Create a form using a wizard that includes all of the fields from the Films table. Make any modifications to the form layout to make it visually appealing. Add the label **Favorite Films** to the Form Header.

f. Enter the data for the 10 films you found on your Internet search. Type your name in the DATA ENTRY BY field.

g. Filter the database to show all the films you would see again. Print the datasheet.

h. Sort the database in alphabetical order by title. Print the datasheet again.

i. Create a query containing the fields for CATEGORY, FILM TITLE, RATING and RELEASE YEAR that shows films that were released after 1998 that have a PG rating. Save the query as "Favorite Recent PG Films".

j. Print the form for six of the records you entered.

k. Close the database, then exit Access.

Access 2002

► Visual Workshop

Use the Choose file command to open a copy of the database Charity Run from the drive and folder where your Project Files are located. Modify the *Runners* form in Design view so that it looks similar to the form shown in Figure B-25. (*Hint*: Insert the image file Runner.jpg in the position shown in the Detail section.) When you have finished, open the form in Form view, type your name in the Data Entry By field value text box for the first record, then print the first three records in Form view.

FIGURE B-25

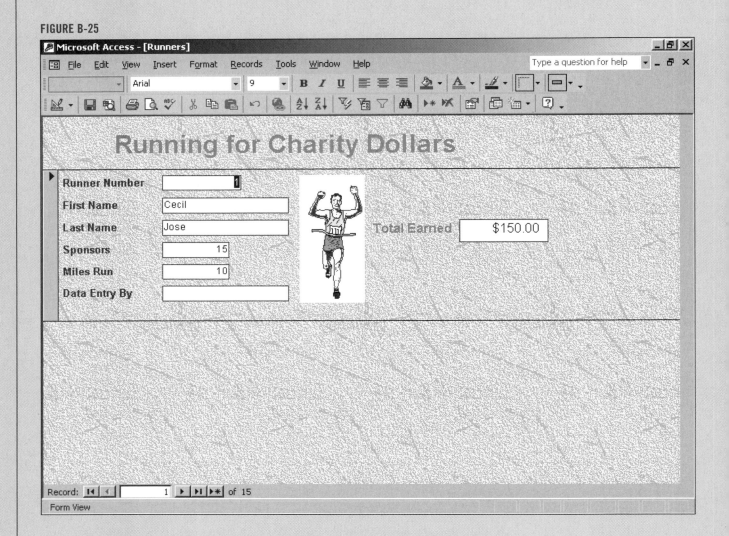

Creating
Database Reports

Objectives

- ► Create a report
- ► Resize and move controls
- ► Format a report
- ► Work with a report in Print Preview
- ► Create a report from a query
- ► Add summary information to a report
- ► Add an expression to a report
- ► Create mailing labels

In this unit you will learn how to organize the fields of a database into reports. A **report** is a summary of database information designed specifically for printing. A report can include one or more database fields, summary information, clip art, and descriptive labels. You create reports from tables or queries in the database. ✐ Elizabeth Fried, the database administrator for Outdoor Designs, has asked you to help her create a series of reports containing summary information from the Outdoor Designs customer database. She wants you to create, print, and distribute the reports to the Outdoor Designs sales managers.

Creating a Report

When a database grows large, spotting statistical trends in the data can be difficult. For example, if a sales database contains hundreds of records, it's hard to determine the amount of an average sale, or the total sales. You can solve this problem by creating summary reports of your database. You can create new reports manually in Design view or with the help of the Report Wizard, which automatically creates a report based on your specifications. Each report is stored as an object in your database file so you can print it or refer to it later. ✐ Elizabeth asks you to create a new report, organized by a sales representative, that lists all of the customer information contained in the Customers table within the Outdoor Designs database.

Steps

1. Start Access, then use the Choose file command on the New File task pane to open a copy of the file **Outdoor Designs Sales** from the drive and folder where your Project Files are located

2. In the Outdoor Designs Sales1: Database window click **Reports** in the Objects list, then click **New**

   The New Report dialog box displays options for creating a new report. The Design View option lets you manually add controls to a new report. You can use one of the two AutoReports to create a report based on the chosen table or query with predefined settings. You can use one of the three wizards to create a report, a chart, or a set of labels.

3. Click **Report Wizard** in the New Report dialog box, click the **Choose the table or query where the object's data comes from list arrow**, click **Customers**, then click **OK**

   The Customers table contains the fields needed for this report, as shown in Figure C-1.

4. Click the **Select All Fields button** >>

   All the fields now appear in the Selected Fields box. You do not need the Sales field in this report.

5. Click **SALES** in the Selected fields box, click the **Remove Field button** <, then click **Next**

   The Sales field is removed from the Selected fields list. The next dialog box determines how the records are grouped. **Grouping** organizes a report by field or field values so you can spot trends or find important information more easily. You want to group the customers by sales rep.

6. Click **REP**, click the **Select Field button** >, notice that the REP field appears in blue text above the remaining fields in the list, then click **Next**

   The next dialog box determines how the records in the report will be sorted.

QuickTip

The Sort Order button in this dialog box is a toggle button. Click it to switch between ascending and descending sort order.

7. Click the first **Sort list arrow**, then click **BUSINESS**

   This sorts the records in ascending alphabetical order by the name of the business.

8. Click **Next**, verify that that **Stepped Layout option button** is selected, click the **Landscape Orientation option button**, verify that the **Adjust the field width so all fields fit on a page check box** contains a check mark, then click **Next**

9. Click **Compact** in the style list, click **Next**, type **Customers by Sales Rep** as the report title, click **Finish**, maximize the report window, save your changes, then scroll to the right to see the Phone column

   The Report is displayed in Print Preview, as shown in Figure C-2. You can see that the Phone numbers are too wide to fit in the column so that only part of each number is visible. In Print Preview you can't make any changes, but you can see exactly how your report will be printed. You see that you need to make formatting modifications.

FIGURE C-1: Report Wizard dialog box

Report will be based on Customers table

Available fields in Customers table

Select All Fields button

Remove Field button

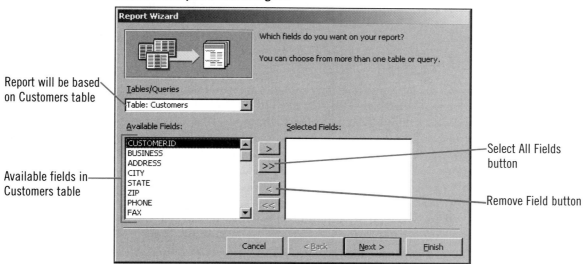

FIGURE C-2: Customers by Rep report in Print Preview

Report will print in landscape orientation

Data grouped by Rep

Within each group, data is sorted by Business

Phone column is too narrow to show full phone numbers

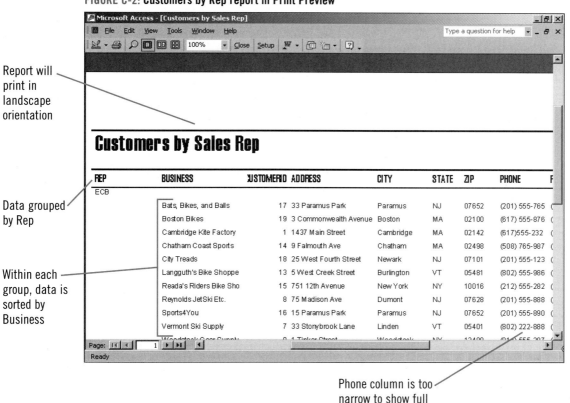

Access 2002

Resizing and Moving Controls

After you create a report using the Report wizard, you usually have to make modifications to improve its appearance. Often you need to resize or move controls so that all the information in the report is visible. To make changes to the report's layout, you need to open the report in Design view. In Design view, the report is divided into sections, much as in Form Design view. The **Report Header** section contains the report name and appears only at the top of the first page. The **Page Header** section contains the field labels and appears at the top of every page. The **Details** section contains the field values for all the records in the underlying table. See Table C-1 for descriptions of the other sections. You can use Design view to move, resize, and delete controls. ✐ The phone column of the Customers by Sales Rep report is too narrow so that only part of each phone number appears. You decide to make the REP column smaller, move the middle columns over to the left to create more space, and widen the phone column so that all the numbers fit. You also want to delete the CITY, STATE, and ZIP labels from the Page Header.

Trouble?

If the Customers field list and the Toolbox are in the way, close them by clicking the Close button in the title bar of each.

1. Click the **Design View button** 🖾 on the Print Preview toolbar
   The report opens in Design view.

2. Click the **CITY field label** in the Page Header, press and hold **[Shift]**, click the **STATE field label**, click the **ZIP field label**, release **[Shift]**, then press **[Delete]**
   These labels aren't necessary since all these fields fit under the label "Address."

3. Click the **REP field label** in the Page Header, press and hold **[Shift]**, click the **REP field value text box** in the Rep Header, release **[Shift]**, point to one of the right-middle sizing handles so that the pointer changes to ↔, drag to the ½ inch mark on the horizontal ruler, then click away from the selection
   The REP field label and field value text box are now much smaller, giving you more room to resize and reposition the other controls in the report. See Figure C-3. Clicking away from the selection deselects it, so that you don't make additional inadvertent changes to it.

4. Press and hold **[Shift]**, click the **BUSINESS label**, **CUSTOMERID label** and **ADDRESS label** in the Page Header, click the **BUSINESS, CUSTOMER, ADDRESS, CITY, STATE, and ZIP field value text boxes** in the Detail section, then release **[Shift]**

5. Position the pointer over the **BUSINESS field label** until it changes to 🖑, then drag it to the left until the left edge is at the ½ inch mark on the horizontal ruler
   All the selected controls are now repositioned further to the left, giving you room to enlarge the phone field.

QuickTip

After you move or resize selected controls, make sure that you click away from the selected fields to deselect them.

6. Click away from the selection

7. Scroll to the right, click the **PHONE field label**, press and hold **[Shift]**, click the **PHONE field value text box** to select both, then drag one of the **left-middle sizing handles** to the 6½ inch mark on the horizontal ruler
   As Figure C-4 shows, the PHONE field value text box and label are now wider and should be able to accommodate all the digits in a phone number.

8. Save your changes

FIGURE C-3: Resized REP controls in Design view

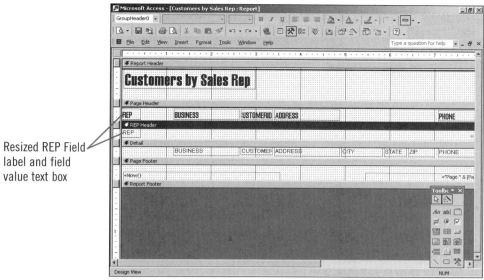

Resized REP Field label and field value text box

FIGURE C-4: Resized PHONE controls in Design view

Resized PHONE controls

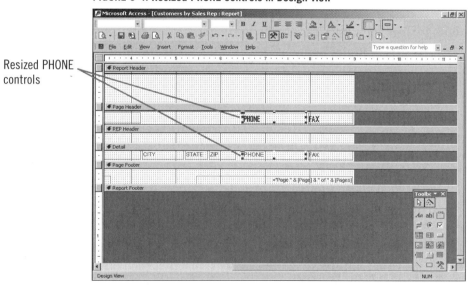

TABLE C-1: Report sections

section	description
Report header	Contains the report name or company logo, and appears only at the top of the first page of the report
Page header	Contains field labels and appears at the top of every page (but below the report header on the first page)
Group header	Contains the chosen group field name, and appears at the beginning of a group of records ("Group" is replaced by the chosen field name)
Detail	Usually contains bound controls and appears once for every record in the underlying datasheet
Group footer	Contains the chosen group field name, and appears at the end of each group of records ("Group" is replaced by the field name)
Page footer	Usually contains the current date and page number and appears at the bottom of each page
Report footer	Appears at the end of the last page of the report, just above the page footer

Formatting a Report

You can use Design view to enhance the appearance of a report in many ways. You can change the alignment of labels and field values, apply formatting to labels and field values, and change the properties of any report element. You can also add additional text using the label button on the Toolbox. ✐ You continue to improve the appearance of the Customers by Sales Rep report by making changes to it in Design view. You decide to change the field label CUSTOMERID to simply ID, center the field labels, and add color and bold formatting to certain controls to make them stand out. You will also add your name to the Report Header.

Steps

1. Click the **CUSTOMERID field label** in the Page Header section, then click the **Properties button** 🔲 on the Report Design toolbar
   The Properties sheet opens.

2. Click the **Format tab** if necessary, click in the **Caption property text box**, type **ID**, as shown in Figure C-5, then click 🔲
   The Property sheet closes, and the CUSTOMERID label now reads simply "ID."

3. With the ID label control selected, press and hold **[Shift]**, click the **CUSTOMERID field value text box** in the Detail section, then click the **Center button** 🔳 on the toolbar

4. Position the pointer in the left margin of the Page Header so that the pointer changes to ➡, then click
   This selects all the field labels in the Page Header.

5. With all the labels selected, click the **Font size arrow** on the Formatting toolbar, click **16**, then click the **Bold button** 🅱

6. Click the **REP control** in the Rep Header section, click the **Font/Fore Color list arrow** 🔻, click the **red square**, then click 🅱
   Compare your screen to Figure C-6. The bold red formatting will help make each rep's initials stand out on the report.

Trouble?
If the Toolbox is not open, click the Toolbox button 🛠 on the Report Design toolbar.

7. Click the **Label button** 🔤 on the Toolbox, position the pointer just below **Customers by Sales Rep** in the Report Header, then drag down and to the left to create a text box that is approximately 2 inches wide and ¼ inch high
   Compare your screen to Figure C-7.

8. Type your name in the text box

9. Save your changes

FIGURE C-5: Format tab of Properties sheet

Format tab ——————

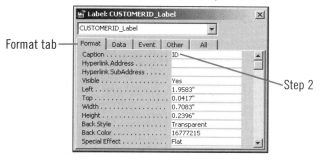

Step 2

FIGURE C-6: Formatting applied to labels and controls

Bold button

Font/Fore color list arrow

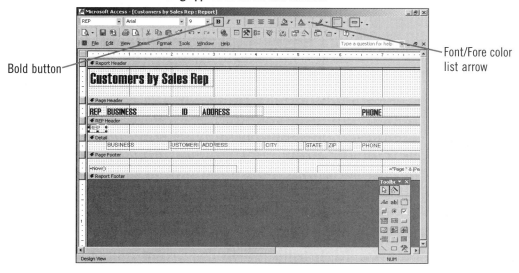

FIGURE C-7: Dragging a text box using the Label button

Inserted text box created with Label button

Toolbox

Label button

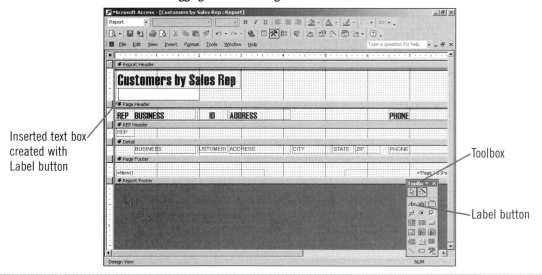

Access 2002

Working with a Report in Print Preview

You can see how a report will look when printed by viewing it in Print Preview. Examining the report in Print Preview is an important step because you can catch any formatting problems before you print. You can view one page at a time or see multiple pages at once, and you can zoom in to get a closer look at any page. You can navigate from one page to the next using the page navigation buttons at the bottom of the Print Preview window. ✒️ To verify that all your formatting changes have improved the appearance and readability of the Customers by Rep report, you decide to preview the Customers by Sales Rep report before printing it for your colleagues.

Steps

1. Click the **Print Preview button** 🔍 on the Report Design toolbar
   The Print Preview window opens. You can see that the ID column is much easier to read now that it is center-aligned. Notice that the zoom level in the Zoom list box is set to Fit, meaning that your view of the page is sized to fit completely within the program window. You can also see that the pointer changes to 🔍. You can use this pointer to zoom in on any section of the report to get a good look at the details.

2. Position the pointer 🔍 in the middle of the page over the PHONE column, then click
   The page is magnified so that you can see the phone column and surrounding text up close. See Figure C-8. Notice that the zoom level is now at 100% and the pointer changes to 🔍.

3. Scroll down to the bottom of the page until you see the footer
   You can see that the page number appears on the right side of the footer, and the date appears on the left side.

4. Click anywhere on the page
   The zoom level returns to Fit, and the pointer changes back to 🔍.

QuickTip

If your report has several pages, you can click the Multiple Pages button 🔳 then click the number of pages you want to view.

5. Click the **Two Pages button** 🔳 on the Print Preview toolbar
   Both pages of this report appear on the screen, as shown in Figure C-9. The report is looking good.

6. Click the **Print button** 🖨️ on the Print Preview toolbar

7. Save your changes, click File on the menu bar, then click Close
   The Print Preview window closes and you return to the database window.

FIGURE C-8: Magnified report page in Print Preview

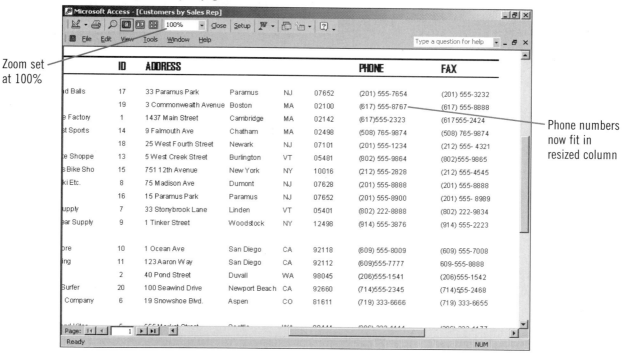

Zoom set at 100%

Phone numbers now fit in resized column

FIGURE C-9: Viewing two pages of the report

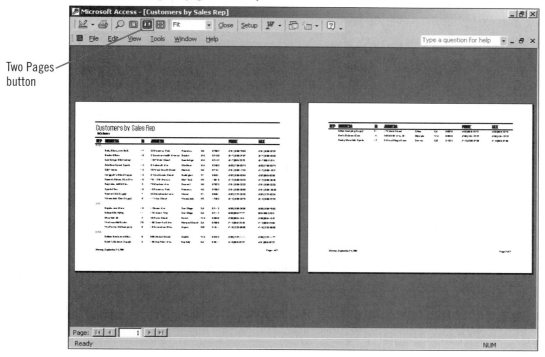

Two Pages button

Access 2002

Access 2002

Creating a Report from a Query

Queries answer questions about data in your database. Although you can print query results in Datasheet view as a simple table, you can also create great looking reports from your queries using the Report Wizard. ✍ Elizabeth wants you to create a report that shows all the customers who have placed orders greater than $5000; Outdoor Designs identifies these as Gold level customers. She has already created a query that displays the total orders placed by each customer. You first need to modify this query so that the query displays only customers who have ordered more than $5000, then you can create a report based on this revised query.

Steps 1 2 3 4

1. In the Outdoor Designs Sales: Database window, click **Queries** in the Objects list, click **Customers Query**, then click **Design**

2. Maximize the Query window, if necessary, scroll to the **SALES column**, click the **SALES field Criteria cell**, type **>5000**, then click the **Datasheet View button** 🖩 on the Query Design toolbar
   The query shows all the customers whose orders total more than $5000, as shown in Figure C-10.

3. Click **File** on the menu bar, click **Save As**, type **Gold Customers** in the Save Query to box, click **OK**, click **File** on the menu bar, then click **Close**
   The Query window closes, and you are now back in the database window.

4. Click **Reports** in the Objects list, click **New**, click **Report Wizard** in the New Report dialog box, click the **Choose the table or query where the object's data comes from list arrow**, click **Gold Customers**, then click **OK**

5. Click **BUSINESS**, click the **Select Field button** ▶, click **STATE**, click ▶, click **SALES**, click ▶, click **REP**, click ▶, then click **Next**
   Now, instead of showing all the fields contained in the query, the report will show just the BUSINESS, STATE, SALES, and REP fields.

6. Click **REP**, click ▶, then click **Next**
   The report will group the customers by sales rep.

7. Click the first **Sort list arrow**, click **BUSINESS**, then click **Next**
   This sorts the records in ascending alphabetical order by the name of the business.

8. Click the **Outline 1 Layout option button**, verify that the **Portrait Orientation option button** is selected, click **Next**, click **Bold** in the style list, click **Next**, type **Gold Customers Report** as the report title, verify that the **Preview the report option button** is selected, click **Finish**, then maximize the report window if necessary
   Compare your screen to Figure C-11.

9. Preview the report, click the Print button 🖨 on the Print Preview toolbar, click Close on the Print Preview toolbar, click File on the menu bar, then click Close

FIGURE C-10: Gold Customers Query results

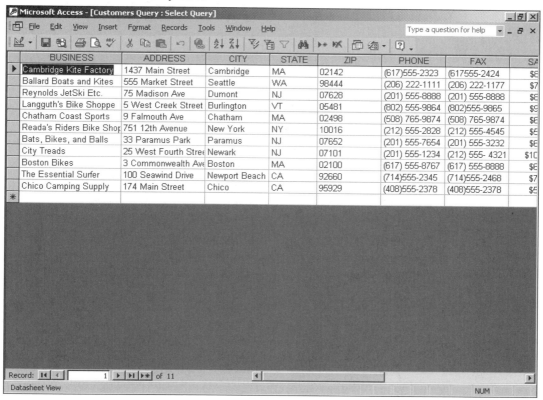

FIGURE C-11: Finished Gold Customers report

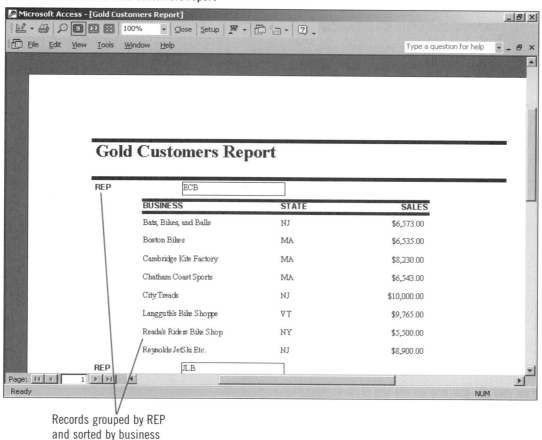

Records grouped by REP
and sorted by business

Adding Summary Information to a Report

Summary information in a report displays statistics about one or more fields in a database. Summaries can include statistics for the sum, average, minimum, or maximum value in any numeric field. Table C-2 describes the five summary calculations you can use in your database reports. You can add summary information to a report while creating the report with the Report Wizard, or in Design view. ✐ Elizabeth has asked you to prepare a report that shows sales of each customer grouped by state. She wants the report to show only the BUSINESS, STATE, SALES and REP fields. You need to use the Customers table to create this report, because it must include all Outdoor Sales customers, not just Gold level customers.

Steps

1. In the Outdoor Designs Sales: Database window, click **Reports** in the Objects list if necessary, double-click **Create report by using wizard**, click the **Tables/Queries list arrow**, then click **Table: Customers** if necessary

2. Click **BUSINESS**, click the **Select Field button** ⎣>⎤, click **STATE**, click ⎣>⎤, click **SALES**, click ⎣>⎤, click **REP**, click ⎣>⎤, then click **Next**
   Only the BUSINESS, STATE, SALES, and REP fields will be included in the report.

3. In the next dialog box click **STATE**, click ⎣>⎤, then click **Next**
   The customer records will be grouped by state. The next dialog box lets you choose how you want to sort the records in the report, and also lets you choose summary options.

4. Click **Summary Options**
   The Summary Options dialog box opens, as shown in Figure C-12. Of the fields you selected for this report, summary options are available only for the SALES field because this is the only field containing numeric values.

5. Click the **Sum check box**, click the **Avg check box**, click the **Min check box**, click the **Max check box**, click the **Calculate percent of total for sums check box**, then click the **Detail and Summary option button** if necessary
   By selecting these options, you specify that you want to see the total sales, the average sales, the minimum sales, and the maximum sales for each state, and that you want to see the details (sales for each account) in addition to the summary information (calculated for each state).

6. Click **OK**, click the first **Sort list arrow**, click **BUSINESS**, click **Next**, click the **Block option button**, verify that the **Portrait option button** is selected, click **Next**, click the **Soft Gray** style, then click **Next**

7. Type **Sales by State Report** as the report title, click the **Preview the report option button** if necessary, then click **Finish**
   The report opens in Print Preview.

8. Scroll down so that all the information for California and Colorado are visible
   Your screen should look similar to Figure C-13.

9. Save your changes

FIGURE C-12: Summary Options dialog box

Click to select the summary fields you want to add

Only SALES field available because no other fields have numeric values

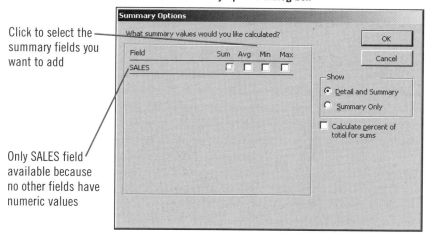

FIGURE C-13: Sales by State Report with summary information

Summary information

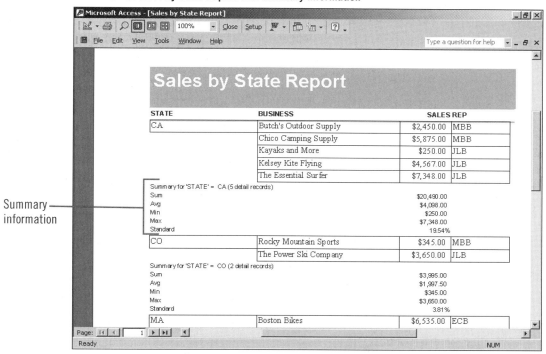

TABLE: C-2: Common summary calculations available in database reports

summary	statistic	calculates
SUM	Sum	Total of all values in the field
AVG	Average	Average of all values in the field
COUNT	Count	Number of records in the database
MIN	Minimum	Smallest value in the field
MAX	Maximum	Largest value in the field

Access 2002

Adding an Expression to a Report

Access 2002

You can include calculated expressions in a report. An **expression** is a mathematical equation that performs a calculation. Expressions can include built-in functions or manually written calculations, as well as field names. To ensure database integrity, you should use fields from the underlying table or query when creating expressions, rather than adding a new field. That way, any time you update the data in the database, the expression's results will automatically be updated. ✐━━ You want to include commissions in the Sales by State Report. The Customers table does not contain a commissions field, so you decide to add a control that contains an expression that calculates this information. You want the information (which is calculated as 15% of sales) to appear in the STATE footer section of the report with the rest of the summary information.

1. Click the **Design View button** 🖾 on the Print Preview toolbar

2. Place the pointer on the top of the **Page footer bar**, then when the pointer changes to ✛, drag the divider down ½ inch on the vertical ruler

Trouble?

If the Toolbox is not open, click the Toolbox button 🛠 on the Report Design toolbar to open it.

3. Click the **Text box button** 🔤 on the Toolbox, then click the **Text box pointer** ⁺🔤 directly below the =Sum([SALES])/)[field value text box in the State footer section at the 4½ inch mark on the horizontal ruler, as shown in Figure C-14
   A blank label with a placeholder name and an empty field value text box are inserted.

4. Click the **Properties button** 🖾, click the **Data tab** on the property sheet, click the **Control Source box**, type =[SALES]*0.15, then press [Enter]
   As shown in Figure C-15, =[SALES]*0.15 is entered in the control. This expression will calculate commissions by multiplying the value in the SALES field in the Customers table by 15%.

5. Click the **Format tab** on the Property sheet, click the **Format down arrow**, then click **Currency**
   This specifies that the calculated commissions result will be formatted as currency.

QuickTip

You can also resize a label by dragging its resizing handle.

6. Click the new **text box label** in the STATE footer section, click the **Format tab** on the property sheet, type **Commissions** in the Caption text box, select the text in the Width box, type 1, then press [Enter]
   The label now reads "Commissions" and the whole word fits in the text box, because you adjusted the width to 1 inch.

7. Click the **Properties button** 🖾 to close the Properties sheet, click the =[SALES]*0.15 text box, press and hold [Shift], click the **Commissions label**, click the **Font list arrow** on the toolbar, click **Arial**, click the **Font size list arrow**, then click 8

8. Click away from the selection, click the **Commissions label**, click 🅱, point to the **black square selection handle** in the label's upper-left corner until the pointer changes to a 👆, then drag the label to the left edge of the screen, under the Standard label
   Dragging the 👆, drags the label text box separately from the field value text box. The Commissions label and field value text box now are formatted like the other controls in the report.

9. Click the **Print Preview button**, click to zoom in, scroll to view the Summary information, compare your screen to Figure C-16, save your changes, click **File** on the menu bar, then click **Close**

FIGURE C-14: Text box control in State Footer

Step 3

Drag Page Footer
bar to here

Toolbox button

Text box button

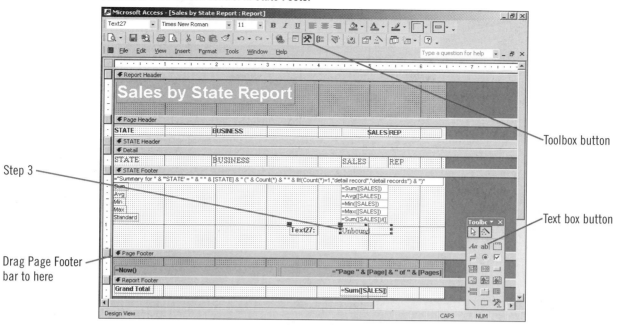

FIGURE C-15: Expression entered in Control Source box of Property sheet

Your text box
placeholder
number will vary

Control Source box

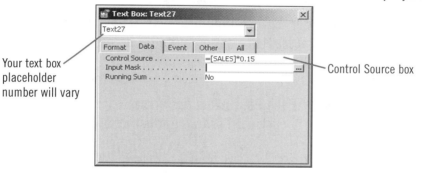

FIGURE C-16: Report in Print Preview showing added expression

Formatted and
repositioned label

Expression
formatted
as currency

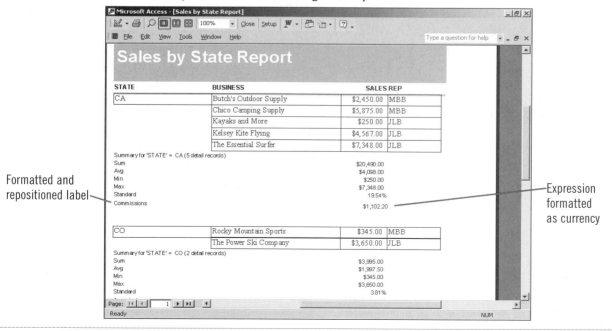

Access 2002

Creating Mailing Labels

Access 2002

Reports don't have to be printed on sheets of paper. You may want to use the data in a database to create other forms of printed output, such as labels or envelopes. Access includes a Label Wizard to help you create labels containing data from any fields in the database. You can create labels based on queries or filters to generate a report for specific needs, such as a mailing to all clients in New Jersey or all employees in the legal department. Elizabeth asked you to create mailing labels for a promotional mailing that will be sent to all Outdoor Designs customers announcing some new product lines. You decide to use the Label Wizard to create the labels.

1. In the Outdoor Designs Sales1: Database window click **Reports** in the Objects list if necessary, then click **New**
   The New Report dialog box opens.

QuickTip

The labels in this dialog box are organized in numerical order.

2. Click **Label Wizard**, click the **Choose the Table or query where the object's data comes from list arrow**, click **Customers**, then click **OK**
   In the first dialog box of this wizard, there is a list of predefined formats for labels made by several manufacturers from which you can choose.

3. Click the **Filter by manufacturer list arrow**, click **Avery** if necessary, click the **English Unit of Measure option button** if necessary, scroll down the Product number list, then click **5390**
   This form has two labels that are each 2⅙ x 3½" across a sheet.

4. Click **Next**, click the **Font name list arrow**, click **Arial Black**, click the **Font size list arrow**, click **10**, click the **Font weight list arrow**, click **Normal**, then click **Next**
   In this dialog box, you choose which fields you want to include on each label, as well as their placement. You select each field from the Available fields list in the order in which you want them on the label. You need to enter any spaces, punctuation, or hard returns using the keyboard.

QuickTip

Double-click the field name in the Available fields list to move it to the Prototype label text box.

5. Click **BUSINESS**, click the **Select Field button** `>`, press **[Enter]**, click **ADDRESS**, click `>`, press **[Enter]**, click **CITY**, click `>`, type **, (a comma)**, press the **[Spacebar]**, click **STATE**, click `>`, press the **[Spacebar]**, click **ZIP**, then click `>`
   Your screen should look similar to Figure C-17.

6. Click **Next**
   In this dialog box, you specify how the records should be sorted when they are printed.

QuickTip

If an error message appears saying there is not enough space between the columns, click OK.

7. Scroll to and click **REP**, click `>`, click **BUSINESS**, click `>`, click **Next**, type **Customer Labels** as the report name, click **Finish** to accept the default report name, then maximize the Print Preview window
   The labels appear in Print Preview, as shown in Figure C-18. They are sorted alphabetically by sales rep name and then within each sales rep category by business name. If you have a sheet of Avery 5390 labels, you can put it in your printer and print this report, or you can print the labels on an 8½ x 11 inch sheet of paper to see what they would look like.

8. Save your changes, then click the **Print button** 🖨 on the Print Preview toolbar

9. Click **File** on the menu bar, then click **Exit**

FIGURE C-17: Label Wizard dialog box

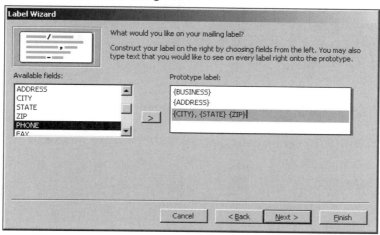

FIGURE C-18: Completed labels in Print Preview

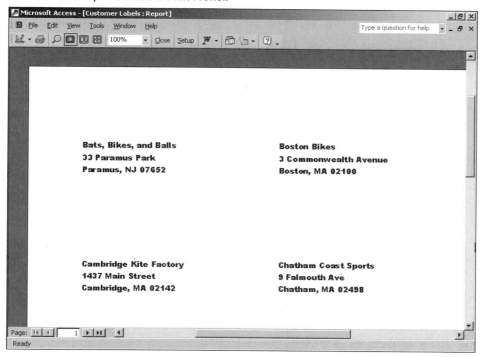

Modifying labels in Design view

Because labels are a type of report, you can modify them in Design view, just as you do other kinds of reports. Experiment with adding formatting and color to create interesting, eye-catching labels. Note, however, that the wizard sets the important label parameters for printing, so do not change the size if you want to print on preprinted label forms.

Practice

▶ Concepts Review

Label each of the elements of the Access window shown in Figure C-19.

FIGURE C-19

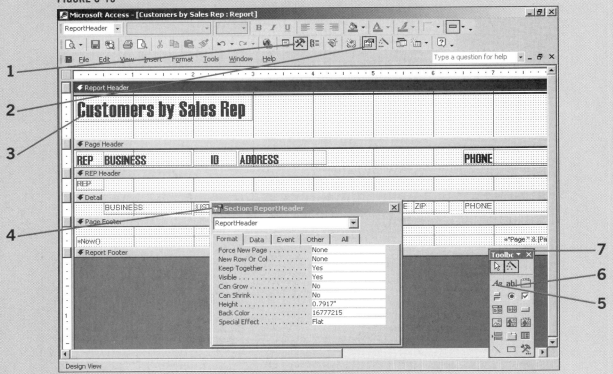

Match the report section in Design view with the type of data it is likely to contain.

8. Page Header	**a.** Bound controls
9. Report Header	**b.** Date and page number
10. Group Header	**c.** Report name
11. Detail	**d.** Field labels
12. Page footer	**e.** Field name by which the report is ordered

Select the best answer from the list of choices.

13. A report is a summary of database information specifically designed for:
    a. Printing.   **c.** Examining in Form view.
    b. Sorting.   **d.** Searching.

14. Which section of a form contains the field values for the records in the underlying data source?
    a. Page Header   **c.** Group Header
    b. Details   **d.** Report Footer

15. Which of the following calculations is not available in a Summary report?
    a. Maximum value
    b. Minimum value
    c. Average
    d. Present value

16. Which view do you use to resize controls or apply formatting to labels in a report?
    a. Print Preview
    b. Design view
    c. Form view
    d. Datasheet view

17. To change the name of a field label, you can use the:
    a. Toolbox.
    b. Field list.
    c. Task pane.
    d. Property sheet.

18. Which of the following can not be included in an expression?
    a. Field names
    b. Built-in functions
    c. Hyperlinks
    d. Manually written calculations

▶ Skills Review

1. **Create a report.**
    a. Start Access, then use the Choose file command on the New File task pane to create a copy of the file Outdoor Designs Stock.
    b. Use the Report Wizard to create a new report based on the Inventory table.
    c. Select all the fields except for Description.
    d. Group the report by Department.
    e. Sort in descending order by Price. (*Hint*: Click the Ascending Sort button on the Wizard dialog box to switch to a descending sort order.)
    f. Select the Stepped Layout and Portrait Orientation.
    g. Select the Corporate style and type **Inventory Report** as the report title.
    h. View the report in Print Preview.

2. **Resize and move controls.**
    a. View the Inventory Report in Design view.
    b. Delete the SIZE label and field value text box, the YTD UNITS SOLD label and field value text box, and the COLOR label and field value text box from the report.
    c. Select the PRICE, ITEM NUMBER, ITEM labels and field value text boxes, then drag them over to the right ½ inch.
    d. Increase the width of the DEPARTMENT label and DEPARTMENT field value text box so that the entire word is visible.
    e. Resize and move the remaining controls as necessary so that the PRICE, ITEM, ONHAND, and YTD SALES labels are all visible on the report. (You will fix the remaining labels in the next set of steps.)
    f. Save your changes.

3. Format a report.

    a. Use the property sheet to change the ITEM NUMBER label to **NO.**, the REORDER DATE label to **REORDER**, and the REORDER QUANTITY label to **QTY**.

    b. Center align the NO. label and the ITEM NUMBER field value text box.

    c. Center align the REORDER label and REORDER DATE field value text box.

    d. Center align the ONHAND label and field value text box.

    e. Change the font size of all the field values in the Details section to 10 points.

    f. Apply green bold formatting to the DEPARTMENT label in the DEPARTMENT Header, then save the report.

4. Work with a report in Print Preview.

    a. View the Inventory report in Print Preview.

    b. Use the Magnifier to zoom in on all sections of the report to make sure all data is visible.

    c. If any labels or field values are not visible in Print Preview, return to Design view and make any adjustments to the controls so that all information is visible.

    d. Add a label containing your name to the Report Header, then save and close the report.

5. Create a report from a query.

    a. Create a new report using the Report Wizard based on the Bestselling Items query.

    b. Select all the fields, group by DEPARTMENT, sort in descending order by YTD SALES, use the Stepped layout, use Portrait orientation, use the Formal style, and type **Bestselling Items Report** as the report title.

    c. View the results in Print Preview.

    d. Make any necessary formatting adjustments in Design view so that the report is attractive and easy to read. Switch between Design view and Print Preview as necessary until you are satisfied with the result.

    e. Add your name to the Report Header, then save, print, and close the report.

    f. Open the Bestselling Items query, then modify it to select only those items whose sales are less than $2000 YTD.

    g. Save the query as *Low Selling Items*.

    h. Create a new report using the Report Wizard, based on the Low Selling Items query. Select all the fields, group by DEPARTMENT, sort in ascending order by YTD SALES, use the Stepped layout, use the Portrait orientation, use the Casual style, and title the report Low Selling Items Report.

    i. Switch to Design view, then resize, move, rename, and realign field labels and field value text boxes as necessary so all the information is displayed clearly.

    j. Add your name in the Report Header, then print and close the report.

6. Add summary information to a report.

    a. Create a new report using the Report Wizard based on the Inventory table.

    b. Select all the ITEM NUMBER, DEPARTMENT, ITEM, PRICE, and ONHAND fields, then group by Department.

    c. Open the Summary Options dialog box, click to add check marks to the all the summary calculation checkboxes for the PRICE field, and click to add a check mark to the Sum check box for the ONHAND field.

    d. Sort in descending order by ONHAND, use the Outline1 layout, use the Soft Gray style, and type **On-Hand Inventory** as the report title.

    e. Preview the report.

    f. Use Design view to format the ONHAND, ITEM NUMBER, ITEM, and PRICE field labels as red, Arial, 10-point.

    g. Format the statistics field values in the DEPARTMENT Footer section as Currency.

    h. Make any necessary formatting changes to the report to make all the information visible and easy to read. Change label names if necessary, to make the information look attractive and easy to read.

    i. Add your name to the Report Header, then preview and print the report.

    j. Save and close the report.

7. Add an expression to a report.

a. Create a new report using the Report Wizard, based on the YTD Sales query. Select all the fields, do not add any grouping levels, sort by Item in ascending order, choose the tabular layout option, choose the Soft Gray style, then type **YTD Sales with Tax** as the report title.

b. View the report in Design view, then drag the top of the Page Footer bar down ½ inch to make room in the Detail section.

c. Use the Toolbox to add a Text box control to the Detail section, below the PRICE field value text box.

d. Change the TEXT 24 label to "TAX." (Your text label number may vary.)

e. You want to know the applicable tax for each DEPARTMENT item. The formula is PRICE multiplied by 7%. Open the property sheet for the new control, then click the Data tab. Type the expression **=[PRICE]*.07** in the Control Source text box, then press [Enter]. Do not close the property sheet.

f. Click the Format tab, click the Format list arrow, then click Currency. Close the property sheet.

g. View the report in Print Preview, and make any necessary formatting changes so that the report is professional looking and easy to read. Change label names, if necessary, to enhance the appearance of the information.

h. Add a label containing your name to the Report Header. Save and close the report.

8. Create mailing labels.

a. Create a new report using the Label Wizard.

b. Base the labels on the Label Query.

c. Click the Filter by Manufacturer list arrow, click Avery, click the English option button, then scroll to and click 5198.

d. Change the font to Franklin Gothic Book Normal 10-point or a font of your choice.

e. Set up the label as shown in Figure C-20.

f. Sort the records by Item Number.

g. Title the report *Inventory Labels*.

h. Preview, then print the labels.

i. Save the labels, then close the report and exit Access.

FIGURE C-20

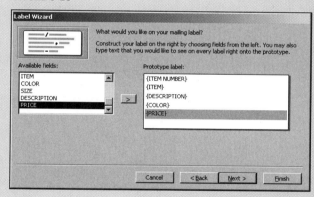

► Independent Challenge 1

Stuff for Pets is planning a campaign to target good customers. You need to create several reports to present to the sales force to help their effort to generate new business.

a. Start Access, then use the Choose file command to open a copy of the file *Pets Customers* from the drive and folder where your Project Files are located.

b. View the Customers Sales Query Report in Print Preview.

c. Modify the Customers Sales Query to select only customers who purchased cats; save this query as *Cat Customers*, then close the query.

d. Create a report using the Report Wizard, based on the Cat Customers query. Select all the fields, group by BREED, and do not specify a sort order. Choose any layout and style you like. Type **Cat Customers** as the report title.

e. View the report in Print Preview, then open it in Design view and make any modifications necessary to make the report attractive, professional, and easy to read.

f. Add your name to the Report Header.

g. Preview and print the report.

h. Create a mailing label for all customers based on the Cat Customers query. Use Avery label 5160, choose any professional-looking font style you like, and include the customer's first and last name, address, city, state, and zip code on the label, inserting spaces and punctuation where appropriate. Save the report as *Cat Customers Labels*, then preview, print, and close it.

▶ Independent Challenge 2

The president of Stuff for Pets, Donna Rand, has asked you to run and print three reports based on data in the Pets Profits database. She is trying to expand the business and needs to see what inventory is in stock, her cost basis, and how the business has been performing in each product area.

a. Start Access, then open a copy of the file *Pets Profits* from the drive and folder where your Project Files are located.

b. Use the Report Wizard to create a report based on the Animals table.

c. Include all the fields, group by CATEGORY, sort by BREED, and choose an appropriate layout and style. Type **Pets Profits** as the report title.

d. Modify the report so you can see all the fields clearly.

e. Delete the TIME field value text box in the Detail section.

f. Select the TIME field label, then use the Property sheet to change the caption to PROFIT.

g. Create a text box in the Detail section in the blank space where the TIME field value text box used to be. Delete the unbound field label.

h. Use the control source box of the Property Sheet to enter the expression =[RETAIL]–[COST] in the new text box control. Use the Format tab of the Property sheet to format this text box as Currency.

i. Resize and move controls as necessary so that all information is attractively laid out and easy to read. Use color to enhance the report.

j. Add your name to the Report Header, preview and print the report, then save and close the report.

k. Create a new query from the Animals query that only shows records that are dogs. (*Hint:* Set the criteria to =dog in the Category field.) Save the query as *Dog Query*.

l. Create a report from the Dog Query that includes only the BREED, DOB, COST, and RETAIL fields in the report. Choose any layout and style you want. Type **Dog Report** as the report title.

m. Add your name to the Report Header, preview and print the report, then save and close it.

n. Modify the Animals query by changing the Category criteria to "=cat". Save the query as *Cat Query*, close it, then create a report for all cats using the Cat Query as a basis. Include the CATEGORY, GENDER, BREED, DOB, COST, and RETAIL fields. Title this report *Cat Report*.

o. Make any modifications necessary to create an attractive and professional report. Add your name to the Report Header, then preview and print the report.

p. Save and close the report, then exit Access.

▶ Independent Challenge 3

As director of the Human Resources department for Little Guy Toys, you need to provide the department heads with information about the staff. You create a confidential report to distribute to the department heads.

a. Start Access, then open a copy of the file *Human Resources* from the drive and folder where your Project Files are located.

b. Use the Report Wizard to create a report based on all the fields in the Employees table.

c. Group the report by DEPT, and sort in ascending order by LAST NAME.

d. Include summary information on salary that includes the minimum and the maximum fields, in both the detail and summary forms.

e. Choose a layout, title, and style for the report that appeals to you. Title the report *Employees Report*.

f. Modify the report so that all fields are visible. Resize and move controls as necessary. Delete and change labels as needed. Format the salary field as currency.

g. Use color to enhance the report. Add a label reading *Confidential* to the Report Header.

h. Add an expression to the Details section that calculates a bonus for each employee that is based on 5% of their salary. Position this new text box below the SALARY field value text box. Rename the field label for this new field value text box **bonus**. Format and position the label and field value text box attractively.

i. Add your name to the Report Header.

j. Preview and print the report, then close it and exit Access.

 Independent Challenge 4

You and a group of friends are taking a trip to a city in one of the following places: England, Scotland, Ireland, or Australia (your choice). You have promised everyone that you will create a list of attractions for your chosen destination containing information about each attraction.

a. Log on to the Internet, go to a search engine site such as Google (www.google.com) or AltaVista (www.altavista.com) and research information about 10 sightseeing attractions in your chosen city.

b. Start Access, then create a new database named *Attractions.mdb*.

c. Create a table that contains the following fields: ATTRACTION NAME, CATEGORY, ADDRESS, CITY, COUNTRY, HOURS, ADMISSION FEE. Apply the data type currency to the ADMISSION FEE field. Include any additional fields that would be of interest to you and your friends. Name the table *Attractions*.

d. Create a form based on the table, called *Attractions*, then enter at least 10 records into the database.

e. Create a report based on the Attractions table. Choose a layout and style that you like. Group the report by CATEGORY, and sort by ATTRACTION NAME. Include at least one type of Summary Information for the PRICE field.

f. Title the report *Attractions Report*.

g. Add an expression to the report that calculates the total admission fee for everyone in your group. Place it in an appropriate place.

h. Make any modifications necessary to the report in Design view so that it is professional looking.

i. Add your name to the Report Header.

j. Preview and print the report, save your changes, close the report, then exit Access.

▶ Visual Workshop

Open a copy of the database *Runners* from the drive and folder where your Project Files are located. Create the report shown in Figure C-21, based on the Runners table.

FIGURE C-21

Runners Report

SCHOOL	TOTAL	NAME		SPONSORS	PLEDGED	MILES
Hammond Public						
	$220.00	Felicia	Chan	20	$220.00	10
	$300.00	Melissa	Doran	22	$300.00	10
	$325.00	Maria	Gomez	30	$325.00	10
Jefferson						
	$110.00	Katy	Roman	15	$150.00	7
	$225.00	Joannie	Dea	15	$225.00	10
	$250.00	Stacey	Linwood	21	$285.00	9
	$250.00	Jay	Arthur	10	$250.00	8
	$300.00	Anne	Harris	25	$300.00	10
Lincoln Academy						
	$120.00	Debbie	Nelson	12	$120.00	10
	$220.00	Paul	Vita	25	$240.00	9
	$245.00	Mary	Barton	15	$245.00	10
	$260.00	Linda	Lynch	17	$275.00	9.5
	$325.00	Nancy	Cho	22	$325.00	10
	$375.00	Rebecca	Brown	20	$400.00	9
	$800.00	Beth	Brummel	35	$800.00	10

Unit
A

Creating
and Modifying a Presentation

Objectives

► **Create a presentation**
► **Navigate a presentation**
► **Enter text in the Outline tab**
► **Enter text in the Slide pane**
► **Format text**
► **Use the Drawing toolbar**
► **Add text boxes**
► **Check spelling and preview a presentation**

Microsoft PowerPoint is a **presentation graphics** program, a program that makes it easy to create on-screen slide shows, overheads, 35mm slides, and other commonly used business presentation materials. It takes just minutes to turn basic information about a company, product, or other topic into a professional-quality presentation, complete with speaker notes for you and handouts for your audience. ✒ Kimberly Ullom, a sales representative at Outdoor Designs, is preparing for a tour of her retail accounts, where she will present the fall product line. She asks you to prepare a PowerPoint presentation that she can use on these sales calls.

Creating a Presentation

PowerPoint 2002

To create an effective presentation, you need to decide what information you want to convey and how you want to convey it. There are several presentation options with PowerPoint, including **on-screen presentations**, where you run a slide show from your computer; 35mm slides, which requires you to take PowerPoint slide files to a film-processing service for conversion; black-and-white or color overheads, which you can print directly on transparencies; and supporting materials, including notes for the presenter, audience handouts, and presentation outlines, which are usually printed on paper. ✎ The purpose of Kimberly's presentation is to present the new fall product line to retailers. She will be making one-on-one presentations at the headquarters of each retail account, usually in the buyer's office or a small conference room. You decide to create both an on-screen slide show, so she can run the presentation on her laptop computer, and speaker notes she can refer to if necessary.

Trouble?

The first time you start PowerPoint, the task pane is automatically open in the program window. After you save a presentation and close PowerPoint, the next time you open PowerPoint the task pane might not be open; to open it, click View on the menu bar, then click Task Pane.

QuickTip

To add text that will appear at the bottom of every slide, type it in the Footer text box in the Presentation Options dialog box.

1. Start **PowerPoint**

   The PowerPoint program window opens, as shown in Figure A-1. In the New Presentation task pane, you can choose to start a new presentation by using a blank presentation, a PowerPoint template, or the AutoContent Wizard. Or, you can open an existing presentation, either by clicking Presentations and locating the file in the Open dialog box or, if anyone has saved a presentation on your computer, by clicking one of the presentations in the list of recently opened files or by clicking More Presentations.

2. Click **From AutoContent Wizard** in the New Presentations task pane

   The AutoContent Wizard opens, as shown in Figure A-2. This method offers a quick and easy way to create a presentation. The chart along the left side of the dialog box shows that you complete three simple steps to create the basic presentation: you choose a presentation type, a presentation style, and presentation options. After you have completed the steps in the Wizard, you replace prompt text with the text of your presentation.

3. Click **Next**

   In this dialog box, you can choose from a variety of presentation types. By default, Generic is selected, showing the most common presentation types. To see a different category, you click a different button.

4. Click **Sales/Marketing**, click **Product/Services Overview**, then click **Next**

   In the Presentation style dialog box, you specify how the presentation will be **output**, or produced, so that PowerPoint can format it correctly.

5. Click the **On-screen presentation option button** if necessary, then click **Next**

   In the Presentation options dialog box, you specify a name for the presentation and any additional information you want to appear on the slides.

6. Click in the **Presentation title text box**, type **Fall Product Highlights**, then click the **Date last updated check box** and the **Slide number check box** to deselect them

   Compare your screen with Figure A-3.

7. Click **Finish**

8. Click the **Save button** 🖫 on the Standard toolbar, display the drive and folder where your Project Files are stored, then save the presentation as **Outdoor Designs Sales Presentation**

FIGURE A-1: Starting a new presentation

When the Slides/Outline pane is narrow, these tabs appear as icons, as shown here

New Presentation task pane

AutoContent Wizard

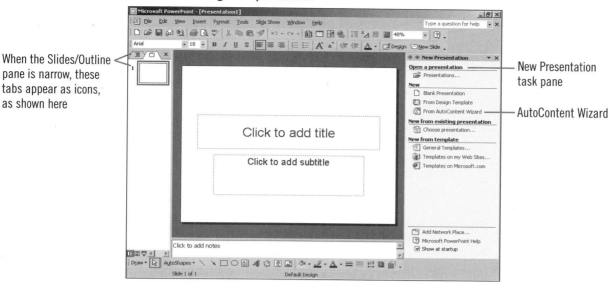

FIGURE A-2: AutoContent Wizard dialog box

FIGURE A-3: Presentation options dialog box of AutoContent Wizard

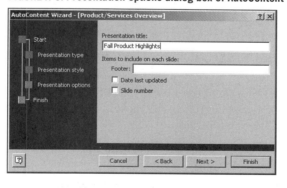

CLUES TO USE

Working with PowerPoint templates

The presentations available through the AutoContent Wizard are also available to you without using the wizard. They are available without the suggested content as design templates, or with the suggested content as presentation templates. To locate these templates, click General Templates in the PowerPoint New Presentation task pane. In the Templates dialog box, click the Design Templates tab or the Presentations tab. The Preview window shows the design of the selected template. Click a design, then click OK. If the template is not installed on your system, click OK to install it. You can also add your own presentation to the AutoContent Wizard, so that you can use it to create future presentations. To do so, click the category you want to place it in within the second wizard dialog box, click Add, locate your file in the Select Template dialog box, then double-click it to insert it in the wizard list.

Navigating a Presentation

Because a PowerPoint presentation can take many forms, such as an on-screen presentation, printed slides, or transparencies, you can work in a variety of views: Normal view; Slide Sorter view; Notes Page view; and Slide Show (from current slide) view. Normal view, the default PowerPoint view, displays the presentation in three scrollable panes. The Outline/Slides pane on the left contains a Slides tab, where you can work with thumbnails of all the slides in the presentation, and an Outline tab, where you can work with the text of the presentation. In the Slide pane in the center, you can work with all slide elements, and see them exactly as they will appear in an on-screen presentation or a printout. In the Notes pane under the Slide pane, you can add notes to remind you of key points. Before customizing the presentation the AutoContent Wizard created, you decide to review its contents and familiarize yourself with the PowerPoint program window.

1. **Click Tools on the menu bar, click Customize, click the Show Standard and Formatting toolbars on two rows check box to select it if necessary, click the Always show full menus check box to select it if necessary, click Reset my usage data button, click Yes in the message box, then click Close**
   Now there is room to display more buttons on each toolbar, and all the menu commands will appear at once when you open a menu. Figure A-4 identifies many important elements in the PowerPoint program window.

2. **Click the Close button in the upper-right corner of the task pane if necessary**
   The task pane closes. Now you have more room to display your presentation while you work on it.

   QuickTip
   To enlarge the Outline/Slides pane, point to the right border of the pane, then when it changes to ←‖→, drag it to the right.

3. **Click the Outline tab if necessary, then drag the scroll box in the vertical scroll bar down to the end of the outline**
   The AutoContent Wizard created a presentation with seven slides. In the Outline tab, you can see only the text of each slide, with slide titles and bulleted text indicated in outline levels, but with no indications of graphics or slide formats. In the Slide pane, you can see the slide that is selected in the Outline pane, complete with the background and the formatting of the slide elements (such as the title, the bulleted points, and the fonts and font sizes).

4. **In the Outline tab, click anywhere in the slide title Availability to the right of the Slide 7 icon**
   Notice that the Slide pane now displays Slide 7. When you change to a different slide in one pane, the other panes reflect the move. The status bar displays "Slide 7 of 7" because you are currently viewing that slide.

5. **In the Slide pane, click the Previous Slide button ▲ in the vertical scroll bar**
   The Slide pane now displays Slide 6, titled "Pricing," and the status bar displays "Slide 6 of 7."

6. **In the Outline pane, select the word available in the bulleted text in Slide 6, then press [Delete]**
   The deletion is reflected in both the Outline tab and the Slide pane, as shown in Figure A-5.

7. **Click the Slides tab, then click the Slide 3 thumbnail**
   The Slide pane now displays Slide 3, titled "Features & Benefits." When a slide is selected in the Slides tab, a border appears around it.

   QuickTip
   To enlarge the Notes pane, point to the top border of the pane, then when it changes to ↕, drag it up.

8. **Click in the Notes pane, then type Kite kits aren't just for kids. Our marketing research shows that sales to adults in the 40-65 age range have increased 38% in the past year.**
   This text does not appear in the Outline or Slides tab because it does not appear on the slide itself, only in the notes.

FIGURE A-4: PowerPoint program window in Normal view

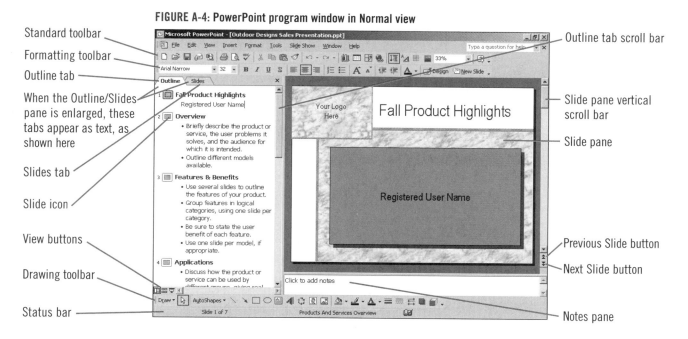

Standard toolbar
Formatting toolbar
Outline tab
When the Outline/Slides pane is enlarged, these tabs appear as text, as shown here
Slides tab
Slide icon
View buttons
Drawing toolbar
Status bar

Outline tab scroll bar
Slide pane vertical scroll bar
Slide pane
Previous Slide button
Next Slide button
Notes pane

FIGURE A-5: Navigating through a presentation

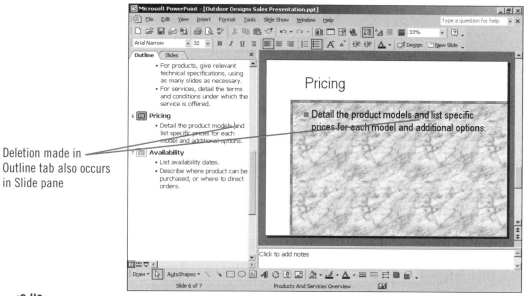

Deletion made in Outline tab also occurs in Slide pane

Working with PowerPoint views

You can quickly switch from view to view by using the View menu or the View buttons at the bottom of the Outline/Slides pane. The current slide in Normal view displays a slide as it will appear when it is output, including the layout, formatting, and any graphics. The Outline tab displays the text of the entire presentation in outline format, which is ideal when you are writing or editing content. The Slides tab displays thumbnails of all the slides, which is useful for navigating slides or rearranging slide order. Slide Sorter view conveniently displays miniatures of all your slides at once, which is useful when you want to view how the slides look in relationship to each other, rearrange them, or make design changes. Slide Show runs the on-screen presentation. Notes Page view (available only on the View menu) lets you add notes to your presentation, which you can then print with or without the accompanying slides. Because Normal view contains the Outline/Slides pane, the Slide pane, and the Notes pane, you may find this the preferred view for most of your work.

Entering Text in the Outline Tab

The **Outline tab** displays the text of a presentation in outline format, making it easy to enter and edit text, and organize the flow of information. You are ready to customize the content provided by the AutoContent Wizard to match your presentation goals, and decide to accomplish this task in the Outline tab.

Steps

1. Click the **Outline tab**, click the **Slide 1 thumbnail**, select the first line of text below the heading "Fall Product Highlights," then type **Kimberly Ullom**

   Because Kimberly will be making the sales presentation, you want her name to appear on the first slide of the presentation. Notice that when you make the change in the Outline tab, the text in the Slide pane changes as well. See Figure A-6.

2. Click **View** on the menu bar, point to **Toolbars**, then click **Outlining**

   The Outlining toolbar opens along the side of the Outline tab. Take a moment to familiarize yourself with the Outline tab, using Figure A-7 as a reference. This tab displays the presentation text in outline format. The Outlining toolbar makes it easy to work with the levels of text in the outline.

3. Select the text **Briefly describe the product or service, the user problems it solves, and the audience for which it is intended.** under the title "Overview" in Slide 2

4. Type **Exciting New Products**

5. Select the second line of bulleted text, **Outline different models available.**, then type **Exciting New Product Line**

6. Press **[Enter]**, then type **Fantastic New Discount Policy**

   To create a new bullet, you simply press [Enter]. The current outline level is automatically assigned to a new line of text, and the current slide layout is assigned when a new slide is added.

7. Select the text beginning with the title **Features & Benefits** in Slide 3 and ending with the last bulleted text in Slide 7 (**Describe where product can be purchased, or where to direct orders**), press **[Delete]**, then click **OK** to confirm the deletion

   The slides you deleted do not match your plans for this presentation.

8. Press **[Enter]**, click the **Promote button** 🔲 on the Outlining toolbar, then type **New Products for Fall**

   Creating new slides in Outline view is easy. You press [Enter] to start a new line of text, and use the buttons on the Outlining toolbar to **promote** text, moving it up one outline level, or **demote** it, moving it down one level. The highest level you can promote a line of text to is the slide title. There are several subordinate levels available. PowerPoint formats the text as title text and assigns a number and slide layout to the slide, as shown in Figure A-7.

9. Press **[Enter]**, click the **Demote button** 🔲 on the Outlining toolbar, type **Nightsky 3000 Tent**, press **[Enter]**, type **North by North Beach Kite Kit**, then save your changes

> **Trouble?**
>
> If you deleted the paragraph return between the first and second bulleted points, simply press [Enter] after typing the text.

FIGURE A-6: Outline tab

Outline tab

Selected text changed in the Outline tab and in the Slide pane

Normal View button

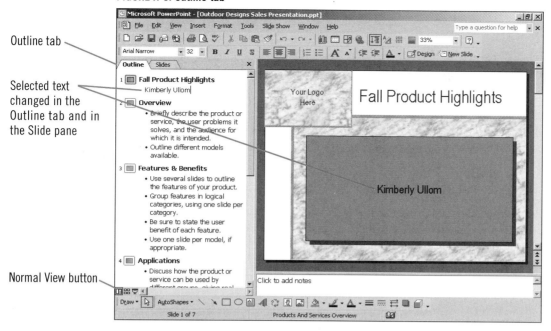

FIGURE A-7: Promoting a line of text

Promote button (active when selected text is not already at the highest level)

Demote button

Outlining toolbar

Text is promoted to a slide title for a new Slide 3, formatted like the previous slide

Some outlining buttons are also available on Formatting toolbar

Bullet point

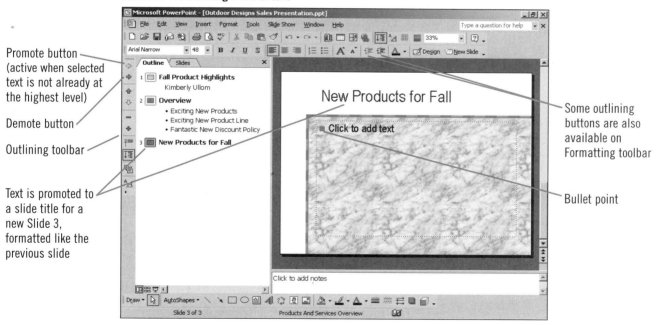

Working with text in Outline view

You work with text in Outline view just as you do with an outline in a word processor such as Microsoft Word. An Outlining toolbar, which appears along the left edge of the screen, provides shortcuts to common outlining actions such as promoting or demoting text, viewing selected levels of the outline, and moving text around. For example, the Collapse button ☐ displays only the titles of the selected slide or slides,

so you can view them without being distracted by the slide text. The Move Up button ⬆ moves the selected text above the previous line. To change the layout of a slide while in Outline view, click anywhere in the slide text, click Format on the menu bar, then click Slide Layout. The Slide Layout task pane opens to let you choose a different layout.

PowerPoint 2002

Entering Text in the Slide Pane

The Slide pane in Normal view lets you see exactly how a slide will appear as you enter and edit text, graphics, and other elements. On the current slide, each graphic or line of text is an **object**, which can be moved, resized, or edited. To edit the text within a text object, click the object, then move the insertion point to the appropriate location.  You can easily insert new slides into a presentation by using the New Slide button, which automatically opens the Slide Layout task pane. You decide to create three new slides and use the Slide pane to enter text for them, while using the Slides tab to navigate the presentation.

Steps

1. Click the **New Slide button** on the Formatting toolbar
   You want to create a new slide to contain information about the new product line. A new slide appears as the current slide, and the Slide Layout task pane opens, as shown in Figure A-8. In this task pane, you specify a layout for the new slide you want to create, which contains formatting and **placeholders** for text and graphics. The currently selected layout is shown in the preview box. If you rest the pointer over the layout, a ScreenTip shows its name.

2. In the Slide Layout task pane, scroll down to the Text and Content Layouts section, point to the **first box in the top row** (Title, Text, and Content), click the **arrow button**, then click **Apply to selected slides**
   You decide to use this layout for the food kits product line, which contains placeholders for text and graphics content, as shown in Figure A-9.

3. Click the **title placeholder**, which is labeled "Click to add title"
   A **selection box** appears around the placeholder, indicating that you can enter or edit text at the insertion point, use the sizing boxes to resize the placeholder, or drag any edge to move it.

4. Type **Back Country Gourmet Kits**, click in the **bulleted list placeholder**, type **Dehydrated Food Kits for Gourmet Campers**, press [Enter], type **Lightweight**, press [Enter], type **Nutritious & Delicious!**, press [Enter], then type **Available in September**
   You will insert clip art for this slide in the next unit.

QuickTip
To move to a different slide, you can use the vertical scroll bar in the Slide pane, click the Next Slide and Previous Slide buttons, click the desired slide icon in the Outline/Slides pane, or press [PgUp] and [PgDn].

5. Create and enter text for two more slides based on the information below:

Use this Slide Layout:	In Title Placeholder type:	In Bulleted List Placeholder type:
Title and Text	Improved Discount Policy	• 60% discount for orders over $1000
		• 62% discount for orders over $2000
		• 64% discount for orders over $3000
Title and Text	Thanks for a Great Year So Far!	• Sales are up 58%!
		• 78 new retail partners!
		• Let's keep the business booming!

6. Click the **Slide 1 thumbnail** in the Slides tab

7. Click the **Close button** in the Slide Layout task pane

Trouble?
If the AutoFit Options button (a button that helps you control the look of text) appears, rest the pointer over it, click the arrow to view the options, then click away from the button to accept the default option.

8. Click after the text "Kimberly Ullom," press [Enter], type **Outdoor Designs**, then save your changes
   Compare your screen with Figure A-10.

FIGURE A-8: Current slide with Slides tab open

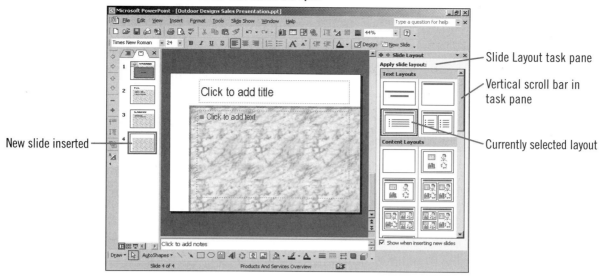

New slide inserted

Slide Layout task pane

Vertical scroll bar in task pane

Currently selected layout

FIGURE A-9: Slide Layout task pane

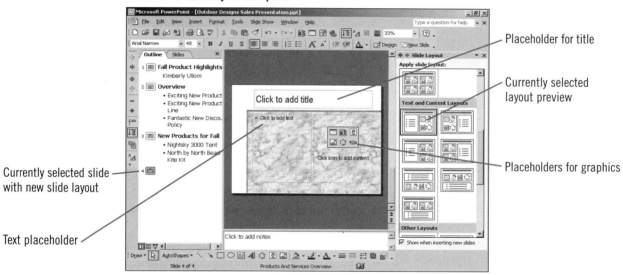

Currently selected slide with new slide layout

Text placeholder

Placeholder for title

Currently selected layout preview

Placeholders for graphics

FIGURE A-10: Edited slide

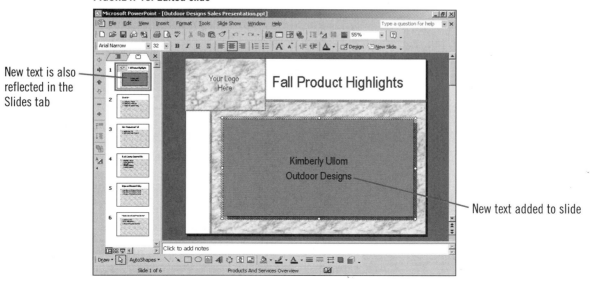

New text is also reflected in the Slides tab

New text added to slide

PowerPoint 2002

Formatting Text

You can format text in a presentation to make certain messages stand out. For example, in a bulleted list you might want to distinguish one bulleted point by changing its color or selecting a different font type. You can format selected text or turn on formatting options before typing new text. As with entering and editing text, you can format text in the Outline tab or in the Slide pane. ✐ You want to format the text in Kimberly's sales presentation to highlight important information, such as her name, the company name, and the agenda for the presentation. You should still be in Normal view, with the first slide active.

Steps 1 2 3 4

1. Press and hold **[Shift]**, then click in the **text placeholder** containing Kimberly Ullom's name
   This keyboard shortcut selects all the text in the placeholder. The Font Size list box shows that the current font size is 32 points.

2. Click the **Font Size list arrow** 🔟 on the Formatting toolbar, then scroll to and click **48**

3. Select the text **Outdoor Designs**, then click the **Increase Font Size button** Ａ on the Formatting toolbar twice
   The size of the selected text changes to 60 points. See Table A-1 for a description of the buttons on the Formatting toolbar.

4. Click **Format** on the menu bar, then click **Font**
   The Font dialog box provides a variety of formatting options, including font, font style, font size, effects, and colors.

5. Click the **Color list arrow**, click **More Colors**, then click the **Standard tab** if necessary
   The Colors dialog box contains a large palette of colors from which to choose. Below the color palette is a black and white palette, which is useful when you are preparing a presentation that will be printed on a black-and-white printer. In the lower corner, the New and Current preview box provides a comparative view of the two colors.

6. Click the shade of green shown in Figure A-11, click **OK**, click **OK** in the Font dialog box, then click away from the text to deselect it
   The new color reflects the active, natural image of Outdoor Designs.

7. Select the text **Kimberly Ullom**, click the **Font Color list arrow** 🅰 on the Drawing toolbar, then click the **color white** (the first box in the second row)

8. Click the **Slide 2 thumbnail** in the Slides tab, Press **[Shift]**, click anywhere in the bulleted text, click the **Bold button** Ｂ on the Formatting toolbar, then click the **Shadow button** 🅂 on the Formatting toolbar

9. Click **Format** on the menu bar, click **Line Spacing**, click the **up arrow** in the **Line spacing box** to set the spacing at **1.5**, click **OK**, then click away from the bulleted text to deselect it
   The bold and shadow attributes and the increased line spacing help make each point stand out, as shown in Figure A-12.

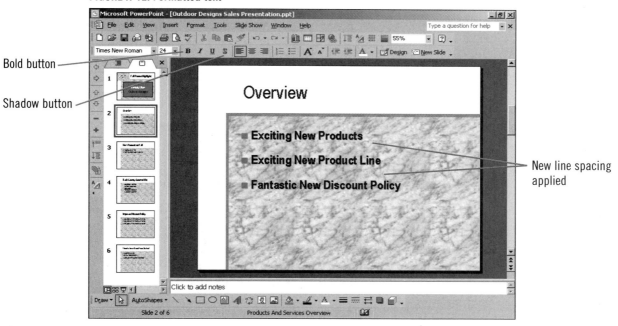

FIGURE A-11: Changing the font color

Standard tab is selected

Step 6

New color selected in the color wheel

Color currently in use

FIGURE A-12: Formatted text

Bold button

Shadow button

New line spacing applied

Overview

- Exciting New Products
- Exciting New Product Line
- Fantastic New Discount Policy

TABLE A-1: Formatting toolbar buttons

toolbar button	description	toolbar button	description
B	Turns bold formatting on or off		Formats text in bullets
I	Turns italic formatting on or off	A	Increases font size
U	Turns underlining on or off	A	Decreases font size
S	Turns text shadow formatting on or off	A	Opens Font Color list
	Turns left-alignment on or off		Decreases Indent
	Turns center-alignment on or off		Increases Indent
	Turns right-alignment on or off		Opens Slide Design task pane
	Formats text in numbered bullets		Opens Slide Layout task pane

Using the Drawing Toolbar

The Drawing toolbar contains drawing tools that let you enhance your presentations with shapes, lines, and simple pictures. Like text boxes and graphics, the shapes and lines you create are objects that can be moved, resized, and formatted. The AutoShapes button opens a list of several custom shape categories to speed up your drawing tasks. ✎ You decide to add graphics—a sun and a moon—to two slides in Kimberly's presentation.

Steps

1. Click the **Slide 1 thumbnail** in the Slides tab
   The first slide in the presentation contains a placeholder box for inserting a company logo.

2. Select the placeholder text **Your logo here**, then press **[Delete]**

3. Click **AutoShapes** on the Drawing toolbar, then point to **Basic Shapes**
   The Basic Shapes palette opens, as shown in Figure A-13. Refer to the figure for guidance in locating the shape and drawing it on the slide.

4. Click the **Sun AutoShape**, click in the upper-left corner of the logo area, then drag down and to the bottom-right corner of the logo area, as shown in Figure A-13

5. Make sure the Sun shape is selected, click the **Fill Color list arrow**, click **More Fill Colors**, then click the **Custom tab** in the Colors dialog box if necessary

6. Click the **yellow color** in the palette and drag the **slider** up, as shown in Figure A-14, then click **OK**
   The color of the new AutoShape brightens up. In the Colors dialog box, you can choose a custom color by clicking anywhere in the palette or entering values in the text boxes below it, and adjust the luminosity of the selected color by dragging the slider to achieve the effect you want.

7. Click the **Slide 3 thumbnail**, click **AutoShapes**, point to **Basic Shapes**, click the **Moon shape**, press and hold **[Shift]**, click to the right of the bulleted text and drag down to the bottom-right corner to draw a moon, release the mouse button and [Shift], click the **Fill Color list arrow**, then click the **white color**
   Pressing and holding [Shift] while you draw or resize a shape maintains its original proportions. See Table A-2 to learn more about working with objects.

8. Click **Draw** on the Drawing toolbar, point to **Rotate or Flip**, then click **Flip Horizontal**
   The moon looks better facing this new direction.

9. Click the **Shadow Style button**, click the **second box in the second row** (Shadow Style 6) of the Shadow palette, click away from the shape, then save your changes
   Compare your screen with Figure A-15.

FIGURE A-13: Drawing with an AutoShape

In Step 4, click here to begin drawing

In Step 4, release the mouse button to finish drawing here

Sun shape

FIGURE A-14: Custom tab of the Colors dialog box

In Step 6, select this color

In Step 6, drag the slider here

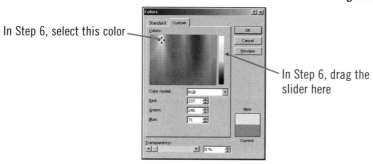

FIGURE A-15: Formatted AutoShape

Moon AutoShape with new fill color

Shadow Style Six added to the moon shape

Shadow Style button

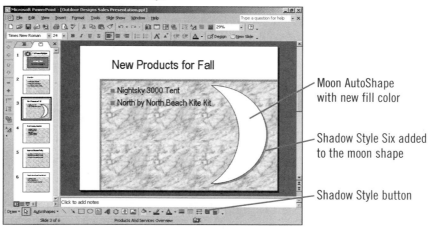

TABLE A-2: Working with objects

if you want to	do this
Select an object	Click the Select Objects button 🔂 on the Drawing toolbar if necessary, then click the object you want to select.
Move an object	Select the object, then click in the middle of the object and drag the Move pointer in the desired direction.
Resize an object	Select the object, then drag a corner sizing handle in the desired direction. Press [Shift] while dragging to maintain the object's proportions.
Delete an object	Select the object, then press [Delete].
Draw a proportional object	Press [Shift] while drawing a circle or square to make it proportional from the edge of the object; press [Ctrl] to make it proportional from the center of the object.

Adding Text Boxes

You can use the Drawing toolbar to add text boxes to a slide. **Text boxes** are similar to text placeholders but allow more flexibility in terms of the shape and format of the text. You can create text boxes in which text automatically wraps to the next line. These are useful for labels and brief messages. Whether you add text directly to existing shapes or create new text boxes, you can bring important messages to life. ✏ Kimberly asks you to add a last-minute addition to the discount policy: all orders posted by August 15 receive free shipping. You decide to use a text box on the "Improved Discount Policy" slide to make the new information stand out.

1. Click the **Slide 5 thumbnail**

   Under the last bullet on the slide titled "Improved Discount Policy" there is room to insert a text box to contain the new discount information.

QuickTip

You can also add text directly to a shape by right-clicking in the shape where you want to begin typing. Press [Shift][Enter] or [Enter] when you want the text to wrap to a new line or paragraph within a shape.

2. Click the **Text Box button** 🖾 on the Drawing toolbar, click and hold in the upper-left area under the last bulleted item, then when the pointer changes to ┼, drag down and to the right to draw a rectangle that fits approximately in the center of the space

   If necessary, move or resize your shape so that it matches Figure A-16. When you enter text into the text box, the size of the box will increase to contain it.

3. Type **Free Shipping**, press **[Shift][Enter]** if you have not reached the end of the text box, then type **til August 15!**

   Pressing [Shift][Enter] inserts a new line, so that the remaining text wraps. Pressing [Enter] within a text box inserts a new paragraph, which would create too much space between the two lines for your purposes.

QuickTip

When you create a text box, you do not need to click in the box before entering text. Once you release the mouse button after drawing the box, simply begin typing.

4. Select the two lines of text, press **[Ctrl][B]**, click the **Font list box** on the Formatting toolbar, click **Arial Narrow**, click the **Font Size list box**, click **32**, then click away from the text box

   This formatting makes the text easier to read. You format text in a text box just as you do other slide text: by selecting it, then using the Format menu, the Formatting toolbar, or a keyboard shortcut. Text you type wraps automatically to maintain the width of the text box.

QuickTip

Remember that you can often select any object simply by clicking it. The Select Objects button ▨ is selected by default.

5. Click the **text box**, select the two lines, click the **Center button** 🔳 on the Formatting toolbar

6. Click the **Fill Color button list arrow** 🖌▾ on the Drawing toolbar, click the **yellow color** (the first box in the second row), then click away from the text

   Because you used this custom color elsewhere in the presentation, it now appears on the Standard fill palette. The slide is complete. Compare your screen with Figure A-17.

7. Save your changes

FIGURE A-16: Creating a text box

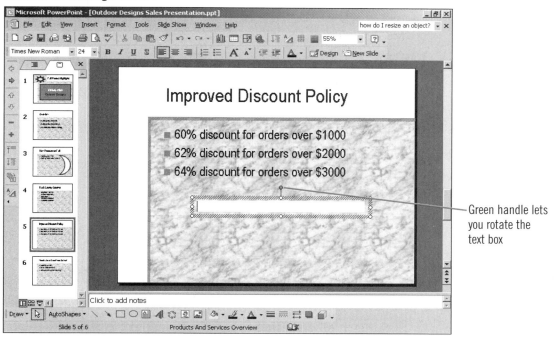

Green handle lets you rotate the text box

FIGURE A-17: Completed text box

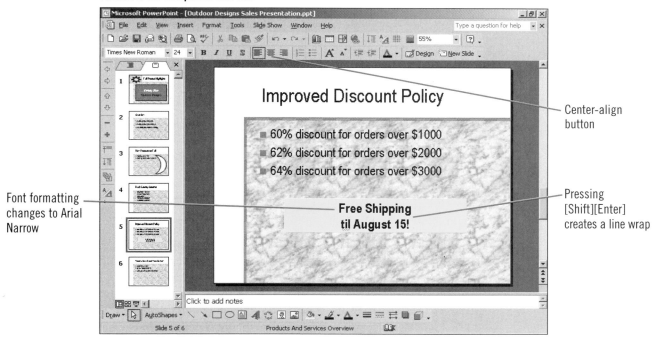

Center-align button

Font formatting changes to Arial Narrow

Pressing [Shift][Enter] creates a line wrap

Working with stacked objects

Inserting one object on top of another object is called **stacking** the objects. The last object you insert is on top, or in the front, of the stack. You can change the stacking order by right-clicking an object, pointing to Order on the submenu, then clicking an option to send the object farther to the back or closer to the front of the stacking order. Click Bring to Front or Send to Back to move the object to the very front or back of a stack of objects. Click Bring Forward or Send Backward to move the object only one layer in either direction.

PowerPoint 2002

Checking Spelling and Previewing a Presentation

PowerPoint contains tools for ensuring that your presentation is free of errors before you run it in front of an audience. The AutoCorrect feature corrects common spelling and typing errors as you work. The Spelling feature underlines additional misspellings as you type, and you can run a spelling check to find and correct these additional errors all at once. You can preview your work in Slide Sorter view to check the flow of information and the overall design, then switch to Slide Show view to view the slides, full-screen, progressing through the presentation one at a time. ✐ You're almost ready to show Kimberly the first draft of the sales presentation. First, you want to check the spelling. Then you want to review your work in Slide Sorter view to decide whether the flow of information is logical.

QuickTip

You can also use the keyboard shortcuts [Ctrl][Home] to move to the first slide in a presentation, and [Ctrl][End] to move to the last slide.

1. Click the **Slide 1 thumbnail**

2. Click the **Spelling button** 📝 on the Standard toolbar
   The spelling check begins. The Spelling dialog box opens when it finds a word it doesn't recognize. As shown in Figure A-18, the first word it finds is "Ullom." (If you made typing errors before this point, another word might appear here.)

3. Click **Add**
   Although the spelling check suggests alternate spellings, you want to add Kimberly's last name to the dictionary. The next word is "Nightsky." The spelling check doesn't recognize this word either, but you know it is spelled as the manufacturer intended.

4. Click **Ignore All**
   The spelling check continues. The next misspelled word is "til". The suggested correction, "till," is selected in the Change to text box.

5. Scroll through the list of suggestions to find the word "Until"
   This word does not appear in the list.

6. Type **Until**, click **Change**, respond to any additional prompts in the Spelling dialog box if necessary, then click **OK** when you get the message that the spelling check is complete

7. Click the **Slide Sorter View button** 🔳 at the bottom of the Slides tab
   Slide Sorter view displays all the slides in the presentation in miniature and allows you to move them easily. There is a Notes button on the Formatting toolbar in this view, which lets you easily add speaker notes to each slide without returning to Normal or Notes Page view. The Summary Slide button lets you create a slide that contains a bulleted list of all the titles of the slides you select in Slide Sorter view, which is useful when introducing or recapping a presentation. When you select a slide, and then click the Hide Slide button, that slide remains in the presentation, but is not displayed during your slide show unless you specifically call it up.

QuickTip

To move a slide in Slide Sorter view, you simply drag it to the desired location until the insertion point appears where you want to position the slide. You can also rearrange slides by dragging them on the Slides tab.

8. Click **Slide 5** to select it if necessary, then drag it on top of **Slide 6** so that the insertion point appears to the right of Slide 6
   The "Improved Discount Policy" slide becomes Slide 6, changing places with the "Thanks for a great year so far!" slide, as shown in Figure A-19. It makes more sense to discuss the new discount policy after thanking buyers for a great year.

9. Click **Slide 1**, **click the Slide Show (from current slide) button** 🖵 to the lower-left of the horizontal scroll bar, press **[Spacebar]** to move through each slide in order, click any key when the slide show ends, then save and close the presentation

FIGURE A-18: Spelling dialog box

Spelling check stops at many proper names

Adds current word to the dictionary

FIGURE A-19: Slide Sorter view

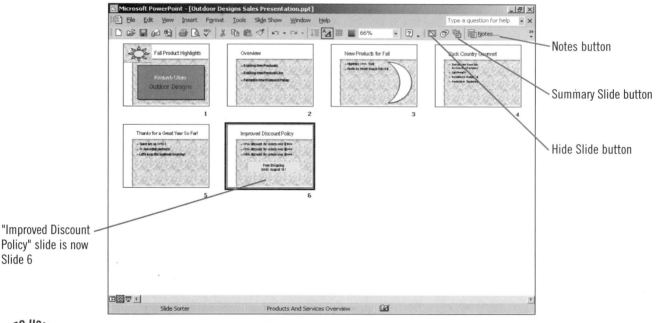

Notes button

Summary Slide button

Hide Slide button

"Improved Discount Policy" slide is now Slide 6

PowerPoint 2002

Working with the Spelling Checker

The Spelling feature works by finding words within the main text of a presentation that are not contained in PowerPoint's dictionary files, and suggesting alternate spellings. You should also review the text of a presentation to find any grammatical or word usage errors (such as "it's" instead of "its"). In the Spelling dialog box, you can leave the word as it is by clicking Ignore or Ignore All (to ignore all instances of this word in the presentation), change the spelling to the highlighted suggestion by clicking Change or Change All (to change all instances of this word to the suggested alternative), choose a different spelling in the Suggestions list by clicking it, enter your own correction in the Change to text box, add the word to your custom dictionary file so that PowerPoint never flags it again, or stop checking spelling by clicking Close.

Practice

► Concepts Review

Label each of the PowerPoint elements shown in Figure A-20.

FIGURE A-20

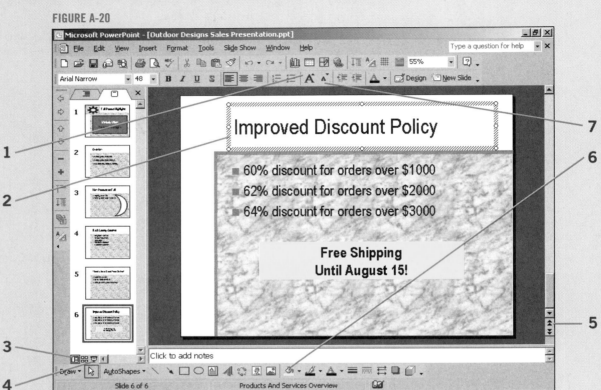

Match each of the following views with the activity for which it is most useful.

8. Outline tab   **a.** Viewing all the slides in a presentation at once
9. Normal view   **b.** Working with presentation content, individual slides, and notes all at once
10. Slide Sorter view   **c.** Working with slide text
11. Slide Show view   **d.** Running the presentation full-screen, one slide at a time

Select the best answer from the list of choices.

12. A presentation graphics program is primarily used to:
   a. Create presentation materials such as slides and transparencies.
   b. Compose lectures.
   c. Run videos on personal computers.
   d. Create clip art.

13. A PowerPoint presentation may include:
   a. Notes.
   b. 35mm slides.
   c. Handouts.
   d. All of the above

14. An on-screen presentation involves:
   a. Demonstrating the use of a computer program using a laptop computer.
   b. Processing PowerPoint slides into 35mm color slides.
   c. Opening Word files and scrolling through them with a client or customer.
   d. Running a PowerPoint slide show from a computer.

15. Which of the following is *not* a valid way to start creating a PowerPoint presentation?
   a. Use a Presentation template
   b. Use the AutoContent Wizard
   c. Use the Blank Presentation template
   d. Use Slide Sorter view

16. The New Slide button is located on the:
   a. Standard toolbar.
   b. Formatting toolbar.
   c. Outline tab.
   d. Menu bar.

17. When you click the 🄰 button on the Formatting toolbar, it:
   a. Promotes the current line of text to the next level.
   b. Decreases the current font size.
   c. Changes the current font color.
   d. Increases the current font size.

18. You can use the AutoShapes button to:
   a. Fill shapes with color.
   b. Draw freestyle designs.
   c. Import clip art.
   d. Change slide shapes.

PowerPoint 2002

19. Which view button do you click to switch to run a slide show starting with the current slide?

   a.

   b. ▦

   c. ▣

   d. None of the above

▶ Skills Review

1. Create a presentation.

   a. Identify three goals for a new presentation: make an informational presentation to the Outdoor Designs staff regarding company performance, inform employees about the status of sales and marketing goals, and recognize outstanding individuals.

   b. Start PowerPoint.

   c. Start a new presentation using the AutoContent Wizard.

   d. In the Presentation Style dialog box of the AutoContent Wizard, choose the Company Meeting presentation type in the Corporate category. If prompted to install this template, insert your Office XP CD, then click Yes.

   e. In the Presentation dialog box, choose the On-Screen presentation type.

   f. In the Presentation Options dialog box, do not type a title or deselect any check boxes.

   g. After completing the wizard, save the presentation as *Fall Company Meeting*.

   h. In the Registered User Name placeholder, type your name.

2. Navigate a presentation.

   a. If necessary, close the task pane.

   b. In the Outline tab, drag the scroll box in the vertical scroll bar down, pausing and releasing the mouse button to read the content of the entire presentation.

   c. Click anywhere in the text of Slide 13.

   d. In the Slide pane, click the previous slide button on the vertical scroll bar to move to Slide 12.

   e. In the Outline tab, scroll to and click in the bulleted or title text of Slide 7 to move to that slide.

   f. In the Slides tab, click the Slide 4 thumbnail.

   g. Drag the top border of the Notes pane up to create more space for entering notes.

   h. Click in the Notes pane, then type **Outdoor Designs has increased its market share by 10% in the past year**.

   i. Save your changes.

3. Enter text in the Outline tab.

   a. Display the Outlining toolbar if necessary.

   b. Click after the title Agenda in the second slide, then press [Enter].

   c. Click the Demote button on the Outlining toolbar.

   d. Enter the following text as bulleted list items: **Review Key Objectives, Review Our Progress, Discuss Top Issues, Gather Consensus on Goals, Summary.**

   e. Select all the slide text from Slide 5 through Slide 11, then delete it.

   f. Save your changes.

4. Enter text in the Slide pane.

   a. Click the New Slide button on the Formatting toolbar.

   b. In the Slide Layout task pane, choose the layout containing a title and two-column text, position the pointer over the selection until the arrow button appears, click it, then click Apply to Selected Slides.

   c. Click in the title placeholder of the new slide, then type **And the Winners Are**.

   d. Click the left placeholder text labeled Click to add text, then type **Jamie Nolan**.

   e. Click the right placeholder text labeled Click to add text, then type **Kimberly Ullom**.

5. Format text.

   a. Change the font size of the names Jamie Nolan and Kimberly Ullom to 36 points.

   b. Select the text Jamie Nolan, then use the Color list box in the Font dialog box to change the font color to the shade of dark green that follows the Accent and Followed Hyperlink Scheme color.

   c. Move to the previous slide, titled How Did We Do?, then press and hold [Shift] to select all of the main text.

   d. Format the selection in bold and italic.

   e. Select the word Brief, then use the Color list box in the Font dialog box to change the font color to the shade of tan that follows the Accent and Hyperlink Scheme color.

   f. Save your changes.

6. Use the Drawing toolbar.

   a. Move to Slide 5, titled And the Winners Are.

   b. Use the Stars and Banners AutoShapes menu on the Drawing toolbar to draw one vertical scroll banner approximately 1" long under Jamie's name and another vertical scroll banner under Kimberly's name. Place each banner approximately one inch below their names. Each banner should span the width of the name above it.

   c. Use the Rotate or Flip command on the Draw menu to horizontally flip the banner under Kimberly's name.

   d. Select the banner under Jamie's name, and use the Line Color button on the Drawing toolbar to change the line color to the shade of dark green that follows the Accent and Followed Hyperlink Scheme color.

   e. Save your changes.

7. Add text objects.

   a. Click the Text box tool on the Drawing toolbar, then click and drag to create a text box in the area above the banners that extends from the middle of one banner to the middle of the other banner.

   b. Enter the text **Achieved Their Goals!** in the text box.

   c. Select the text, and center-align it.

   d. Select Jamie's banner, then enter the text **Marketing initiatives have paid off!** in the banner. (*Hint*: Press Enter after each word to start a new line of text. When the AutoCorrect smart tag appears, click the arrow to view the options, click outside the smart tag to close it. Leave automatic capitalization turned on.)

   e. Select Kimberly's banner and enter the text **Top Sales Rep!** Your screen should look similar to Figure A-21.

   f. Save your changes.

FIGURE A-21

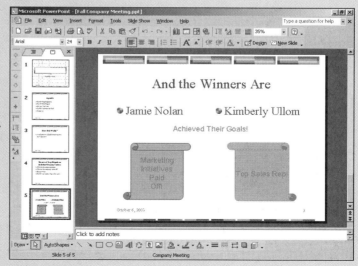

PowerPoint 2002

8. Check spelling and preview the presentation.

a. Run the Spelling Checker, and correct any spelling errors in the presentation.

b. Change to Slide Sorter view, and view the slides.

c. Change the order of the third and fourth slides.

d. Move to Slide 1, then change to Slide Show (from current slide) view.

e. Press [Spacebar] to progress through each slide title, bulleted point, and slide.

f. When you return to Slide Sorter view, click the Print button on the Standard toolbar to print a hard copy of the presentation using the default print settings.

g. Close the presentation, saving your changes when prompted then exit PowerPoint.

▶ Independent Challenge 1

The Wacky Words Card Company is looking for ways to explore new greeting card markets and distribute their cards through more retail channels. You've been assigned the task of creating a presentation that discusses how to sell Wacky Words to a larger market. You decide to use a template in the AutoContent Wizard to help to create your presentation.

1. Start PowerPoint or, if PowerPoint is currently running, open the New Presentation task pane.

2. Click the AutoContent Wizard, click the General button, click the template titled Recommending a Strategy, then click Next.

3. Select an on-screen presentation, title the presentation Wacky Words, and enter your name in the Footer placeholder. Clear the date and slide number check boxes.

4. Switch to Slide Show view, and view the slide show.

5. Enter your name in the Registered User placeholder, and save the presentation as *Wacky Words Introduction*.

6. Switch to the Outline tab of Normal view, if necessary, move to the first slide in the presentation, then modify text throughout the presentation to achieve your goal of presenting the Wacky Words company to prospective new customers in the best possible light. Follow the Wacky Words philosophy that greeting cards enhance the quality of life of those who give and receive them. Use testimonials from happy customers and any tools to prove that Wacky Words cards are a valuable resource that no retailer should be without.

7. Delete any slides that do not meet your needs, and add new slides as necessary.

8. Use drawing shapes and formatting to enhance your message as appropriate.

9. When you are finished, check the spelling in the presentation, preview your work in Slide Sorter view, and adjust the placement of individual slides if necessary.

10. Run the slide show in Slide Show view.

11. Save your changes, then close the presentation.

▶ Independent Challenge 2

Travel the World is a travel company that organizes active vacations for small groups. You've been hired to promote a trip to a country outside the North American continent, and you'll create a PowerPoint presentation that describes the benefits of taking a Travel the World vacation to this country. Chose a country that you're interested in, would like to visit, or know something about already. Include information in your presentation about the opportunities for rock climbing, hiking, kayaking, swimming, or other activities available in the country you've chosen.

1. Start PowerPoint if necessary.

2. Use the AutoContent Wizard to create a Sales/Marketing presentation for Selling a Product or Service. The presentation will be presented using a slide projector, so plan to output PowerPoint slides and take them to a film processor to be developed into 35mm slides. Type your name in the footer placeholder so that it appears on every slide.

3. Save the presentation as *Travel Presentation*.

4. Customize the content, formatting, and other elements to create an effective, inspiring plan that will sell your audience on taking the trip.

5. Check the spelling of the presentation before viewing it in Slide Show view.

6. When you are satisfied with the presentation, then save and close it.

▶ Independent Challenge 3

Office Assistant can extend your knowledge of PowerPoint by answering specific questions. As you continue working in PowerPoint, you may want to create presentations that are more interactive, especially for clients and coworkers with whom you communicate over the Internet. Find out how you can use the Internet to collaboratively produce and enhance your PowerPoint presentations.

1. Start PowerPoint if it is not currently open.

2. Open the Office Assistant by clicking Help on the menu bar, then clicking Show the Office Assistant.

3. Type **reviewing a presentation**.

4. Explore the topics the Office Assistant provides, clicking links to read related text and topics.

5. Print at least two topics concerning collaborating with others on a presentation, combining reviewed presentations, or discussing a Web page or document. (*Hint*: To print, click the Print button 🖨 at the top of the Help window.)

6. When you are finished, close the Office Assistant.

Independent Challenge 4

The Microsoft Office XP Web site offers several tools for becoming a more effective PowerPoint user. The PowerPoint Web site contains several resources for learning more about PowerPoint, communicating with PowerPoint experts, and downloading additional materials related to PowerPoint. Explore the PowerPoint Help articles on the Web now, and use the tips there to try out a new feature in PowerPoint 2002.

a. Start PowerPoint if necessary.

b. If necessary, connect to the Internet.

c. Click Help on the menu bar, click Office on the Web, then if a regional map appears click your region on the map.

d. On the Assistance Center page, click the link to PowerPoint to move to the PowerPoint 2002 Web page.

e. On the PowerPoint 2002 page, click the link to the presentation tips from Dale Carnegie, and read the article.

f. Move back to the PowerPoint 2002 page, if necessary, and select another PowerPoint Help article that contains a tip or technique you want to try, such as adding information to the footer placeholder on a slide.

g. Print the Help article, then write your name at the top of the printout.

h. Switch to PowerPoint, which is open on your desktop, and apply the new tip or technique in a presentation. Create a new presentation, by clicking Blank Presentation under New in the task pane. Select a slide layout for one slide that contains a title placeholder and a subtitle placeholder. Enter the name of the tip or technique in the title placeholder, and then type your name in the subtitle placeholder. Apply the new tip or technique, such as adding the word Confidential to the footer of your slide. Save your presentation using the filename *Help on the Web*. Print the slide that contains the new skill.

i. When you are finished, exit your browser.

j. Disconnect from the Internet if necessary, then close the presentation and exit PowerPoint.

▶ Visual Workshop

Create the slide shown in Figure A-22 using the skills you have learned in this unit. The Presentation template is available in the New Presentations task pane after clicking From Design Template. (*Hint*: The bagel graphic was created using three tools on the Drawing toolbar, including the More Colors option of the Fill Colors menu. The second bagel was copied from the first.) Enter your name on the slide by adding a bulleted item to the end of the list of bulleted items. When you have finished, save the presentation as *Laurie's Bagel Bakery*.

FIGURE A-22

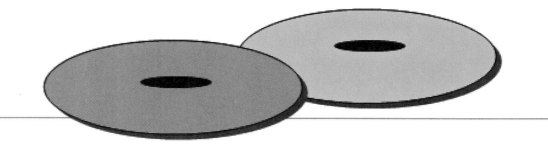

Laurie's Bagel Bakery

- Established in 1974
- Located in Historic Old Town
- All Natural Ingredients
- No Franchises — One of a Kind

Polishing

and Running a Presentation

Objectives

► **Change the color scheme of an existing presentation**
► **Insert clip art**
► **Work with pictures**
► **Run an online slide show**
► **Set timings and transitions**
► **Apply animation schemes and custom animation**
► **Create speaker notes and printed materials**

You can enhance a PowerPoint presentation by changing colors, adding graphics, and customizing other visual elements. If you plan to run your presentation on a PC, you can use PowerPoint controls to advance through the presentation at your own pace. If you prefer, you can set the timing of the slides to advance automatically, and use special effects to add impact. Kimberly Ullom, sales representative for Outdoor Designs, is pleased with the progress of her sales presentation. She suggests that you modify the colors of the slide show to suit the fall theme and add a graphic to highlight a new product. She plans to run the slide show automatically, so you'll need to apply an animation scheme and set additional timing and transition effects. Finally, she asks you to add some speaker notes to help her remember key points.

Changing the Color Scheme of an Existing Presentation

Each PowerPoint presentation template contains a preset color scheme, a set of eight coordinated colors for each element in a presentation, including the slide background, title text, and fills and shadows. Every slide or element you create is automatically formatted with these colors so the entire presentation looks professional. You can choose a different color scheme or modify aspects of it to customize your presentation. ✒️ You decide to change the color scheme of the sales presentation to include a fall color.

Steps 1 2 3 4

QuickTip

If PowerPoint is already running and the New Presentation task pane is not open, click File on the menu bar, click Open, navigate to the drive and folder where your Project Files are located, double-click the filename PPT B-1, then skip to Step 3.

1. Start PowerPoint, then in the New Presentation task pane, click **Choose Presentation** in the New from Existing Presentation section
   The New from Existing Presentation dialog box opens. This dialog box lets you create a new presentation based on an existing one without the risk of inadvertently modifying the existing presentation.

2. Click the **Look in list arrow**, navigate to the drive and folder where your Project Files are located, click the filename **PPT B-1**, then click **Create New**

3. Click **File** on the menu bar, click **Save As**, make sure that the Save in list box displays the drive and folder containing your Project Files and that the filename in the File name text box is selected, type **Fall Sales Presentation**, then click **Save**

4. Click the **Next Slide button** 🔽 in the Slide pane to view each slide in the presentation

Trouble?

If necessary, maximize the PowerPoint program and presentation windows.

5. Click the **Slide Design button** 📃 on the Formatting toolbar, click **Color Schemes** in the Slide Design task pane, then click **Edit Color Schemes**
   In the Edit Color Scheme dialog box, you can change the entire color scheme of a presentation by choosing one of the schemes listed on the Standard tab, or change selected color scheme elements by using the Custom tab.

6. If necessary, click the **Custom tab**
   As shown in Figure B-1, this tab lists the eight elements whose colors you can change in a PowerPoint presentation: Background, Text and lines, Shadows, Title text, Fills, Accent, Accent and hyperlink, and Accent and followed hyperlink. The last two options apply only to Web presentations. The preview box shows the currently selected colors for the elements in the current presentation, so you can easily make color choices using the dialog box.

7. Click the **Background color box**, as shown in Figure B-1, then click **Change Color**
   In the Background Color dialog box, you can choose one of the colors on the Standard tab, or specify a custom color on the Custom tab.

8. Click the **Standard tab** if necessary, click the **shade of orange** shown in Figure B-2, then click **OK**

QuickTip

To apply a scheme to selected slides, select the slides in the Slides tab, place the pointer over the scheme, click the arrow in the scheme, then click Apply to Selected Slides.

9. In the Color Scheme dialog box, double-click the **Title text color box**; click the **Standard tab** if necessary; click the **shade of white** in the color palette; click **OK**; click **Apply**; then save your changes
   The color of the title text on all the slides changes to white, which contrasts nicely with the new background color. After you change a color scheme, the new scheme is included in the list of available color schemes in the Slide Design - Color Schemes task pane.

FIGURE B-1: **Edit Color Scheme dialog box**

Contains preset color schemes

Step 7

Opens the color palette

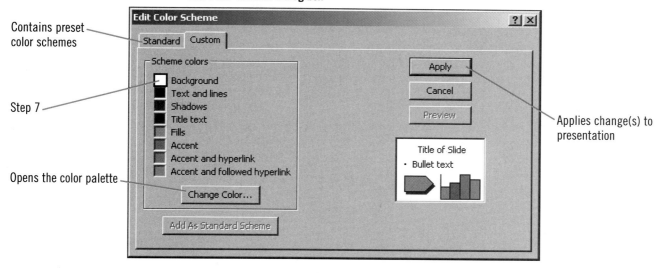

Applies change(s) to presentation

FIGURE B-2: **Background Color dialog box**

Contains colors that are not on the Standard palette

Color choices for a color presentation

Choices for a black and white presentation

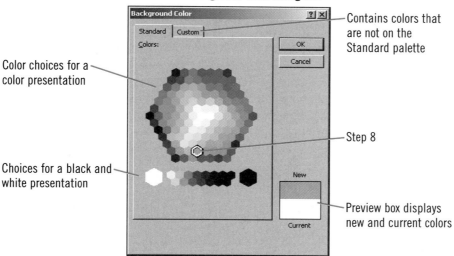

Step 8

Preview box displays new and current colors

Designing your presentation

When designing your presentation, remember these basic design principles:

- Use colors that contrast and complement each other within a slide and within the whole presentation. The color combinations provided in a design template provide a solid base to work from. Changing more than two or three colors throughout a presentation can weaken the unified, professional look of the finished product.
- If you plan to present on a PC or are using color slides, choose dark colors for backgrounds and lighter colors for text; if you plan to use transparencies or black and white printouts of your slides, light background and dark text colors are

more effective. The Standard tab of the Color dialog box offers color schemes suitable for both these situations.

- Make choices that support the desired tone of your presentation. A wild combination of colors might be fun to create but detract from your message.
- Edit text as necessary to keep your messages short and simple. A few words in a bulleted item create more impact than a long, detailed sentence.
- Use clip art and other pictures that convey information clearly. Detailed illustrations are difficult to recognize when shrunk to a small size to fit on a slide, and can confuse rather than enlighten.

Using Clip Art

Graphics files you insert into an electronic document are known as **clip art**. You can insert a clip-art image anywhere in a PowerPoint slide (some slide layouts contain a clip-art placeholder which can be helpful when planning a slide layout). Hundreds of clip art images are available on the Microsoft Office XP Media Content CD-ROM, and many of these are installed with PowerPoint. Clip-art images are referred to as "media files" in PowerPoint 2002. To make it easy to add, organize, and find clip art on your system, on the Office XP Media Content CD-ROM, or on the Web, use the Microsoft Clip Organizer. ✒️ Kimberly wants to illustrate the food kits from Back Country Gourmet, but the manufacturer did not provide a picture of the new product. You decide to find a piece of clip art to convey the high quality and sophistication of these ready-to-travel meals.

Steps

QuickTip

To insert clip art on a slide that does not have a clip art placeholder, click Insert on the menu bar, point to Picture, then click Insert Clip Art. If you want to insert a picture that is not in the Clip Organizer, click Insert on the menu bar, point to Picture, click From File, locate the file in the Insert Picture dialog box, then click Insert.

1. Move to **Slide 4**, then double-click the **Double click to add clip art icon**

   The Search Picture dialog box opens, as shown in Figure B-3, so that you can search the clip art currently installed on your system or import new clips. To search for clip art that is filed under a specific keyword or keywords, type the word or words in the Search for clips text box, click Search, then scroll through the available choices. You can also click the Import Clips button to import clip art from the Office XP Media Content CD-ROM or from another location, such as a disk, to the Clip Organizer. In the Insert Clip Art task pane, you can click the Clips Online link to search for more clips on the Web, or click Clip Organizer to open it in freestanding mode, as a small, separate program within PowerPoint. The mechanics of searching and inserting images are slightly different when you work with the Clip Organizer in freestanding mode, for example, you must copy the clip from Clip Organizer to the Office Clipboard, then use PowerPoint's Paste command to paste it onto the slide. You would open Clip Organizer in freestanding mode if you wanted to view or organize your clips by collections of clips.

2. Type **Food platter** in the Search text box, then click **Search**

Trouble?

If the clip shown in Figure B-4 does not appear on your screen, or if you locate the image but a message box opens requesting that you insert the source CD, insert the appropriate Office XP CD, then click Try again. This image is also available on your Project Disk. To use it, click Insert on the menu bar, point to Picture, click From File, locate your Project Files, then double-click the Food Platter file.

3. Scroll to the clip, as shown in Figure B-4, then double-click the **food platter clip** to insert it

   The clip image is inserted in the slide in place of the placeholder.

4. Point to the **center of the picture**, then click and drag to the **lower-right corner of the slide**, as shown in Figure B-5

   Clicking the center of a clip art image and dragging moves the image. Clicking and dragging a sizing handle changes its size.

5. Compare your screen with Figure B-5 to decide whether you need to resize your image, then if necessary, click the **upper-left corner sizing handle** and drag up and to the left to resize the image

   Your screen should look similar to Figure B-5.

6. Save your changes

Inserting other types of pictures

In addition to inserting clip art, you can insert almost any kind of graphic file in a PowerPoint presentation. These are identified as pictures in PowerPoint and may include a scanned photograph, a piece of line art created in a drawing program, or a graphic file such as a JPEG, GIF, or TIF file. To insert a picture, click Insert on the menu bar, point to Picture, and then click From File. Use pictures to customize a presentation by adding your company logo, the picture of a featured product, or other specific visual references to selected slides.

FIGURE B-3: **Select Picture dialog box**

Search text text box

Search button

The previews in this dialog box may be different, depending on which images are stored on your system

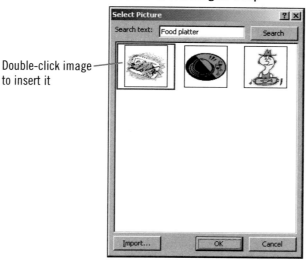

FIGURE B-4: **Searching for a clip**

Double-click image to insert it

FIGURE B-5: **Moving the clip-art image**

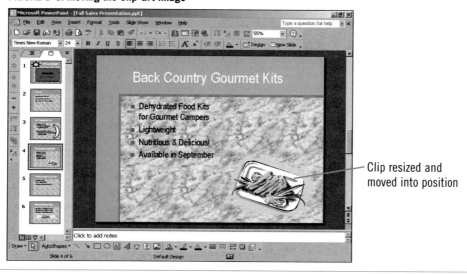

Clip resized and moved into position

PowerPoint 2002

Unit B

PowerPoint 2002

Working with Pictures

You can change the formatting and properties of pictures in PowerPoint to suit the needs of your presentation. In addition to simply moving and resizing an image, you can change **image properties**, such as brightness and contrast, change the colors, and even crop an image to use only part of it. When you select a picture (unless the Picture toolbar is hidden), the Picture toolbar opens. The Picture toolbar contains commands for adjusting the image properties of the selected picture. You decide to change the picture on the Back Country Gourmet Kits slide to better coordinate it with your presentation's color scheme.

Steps

Trouble?

If the Picture toolbar is not open on your screen, click View on the menu bar, point to Toolbars, then click Picture.

1. Click the **picture** to select it if necessary, then click the **Color button** on the Picture toolbar
A list of color options opens. See Table B-1 for a description of the Picture toolbar buttons.

2. Click **Black & White**, review the change, click again, then click **Automatic** to return to the default colors

3. Click the **More Contrast button** on the Picture toolbar three times, then click the **More Brightness button** once
Note the increase in contrast and brightness as you click.

4. Click the **Recolor Picture button** on the Picture toolbar
The Recolor Picture dialog box opens, as shown in Figure B-6. In this dialog box, you can change the background colors and fill colors in a picture. Background color is the color of the slide background; fill color refers to the color that fills a frame.

5. In the Change area, click the **Fills radio button** to display the fill colors, click the **shade of pink check box**, which is the color of the plate, in the Original list, then click the **New color list arrow** next to that color
A color palette opens. In the top row are colors that match the current color scheme of the presentation. In the bottom row are custom colors.

6. Click the **darker green box**, click **OK**
The color of the plate changes to green. It looks slightly brighter than it did in the dialog box because of the previous formatting changes you made to the picture.

7. Click the **Format Picture button** on the Picture toolbar
In the Format Picture dialog box, you can make all of the changes available on the Picture toolbar, such as cropping, changing fill and line colors, and changing image control, plus many more, and you can make some changes with a greater degree of control. For example, when cropping, you can enter the exact amount you want to trim from the picture.

QuickTip

When you print a slide that contains a transparent color, the color appears solid.

8. Click the **Colors and Lines tab**, in the Fill area click the **Color list box**, click the **white box** in the top row, drag the **scroll bar** in the Transparency area until the Transparency text box displays 50%, click **OK**, then click anywhere away from the picture to deselect it
The semitransparent fill makes the picture stand out more distinctly from the rest of the slide. Compare your screen with Figure B-7.

9. Save your changes to the presentation

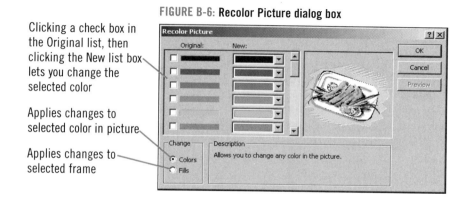

FIGURE B-6: Recolor Picture dialog box

Clicking a check box in the Original list, then clicking the New list box lets you change the selected color

Applies changes to selected color in picture

Applies changes to selected frame

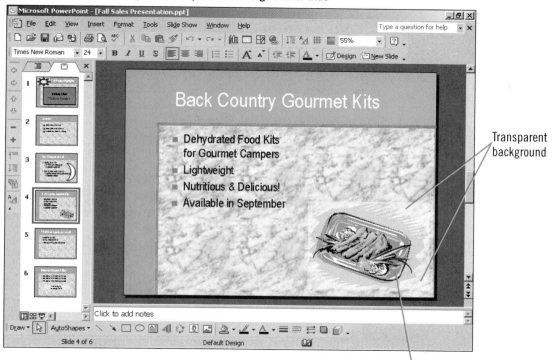

FIGURE B-7: Background of picture complements background of slide

Transparent background

Green fill applied to plate

TABLE B-1: Picture toolbar buttons

button	function	button	function
	Insert Picture from File		Rotate Left
	Color		Line Style
	More Contrast		Compress Pictures
	Less Contrast		Recolor Picture
	More Brightness		Format Picture
	Less Brightness		Set Transparent Color
	Crop		Reset Picture

Running an Online Slide Show

PowerPoint lets you run an online slide show on any compatible computer. You can use the keyboard or mouse to control the progression of slides, annotate the current slide, and navigate among slides in any order, so you can tailor the presentation to your current audience. An online slide show is often a good alternative to printing transparencies or slides because you don't need any equipment other than a computer to run the presentation. You practice running the slide show so you can make suggestions to Kim about how to run her presentation effectively.

Steps

1. Click **Slide 1** in the Slides tab, then click the **Slide Show (from current slide) button** to the left of the horizontal scroll bar
   The first slide in the sales presentation fills the screen.

2. Point anywhere on the screen to display the **Slide Show menu icon** (the semitransparent icon in the lower-left corner of the screen), then click it
   The Slide Show menu opens. You can point anywhere on the screen to display the Slide Show menu button or right-click anywhere on the screen to open the shortcut menu at the location of the mouse pointer button. This menu offers several choices for running the slide show, including navigating through slides, annotating your presentation with an on-screen pen, displaying speaker's notes, and ending the slide show.

3. Point to **Go**, then click **Slide Navigator**
   The Slide Navigator dialog box opens, as shown in Figure B-8. In this dialog box, you can move to any slide using the title of the slide. This dialog box is especially useful when working with a presentation that contains a large number of slides.

4. In the Slide titles list box of the Slide Navigator dialog box, click **6. Improved Discount Policy**, then click **Go To**
   Slide 6 fills the screen.

> **QuickTip**
>
> To remove a Pen mark immediately, press [E].

5. Right-click anywhere on the screen, point to **Pointer Options** on the pop-up menu, then click **Pen**
   You can use the pen to highlight important information as you're delivering the presentation.

> **QuickTip**
>
> Right-click within the slide, point to Pointer Options on the pop-up menu, then click Automatic to remove the pen pointer.

6. When the pointer changes to ✎, press and hold the **mouse button**, then drag a circle around the last bulleted item in the list
   As shown in Figure B-9, the last bulleted point is now circled with a pen. This mark lasts only until you move to a different slide.

7. Press **[←]**
   Slide 5 fills the screen.

> **QuickTip**
>
> To view a list of keyboard shortcuts to use during a slide show, right-click anywhere on the screen during an online slide show, then in the pop-up menu click Help.

8. Press **[B]**, note the effect, press **[B]** again to restore the screen, press **[W]**, then press **[W]** again
   You can use these shortcut keys to change the screen to black or white; this can be helpful when you want to direct attention away from the screen for a moment to discuss something with the audience, then move back when finished.

9. Press **[Home]** to return to the first slide, press **[Spacebar]** to progress through the presentation slide by slide, then press any key to end the slide show
   After the slide show ends, you return to the previous view, Normal view.

FIGURE B-8: Slide Navigator dialog box

Slide title list ——————

Click Go To button
to display the
selected slide

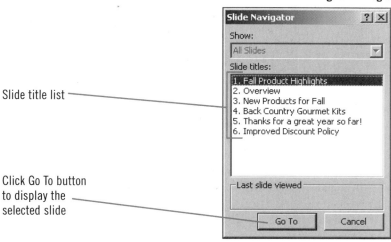

FIGURE B-9: Annotating a slide

Drag pen to
circle this
bullet point

Slide Show
button

Using PowerPoint Viewer when PowerPoint isn't installed

Sometimes you want to run a PowerPoint slide show on a computer that does not have PowerPoint installed. You may have a laptop computer without enough free disk space to install PowerPoint, or need to run a presentation on someone else's computer. You can run a PowerPoint presentation on any compatible computer as long as the computer can run a small program called PowerPoint Viewer. To use PowerPoint Viewer, you copy the program onto the disk where you save your presentation, then use it when you insert the disk in the other computer. PowerPoint contains a wizard that makes this process easy. Click File on the menu bar, then click Pack and Go. If the Pack and Go feature is not installed on your system, insert the appropriate Office XP CD before proceeding. When the Pack and Go Wizard opens, proceed through the steps to prepare your presentation.

PowerPoint 2002

Setting Preset Timing and Transitions

Sometimes you want to run a presentation without manually controlling the progression of slides. PowerPoint makes this easy by letting you set timing and transition effects ahead of time in the Slide Transition task pane in Normal or Slide Sorter view. Working in Normal view is easy because you can see icons on the Slides tab that represent your settings, and preview them before you run the slide show. Then, in Slide Show view, you can let the presentation run itself, or make manual moves only when you wish to. You can set timing and transitions in Normal view or Slide Sorter view. You decide to set timing and transitions so Kimberly can focus on her customers instead of on running the slide show. First, you set the timing for all slides in the presentation to 20 seconds, but also enable Kimberly to advance a slide manually to move more quickly when she chooses.

QuickTip
You can also open the Slide Transition task pane by right-clicking any slide in Slide Sorter view and then clicking Slide Transition on the pop-up menu, or by clicking the Other Task Panes button if another task pane is open.

1. **Click Slide Show on the menu bar, then click Slide Transition**
The Slide Transition task pane opens, as shown in Figure B-10. In this task pane, you can set **timing**, the amount of time each slide appears before the next is displayed, and set **transitions**, which controls how a slide appears, such as whether it appears to fade in or expand like a box. You can also modify the speed of the transition and add sound files to the effect. If the AutoPreview check box contains a check mark, you can preview the transitions you set in the Slide pane.

2. **Click the AutoPreview check box to add a check mark if necessary**

3. **Click the Automatically after check box in the Advance slide section to add a check mark, then click the up arrow until 20 appears in the text box**
You leave the On mouse click check box selected so Kimberly has the option of advancing to the next slide using the mouse if she finishes speaking in less than 20 seconds.

QuickTip
You can also apply timing or transition effects to only the current slide, by selecting that slide, then clicking the transition effect you want to apply from the Apply to selected slides list of effects, or to selected slides by pressing and holding [Ctrl] while clicking the noncontiguous slides to which you want to apply the effect.

4. **Click Apply to All Slides**
This applies the transition to all slides in the presentation.

5. **With the first slide selected, press and hold [Shift], click Slide 2, then click Blinds Horizontal in the Apply to selected slides section**
A preview of the transition effect runs in the Slide pane. This effect causes the first two slides in the presentation to appear in a blind-like design, making it look as if you are opening the blinds to show a new slide. See Table B-2 for a description of popular transition effects.

6. **Click the Speed list arrow in the Modify transition section, then click Medium**
A preview of the effect at medium speed appears in the Slide pane. Fast is the default speed for transitions, so this modification slows the effect slightly.

Trouble?
Be careful not to click Apply to All Slides at the end of this step or you will apply this effect to all slides in the presentation; if this happens, press [Ctrl][Z], then repeat Step 6.

7. **Click Slide 3 in the Slides tab, click Box Out in the transition list, click the Speed list arrow in the Modify transition section, click Slow, enter 30 in the Automatically after text box, click the Sound list arrow, then click Whoosh**
This sets a timing of 30 seconds for this slide and a transition effect that makes the slide appear as a small box that slowly expands to fill the screen. To hear sound effects during a presentation, you must have a sound card installed. Kimberly has a sound card on her PC, so this sound effect will be a great addition. In the Slides tab, an icon for the transition or preset animation effect appears for the slide.

8. **Click the Slide Sorter View button** ⊞
In Slide Sorter view, you can easily review timing and transition effects. As shown in Figure B-11, the timing for each slide appears below it, along with an icon if a transition (or animation) has been preset for the slide.

FIGURE B-10: Slide Transition task pane

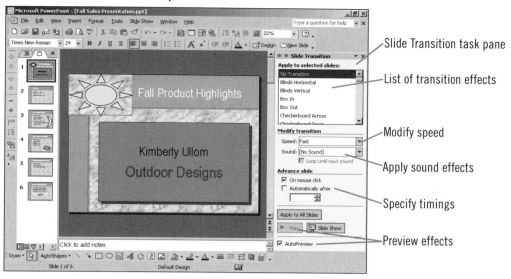

Slide Transition task pane

List of transition effects

Modify speed

Apply sound effects

Specify timings

Preview effects

FIGURE B-11: Timing and transition effects appear in Slide Sorter view

Icon signifies that a transition or animation effect is set for this slide

Number indicates that timing is set for this slide

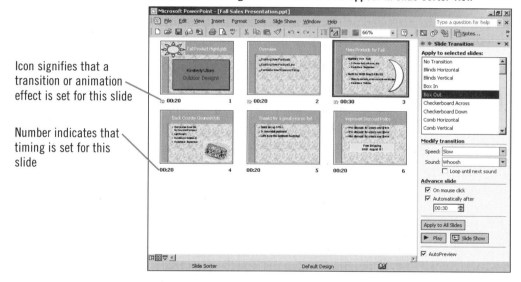

TABLE B-2: Popular transition effects

effect	description
Box In	Edges of slide appear first and fill in toward the center
Box Out	Slide appears as a small box that expands to fill the screen
Dissolve	Previous slide appears to dissolve into the current slide
Random Transition	Sets a different transition effect for each selected slide, or for all the slides in a presentation
Wipe Left	Slide appears to move over previous slide from right to left
Wipe Right	Slide appears to move over previous slide from left to right

PowerPoint 2002

Applying Animation Schemes and Custom Animation

Animation schemes are special sets of transition effects and graphics effects you can apply to make elements on a slide appear more interesting. You can apply an animation scheme to all the slides in your presentation, or to selected slides within your presentation. You can even specify the order in which you want the elements on the slide to animate. You can make all animation choices in the Animation Schemes task pane, or you can select one or more elements on a slide and use the Custom Animation command on the Slide Show menu to apply them. You can work in the Animation Schemes panes while in Normal view or Slide Sorter view; you can work in the Custom Animation slide only while in Normal view. After you apply animation effects, an icon appears on the selected slide or slides in the Slides tab. ✒ You decide to apply an animation scheme to the presentation as a whole and add custom animation effects to a selected slide element.

1. Click the **Normal View button** 🖫, click **Slide 1** in the Slides tab, click the **Other Task Panes button** ▫▾ in the task pane, then click **Animation Schemes**
   The Animation Schemes task pane opens, containing a list of preset animation effects you can apply to one slide or to all slides. When you rest the pointer over an animation effect, a ScreenTip appears telling you what the effect contains, as shown in Figure B-12.

2. Click **Slide 4**; press and hold [Shift]; click **Slide 5** and **Slide 6**; in the Apply to selected slide list, click **Zoom** in the Moderate category

3. Move to **Slide 6**, click **Slide Show** on the menu bar, then click **Custom Animation**
   The Custom Animation task pane opens, as shown in Figure B-13. The transition and animation effects you've already applied are indicated in the task pane for the selected slide.

4. Click the **Free Shipping text box**, click **Add Effect** in the task pane, point to **Entrance**, then click **Checkerboard**
   The Animation order list box shows the animated items listed in the order in which they are set for animation.

5. Click **Play**, click the **list arrow** next to the Shape 3 effect, then click **Effect Options**
   When you preview a custom animation, a moving timeline appears at the bottom of the task pane, which displays the seconds each animated item takes to move through its sequence. The Effect Options dialog box contains additional options for effects.

6. Click the **Effect tab** if necessary, in the Enhancements section click the **Sound list arrow**, then click **Applause**; if PowerPoint asks if you want to install this feature now, insert the Office XP CD, click **Yes**, then click **OK**

7. Move to **Slide 5**, click the **slide title text box** to select it, click **Add Effect** in the task pane, point to **Emphasis**, then click **Grow/Shrink**
   Now the title appears with a custom animation, which is numbered "4" on the slide.

8. In the Custom Animation list in the task pane, click the **Title 1** effect you just added, and drag the animation effect to the top of the list, then click the **Play button**
   Now that you have changed the animation order to list the Emphasis effect before the title animation contained in the custom animation scheme, the Emphasis effect is now numbered "1."

9. Move to **Slide 1**, then click the **Slide Show button** 🖳 to run the slide show

FIGURE B-12: Animation Schemes task pane

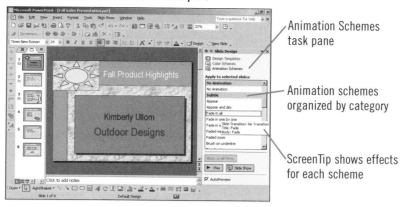

Animation Schemes task pane

Animation schemes organized by category

ScreenTip shows effects for each scheme

FIGURE B-13: Custom Animation task pane

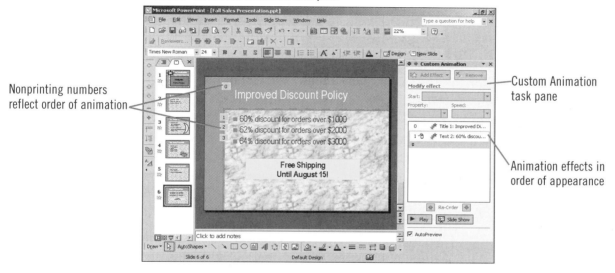

Nonprinting numbers reflect order of animation

Custom Animation task pane

Animation effects in order of appearance

Preparing for an off-site presentation

When preparing for an off-site presentation, do as much information gathering and planning as possible to ensure your success. If you plan to use an overhead projector or a slide projector, set up the equipment ahead of time so you can test it with your materials. If you plan to use a PC, make sure that PowerPoint or PowerPoint Viewer is installed and that the audience will be able to see the screen; you may want to arrange to connect the PC to a projection device if the audience is larger than three or four. Find out where the light switches are for the room, and make sure that you or someone you designate can turn off or dim the lights so that the audience can see the monitor or projection screen more clearly. If you plan to use handouts or refer to notes during the presentation, be aware that the altered lighting may not allow you or your audience to read printed handouts easily. If possible, arrange time for a rehearsal at your presentation site. Sightlines and acoustics vary from space to space and can greatly affect the success of your presentation.

Creating Speaker Notes and Printed Materials

Speaker notes accompany slides to help you remember important information that you do not want to appear on the slides. You can use speaker notes on-screen or print them out. You can create and work with speaker notes in either Notes Page View or Normal view. ✐ Kimberly will need some notes to help her remember important information as she makes her sales presentation.

Steps 1234

1. Click the **Close button** ☒ on the task pane, move to **Slide 1**, click **View** on the menu bar, then click **Notes Page**

2. Click the **text placeholder** below the slide
   The insertion point appears in the placeholder.

3. Click the **Zoom list arrow** on the Standard toolbar, then click **75%**
   The view is enlarged, as shown in Figure B-14, making it easier to enter text.

> **QuickTip**
> If you misspell any words, a red wavy line appears below them.

4. At the insertion point, type **Thanks for taking the time to meet with me today. I'm looking forward to working directly with you. At Outdoor Designs, our goal is to get into the field as much as possible, to answer questions, solve problems, and tell you about our exciting line of products. My goal is to help you increase your business, so don't hesitate to ask questions or make suggestions. Are there any issues you'd like to address before we get started?**
   As you type, the text wraps automatically.

> **QuickTip**
> If you have graphics that will enhance your printed notes, you can insert them in the Notes page; from Notes Page View, click Insert on the menu bar, then click the appropriate command (Picture, Diagram, Chart, Table, etc.) to add an element that further illustrates your point.

5. Click the **Next Slide button** ⬇ twice to move to **Slide 3**, click the **Click to add text placeholder**, then type **Both of these new products are manufactured by El Jardin, a major European manufacturer of outdoor products based in Barcelona, Spain. We hold exclusive distributorship of El Jardin products in North America.**

6. Click the **Normal View button** ▣, move to **Slide 1**, click in the **Notes pane**, scroll down using the Notes pane vertical scroll bar, as shown in Figure B-15, select all the text from **My goal is** to **before we get started.**, then click the **Cut button** ✂
   You want to move this text to Slide 6, where it will be more pertinent to Kimberly's presentation.

7. Move to **Slide 6**, click in the **Notes pane**, then click the **Paste button** 📋
   The text is pasted into the new location.

> **QuickTip**
> You can click Handouts in the Print what list to choose how many slides per page to print. If you print three slides to a page, your handouts feature a lined area to the right of the slides for your audience to take notes.

8. Click **File** on the menu bar, click **Print**, click the **Print what list arrow**, as shown in Figure B-16, click **Notes Pages**, then click **OK**
   A copy of your notes prints with the slide attached to make it easy to refer to.

9. Save your changes to the presentation, click the **Close button** to close the presentation, then exit PowerPoint

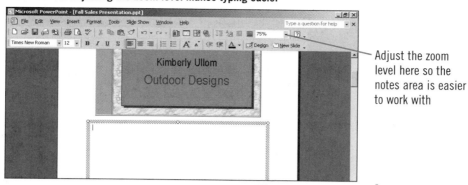

FIGURE B-14: Adjusting the zoom level makes typing easier

Adjust the zoom level here so the notes area is easier to work with

FIGURE B-15: Working with notes in Normal view

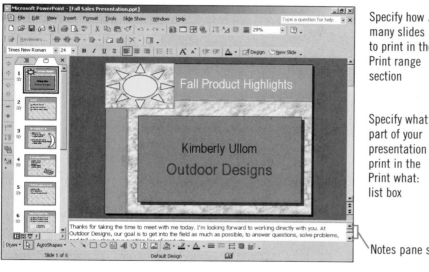

Notes pane scroll bar

FIGURE B-16: Working in the Print dialog box

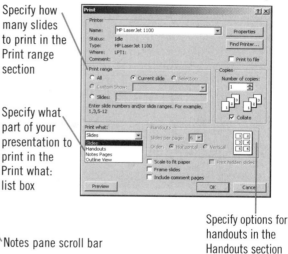

Specify how many slides to print in the Print range section

Specify what part of your presentation to print in the Print what: list box

Specify options for handouts in the Handouts section

CLUES TO USE

Previewing printed materials

Before you print a presentation, you can switch to Print Preview to get an idea of the overall appearance of the printed presentation and any supporting materials such as speaker notes. To open Print Preview, click File on the menu bar, then click Print Preview. The current slide appears in Print Preview. You can move to the next or previous slide by clicking the Next Slide or Previous Slide button on the vertical scroll bar. In this view, you can also set a variety of options, among them: change the **orientation** of the printed page, which can be either **landscape** mode, in which the width of the page is printed so it is larger than the height, or **portrait** mode, in which the height of the page is printed so that it is larger than the width. You can also add a header or a footer to the selected page or

all pages. A **header** lets you add information in a frame that appears in the background at the top of selected slides, while a **footer** lets you add this information at the bottom. You can also specify color choices, add a frame around slides, or print hidden slides. When previewing notes pages, you might see that there is enough space on the page to allow for additional content, such as an organization chart or diagram. In Print Preview, you can also specify how to print **handouts**, hard copies of a presentation that you can distribute to your audience, so that they print one slide per page, two slides per page, or up to nine slides per page. To include a lined area for taking notes, chose to print three slides per page, which includes a convenient lined space that is not visible in PowerPoint's other views.

Practice

▶ Concepts Review

Label each of the elements shown in Figure B-17.

FIGURE B-17

Match each of the following tasks with the task pane, dialog box, or tab best used to complete it.

7. Change one color in a presentation.
8. Change a picture's fill and line colors, position, and size.
9. Change one color in a picture.
10. Change all the colors in a presentation.
11. Insert a piece of clip art in a slide.

a. Insert Clip Art task pane
b. Standard tab in the Edit Color Scheme dialog box
c. Recolor Picture dialog box
d. Format Picture dialog box
e. Custom tab in the Edit Color Scheme dialog box

Select the best answer from the list of choices.

12. A color scheme is:
a. The combination of design elements in a presentation.
b. A combination of eight colors applied to a presentation.
c. A combination of three colors applied to a presentation.
d. The combination of colors in a piece of clip art.

13. Annotating a slide with the Pen tool causes which effect?
a. The slide text is highlighted in yellow.
b. The slide is printed with whatever marks you create.
c. The slide text displays the marks you create until you move to a different slide.
d. The slide is deleted from the presentation.

14. When you set the transition in a slide, you are controlling:
a. The size of the slide when it is displayed.
b. The manner in which the slide is displayed.
c. The manner in which objects on the slide are displayed.
d. The color scheme of the slide.

15. In Slide Show view, what happens when you point anywhere on the screen?
a. The Slide Show menu button appears.
b. You move to the next slide.
c. You move to the previous slide.
d. The slide show ends.

16. When you preset the timing of a slide, you are controlling:
a. How long it remains on-screen before ending the slide show.
b. How long it remains on-screen before changing to a black screen.
c. How long it remains on-screen before changing to Slide Sorter view.
d. How long it remains on-screen before advancing to the next slide.

17. In Slide Show view, what key can you press to move to the previous screen?
a. [Spacebar]
b. [Enter]
c. [N]
d. [←]

18. What is the best way to run a PowerPoint presentation on a compatible computer that does not have PowerPoint installed?
a. Convert the slides to .GIF files, and open them on the compatible computer.
b. Install Microsoft Office XP on the compatible computer.
c. Use PowerPoint Viewer on the compatible computer.
d. Try opening the presentation in a different presentation graphics program installed on the compatible computer.

▶ Skills Review

1. **Change the color scheme of an existing presentation.**
   a. Start PowerPoint. Create a new presentation based on the existing file PPT B-2 from the drive and folder where your Project Files are stored.
   b. Save the new presentation as *Fall Meeting*.
   c. Open the Slide Design–Color Schemes task pane.
   d. Apply the first color scheme in the Apply a color scheme list to all slides in the presentation.
   e. Save your changes.

2. **Use clip art.**
   a. Move to Slide 7.
   b. Click in the title placeholder and type **1st Annual Employee Volunteer Contest!**.
   c. Click the text placeholder, type **Log your volunteer hours with Human Resources**, press [Enter], type **1st prize is a weekend getaway in Aspen**, press [Enter], type **Support your favorite cause!**, press [Enter], then type **Prepared by** and add your name.
   d. Double-click the clip-art placeholder.
   e. In the Select Picture dialog box, search for clips of skiers, then insert the first clip of a downhill skier you find.
   f. Drag the upper-right corner sizing handle of the inserted picture until the skier's head and shoulder are inside the title text frame.
   g. Save your changes.

3. **Work with a picture.**
   a. If necessary, click the picture to select it, then increase the contrast of the picture three times.
   b. Open the Format Picture dialog box for the selected picture.
   c. In the Format Picture dialog box, change the fill color of the picture to the shade of gold, the fourth color in the top row.
   d. Set the transparency of the picture at 50%, then close the dialog box.
   e. Move the picture down so that it is directly below the title text and so that the left edge of the fill does not obscure the bullets.
   f. Open the Recolor Picture dialog box for the selected picture, then change the third color in the Original list to the shade of gold in the first row of the New color palette.
   g. Compare your screen to Figure B-18, then save your changes.

FIGURE B-18

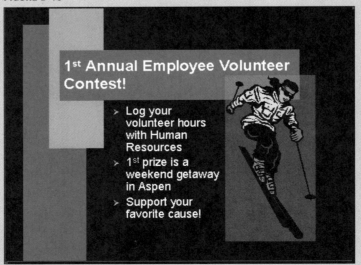

4. Run an online slide show.

    a. Start the slide show at Slide 1.

    b. Open the Slide Navigator to move to the third slide, titled Secrets of Our Success.

    c. Open the title and bulleted items.

    d. Select the Pen from the Pointer Options.

    e. Drag to circle the bulleted point, Emphasis on Quality of Life.

    f. Using the shortcut menu, point to By Title, then click Goals for Fall Quarter.

    g. When the Volunteer Initiative bullet appears, press [Spacebar] to move to the next slide.

    h. Press [←] to move to the previous slide.

    i. Press [End] to move to the last slide.

    j. Use the [Spacebar] to return to Normal view.

5. Use preset timing and transitions.

    a. Open the Slide Transition task pane.

    b. Move to Slide 4, and set it to run automatically after 10 seconds.

    c. Apply the Split Horizontal In transition effect.

    d. Apply these effects to all the slides.

    e. Click Slide 3, then change the timing for this slide only to 30 seconds.

    f. Change the transition effect for this slide only to Uncover Up.

    g. Apply an applause sound effect to this transition.

    h. Save your changes.

6. Apply animation schemes and custom animation.

    a. Open the Custom Animation task pane.

    b. Move to Slide 1.

    c. Select both the title placeholder and the text placeholder on the slide.

    d. Add an Entrance effect, the Fly in effect.

    e. Set it to fly in from the right at medium speed.

    f. Move to Slide 2, and add an entrance animation effect that makes the slide text crawl in at slow speed.

    g. Move to Slide 3, and add an emphasis effect that makes the bulleted items grow and shrink.

    h. Save your changes.

    i. Move to the first slide.

    j. Switch to Slide Show view, and view the presentation.

7. **Create speaker notes and print materials.**

   a. Move to Notes Page view, and increase the zoom level to 75%.

   b. Move to Slide 5.

   c. In the notes area, type **Jamie implemented two co-marketing ventures with major retailers and also designed a direct mail campaign that drew a 12% return.**

   d. Create a new paragraph and type **Kimberly increased orders in her new sales region by 70%, a company record.**

   e. Move to Slide 7.

   f. Click in the text placeholder, and type **In this annual contest, we will recognize the Outdoor Designs employee who donates the most hours to volunteer service. The winner will receive a weekend ski package for two at a luxury spa in Aspen. In addition, the charity of his or her choice will receive a $1000 donation!**

   g. Save your changes.

   h. View the notes page in Print Preview and change the page orientation to landscape.

   i. Move to Slide 7, click the Magnifier to view the notes, then click the Close button to return to the Normal view.

   j. On the File menu, click Print, in the Print dialog box, print the presentation as Notes pages.

   k. Close the Fall Meeting presentation, then exit PowerPoint.

▶ Independent Challenge 1

At Stuff for Pets, you are preparing to present your expansion plan to potential investors. You have completed a marketing plan presentation that outlines the goals and projections for the establishment of a new retail outlet on the south side of town. You decide to enhance your presentation before producing the 35mm slides needed for your slide projection presentation.

   a. Start PowerPoint if necessary.

   b. Create a new presentation based on the file PPT B-3 from the drive and folder where your Project Files are located.

   c. Save the presentation as *Final Stuff For Pets Presentation*, and replace the placeholder text on Slide 1 with your name.

   d. Enhance the presentation by changing the color scheme or individual color elements.

   e. Add clip art to the presentation. (*Hint*: Remember that you can add clip art to any slide by clicking Insert on the menu bar, pointing to Picture, then clicking Clip Art.)

   f. Add speaker notes to help you remember key points.

   g. You do not need to set transitions, timing, or animation effects for this slide show because you plan to output it on 35mm slides. Instead, take this opportunity to learn about how to output a presentation for a film-processing bureau. Start PowerPoint Help, and search for information on 35mm slides. You plan to send your files to a service bureau to produce the slides.

   h. Preview the slides in Print Preview as notes pages, then add a clip-art image to one of the notes pages. (*Hint*: For example, move to Slide 4 and insert a tropical fish clip.)

   i. When you are finished, print the slides as Notes pages.

   j. Close the presentation, saving changes when prompted, and exit PowerPoint.

Independent Challenge 2

The Literary Loft is starting a book club. To encourage customers to join the book club, staff members will take turns leading the first several meetings. To lead the book club meeting, you must choose a book and create a brief presentation raising issues or questions that encourage discussion about the book. You have been asked to lead the first book club meeting. You anticipate attendance at the first meeting to be small, so you plan to use your PC to make your presentation.

a. Choose a favorite book.

b. Plan your presentation by thinking about what you like best or least about the book and the author. Think about the tone you want to establish and the types of discussion questions that would encourage a greater appreciation of the book. If the author is a favorite of yours, you might want to include information about the author or other books she has written.

c. Start PowerPoint if necessary.

d. Use the AutoContent Wizard or another template to create your presentation. Be sure to include your name on the first slide.

e. Save the presentation as *Book Presentation*.

f. Use your skills and your imagination to create interesting slides that complement the tone of the book and the goals of your discussion.

g. Enhance the presentation with colors, clip art, animation schemes, custom animation effects, and transitions.

h. If you wish, create speaker notes to help you remember key points and illustrate them with inserted clips.

i. Run the slide show, pausing the presentation as necessary. Use the Pen pointer to annotate key points.

j. When you are finished, preview the presentation in Print Preview, print the presentation as Notes pages, save and close the presentation, and exit PowerPoint.

► Independent Challenge 3

The Wacky Words Card Company is preparing sales representatives to create several presentations while they are on the road. The presentations will instruct retailers on stocking and inventory during special promotional seasons. The sales representatives travel with PCs and black and white printers. They plan to make group presentations to the entire staff of one or more stores, so they will not be able to use their PCs. They will need to print black and white transparencies to use with overhead projectors. You have volunteered to help the reps achieve the best results with their limited resources.

a. Start PowerPoint if necessary.

b. Type a question for help, using the keywords black and white printing.

c. Read the "About Printing" topic.

d. Learn how to work and print in black and white. Find out how text and objects in a color presentation will be printed on a black and white printer, and how to work in black and white so that what you see on the screen is what you get when you print.

e. Create a black and white presentation that summarizes the information you learned. Use the Design Template of your choice to start the presentation, then change the slide color scheme to black and white. Use the information you learned in Help to make design and formatting decisions. Be sure to include your name on one of the slides.

f. Save the presentation as *Card Company*.

g. Add at least one piece of full-color clip-art image to the presentation, then convert it to black and white (*Hint*: Use the Color button on the Picture toolbar). Use tools on the Picture toolbar to enhance the appearance of the image in black and white.

h. When you are finished, print the presentation as slides, then save and close the Help system and exit PowerPoint.

Independent Challenge 4

The Microsoft Clip Organizer makes it easy to organize and use clip art. In addition to the clip art in the organizer, you can access additional clip art on the Microsoft Office XP Media Content CD-ROM and from other sources, including the Web. Add a new piece of clip art to one of the presentations you created in this unit.

a. Start PowerPoint if necessary.

b. Create a new presentation based on the file PPT B-4 from the drive and folder where your Project Files are located. Replace the placeholder text on Slide 1 with your name.

c. Save the presentation as *Fishing Clips*.

d. Move to the slide that contains the clip art placeholder.

e. Open the Insert Clip Art task pane, then click the Microsoft Clip Organizer link to open it in freestanding mode.

f. In the Microsoft Clip Organizer, click the Clips Online link.

g. Connect to the Internet if necessary.

h. You'll come back to the Microsoft Web site, but now that you're connected to the Internet, use a favorite search engine such as www.google.com to search for Web sites that offer collections of clip art. (*Hint*: Search using the keywords clip art.) You want to locate clips to illustrate a slide show about fly fishing, so search the clip art collection sites you visit for clips about fishing or fish.

i. When you find a Web site that contains clips available for downloading, read the end-user terms carefully before downloading any clips, so you're sure that they are royalty-free for your use.

j. Download an appropriate fishing clip to illustrate Slide 2 in the Fishing Clips presentation.

k. Point your browser to the Microsoft Clips Online site. (*Hint*: Either click the Back button in your browser, or return to PowerPoint and click the link in the task pane again.)

l. Read and accept the terms of the end-user agreement.

m. Use the Browse by category list box to choose a clip-art category of interest to you, then browse the clips to find a picture you like.

n. Scroll through the available choices to find clip art you want to download.

o. When you find a piece of clip art you want, click it. A large preview of the clip appears in the lower-left corner of the screen, along with keywords links to related pictures.

p. Click the preview of the clip to download it.

q. Disconnect from the Internet if necessary.

r. Add a new title, clip art, and text slide to the end of the presentation. Then, in the Insert ClipArt task pane, locate the clip in the Downloaded clips category, then insert it in Slide 3. Move and resize the clip as necessary, then complete the slide by adding a title and text that reflects your thoughts about fly fishing.

s. Print the slides that contain the clip art, save and close the presentation, then exit PowerPoint.

PowerPoint 2002

▶ Visual Workshop

Use the skills you have learned in this unit to create the presentation slides shown in Figures B-19 and B-20. To begin, open the file PPT B-5, and save it as *Star Gazers Club*. Add your name as the last bulleted item on Slide 2. Print each slide when you have finished.

FIGURE B-19

FIGURE B-20

Integrating

Office XP Programs

Objectives

- ► **Embed an Excel chart in a PowerPoint slide**
- ► **Send a PowerPoint presentation to Word**
- ► **Insert a Word file in a Word document**
- ► **Link an Excel worksheet to a Word document**
- ► **Update a linked Excel worksheet**
- ► **Insert Access fields in a Word form letter**
- ► **Merge Access data and Word text to create a form letter**
- ► **Save an Office document as a Web page**

So far you've created many documents, worksheets, databases, and presentations using individual Office programs. Sometimes, however, you may want to create documents that combine information from different Office documents, such as a newsletter you create with Word that also contains a chart created with Excel. You also can save any Office document as a Web page for use on the Internet or an intranet. ✎ The staff at Outdoor Designs would like your help in creating a report in Word for investors that will include information from a PowerPoint presentation and an Excel workbook. They want you to send the report as a form letter to each investor, and have provided an Access database of the investors' names and addresses so that you can accomplish this quickly. Finally, you need to convert the final report to a document that can be published on the company's Web site.

Integration

Embedding an Excel Chart in a PowerPoint Slide

Inserting an Excel chart into a PowerPoint slide takes just a few steps. The Excel chart becomes an **embedded object**, which is a separate copy of the original file (called a **source file**) that you can edit using the menus and toolbars of the program in which it was created. ➤ Sue Ellen has prepared her six-month sales summary presentation for the sales staff, except for a slide showing the total sales by region for the previous two quarters. You need to embed an Excel chart with this information into a slide for her.

Steps

1. Start PowerPoint, navigate to the drive and folder where your Project Files are located, open the presentation **INT A-1**, then save it as **July Presentation**

2. Click **View** on the menu bar, point to **Toolbars**, click **Customize**, click the **Options tab** if necessary, click the **Show Standard and Formatting toolbars on two rows check box** to add a check mark if necessary, click the **Reset my usage data button**, click **Yes** in the message box, then click **Close**

Trouble?

If the task pane is not visible, click View on the menu bar, then click Task Pane.

3. Click the **Slide 2** thumbnail in the Slides tab, click the **New Slide button** 🖼 on the Formatting toolbar, click the **Blank content layout** in the Slide Layout task pane, then click the **Close button** in the task pane
   A new, blank slide appears as the third slide in the presentation.

4. Click **Insert** on the menu bar, then click **Object**
   The Insert Object dialog box opens, as shown in Figure A-1. You can insert an embedded object by choosing a new object to create or by inserting an existing file.

5. Click the **Create from file option button**, click **Browse**, navigate to the drive and folder where your Project Files are stored, double-click **INT A-2** on your Project Disk, then click **OK**
   The embedded Excel chart appears in the slide as a selected object, as shown in Figure A-2.

6. Double-click the **chart object**
   The Excel menu bar and toolbars replace the PowerPoint menu bar and toolbars, and the Excel Chart toolbar opens, giving you access to these features so that you can work with the chart just as you would in Excel.

Trouble?

If you don't see the Chart toolbar, right-click any toolbar to open a pop-up menu, then click Chart.

7. If the Standard and Formatting toolbars appear on one row, click the **Toolbar Options button** ⏷ at the end of the toolbar, then click **Show Buttons on Two Rows**

8. Click the **Chart Objects list arrow** on the Chart toolbar, click **Chart Title**, click the **Font Size list arrow** on the Formatting toolbar, then click **28**
   Because the chart is an embedded object, the title size changes only in the copy on the PowerPoint slide, not in the original Excel chart. See Figure A-3.

Trouble?

If an Excel toolbar appears as you try to drag the object, click in the Presentation window away from the chart object, then try Step 9 again.

9. Click anywhere outside the chart object to return to PowerPoint, click the **chart** to select it, drag it up until the title is slightly above the black line and the plot area is just below the line, then save your changes to the presentation

FIGURE A-1: Insert Object dialog box

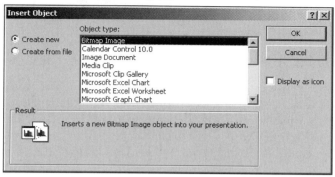

FIGURE A-2: Embedded Excel chart

Excel chart embed-
ded in PowerPoint
slide

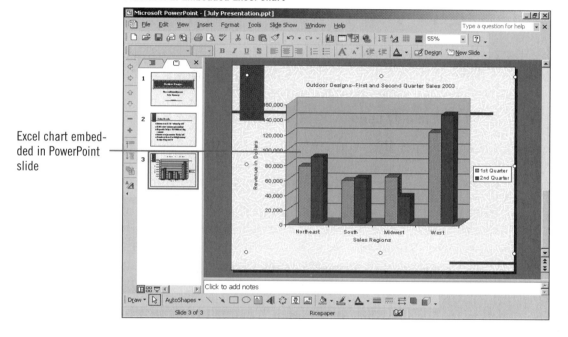

FIGURE A-3: Embedded Excel chart with source file commands

Reformatted title

Chart toolbar

Excel interface

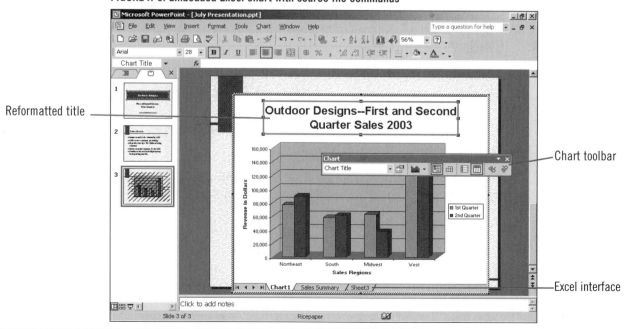

Sending a PowerPoint Presentation to Word

Sometimes you want to **export** a document, or change it from one file type to another. For example, you can easily save an existing PowerPoint presentation as a Word document. You can choose from five layout styles for the new Word document. Four of the layout styles include slides, and the fifth includes only the text outline. After you export the presentation to Word, you can save, edit, and format it just as you would any other Word document. ✐ Dean Holmes, marketing manager for Outdoor Designs, wants to incorporate the sales goals from Sue Ellen's sales presentation into a report he is working on. He asks you to export an outline of Sue Ellen's six-month sales summary presentation to a Word document.

QuickTip

When you click an option other than Word document on the Send To menu, such as Mail or Routing Recipient, you are choosing an actual recipient, not a different file type for the presentation.

1. Click **File** on the menu bar, point to **Send To**, then click **Microsoft Word**
   The Send To Microsoft Word dialog box opens.

2. Click the **Outline only option button**, as shown in Figure A-4

3. Click **OK**, maximize the Word program window, if necessary, then switch to Print Layout View
   Word starts, and the PowerPoint slide outline appears in a new Word document. This might take a minute or two. See Figure A-5. PowerPoint remains open, and the new Word document, Document1, contains the title slide text formatted as heading 1 and heading 2, with the title and bulleted items from Slide 2 formatted as heading 1 text with bullet points. Note that Slide 3 does not appear in the outline because it contains a chart object only.

4. Click the **Toolbar Options button** ⬚ on the toolbar, then click to select **Show Buttons on Two Rows**

5. If necessary, click the **Show/Hide button** ¶ on the Standard toolbar
   The Show/Hide feature lets you view the nonprinting characters in a Word document, such as manual line breaks, tabs, and paragraph marks, so you can make sure your document will print correctly. When you display these characters, you can catch mistakes, such as extra spaces inserted between words or at the end of a sentence, more easily than you can by simply scanning your document.

QuickTip

To apply a text style to text, select the text, click the Style list arrow on the Formatting toolbar, then click the name of the style you want to apply.

6. Delete the first four lines of text from **Outdoor Designs** through **Sales Goals**, including the paragraph mark and the two blank lines below the bulleted text, then apply the **Normal style** to the five sales goals
   The text changes to 12-point Times New Roman, and the bullets are removed.

7. Click **File** on the menu bar, click **Save As**, navigate to the folder and drive where your Project Files are stored, click the **Save as type list arrow**, click **Word Document** if necessary, then save the document as **Sales Goals**

8. Close the **Sales Goals** document

9. Maximize the **PowerPoint program window**, save your changes, close the **July Presentation** presentation, then exit **PowerPoint**
   Word remains open.

FIGURE A-4: Send to Microsoft Word dialog box

FIGURE A-5: Word document with exported PowerPoint outline

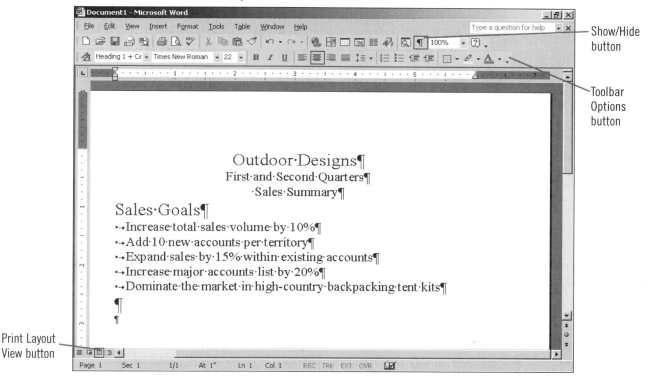

Show/Hide button

Toolbar Options button

Print Layout View button

Inserting Word text in a PowerPoint slide presentation

You can use an outline that you've created in Word as the starting point for a PowerPoint presentation. Make sure to use the built-in heading styles in Word when you create your outline, because those heading tags determine the structure of the outline when it's imported by PowerPoint. Type your outline in Word, using the Heading 1 style for slide titles, Heading 2 for the first level of indented text, and so on. When the outline is complete, save and close the Word document.

Start PowerPoint, create a new presentation, click Insert on the menu bar, then click Slides from Outline. Navigate to the Word document containing the outline, then click Insert. If a dialog box prompts you to install a converter to complete the procedure, click Yes. You can edit the outline and design your slides as usual. If the imported outline doesn't fit on your slides the way you'd like, use the Outlining toolbar to promote or demote elements.

Integration

Inserting a Word File in a Word Document

As you work, you might want to combine two files into one, or insert someone else's entire document into your own. Although you can easily copy and paste information between open documents, it's sometimes easier to **import**, or insert, the entire contents of a closed file into an open document. ✐ Dean wants to include Sue Ellen's Sales Goals document in a report that will be sent to the company's investors. He asks you to import the Word document containing the sales goals into the report, which is also a Word document.

1. Open the file Word **INT A-3** from the drive and folder where your Project Files are stored, then save it as **Investors Report**
   This is Dean's report.

2. Click **to the left of the paragraph mark** of the second blank line following the first paragraph in the body text, which ends with "Our sales goals for Outdoor Designs include:"
   This is the location where you want to insert the Sales Goals document.

3. Click **Insert** on the menu bar, then click **File**
   The Insert File dialog box appears. This dialog box looks and functions similarly to the Open dialog box. See Figure A-6.

4. Navigate to the drive and folder where your Project Files are stored, click **Sales Goals**, then click **Insert**
   The entire Sales Goals document, which you created in the previous lesson, appears in the report.

5. Select the entire list of goals, then click the **Bullets button** 📇 on the Formatting toolbar
   The sales goals are formatted in a bulleted list, as shown in Figure A-7.

6. Click away from the selected text to deselect it

7. Save your changes

Using drag and drop to insert an Access table into Word

You can insert an Access table into a Word document by using drag and drop. Open the Access database containing the table you want to insert, and then click the Tables button in the Objects list, but don't open the table. Start Word and open the document into which you want to insert the table. In the Access window, select (but don't open) the table in the Objects list, then drag the table to the taskbar button for the Word document you want to copy it to. The mouse pointer changes to ⬚. Hold the mouse pointer on the taskbar button until the document maximizes, position the copy object pointer at the exact location in the document where you want to insert the table, then release the mouse pointer. The table is inserted as a regular Word table, not as an Access object, so you can edit it as you would any Word table.

FIGURE A-6: Insert File dialog box

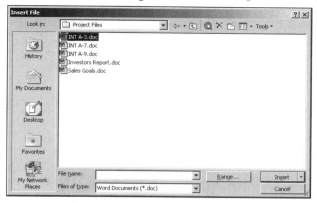

FIGURE A-7: Sales goals formatted as a bulleted list

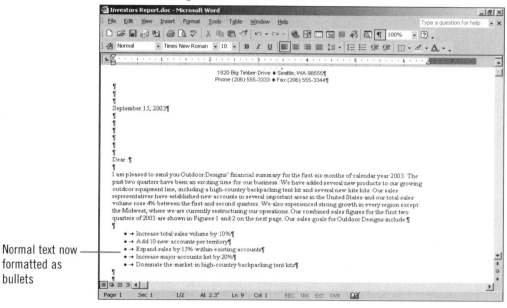

Normal text now formatted as bullets

CLUES TO USE

Inserting Excel data in a Word file

It takes just a few steps to insert all or part of an Excel worksheet or an entire Excel workbook into a Word document. Move the insertion point to where you want to insert the worksheet. Click Insert on the menu bar, click File, click the Files of type list arrow, click All Files, click the Excel file to import, click Range and enter a range in the Set Range dialog box if you only want to insert part of the worksheet, then click Insert. If prompted to install this feature, insert your Office XP CD and click OK. In the Open Worksheet dialog box, shown in Figure A-8, click the Open document in Workbook list arrow, click the worksheet you want to import, then click OK. The Excel data appears in the Word document as a table, which you can edit and format as usual using the table commands in Word.

FIGURE A-8: Open Worksheet dialog box

Open Worksheet

Open document in Workbook:
Entire Workbook

Name or Cell Range:
Entire Worksheet

☐ **Format for Mail Merge**

OK

Cancel

Linking an Excel Worksheet to a Word Document

Another way to share information between files is to link them. A **link** displays information from one file called the **source** in another file called the **destination**. In a document, linked data looks just like inserted or embedded data; the difference is that if you edit linked data, any changes you make in one file also appear in the other file. ✐▬▬▬ Dean asks you to link the Excel worksheet and chart with the sales figures to the Investors Report so if Sue Ellen updates a number, the change will be made automatically in the report. He suggests that you tile the Word and Excel program windows to make it easier to work in both programs.

QuickTip

If any programs other than Word and Excel are open, exit them now.

1. Start Excel, open **INT A-2** from the drive and folder where your Project Files are located, then save the workbook as **July Sales Summary**
   Both Word and Excel are now open.

2. Right-click the **taskbar** but not on a program button, then click **Tile Windows Vertically** in the pop-up menu
   Now you can see both program windows at once.

3. Click in the Excel program window, click the **Sales Summary sheet tab**, select the range **A3:C8**, click **Edit** on the menu bar, then click **Copy**
   The cells are copied to the Clipboard.

QuickTip

If Word and Excel appear on the opposite sides from Figure A-9, the steps will work the same. Just make sure you click in the specified program window.

4. Click in the **Word program window** to make it active, then click in the **blank line** below the Figure 1 caption on page 2 of the document, as shown in Figure A-9

5. Click **Edit** on the Word menu bar, click **Paste Special**, click the **Paste link option button**, click **Microsoft Excel Worksheet Object**, click **OK**, then save your changes to the **Investors Report** document
   The Excel cells appear in the Word document as a selected object, as shown in Figure A-10.

6. Click in the **Excel program window** to make it active, click the **Chart 1 sheet tab**, click the **Chart Objects list button** on the Chart toolbar, click **Chart Area**, then click the **Copy button** 🖺 on the Standard toolbar
   A copy of the chart is stored on the Office Clipboard.

QuickTip

If the Clipboard task pane opens, click the Clear All button, then click the Close button on the Clipboard task pane.

7. Click in the **Word program window**, click in the **first blank line** below the Figure 2 caption, click **Edit** on the Word menu bar, click **Paste Special**, click the **Paste link option button**, click **Microsoft Excel Chart Object**, then click **OK**
   The Excel chart appears in the document, but is much too large.

8. With the chart object selected, click **Format** on the Word menu bar, click **Object**, then in the Format Object dialog box, click the **Size tab**

9. In the Scale section, click the **Lock aspect ratio check box** to add a check mark if necessary, type **55%** in the Height text box, click **OK**, then save your changes
   Your screen should look similar to Figure A-11.

FIGURE A-9: Excel worksheet cells copied to the Office Clipboard

Inactive program window (title bar is gray)

Active program window (title bar is blue)

Copied cells

Step 4

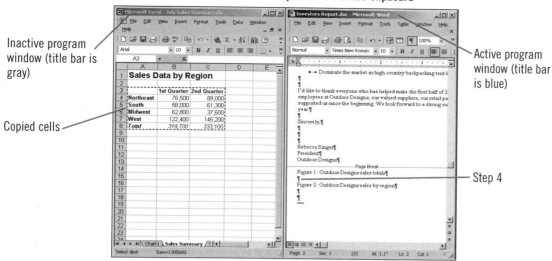

FIGURE A-10: Excel cells pasted into a Word document

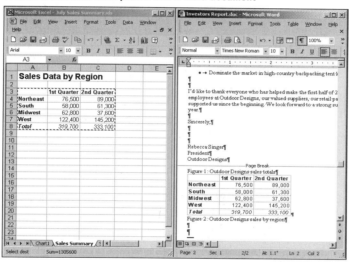

FIGURE A-11: Linked objects in a Word document

Linked objects

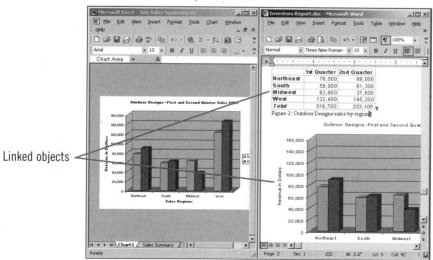

Integration

Updating a Linked Excel Worksheet

The beauty of working with linked files is that when you change the information in one file, it is updated automatically in the other file. You can also update a linked object manually by selecting the linked object and pressing [F9]. The [F9] key is the keyboard shortcut for updating links. Sue Ellen just determined that the second quarter sales total for the Midwest region should be $39,200, not $37,600, as recorded in both the July Sales Summary and the Investors Report. Because the two files are linked, you only need to make the change once.

Steps 1 2 3 4

1. Click in the **Excel program window**, then click the **Sales Summary sheet tab**

2. Click cell **C6**, type **39200**, then press **[Enter]**
   The new figure appears in the Excel worksheet and also in the Word document. See Figure A-12.

3. Save your changes to **July Sales Summary**

4. Click the **Chart 1 sheet tab**, then point to the second quarter bar for the Midwest
   A ScreenTip appears, showing the new value of the bar, 39,200, as shown in Figure A-13. Because the chart is linked to the worksheet cells, the chart is updated whenever data in the worksheet changes.

> **Trouble?**
> If the linked worksheet cells and chart are not updated, click the linked worksheet cells in Word to select them, then press [F9]. Repeat to update the chart.

5. If necessary, click in the **Word program window** and scroll until you can see the updated chart in Figure A-12
   The change is also made in the linked chart. If the change does not appear in the linked chart, you can update the link manually.

6. Click in the **Excel program window**, close **July Sales Summary**, then exit Excel

7. Maximize the **Word program window**, then save the document as **Investors Report Letter**
   You'll use this document to create form letters in the next lesson.

FIGURE A-12: Linked Excel worksheet updated in Word document

New data entered here

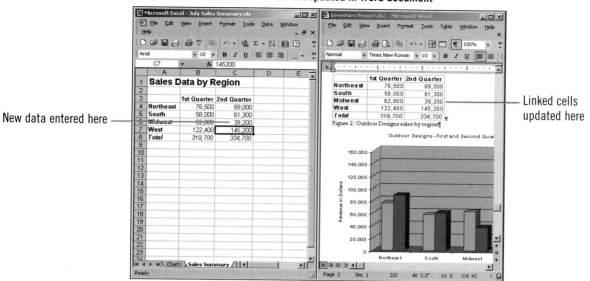

Linked cells
updated here

FIGURE A-13: Excel chart with updated value

Excel charts and
worksheets are
automatically
linked, so data is
updated here

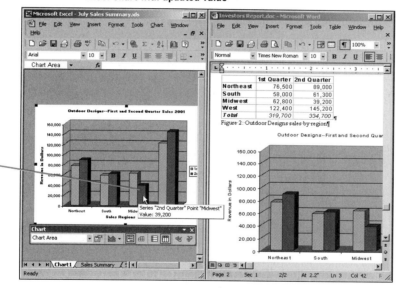

Unlinking files

If you decide that you no longer want changes you
make in one file to affect another file, you can break
the link between them. The linked object in the destination file will become an embedded object. You can
still edit the embedded object using the source file's
menus and commands, but the changes you make
won't appear in the source file. Click the linked object
in the destination file to select it. Click Edit on the
menu bar, then click Links to open the Links dialog
box. See Figure A-14. Click the name of the source
file, click Break Link, then click OK. The object in the
destination file is now an embedded object.

FIGURE A-14: Links dialog box

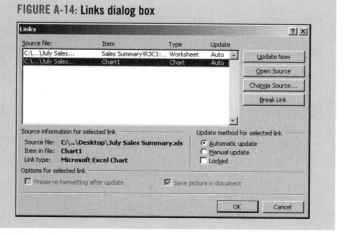

Inserting Access Fields in a Word Form Letter

A **form letter** is a document that contains standard body text and a custom heading for each recipient. The letter itself is usually written in Word, and the data for the custom headings usually are compiled in a table, worksheet, or database such as Access. From these two documents you create a third document that merges the appropriate information into one or more personalized documents. ✒ Dean wants to send the Investors Report to all of Outdoor Designs' investors. He asks you to set up a form letter using Investors Report Letter as the standard body text. You use names and addresses from a database compiled by Elizabeth.

Steps 1234

1. Click **Tools** on the menu bar, point to **Letters and Mailings**, then click **Mail Merge Wizard**
The Mail Merge task pane opens, as shown in Figure A-15. The options in this task pane lead you through the three basic steps involved in creating a form letter: choosing the **main document**, the document that contains the text that should appear in each letter; the **data source**, the file that contains the variable information, such as names and addresses; and the **merged document**, the file or printout that contains all the personalized letters.

2. In the Select document type if necessary section, click **Letters** if necessary, click **Next: Starting document**, then click the **Use the current document option button**, if necessary, to use the Investors Report Letter as the main document

3. Click **Next: Select recipients**, click the **Use an existing list option button** if necessary, click **Browse**, in the Select Data Source dialog box navigate to the drive and folder where your Project Files are stored, then double-click **INT A-4**
Access starts, and a link containing the investors' names and addresses is established between the Word document and the Access database. The Select Table dialog box opens, so that you can choose which table from the Access database you want to use as a data source.

4. Double-click **Investors** in the list of tables in the Select Table dialog box
The Mail Merge Recipients dialog box opens, as shown in Figure A-16. A review of this list shows that the appropriate recipients are included.

5. Click **OK** to close the Mail Merge Recipients dialog box, then click **Next: Write Your Letter**
The Mail Merge task pane displays links for inserting merge fields in your document. **Merge fields** are field names that specify which data goes where in your form letter. These fields in the main document will be replaced with names and addresses from the data source when the two are merged into a third, new document.

6. In the Word document, scroll to and click in the **second blank line** below the date, click **More items** in the Mail Merge task pane, in the Insert Merge Field dialog box, double-click **First Name**, then click **Close**
The merge field appears in the document.

Trouble?

To see nonprinting symbols, click the Show/Hide button ¶.

7. Press [Spacebar], click **More items**, click **Last Name**, click **Insert**, then click **Close**
This completes the first line of the return address. The space you inserted will separate the first and last name of each investor.

8. Insert merge fields for the rest of the address and the salutation, as shown in Figure A-17, then double-check the spacing and punctuation around the merge fields for accuracy

9. Save your changes to the document

FIGURE A-15: Mail Merge Wizard task pane

Main document

Mail Merge task pane

Mail Merge Wizard steps

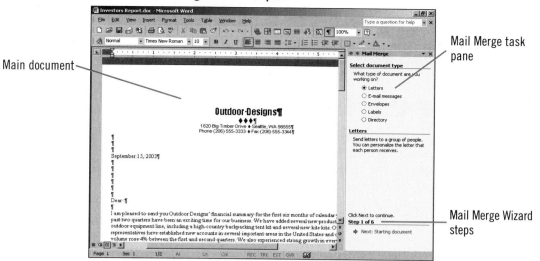

FIGURE A-16: Mail Recipients dialog box

Recipients are listed here

Make any desired changes to data in this dialog box

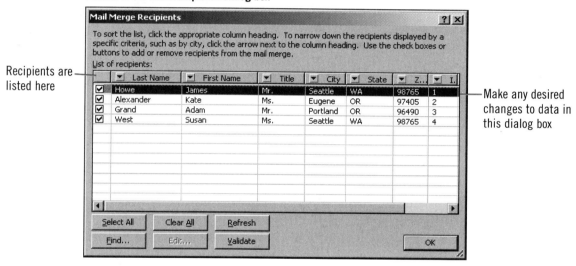

FIGURE A-17: Main document with merge fields

Merge fields entered, with spaces and punctuation

Type a comma followed by a space here

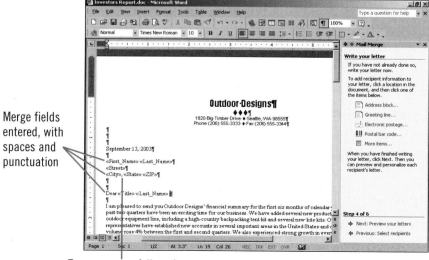

Integration

Merging Access Data and Word Text to Create a Form Letter

After you set up a main document, specify a data source, and insert merge fields, you can **merge**, or combine, the custom information with the standard text to create the personalized form letters. Investors Report Letter is a main document, complete with merge fields that will pull information from the Access data source. You are ready to merge the main document and data source, then print the letters for Dean.

Steps

1. Click **Next: Preview your letters** in the Mail Merge task pane

   The merge fields in the main document show the first record from the data source, which looks accurate, as shown in Figure A-18. You can edit your recipient list in this task pane before going ahead with the mail merge, if you want to exclude any recipients or make changes to any of the merged fields.

2. Click the **Next Recipient button** three times, until you have reviewed the document for each recipient in the data source, then click **Next: Complete the Merge**

   The mail merge is ready to run. You can merge the main document and the data source in several ways. The Print command merges the main document with the data source and immediately prints the results. The Edit individual letters command allows you to store all the letters in a new document, which you can save, preview, modify if necessary, and print.

3. Click **Edit individual letters**, click the **All option button**, if necessary, in the Merge to New Document dialog box, then click **OK**

   Now the four personalized form letters appear in a new document called Letters1.

4. Add your name to the end of the document, then save it as **Investors Report Form Letters**

   Before you print the document, preview it to make sure you don't have any corrections to make.

5. Click the **Print Preview button** 🔍 on the Standard toolbar

   As you scroll through the letters, you can see that in each letter the merge fields were replaced with data from the Access database. Each letter is two pages long, and there are four records in the Access table, so the merged document is eight pages long.

QuickTip

To save on printing costs, you print only one page of the document at this time.

6. Click **File** on the Print Preview menu bar, click **Print**, click the **Current Page option button**, then click **OK**

   The letters now await a signature before they can be mailed. See Figure A-19.

7. Click Close

   Print Preview closes.

8. Save your changes to the **Investors Report Form Letters** document, then close it

9. Save your changes to the **Investors Report Letter** document, then close it

FIGURE A-18: First record viewed in main document

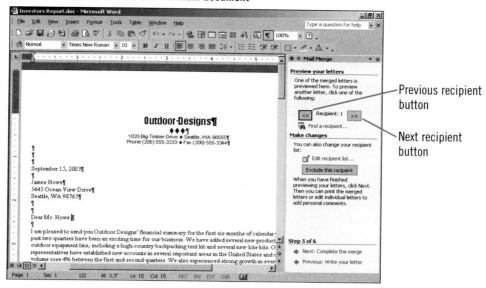

Previous recipient button

Next recipient button

FIGURE A-19: First page of printed form letter for last record

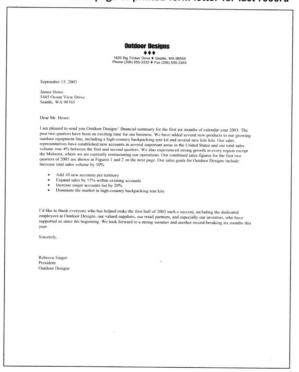

Using the Mail Merge toolbar

The Mail Merge Wizard makes it easy to set up and run a mail merge, but when you become more proficient at the process, you might find it faster to work with the Mail Merge toolbar. To display it, click Tools on the menu bar, point to Letters and Mailings, and then click Show Mail Merge Toolbar. The Mail Merge toolbar contains all the commands available in the Mail Merge task pane, as well as additional ones. For example, you can click the Check For Errors button to test your mail merge and receive a report of any errors in the main document that would prevent a successful mail merge.

Unit A

Integration

Saving an Office Document as a Web Page

In Microsoft Office XP, you can save any file as a Web page so that it can be posted to the Web. When you save an Office XP document as a Web page, you are saving it in **Hypertext Markup Language (HTML)**, the file format for documents posted to the Web. The file extension for Web pages is .htm. A browser program, such as Microsoft Internet Explorer, interprets the HTML codes to determine how to display the document on your screen. ✎ Dean wants to post the Investors Report document on the Outdoor Designs Web site so potential investors can see the latest sales figures for the company. He asks you to save the report as a Web page so he can publish it to the Web.

Steps 1 2 3 4

1. Open the **Investors Report** document from the drive and folder where your Project Files are located
   The version of the report you saved before inserting merge fields appears.

2. Type **Investor** in the salutation after "Dear"

> **QuickTip**
>
> When saving a document as a Web page, any linked or embedded objects are saved as independent graphic images in GIF format, a popular graphics format.

3. Click **File** on the menu bar, then click **Save as Web Page**
   The Save As dialog box opens. Note that the Save As dialog box specifies the default file formats for Web pages, which are .htm and .html. It also contains a Change Title button, which lets you set the name for this page that will be displayed in the title bar of the Web browser.

4. Type **Investors Report Web Page**, navigate to the drive and folder where your Project Files are located if necessary, then click **Save**
   Word saves the document as a Web page, with the modifications.

> **Trouble?**
>
> If a Word message box opens that warns that some of the elements in your letter are not supported by current browser versions, click the Continue button.

5. Minimize the Word document, then double-click the **Investors Report Web Page folder** to view its contents
   When you save a document as a Web page, Office automatically creates a new folder in the folder where you saved the Web page, so that all files needed to display the Web page are stored in one place. The folder contains all the supplementary files created as part of the Web page, including graphics files, frame files, and other essential files. The folder name is based on the Web page filename and contains the additional text "_files." For example, when you save the Investors Report Web Page file, a folder called "Investors Report Web Page_files" is created. In most cases, you never need to open this folder.

6. Maximize the document, which is now called "Investors Report Web Page.htm," click **File** on the menu bar, click **Web Page Preview**, then scroll through the document
   The Web page opens in Internet Explorer (or the browser installed as the default browser on your computer) so that you can see how it will look when posted to the Web, as shown in Figure A-20.

7. Click **File** on the Internet Explorer menu bar, then click **Close**
   You are returned to the Word program window.

> **Trouble?**
>
> If prompted, insert your Office XP CD to install this feature, called the Microsoft Script Editor.

8. Click **View** on the menu bar, then click **HTML Source**
   The coded document appears in a new document window, as shown in Figure A-21. People experienced in HTML can edit the codes in this window if necessary to change how the document will appear in a browser.

9. Click **File** on the Microsoft Script Editor menu bar, click **Exit**, close the Web page, then exit **Word**

FIGURE A-20: Web Page Preview opens a document in the default browser installed on your computer

Report in Internet Explorer window (your Web browser might be different)

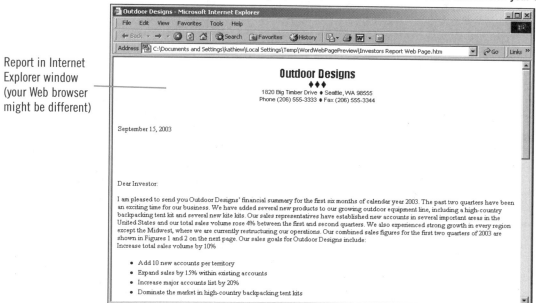

FIGURE A-21: Microsoft Script Editor

Microsoft Script Editor

HTML source code

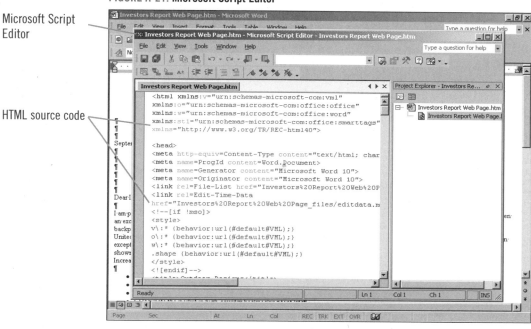

Understanding the World Wide Web

The Internet is a worldwide network that connects computers and computer networks from all over the world. The World Wide Web (also known as the Web) is a part of the Internet that contains Web pages that are linked together. Web pages contain highlighted words, phrases, and graphics called hyperlinks, that open other Web pages when you click them. Web browsers, such as Microsoft Internet Explorer or Netscape, are software programs that allow you to access and view Web pages in a graphical, easy-to-navigate format. The World Wide Web, which debuted in Switzerland in 1990, was created to allow links between documents on the Internet.

Practice

► Concepts Review

Label each element of the window shown in Figure A-22.

FIGURE A-22

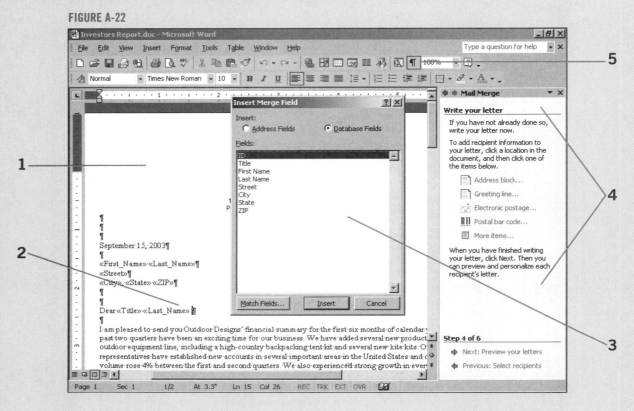

Match each of the descriptions with the correct term.

6. A file containing information you want to link to a destination file
7. A file that stores variable information for a mail merge
8. To change a file from one type to another type, so it can be opened in another program
9. To insert information from one file in another, in a form that allows it to be updated automatically
10. A document intended for multiple recipients, with standard body text and a custom heading for each recipient
11. Names from a specified data source that indicate which data goes where in a form letter
12. To insert the entire contents of a closed file into an open file, in a form that does not allow it to be updated automatically

a. source
b. export
c. form letter
d. link
e. data source
f. import
g. merge fields

Select the best answer from the list of choices.

13. **To edit an embedded object, you must:**
    a. Double-click it.
    b. Click it.
    c. Right-click it.
    d. Drag it.

14. **You can embed an object in another document by using the:**
    a. Insert command.
    b. Embed command.
    c. File command.
    d. Edit command.

15. **Sending only the outline of a PowerPoint presentation to Microsoft Word is an example of:**
    a. Importing.
    b. Embedding.
    c. Exporting.
    d. Linking.

16. **Inserting the entire contents of a closed file into an open document is called:**
    a. Exporting.
    b. Importing.
    c. Embedding.
    d. Linking.

17. **If you want to insert an Excel chart in a Word document so that the contents of the chart are updated in the Word document whenever changes are made to the Excel file, you should:**
    a. Embed the Excel chart to the Word document.
    b. Link the Excel chart in the Word document.
    c. Create a new Excel chart object in Word that contains the same data as the chart you want to insert.
    d. Send the Excel chart to Word using the Write-Up dialog box.

18. **To update linked files, you must make the change in:**
    a. The source file.
    b. The destination file.
    c. Either the destination file or the source file.
    d. Both the destination and the source file.

19. **If you break a link, the object in the destination file becomes a(n):**
    a. Embedded object.
    b. Imported file.
    c. Data source.
    d. Merge field.

20. **The file that stores variable information is the:**
    a. Main document.
    b. Data source.
    c. Source file.
    d. Merge field.

21. **The file format for documents posted to the World Wide Web is:**
    a. HTML.
    b. HTTP.
    c. Styles.
    d. Dynamic Data Exchange.

▶ Skills Review

1. **Embed an Excel chart in a PowerPoint slide.**
    a. Start PowerPoint if necessary, open the presentation INT A-5 from the drive and folder where your Project Files are located, then save it as *Investors Presentation*.
    b. Add a new, blank slide to the end of the presentation, based on the Blank layout under Content Layouts.
    c. Open the Insert Object dialog box.
    d. Create an object from the Excel file INT A-6, located in the drive and folder where your Project Files are stored.
    e. Activate the embedded object for editing.
    f. Enlarge the title Outdoor Designs Revenue to 22 points.
    g. Return to the PowerPoint window.
    h. Use the Format Object dialog box to increase the height of the object to 100% of its original size.
    i. Reposition and resize the table as needed to center it horizontally.
    j. Save your changes to the presentation.

2. Send a PowerPoint presentation to Word.

   a. Send the Investors Presentation file to Word as an outline only.

   b. Save the new document as *Confidential* in Word format.

   c. Activate the Show paragraph marks command, if necessary.

   d. Delete the first three lines of text and any extra blank lines at the end of the document.

   e. Apply the Normal style to the four remaining lines of text.

   f. Save your changes to the Confidential document, then close it.

   g. Save your changes to the Investors Presentation presentation, then close it.

   h. Exit PowerPoint.

3. Insert a Word file in a Word document.

   a. Open the document INT A-7 from the drive and folder where your Project Files are stored, then save it as *Confidential Investor*.

   b. Scroll down until you see the text [Insert Word file here] in the document, then delete this placeholder from the document and the paragraph mark that follows it.

   c. Insert the Confidential file you created previously, at this location in the document.

   d. Format the text you just inserted as a bulleted list.

   e. Save your changes to the document.

4. Link an Excel worksheet to a Word document.

   a. Start Excel.

   b. Open INT A-6 from the drive and location where your Project Files are stored, then save it as *Confidential Data*.

   c. Tile Word and Excel vertically on your screen.

   d. Copy the range A1:F5 to the Clipboard.

   e. Activate the Word program window.

   f. Delete the placeholder [Link Excel table here] and the paragraph mark that follows it.

   g. Open the Paste Special dialog box.

   h. Link the Excel cells to the Word document.

   i. Save your changes to the Confidential Investor document.

5. Update a linked Excel worksheet.

   a. Activate the Excel program window.

   b. Change the value in cell E4 to 950000.

   c. Save the Confidential Data workbook.

   d. Activate the Word program window.

   e. Scroll until you see the linked cells.

   f. Verify that the value changed in the Word document. If necessary, update the link manually (*Hint*: Click the linked object, then press [F9]).

   g. Save the Word document.

   h. Activate the Excel program window.

   i. Close the workbook, then exit Excel.

6. Insert Access fields in a Word form letter.

   a. Maximize the Word window, and save the Confidential Investor document as *Confidential Investor Letter*.

   b. Start the Mail Merge Wizard.

   c. Specify that you want to create letters, and set the current document as the main document.

   d. Use the Investors table in the Access file INT A-4, located in the drive and folder where your Project Files are stored, as the data source.

   e. Replace the bracketed text in the main document with the appropriate merge fields from the data source.

   f. Check the spacing and punctuation around the merge fields for accuracy.

7. Merge Access data and Word text to create a form letter.

   a. Preview the document for each recipient in the data source.

   b. Complete the mail merge process by merging to a new document.

   c. Save the new document as *Confidential Form Letters*.

   d. Add your name at the top of the document, just above the date on Page 1.

   e. Preview the letters in Print Preview, and then print only the first letter.

   f. Save, then close the Confidential Form Letters document .

8. Save an Office document as a Web page.

   a. Open the Confidential Investor document you created in Step 3a.

   b. Replace all the bracketed text after the word Dear in the salutation with Investor.

   c. Delete the bracketed text between the date and the salutation.

   d. Open the Save As Web Page dialog box.

   e. Save the file as *Confidential Investor Web Page*.

   f. Preview the Web page in your browser program, as shown in Figure A-23, then close Web Page Preview.

   g. View the HTML source code.

   h. Save and close the Web page.

   i. Exit Word.

FIGURE A-23

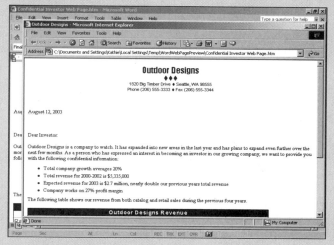

▶ Independent Challenge 1

As the owner of Stuff for Pets, a store catering to the needs of pet owners, you are always on the lookout for new products. You are excited about a new eye medication for miniature poodles that you have just begun to stock. Because miniature poodles tend to have chronic eye problems, you decide to send a letter to all customers who have purchased that breed of dog to inform them of the new eye medication. The sales representative for the product left you his PowerPoint presentation, so you decide to include some information from his slides in your letter.

   a. Start PowerPoint, open the presentation INT A-8 from the drive and folder where your Project Files are located, then save it as *Poodle Presentation*.

   b. Send the outline only from the Poodle Presentation file to Word.

   c. Delete the top line and any extra blank lines at the bottom; apply the Normal style to the remaining lines of text.

   d. Save the document as *Clear Eyes* in Word format, then close the document.

   e. Open the document INT A-9 from the drive and folder where your Project Files are stored, then save it as *Poodle Letter*.

   f. Delete the placeholder text [Insert Clear Eyes here], then insert the Clear Eyes document at that location.

   g. Format the text you just inserted as a bulleted list.

   h. Start Excel, open the workbook INT A-10 from the drive and folder where your Project Files are stored, then save it as *Poodle Data*.

   i. Delete the placeholder text [Link chart here], in the Word document, then link the chart from the Poodle Data workbook to that location.

   j. Format the linked chart in Word so it is easier to read.

   k. Change cell B3 to 42% on the Numbers worksheet, then verify that the Word chart reflects the revision.

   l. Replace the text The Staff at the end of the document with your name.

m. Perform a mail merge, using Poodle Letter as the main document and the Poodle Customers table in the file INT A-11 as the data source.

n. Replace the bracketed text in the letter with the appropriate merge fields.

o. Merge the Access data and Word text to a new document, then save the new document as *Poodle Form Letters*.

p. Print only the first letter.

q. Save and close any open files, then exit all programs.

▶ Independent Challenge 2

Tara Martin plans to start Systems Galore, a computer software mail-order company. Tara has written her business plan and put together an estimate of expenses and sales for the first five years. She needs a $50,000 loan to cover start-up and operating costs. She asks you to help her write a letter with her financial information to send to several banks, requesting the loan. She also asks you to create a document with this information that she can post to the Web to attract potential investors.

a. Use Word to write a letter that Tara can send to banks, requesting a loan. Include the following information in your letter: the date, a salutation, body text with the name and type of company Tara plans to start, three reasons you think the company will be successful, a reference to financial information, and a complimentary closing.

b. Save the letter as *Business Loan Letter*.

c. Start Excel, open the workbook INT A-12 from the drive and folder where your Project Files are located, then save it as *Business Loan*.

d. Embed the worksheet in the appropriate place in your letter. (*Hint*: In the Paste Special dialog box, click the Paste option button.)

e. Change the title in the embedded worksheet to Financial Analysis for 2003-2007.

f. Create an Access database called *Systems Galore Finances* on your Project Disk, and then create a table with the names, addresses, and loan officers of at least four banks. Use real or fictitious information.

g. Use the Business Loan Letter document as the main document of a form letter.

h. Insert appropriate merge fields to address the letter from the Access database you created.

i. Merge the data to a new document. Save the document as *Bank Letters*.

j. Add your name at the top of the last letter in the merged document, print only that letter, then save and close the document.

k. Delete the merge fields from the Business Loan Letter document, then type **Potential Investor** in the salutation.

l. Save the document as a Web page with the name *Potential Investors Web Page* on your Project Disk, then print it.

m. Close any open files, and exit any open programs.

▶ Independent Challenge 3

Theater in the Park is a stage company that performs Broadway plays in San Francisco's Golden Gate Park every year from May through September. This year's season features the plays *Macbeth*, *Proof*, *Into the Woods*, and *Rent*. The group consists of local professional actors and actresses; national stars appear in special engagements. In order to promote the performances, the troupe performs show excerpts at local schools, then gives a presentation about their upcoming shows using PowerPoint. Seung Lee, the manager of Theater in the Park, asks you to put together a presentation for this season that includes the information provided above.

a. Start Word, open a new, blank document, then save it as *Theater Outline*.

b. Using the outline tools or the heading styles, create text for at least three slides. Include information about Theater in the Park, the upcoming season, and special appearances by national stars (real or fictitious).

c. Start a new, blank document, then save it as *Theater Schedule*.

d. Create a Word table in the Theater Schedule document that includes the four plays the company will perform this season. Include the play titles, special appearances, and dates of the performances. Close the document when you have finished.

e. Send the Theater Outline document to PowerPoint to start a new presentation.

f. In PowerPoint, apply a design template and edit and format the slides as necessary. Save the presentation as *Theater Presentation*.

g. Link the Theater Schedule document to a new Title and Text slide to add the upcoming schedule of events to the presentation. Format the linked object if necessary so it is easy to read, and add the title Season Schedule to the slide. When you are finished, close the presentation.

h. In Microsoft Word, open the Theater Schedule document and change one of the dates in the table.

i. In PowerPoint, open the Theater Schedule presentation, let PowerPoint update the link automatically, then verify that the change was made.

j. Save the presentation as a Web page using the name *Theater Web Page*.

k. Add your name to the first slide.

l. Print the presentation as handouts, using the two slides per page option.

m. Close any open files, then exit all programs.

 # Independent Challenge 4

You are an editor at a small, start-up publishing company. You just received a book proposal from an author who wants to write a book about the history of the environmental movement. The proposal seems good, but you want to see what has already been published on the subject. You find out what other books exist, then write a report about the competition.

a. To find out about the competition, log on to the Internet, and use your browser to go to www.amazon.com or another online bookstore of your choice. Search for any books related to environmental history, the environmental movement, and so forth.

b. Create an Excel spreadsheet with the following information: book title, author, publisher, copyright date, sales rank (if the books you choose include this information), and price. Include at least four books in your spreadsheet. Use the sales rank in your analysis of the market for the book. Save the workbook as *Competition*, then close it and exit Excel.

c. Use Word to write a report to the editorial team that includes a description of the proposed book, an analysis of the market for it, and the competition you found. Save the report as *Environmental Books Survey*.

d. Embed the data from the Competition workbook in the appropriate place in your report.

e. Edit the embedded object by adding an appropriate title and changing the font size to 18 points.

f. At the top of the report, add today's date, a To: line, a From: line with your name, and a Re: line that reads Competition for Environmental History Books.

g. Use the active window as the main document of a form letter.

h. Use INT A-13 from the drive and folder where your Project Files are stored as the data source of the form letter.

i. Add the appropriate merge fields to the To: line. Be sure to include the first and last name, and the position of each recipient.

j. Merge the document directly to the printer. Print one letter for the current record only.

k. Save and close the Environmental Books Survey document, then exit Word.

► Visual Workshop

Create the form letter and data source shown below. (*Hint*: You must create a data source, as shown in Figure A-25, in order to have merge fields to insert.) Merge the form letter with the data source to a new document. Add your name at the top of the first letter, just above the date, and right-align it. Save the new document as *Runners Thanks*, then print the letters. When you are finished, save and close all open documents and exit Word and Access.

FIGURE A-24

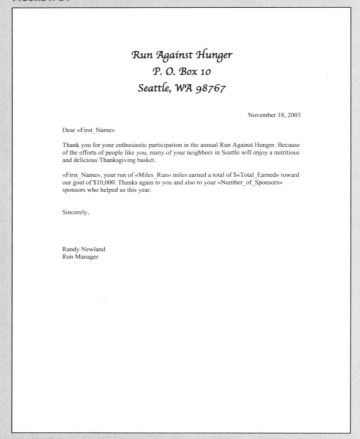

FIGURE A-25

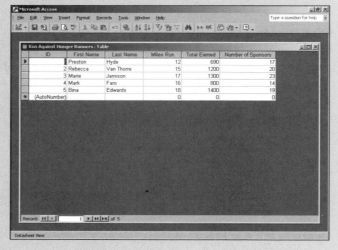

Project Files List

Read the following information carefully!

Find out from your instructor the location of the Project Files you need and the location where you will store your files.

- To complete many of the units in this book, you need to use Project Files. Your instructor will either provide you with a copy of the Project Files or ask you to make your own copy.

- If you need to make a copy of the Project Files, you will need to copy a set of files from a file server, standalone computer, or the Web to the drive and location where you will be storing your Project Files.

- Your instructor will tell you which computer, drive letter, and folders contain the files you need, and where you will store your files.

- You can also download the files by going to *www.course.com*. See the inside back cover of the book for instructions to download your files.

Copy and organize your Project Files.

Floppy disk users

- If you are using floppy disks to store your Project Files, this list shows which files you'll need to copy onto your disk(s).

- Unless noted in the Project Files list, you will need one formatted, high-density disk for each unit. For each unit you are assigned, copy the files listed in the **Project File Supplied column** onto one disk.

- Make sure you label each disk clearly with the unit name (e.g., Word Unit A).

- When working through the unit, save all your files to this disk.

Users storing files in other locations

- If you are using a zip drive, network folder, hard drive, or other storage device, use the Project Files List to organize your files.

- Create a subfolder for each unit in the location where you are storing your files, and name it according to the unit title (e.g., Word Unit A).

- For each unit you are assigned, copy the files listed in the **Project File Supplied column** into that unit's folder.

- Store the files you modify or create in each unit in the unit folder.

Find and keep track of your Project Files and completed files.

- Use the **Project File Supplied column** to make sure you have the files you need before starting the unit or exercise indicated in the **Unit and Location column**.

- Use the **Student Saves File As column** to find out the filename you use when saving your changes to a Project File provided.

- Use the **Student Creates File column** to find out the filename you use when saving your new file for the exercise.

Unit and Location	Project File Supplied	Student Saves File As	Student Creates File	File Type
Office Unit A Project Files				
Note: No project files are supplied with this unit				
Lessons			To Do List	.doc
Lessons			Summer Outing Memo	.doc
Skills Review			My Work Schedule	.doc
Skills Review			Wizard Greeting Letter	.doc
IC1			Kit Names	.doc
IC2			Excel Practice	.xls
IC3			Template Sales Letter	.doc
IC4			Office Product Information	.doc
VW			Germany Memo	.doc
Word Unit A Project Files				
Lessons	WD A-1	Sales Rep Memo		.doc
Skills Review	WD A-2	Meeting Confirmation		.doc
IC1	WD A-3	Sales Meeting Letter		.doc
IC2	WD A-4	Exhibitor Inquiry		.doc
IC3			Recruiter Letter	.doc
IC4			Study Abroad Letter	.doc
VW			Company Picnic	.doc
Word Unit B Project Files				
Lessons	WD B-1	Ski Sack Sheet		.doc
Skills Review	WD B-2	Member Welcome Letter		.doc
IC1	WD B-3	Sales Meeting Agenda		.doc
IC2	WD B-4	Tour Information Sheet		.doc
IC3	WD B-5	Certificate		.doc
IC4			Restaurant Guide	.doc
VW	WD B-6	Juice Menu		.doc
Word Unit C Project Files				
Lessons	WD C-1	Kite Flyer		.doc
Lessons	Kite	(*used in* Kite Flyer *if student cannot access clip art*)		wmf
Skills Review	WD C-2	Special Offer		.doc

Unit and Location	Project File Supplied	Student Saves File As	Student Creates File	File Type
IC1	WD C-3	Price Comparisons		.doc
IC2			Company Picnic Flyer	.doc
IC3	WD C-4	Spa Schedule		.doc
IC4			City Guide	.doc
VW			Scuba Flyer	.doc

PowerPoint Unit A Project Files
Note: No project files are supplied with this unit

Unit and Location	Project File Supplied	Student Saves File As	Student Creates File	File Type
Lessons			Outdoor Designs Sales Presentation	.ppt
Skills Review			Fall Company Meeting	.ppt
IC 1			Wacky Words Introduction	.ppt
IC 2			Travel Presentation	.ppt
IC 3			None	
IC 4			Help on the Web	.ppt
VW			Laurie's Bagel Bakery	.ppt

PowerPoint Unit B Project Files

Unit and Location	Project File Supplied	Student Saves File As	Student Creates File	File Type
Lessons	PPTB-1	Fall Sales Presentation		.ppt
Lessons	Food Platter	(*used in* Fall Sales Presentation *if student is unable to access necessary clip art*)		.wmf
Skills Review	PPTB-2	Fall Meeting		.ppt
IC1	PPTB-3	Final Stuff for Pets Presentation		.ppt
IC2			Book Presentation	.ppt
IC3			Card Company	.ppt
IC4	PPTB-4	Fishing Clips		.ppt
VW	PPTB-5	Star Gazers Club		.ppt

Integration Unit A Project Files
Disks required to complete this unit: 3*

DISK 1

Unit and Location	Project File Supplied	Student Saves File As	Student Creates File	File Type
Lessons	INT A-1	July Presentation		.doc
Lessons	INT A-2	July Sales Summary		.xls
Lessons			Sales Goals (*uses* July Presentation)	.doc
Lessons	INT A-3	Investors Report		.doc

Unit and Location	Project File Supplied	Student Saves File As	Student Creates File	File Type
Lessons	INT A-4	(*used in* Investors Report Form Letters)		.mdb
Lessons			Investors Report Form Letters (*uses* INT A-4)	.doc
Lessons			Investors Report Web Page (*uses* Investors Report)	.htm
Lessons			Investors Report Letter (*uses* Investors Report Web Page)	.doc
Skills Review	INT A-5	Investors Presentation		.ppt
Skills Review	INT A-6	Confidential Data		.xls
Skills Review			Confidential (*uses* Investors Presentation)	.doc
Skills Review	INT A-7	Confidential Investor		.doc
Skills Review			Confidential Investor Letter (*uses* Confidential Investor)	.doc
Skills Review			Confidential Form Letters (*uses* Confidential Investor and INT A-4)	.doc
Skills Review			Confidential Investor Web Page (*uses* Confidential Investor)	.htm
DISK 2				
IC 1	INT A-8	Poodle Presentation		.ppt
IC 1			Clear Eyes (*uses* Poodle Presentation)	.doc
IC 1	INT A-9	Poodle Letter		.doc
IC 1	INT A-10	Poodle Data		.xls
IC 1	INT A-11	(*used in* Poodle Letter)		
IC 1			Poodle Form Letters (*uses* Poodle Letter *and* INT A-11)	.doc
IC 2			Business Loan Letter	.doc
IC 2	INT A-12	Business Loan		.xls
IC 2			Systems Galore Finances	.mdb
IC 2			Bank Letters (*uses* Systems Galore Finances *and* Business Loan Letter)	.doc
IC 2			Potential Investors Web Page (uses Business Loan Letter)	.doc
IC 3			Theater Outline	.doc
IC 3			Theater Schedule	.doc

Unit and Location	Project File Supplied	Student Saves File As	Student Creates File	File Type
IC 3			Theater Presentation (*uses* Theater Schedule *and* Theater Outline)	.ppt
IC 3			Theater Web Page (*uses* Theater Presentation)	.htm
IC 4	INT A-13	(*used in* Environmental Books Survey)		.mdb
			Environmental Books Survey	.doc
IC 4			Competition	.xls
DISK 3				
VW			Runners Thanks	.doc
VW			Run Against Hunger	.mdb

*Because the files created in this unit are large, you will need to organize the files onto three diskettes if you are using diskettes to complete all the exercises. Copy the files as outlined above, and label each disk clearly (e.g., Integration Unit A Disk 1).

Excel Unit A Project Files
Note: No project files are supplied with this unit

Lessons			Product Order 6-30	.xls
Lessons			Web Order form 6-30	.htm
Skills Review			Shipping Ticket 7-30	.xls
			Web Shipping Ticket	.htm
IC1			March Order Summary	.xls
IC2			October Expenses	.xls
IC3			Excel features	.doc
IC4			Weather info	.xls
VW			Regional Sales Analysis	.xls

Excel Unit B Project Files

Lessons	XL B-1	Mountain Air Order		.xls
Skills Review	XL B-2	April Sales		.xls
IC1			Regional Glass Sales	.xls
IC2	XL B-3	Oct-Dec Paper Sales		.xls
IC3	XL B-4	Outdoor Trips 2003		.xls
IC4			Stock Tracker	.xls
VW			Soccer Analysis	.xls

Excel Unit C Project Files

Lessons	XL C-1	Sales Chart		.xls
Skills Review	XL C-2	Outdoor Trips Chart		.xls

Unit and Location	Project File Supplied	Student Saves File As	Student Creates File	File Type
IC1	XL C-3	Annual Sales Chart		.xls
IC2	XL C-4	Animal Visits Chart		.xls
IC3	XL C-5	Art Exhibit Chart		.xls
IC4			Movie Box Office Chart	.xls
VW			Candy Growth Chart	.xls

Access Unit A Project Files
Note: No project files are provided with this unit
Disks required to complete this unit: 2∗

DISK 1				
Lessons			Outdoor Designs	.mdb
Skills Review			Evergreen Camping Supplies	.mdb
IC1			TotWear	.mdb
IC2			Sunset Spa	.mdb

DISK 2				
IC3			Little Guy Toys	.mdb
IC4			Quick Stop Videos	.mdb
VW			Comic Books	.mdb

∗Because the files created in this unit are large, you will need to organize the files onto two diskettes if you are using diskettes to complete all the exercises. Copy the files as outlined above, and label each disk clearly (e.g., Access Unit A Disk 1).

Access Unit B Project Files
Disks needed to complete this unit: 4∗

DISK 1				
Lessons	Outdoor Designs Sales Reps	Outdoor Designs Sales Reps1		.mdb
	tree.jpg	(*used in* Outdoor Designs Sales Reps1)		
Skills Review	Outdoor Designs Inventory	Outdoor Designs Inventory1		.mdb
	logo1.jpg	(*used in* Outdoor Designs Inventory1)		

DISK 2				
IC1	Stuff for Pets Animal Database	Stuff for Pets Animals Database1		.mdb
	logo2.jpg	(*used in* Stuff for Pets Animals Database1)		
IC2	Chef's Delight	Chef's Delight1		.mdb

Unit and Location	Project File Supplied	Student Saves File As	Student Creates File	File Type
DISK 3				
IC3	Toys Employees	Toys Employees1		.mdb
IC4	Films	Films1		.mdb
DISK 4				
VW	Charity Run.mdb	Charity Run1		.mdb
	runner.jpg	(*used in* Charity Run1)		

*Because the files created in this unit are large, you will need to organize the files onto four diskettes if you are using diskettes to complete all the exercises. Copy the files as outlined above, and label each disk clearly (e.g., Access Unit B Disk 1).

Access Unit C Project Files
Disks needed to complete this unit: 4∗

Unit and Location	Project File Supplied	Student Saves File As	Student Creates File	File Type
DISK 1				
Lessons	Outdoor Designs Sales	Outdoor Designs Sales1		.mdb
DISK 2				
Skills Review	Outdoor Designs Stock.mdb	Outdoor Designs Stock1		.mdb
IC1	Pet Customers	Pet Customers1		.mdb
DISK 3				
IC2	Pets Profits	Pets Profits1		.mdb
IC3	Human Resources	Human Resources1		.mdb
IC4			Attractions	.mdb
DISK 4				
VW	Runners	Runners1		.mdb

*Because the files created in this unit are large, you will need to organize the files onto four diskettes if you are using diskettes to complete all the exercises. Copy the files as outlined above, and label each disk clearly (e.g., Access Unit C Disk 1).

Glossary

Absolute cell reference In Excel, a cell reference that does not change when copied to refer to cells relative to the new location. For example, the formula "=B5*C5" in cell D5 does not change to "=B6*C6" when copied to cell D6. *See also* relative cell reference.

Active cell In an Excel worksheet, the current location of the cell pointer.

Active window The window in which you are currently working. If a window is active, its title bar changes color to differentiate it from other open windows and its program button is highlighted on the taskbar.

Alignment The horizontal or vertical position of numbers or text, relative to the page margins. Text can be right-, center-, left-, top-, and bottom-aligned, or justified between the margins.

Animation schemes Special sets of transition effects and graphics effects that control the way elements on a PowerPoint slide are displayed.

Annotation Temporary marks or writing on a PowerPoint slide during an onscreen slide show which disappear when you move to the next slide.

Area chart A line chart in which each area is colored or patterned to emphasize the relationships between pieces of charted information.

Argument A value, cell reference, or text used in an Excel function. Commas separate arguments and parentheses enclose them; for example, AVERAGE(A1,10,5).

Ascending order A way to sort records in a database table or data in a spreadsheet, in which fields are ordered numerically from 0–9 or alphabetically from A–Z.

Ask a Question box A box located at the far right of the menu bar, into which you can type a question to get help from the Help system of the application in which you are working.

Auto fit A feature that automatically resizes an Excel worksheet column so that it is slightly wider than the longest item in the column.

AutoContent wizard A wizard that designs and creates a PowerPoint presentation based on information you provide in a series of dialog boxes.

AutoCorrect A feature that automatically corrects certain words as you type.

AutoCorrect Options button Button that appears after Office makes an automatic text or formatting correction that contains a menu of options you can choose from.

AutoFormat A feature that formats certain elements of your documents, such as numbered lists, bulleted lists and fractions automatically as you type.

AutoNumber field A data type that assigns a unique sequential number to each record.

AVERAGE function Calculates the average value of the arguments.

Back up To save files to another location in case you have computer trouble and lose data.

Bar chart A chart that displays worksheet data as a series of horizontal bars.

Bold A font style that makes text appear in darker type; used to emphasize text in a document, spreadsheet, database, or presentation.

Bound control A control in Access that has a table or query as its data source.

Bound image In Access, a picture or object that is stored in a table as part of an individual record and is specific to each record.

Browser program A program, such as Microsoft Internet Explorer, that allows you to access, view, and interact with pages on the World Wide Web.

Bullet A small graphic, most often a dot, used to identify an item in a list.

Calculated control A control in Access that uses an expression as its data source, which may include a bound control.

Cell The intersection of a row and a column in an Excel worksheet or any table.

Cell reference The name of a worksheet cell; for example, A1.

Chart A graphic representation of selected worksheet data.

Chart title The name assigned to a chart.

Chart Wizard An Excel wizard that helps you to create or modify a chart.

Check box A square box in a dialog box that turns an option on or off.

Click and Type A feature that allows you to begin typing in almost any blank area of a Word document simply by clicking in the desired location.

Clip A media file such as clip art, animations, videos, and photographs available through the Clip Organizer.

Clip art Ready-to-use electronic artwork.

Clip Organizer A program shared by Office applications that helps you organize picture, sound, and animation files.

Close To quit a program or remove a window from the desktop. The Close button usually appears in the upper-right corner of a window.

Color scheme A set of eight coordinated colors for each element in a PowerPoint presentation.

Column A vertical block of text in a document.

Column chart A chart that displays worksheet data as a series of vertical columns.

Column width A cell's horizontal dimension.

Combination chart A chart that displays worksheet data in both line and bar graphs in a single chart.

Common Tasks button A toolbar button that lists common PowerPoint tasks.

Context-sensitive help Information related to your current task.

Control An object on an Access form or report that is composed of the field label and the field value text box and that displays data, performs calculations, or is used for decoration. Examples include fields, text boxes, and graphic images. *See also* bound control, unbound control, and calculated control.

Copy A command that copies selected text in a document to the Windows and Office Clipboard.

COUNT function Calculates the number of values in the argument list.

Criteria In Access, conditions or qualifications that determine whether a record is chosen for a filter or query.

Currency format A type of worksheet formatting that adds a dollar sign ($) and decimal places to selected cells.

Cut A command that removes selected text or objects from a document and places it on the Windows and Office Clipboard.

Data source The file that stores the variable information for a form letter or other mail merge document.

Data types Determines the kind of data a database field contains, such as text, dates, or numbers.

Database An organized collection of data related to a particular topic or purpose and stored electronically in a file.

Database object In Access, one of seven program components that you can create and modify to store, retrieve and work with data.

Datasheet view A view in Access that displays records in a grid format, making records easy to compare, sort, and edit.

Decrypting In Access, reverses the encryption process. *See also* encrypting.

Default A setting that is preset by the operating system or program, such as desktop color or font size.

Descending order A sort in which fields are ordered numerically from 9–0 or alphabetically from Z–A.

Design templates PowerPoint templates that contain suggested design and formatting but no content. *See also* presentation templates.

Design view In Access, the view that shows the structure of a table, form, query, or report. Use this view to modify the object by editing or moving controls or to change the structure of a table by adding, deleting, or editing fields and field properties.

Destination file When linking and embedding data between documents, the target file or program.

Detail section In Access, the section of a form or report that displays the field labels and data for each record.

Dialog box A window in which you enter information needed to carry out a command. Many commands display dialog boxes in which you must select options before Windows can carry out the command.

Document-centric A computer environment in which working with documents is more important than the particular software applications that are used to create the documents. In many respects, Office XP is considered to be a "document-centric" environment.

Document window Area within the Word program window that displays the current document.

Double-spacing A document (or paragraph) that has one blank line between each line of text.

Drag and drop The action of moving or copying selected text in a document by dragging it with the mouse and depositing it at a new location.

Drawing toolbar Toolbar whose buttons provide tools for drawing and working with graphical elements.

Edit To modify the contents of an existing file.

Embedded object A separate copy of a file inserted in a file in a different program that you can edit using the menus and toolbars of the program in which it was created.

Encrypt To compact and scramble a database file so that it is difficult to decipher for security purposes. *See also* decrypting.

Endnote A note or citation that corresponds to a number or symbol in the document and appears at the end of the document. *See also* footnote.

End-of-cell mark The mark in each cell in a table; all text entered in the cell is entered to the left of the end-of-cell mark.

End-of-row mark The mark at the end of each row in a table.

Enter To type information in a document or dialog box.

Exclusive mode A specific way to open a database which makes it available only to the user who has opened it.

Export Change a file from one file type to another.

Expression A mathematical equation that performs a calculation on data in a database; can include field names and mathematical functions as well as built-in functions.

Field Specific category of information in a database such as name, address, or phone number. Usually organized in the smallest possible unit to facilitate organization, such as last name and first name.

Field description In a database table, a descriptive comment that helps document the database by explaining the purpose of a field.

Field label In an Access form or report, the control that describes the contents of its associated field value text box.

Field list List that contains all the fields in a database table; used to add fields to forms or reports.

Field name In an Access table, column headings in a table that indicate the type of information entered for each field value text box.

Field properties Settings and characteristics that determine the way data is stored, displayed or manipulated in a field, such as the length of a text field or the decimal places in a number field.

Field properties pane In Access, a tabbed pane that provides complete information about the currently selected field.

Field value text box The control that contains the data for a particular field.

File An electronic collection of data that has a unique name, distinguishing it from other files.

Filename A name given to a file that distinguishes it from other files.

Fill handle A box that appears on the lower right corner of a worksheet cell that you can drag to the right or down to copy the cell's contents into adjacent cells.

Filter A command that displays only the data that you want to see in an Excel worksheet (or an Access database) based on criteria you set.

Find A command that searches for a word, phrase, or format in a document, spreadsheet, presentation or database.

First Line indent In a Word document, when the first line of text in a paragraph is indented from the left margin.

Font A set of characters in a particular design; for example, Arial or Times New Roman.

Font effects Special enhancements to fonts such as small caps, shadow and superscript that you can apply to selected text in a document, spreadsheet, database or presentation.

Font style Attribute that changes the appearance of a font when applied; bold, italic, and underline are common font styles.

Fontography The process of creating new fonts.

Footer Text that appears just above the bottom margin of every page in a document.

Footnote A note or citation placed at the bottom of a document page.

Footnote reference mark The mark next to a word in a document that indicates a footnote or endnote is associated with the word.

Form A database object that is used to enter, edit, or display records in a database one at a time.

Form footer A section of a database form that appears at the bottom of each form and can contain totals, instructions, or command buttons.

Form header A section of the form that appears at the top of each form and can contain a title or logo.

Form letter A merged document that contains standard body text and a custom header for each recipient.

Format To enhance the appearance of text in a document, spreadsheet, database, or presentation without changing the content.

Formatting toolbar Toolbar in an application whose buttons let you enhance the look of your document, spreadsheet, report, or presentation.

Formula An equation that calculates a new value from existing values. Formulas can contain numbers, mathematical operators, cell references, and built-in equations called functions.

Formula bar The place in the Microsoft Excel application where you enter or edit the formulas of the selected cell.

Function A prewritten formula you can use instead of typing a formula from scratch. Each function includes the function name, a set of parentheses, and function arguments separated by commas and enclosed in parentheses. *See also* formula.

Gridlines Horizontal and vertical lines connecting to the X-axis and Y-axis in a chart.

Group header The part of an Access report that contains the Group field name; used when the information in a report is grouped by a chosen field or fields.

Grouping Organizes information in a report by a field or field values to make spotting trends or finding important information easier.

Handles Small black squares that appear around the perimeter of a selected control or object and are used to resize it.

Handouts In PowerPoint, hard copies of a presentation that are printed for distribution to an audience.

Hanging indent A type of paragraph indent in a Word document where subsequent lines of text in a paragraph indent further than the first line.

Header Text that appears just below the top margin of every page in a document.

Horizontal ruler An onscreen ruler in a program window that helps you place objects in a precise location.

Hyperlink A connection between an element in an electronic document to another element in the same document, or another document, file, or program. The hyperlink itself can be a word or an object that the user clicks to follow the link.

HyperText Markup Language (HTML) A popular file format used for documents posted on the World Wide Web. HTML documents contain formatting codes that produce special effects when viewed in a Web browser such as Internet Explorer.

Image properties Properties of a picture that can be modified using the tools on the Picture toolbar, such as brightness, contrast, and colors.

Import To insert the entire contents of a closed file into an open document.

Indent A set amount of space between the edge of a paragraph and the right or left margin.

Index In a Word document, a list of key terms and their page number locations in the document.

Input mask An optional property that controls the format in which users must enter data in a database field.

Insertion point In a document, a blinking vertical line indicating the point where text will be inserted when you type.

Internet A worldwide collection of millions of computers linked together to share information

Italic A font style that makes text appear slanted; used to emphasize text in a document.

Justified text Text aligned equally between the right and left margins.

Label Descriptive text used to identify worksheet data in Excel, and titles or brief description in Access.

Landscape Layout orientation for a document so that it reads down the length rather than across the width of the page. Used when you want a rectangular page to be wider than it is long.

Legend Area that explains what the labels, colors, and patterns in an Excel chart represent.

Line chart A graph of data mapped by a series of lines. Because line charts show changes in data or categories of data over time, they are often used to document trends.

Link When sharing data between files and programs, displays information from the source file in the destination file. *See also* source file *and* destination file.

List box A box in a dialog box containing a list of items. To choose an item, you click the list arrow and then click the desired item.

Main document A document that stores the standard body text for a form letter or other mail merge document.

Main text Bullet points under a title on a slide.

Margin In a document, the amount of space between the edge of the page and the text in your document.

MAX function Calculates the largest value in the argument list.

Maximize To enlarge a window so that it takes up the entire screen. The Maximize button is usually located in the upper-right corner of a window.

Menu A list of available commands in a program.

Menu bar The bar located directly below the title bar of an application that contains menus available in a program for the tasks you need to perform; changes depending on the active window.

Merge To combine custom information with the standard text to create personalized form letters or other mail merge documents.

Merged document A file or printout that contains all the personalized letters in a mail merge document

Merge fields Field names from the specified data source that act as placeholders for variable information in a form letter or other mail merge document.

Microsoft Office Shortcut bar A toolbar that contains buttons for starting Office programs and performing other common Office tasks.

Microsoft Outlook An email and information manager that comes with Microsoft Office that you use to send and receive email, schedule appointments, maintain to do lists, and store contact information.

MIN function Calculates the smallest value in the argument list.

Minimize To reduce the size of a window to an icon on the taskbar or to a smaller size. The Minimize button is usually located in the upper-right corner of the window.

Mulitple columns Text that is formatted as more than one vertical block of text; as in a newspaper.

Multi-user environment Configuration of computers and software which permits more than one user to modify the same set of data at the same time.

Name box Displays the name or reference of the currently selected cell in the worksheet.

Normal view A view in Word that displays the text and some graphic elements in a document without showing exactly how all the elements in the document will print. A view in PowerPoint that displays the presentation in three areas: an area on the left that alternates between Slides tab and Outline tab, and on the right, a Slide pane and below it, a Notes pane.

Notes Page view View in PowerPoint that displays a slide and a designated area for typing speaker notes to accompany the slide.

Number format A format applied to numbers in cells that represents different number types, such as currency, decimal, date, or percent.

Numeric value A number in a worksheet cell.

Object A graphic or other item or set of items that can be moved and resized as a single unit. In Excel, the components of a chart are called objects. In Access, objects are a collection of principal program components that you can create and modify, including tables, queries, forms, reports, pages, macros, and modules.

Office Assistant Animated character that appears on screen and provides tips and alerts as you work.

Office Clipboard A storage area for storing cut and copied items that can hold up to 24 items at once, and which is accessible from any Office program. *See also* Windows Clipboard.

On-screen presentation A PowerPoint slide show run from a computer.

Open To start a program or display a window that was previously closed; a program that is currently running, but not necessarily displayed in an active window; or the act of loading an existing file into an Office program.

Order of precedence The order in which Excel calculates a formula; the order of precedence is exponents, multiplication and division, addition and subtraction. Calculations in parentheses are evaluated first.

Orphan The first line of a paragraph that appears by itself on the bottom of a page.

Outline tab A part of Normal view that shows the structure of a PowerPoint presentation in selected text levels.

Page break The point at which text in a document flows to the top of a new page.

Page footer The part of an Access report that contains the current date and page number and appears at the bottom of each page.

Page Header section The part of an Access report that contains the field labels and appears at the top of every page of the report.

Password A string of characters that must be typed correctly in order to access a file.

Paste A command that copies information from the Windows Clipboard or Office Clipboard into a document at the location of the insertion point.

Paste function A series of dialog boxes that guides you through entering a function into a worksheet.

Pie chart A circular chart that displays data in one data series as slices of a pie. A pie chart is useful for showing the relationship of parts to a whole.

Placeholder A container for text or graphics in a document template used to reserve space for text or graphics the user will insert in its place.

Point A unit of measurement used to measure characters; a point equals $\frac{1}{72}$ of an inch.

Pop-up menu A menu of common commands that opens when you right-click an item for which a pop-up menu exists.

Portrait Layout orientation for a document so that it reads across the width rather than down the length of the page. Used when you want a rectangular page to be longer than it is wide.

PowerPoint Viewer Program included with PowerPoint that you can use to run a PowerPoint presentation on a computer without PowerPoint installed.

Presentation graphics Software designed for creating on-screen slide shows, 35mm slides, overhead transparencies, and other business presentation materials.

Presentation templates PowerPoint templates that contain suggested design, formatting, content. *See also* Design templates.

Presentation window The area of the PowerPoint program window in which you work with the text or graphics of a presentation.

Primary key field In Access, a field that ensures that each record is unique in a table.

Print Layout view A view in Word that displays layout, graphics, and footnotes exactly as they will appear when printed.

Print Preview A view that shows exactly how a document will look when it is printed and contains options specific to previewing the printed document.

Printer port A special connector on the back of a computer that connects the computer to the printer.

Properties Those characteristics of a specific desktop or program element (such as the mouse, keyboard, or printer, or a document, database field, or object) which you can customize.

Property sheet In Access, a window that displays a control's name and source; can be used to edit the control's properties.

Query A database object that extracts data from one or more tables in a database according to set criteria.

Radar chart A chart that displays worksheet data frequency relative to a center point.

RAM (random access memory) The memory that programs use to perform necessary tasks while the computer is on. When you turn off the computer, all information in RAM is lost.

Range A selected area of adjacent cells.

Range reference The name of a selected range; for example, C5:E15.

Record A collection of related fields that contains all information for an entry in a database such as a customer, item, or business.

Reference mark A number or symbol that is linked to a footnote or endnote.

Relational database A database that contains multiple tables that are related to each other and can share information. Access is a relational database program.

Relative cell reference In Excel, a cell reference that changes when copied to refer to cells relative to the new location. For example, the formula "=B5*C5" in cell D5 changes to "=B6*C6" when you copy the formula to cell D6. *See also* absolute cell reference

Repaginate To renumber the pages in a document.

Replace A command on the Edit menu that lets you search for a word or format in a document, spreadsheet, presentation, or database and insert another word or format in its place.

Report A summary of database information designed specifically for printing.

Report footer Information or images that appear at the bottom of the last printed page of a report.

Report header Section of a report that contains the report name and appears only at the top of the first printed page of a report.

Restore To resize a program or document window to its previous size before it was minimized or maximized. The Restore button is usually located in the upper-right corner of a window.

Right-click To press and release the right mouse button once quickly.

Right indent In Word, when text in a paragraph is indented from the right margin.

Row height A cell's vertical dimension.

ScreenTip A concise description of a toolbar button or other screen element that appears when you point to the item.

Select To click or highlight an item in order to perform some action on it.

Select query A commonly used query in which records are collected and displayed in a datasheet and can be modified.

Selection handles *See* handles.

Serial number A number used in an Excel worksheet that represents a date or time that is used in calculations.

Shading A pattern of dots, lines, or color applied to a worksheet cell, paragraph, page, or other bordered area in order to emphasize it.

Sheet tab In Excel, displays the names of a worksheet in a workbook.

Shortcut A link that you can place in any location that gives you instant access to a particular file, folder, or program on your hard disk or network.

Single spacing A document (or paragraph) that does not have any blank lines between lines of text.

Slide Show view A full-screen view of a PowerPoint presentation in which slide transitions and animation effects are displayed.

Slide thumbnail A reduced view of a PowerPoint slide, displayed on the Slides tab in Normal view, and in Slide Sorter view.

Slide Sorter view Displays all slides in a PowerPoint presentation in reduced size so that you can reorganize them easily.

Slide pane In Normal view, displays text and graphics of a presentation slide in WYSIWYG (what you see is what you get) format.

Smart Tags Items that an application has identified as a particular data type, such as a name, address, or phone number, and upon which you can perform a variety of actions without having to open another Office application.

Sort A command that organizes records in an Access database or columns in an Excel spreadsheet or a Word table numerically or alphabetically, and in ascending or descending order.

Source file When linking or embedding data between two files, the original file or program.

Speaker notes In PowerPoint notes that accompany slides; used to help remember important information that should not appear on the slides themselves.

Spelling and Grammar Checker A tool that checks the spelling and grammar in a document and offers suggestions for fixing possible errors.

Stacking Layering an object on top of another object on a PowerPoint slide. The first object placed in a stack is at the bottom of the stacking order; the last is at the top.

Standard toolbar The toolbar usually located directly below the menu bar in an application whose buttons perform the most common tasks in that application

Statistics Descriptive calculations used in worksheets, such as sum, average, or count.

Status bar Area at the bottom of the program window that displays information such as the current page or record number, and important messages, such as the status of the current print job.

Style A defined set of formatting characteristics for a character or paragraph; can include the font, font size, font style, paragraph alignment, spacing of the paragraph, tab settings, and anything else that defines the format of the paragraph.

Suite A collection of application programs that share a common user interface and are distributed together. Microsoft Office XP is a software suite.

SUM function In Excel, calculates the sum of the arguments.

Summary Information In an Access report, displays statistics about one or more fields in a database including statistics on the sum, average, minimum, or maximum value in any numeric field.

Tab A set position where text following a tab character aligns.

Tab stop A location on the ruler where the insertion point moves to when the Tab key is pressed.

Table In Access, a collection of related records. In Word, information displayed in rows and columns.

Table of authorities List of references in a legal document, such as cases or statues, and their location in a Word document.

Table of contents List of headings in a document and their location in a Word document.

Table of figures List of figures in a document and their location in a Word document.

Taskbar A bar at the bottom of the Windows desktop that contains the Start button and icons for all open programs and files.

Task Pane An interface feature of Office XP that helps you open new files, existing files, templates, or Web documents in Office applications.

Template A special file that contains predesigned formatting, text, and other tools for creating common business documents such as letters, business presentations, and invoices.

Text box Text object that automatically wraps text and can be resized or moved.

Text label Text object that does not automatically wrap text and can be moved or resized.

Text placeholder A designated area on a PowerPoint slide for entering text, such as titles, subtitles, and body text.

Timing The amount of time a slide is displayed during an on-screen presentation.

Title In PowerPoint, the title or first line of text in a slide.

Title bar The horizontal bar at the top of the window that displays the program name and the name of the active file.

Title slide The first slide in a PowerPoint presentation.

Toolbar A customizable set of buttons that allow you to activate commands quickly.

Transition The way a slide first appears in a slide show and obscures the previous slide.

Triple-click To press and release the left mouse button three times quickly. In some programs including Word, this action causes an entire line to be selected.

True Type font A font that appears on screen exactly as it will appear on the printed page.

Unbound control In Access, a label or graphic image with its data source outside the database; used to identify or enhance a database object.

Unbound image In Access, an image or object that is not tied to a data source and stays the same for every record.

Underline A font style that underlines text; used to emphasize text in a document.

Vertical ruler A ruler the runs along the left side of an application window to help place objects precisely.

Vertical scroll bar Moves your view of a document or form up and down through a window.

View A preset configuration that determines which elements of a file are visible onscreen; does not affect the actual content of the document.

Web Layout view A view that shows how a document will look if you save it as a Web page.

Web Page An HTML document that can be viewed in a Web browser, such as Internet Explorer. You can create Web pages in Office XP using the Save As Web Page command on the File menu.

Widow The last line of a paragraph that appears by itself at the top of a page.

Window A rectangular-shaped work area on a screen that might contain icons, the contents of a file, or other usable data.

Windows Clipboard A temporary storage area in your computer's memory for cut and copied items.

Wizard A features that guides you through step-by-step options in a series of dialog boxes to assist you in the process of creating a document or accomplishing a task.

Word processor A program that used to create and manipulate text-based documents, such as memos, newsletters, or term papers.

Word wrap In Word, a feature that automatically pushes text to the next line when the insertion point meets the right margin.

WordArt A kind of stylized text created in Word or PowerPoint with special text formatting features.

Workbook A collection of related worksheets saved in a single Excel file.

Worksheet An Excel spreadsheet comprised of rows and columns of information that is used for performing numeric calculations, displaying business data, presenting information on the Web, and other purposes.

Worksheet window The area in the Excel program window which contains worksheet data.

World Wide Web A part of the Internet that contains Web pages that are linked together. *See also* Internet.

X-axis The horizontal line in a chart that contains a series of related values from the worksheet.

X-axis label A label that describes the X-axis of a chart.

XY (scatter) chart A chart that shows the relationship between two kinds of related worksheet data.

Y-axis The vertical line in a chart that contains a series of related values from the worksheet.

Y-axis label A label that describes the Y-axis of a chart.

Zoom The percentage of normal size at which you view a document on-screen.

Index

Index

Index

Index

Index

Index

Index

Index